Systems Analysis and Design

Donald Yeates and Tony Wakefield

Second edition

FT Prentice Hall
FINANCIAL TIMES

An imprint of **Pearson Education**

Harlow, England • London • New York • Boston • San Francisco • Toronto • Sydney • Singapore • Hong Kong
Tokyo • Seoul • Taipei • New Delhi • Cape Town • Madrid • Mexico City • Amsterdam • Munich • Paris • Milan

Pearson Education Limited
Edinburgh Gate
Harlow
Essex CM20 2JE
England

and Associated Companies throughout the world

Visit us on the World Wide Web at:
www.pearsoneduc.com

First published 1994
Second edition published 2004

ISBN 0273 65536 1

British Library Cataloguing-in-Publication Data
A catalogue record for this book is available from the British Library

10 9 8 7 6 5 4 3 2 1
08   07   06   05   04

Typeset in 10/12½pt Palatino by 35
Printed and bound by Bell & Bain Limited, Glasgow

The publisher's policy is to use paper manufactured from sustainable forests.

Systems Analysis and Design

Contents

Preface

This is a substantially new and different edition of Systems Analysis and Design. We hope that the new materials bring it up to date and that we've kept the best of the old. It has been written for people studying systems analysis and design or who are already working in systems teams. People who are involved in the development of new systems or the development of new systems analysts, or both, have written it.

It is intended to be a practical book, easy to read and easy to use. It follows the same structure as the previous edition and has new and updated material in it. There are more case studies and exercises too and we've cross-referenced the topics to the ISEB syllabus in systems analysis and design.

There is also a web site for the book for the first time. We're excited about the opportunities that this offers. We want to make it interesting and useful to use. You'll find more information about Denton Motor Holdings and some answer pointers to some of the case study problems and exercises. There are also some end-of-chapter quizzes and the answers to them. You could use these to check your understanding as you go through the book. For more information, log on to *www.booksites.net/yeates*.

We hope that you enjoy the book. It can't tell you everything you need to know about analysis and design; no book can do that. There is no substitute for experience.

Finally our thanks to James Cadle, John Koenigsberger, Steve Copson and Murdoch Mactaggart for reviewing some of the material for us, and to the panellists who helped with the final chapter – Debbie Paul, Frank Jones, Jean-Noel Ezingeard, Nigel Underwood and Richard Bevan. Also, we would like to thank Amanda Thompson and Tim Parker at Pearson Education for keeping our noses to the grindstone in the nicest possible way as well as Lionel Browne and David Hemsley the project editors.

Donald Yeates
Tony Wakefield
February 2003

Disclaimer

The publishers and authors do not accept responsibility in any way for the failure of analysis and design work carried out based on ideas in this book or following your reading of the book. Whilst the ideas and good practices are based on hard won experience, they need to be applied with skill and under-standing and take account of project circumstances. Good luck!

Acknowledgements

We are grateful to the following for permission to reproduce copyright material:

Figure 2.7 'Custom Order Workflow', published by Actionworks® – Business Process Management for People Processes; Fig. 4.2 from *The Team Handbook* by Peter Scholtes, published by Oriel Incorporated; Fig. 6.5 from *STARTS Guide 1987*, supported by the Department of Trade and Industry; Fig. 8.10 'NCC clerical document specification', published by National Computing Centre.

In some instances we have been unable to trace the owners of copyright material, and we would appreciate any information that would enable us to do so.

1 The Context for Analysis and Design

1.1 Introduction

Who is this book written for? The whole book is about systems analysis and design, and it's been written for people who are analysts or designers already or people who are thinking about making a career in analysis and design. This book doesn't cover all you need to know about the job. No book can ever do that: there will always be something you'd wish you'd known, and there will always be something you could have done better. Life will present you with new problems every day. However, there's no reason why you should make all of the same mistakes that other analysts and designers have already made. In this book many good and experienced analysts, designers, consultants and trainers offer you their experience in the hope that you will build on it, benefit from it and be better at your job.

The book is organised in a project-chronological sequence. This means that it begins with analysis and ends with implementation. There are some chapters, however, that don't fit neatly into this sequence, so they have been put in at the beginning – like this one – or right at the end – like Change Management. They deal with the environment within which analysis and design takes place and are concerned with business, people, management and quality. There's also a basic assumption running through the book. It is that analysts and designers work for customers. We believe that the word 'customer' is very important. Somebody pays for what analysts and designers deliver. New systems have to be justified by the benefits that they deliver. It is easy to use terms such as 'the users' and 'user management' – they're used in this book – and forget that they are substitutes for 'the customer'. All of the contributors to this book have worked for companies whose very existence depended on their ability to build and deliver new computer-based systems and where customer focus came first, last and everywhere in between. This isn't to say that only those analysts and designers who work for service companies have a customer focus. Indeed, the chapter on Building Better Systems extends the scope of the word 'customer' well beyond its everyday usage and beyond the meaning here in this chapter. We do, however, want you to hold on to the important concept of 'customer' as you read this book. There are three other important points that need to be mentioned here.

- Systems analysis and design involves people. Certainly it involves technology, often technology that we don't really understand and which we rely on other people to manage for us, but the best-designed systems in the world succeed because the people who use them can do their jobs better. This is because their information systems enable them to achieve goals they wouldn't otherwise reach. There are just too many people on trains and planes using laptop machines to believe that we can ever in the future manage without computers. The importance of this 'people aspect' is emphasised later where we consider change management.

- Systems analysts and designers change the world. This is a bold statement, and in one sense everyone changes the world to some extent just by their very existence. The role of the systems analyst, however we may describe it in detail, is to be a change agent. Unless we are interested in changing the way organisations work we have no need for systems analysts. Unless you are interested in changing the way organisations work, you probably have no need to read this book.

- Information systems are expensive to develop and maintain, so it is clear that businesses do not commission them just for the fun of it. The need for an information system must grow out of some perceived business requirement, and the justification for it must be expressed in business terms. Although this is well enough understood in theory, it is surprising how often IS projects do start without clear links back to business plans and strategies. System developers often take the sketchiest of briefs and start to develop something they think meets the need – and are then unpleasantly surprised when the user or sponsor of the system refuses to accept it because it does not properly meet their specific business requirements.

1.2 Business Analysis

1.2.1 Levels of Understanding

A proper analysis of system requirements requires that those carrying out the investigation have a balance of skills and knowledge. This includes a good general understanding of the operation of business and of the factors that affect the viability of all businesses. This involves a broad-based knowledge of finance, accounting, marketing, production and distribution, ideally gained in a variety of business environments. There will also be a need for a more specific grasp of the important features of the particular business being studied. So, for example, an analyst working for a high street chain of shops should have knowledge of the retail sector and be able to discuss retailing matters knowledgeably with the customer. Finally of course a broad knowledge of the possibilities and limitations of information technology is also required.

This balance of skills is needed for three reasons. First, so that the analysts understand what the users of the proposed system are saying to them and can recognise the implications of the requirements they are capturing. Also, because users will not expect analysts to adopt a completely passive role; they will want them to challenge assumptions and interject ideas to stimulate them in thinking out their requirements. Without an understanding of the business of the organisation, or of how other organisations have tackled similar issues, it will not be possible to play this catalytic role. Finally, the users will generally expect the analysts to devise and propose technical solutions to their business problems.

Systems analysts, however, are often generalists and, particularly in service companies, are quite likely to be sent to work with a travel agent on one project, a bank on the next and a manufacturing company on the third. Although this can facilitate cross-fertilisation of ideas between different sorts of business, the disadvantage is, of course, that they sometimes lack the specialist knowledge to deal with users on an equal basis. So if this is the case, what can be done to bring relevant experience to bear on a particular assignment?

First, and most obviously, the project manager should try to find analysts with previous experience of the business to be studied, or something similar. Someone who has worked on a distribution application, for instance, may have achieved a reasonable understanding of areas such as stock-keeping and just-in-time delivery systems, which can be brought into play on a retail assignment. If, however, analysts with relevant backgrounds are not available, additional support will have to be provided by arranging some training for the analysts in the areas of interest in the form of public courses or self-teach packages, or by hiring an expert to coach them in the new business areas. Alternatively, suitable background reading can be provided. Another approach is to provide consultancy support, which can be used either to lead the investigation with the customer or to provide background advice and guidance for the analysis team.

A particular challenge for analysts, and one that seems more difficult for those from a technical background such as programming, is to keep the business requirements as the focus instead of getting hooked up on technological solutions. It is very easy, for example, to take a messy and cumbersome manual system and produce instead a messy and cumbersome computer system. Analysis should at all times be tightly focused on the business objectives that the proposed system is supposed to fulfil, and only when these are thoroughly clear should the identification of technical solutions be attempted. As we shall see in Chapter 2, structured methods, particularly SSADM, provide a very good discipline in this regard, as they tend to conduct requirements analysis and requirements specification at a wholly logical level and deliberately exclude the consideration of technical issues until the business requirements have been settled.

1.2.2 Linkage of IS to Business Objectives

There are many reasons why businesses should want to develop information systems, but some of the most common objectives are:

- *To reduce manpower costs.* The introduction of computer-based systems has often enabled work to be done by fewer staff or, more likely nowadays, has permitted new tasks to be undertaken without increasing staffing levels. The automation of many banking functions, such as cheque clearance, falls into this category.

- *To improve customer service.* Computer systems can often allow organisations to serve customers more quickly or to provide them with additional services. Supermarket point-of-sale systems producing itemised bills provide an illustration of this.

- *To improve management information.* Management decisions can only be as good as the information on which they are based, so many computer systems have been designed to produce more, or more accurate, or more timely information. With modern database query facilities it is even possible to provide systems that do not require the data retrieval requirements to be defined in advance, thereby enabling managers to institute new types of enquiry when changing business conditions demand new or different information.

- *To secure or defend competitive advantage.* This is becoming a major justification for spending on information systems, and is examined in more detail later in this chapter.

Ideally, the analyst should work from a hierarchy of objectives, each one posing a challenge to, and imposing constraints upon, those at a lower level. The lower-level objectives are sometimes referred to as *critical success factors*: that is, they are things that must be achieved if the top-level objective is to be met. The critical success factors will become more detailed and tightly focused as one works down the hierarchy, and perhaps this may be best illustrated by an example.

Let us consider a motor-car manufacturing company. It currently has, say, 10% of the market for its products, and the board has defined a five-year mission of raising that proportion to 20%. But this is a very broad target and, to achieve it, the organisation will have to define a set of more tangible objectives that will lead to its being met – in other words, the critical success factors. It may be felt that one key to increasing market share is to offer a more frequent choice of new models. So, a lower-level objective for the design team may be to reduce the time to develop a new model from, say, five years to two. And the production department will have to be able to switch over assembly lines in less time, say a reduction from six months to three.

Coming down a stage further still, the designers will want to introduce technology that can produce manufacturing instructions, documentation to support the issuing of tenders to subcontractors, component listings and setup instructions for the assembly lines from their drawings. Now, we can derive some very focused critical success factors for our information system based upon these detailed requirements. It can be seen, then, that business objectives and critical success factors 'cascade' from one level to another, and the whole set should form a pyramid supporting the overall aims of the business.

1.3 Constraints

The range of potential solutions that may be proposed by the analyst will be limited by constraints imposed by the user and by the nature of the user's business. The analyst should ideally undertand these constraints before analysis begins but certainly as it progresses, and must keep them firmly in mind as the ideas for the proposed system emerge.

1.3.1 The User's Organisation

The first thing for the analyst to consider is the structure of the user's organisation. It may, for example, operate in a very centralised fashion with nearly all decisions being made at head office. If this is the case, then clearly information systems must reflect this pattern and be designed so that relevant information can be processed rapidly and presented at the heart of the business. If, on the other hand, the organisation allows considerable autonomy to managers in subsidiary parts of the business, then the systems must be designed to provide these managers with what they need to run the business effectively. In other words the systems must reflect the structure of decision-making in the business.

It is important to remember, however, that organisations are not static and tend to oscillate between centralisation and devolution as circumstances, the business and intellectual climate and the most recent theories of management gurus dictate. Nowadays, the difficulty of altering information systems can prove a major obstacle to reorganisation. Some might think this to be a good thing, but it is important not to make systems so inflexible that they actually prevent the organisation from being operated in the way the management decides is necessary.

1.3.2 Working Practices

It is easiest to introduce a new information system if it leaves existing working practices largely undisturbed. Conversely, systems that require a lot of change may prove very difficult to implement.

However, the analyst must not allow a fear of the difficulty of implementation to prevent the best solution – best for the business as a whole, that is – being advocated. The most radical changes will often provide the greatest gains, and if that is so then the problems of implementation must be faced and overcome, and the chapter on change management gives some ideas that help in this difficult process. Alternatively, the management of the organisation may want to use the introduction of new technology as a catalyst for change, to shake up a sleepy, backward-looking department for instance.

The key point is that the analyst must make some assessment of the climate prevailing in the organisation. Will its management wholeheartedly push for change, give it lukewarm support, or just run away from its implications? Finally, at a more prosaic level, some working practices that may appear over-elaborate and cumbersome will turn out to have evolved for good business reasons – such as the maintenance of safety standards on a railway for example.

The analyst must make very sure that these business reasons are not ignored in proposing new and more streamlined systems.

1.3.3 Financial Control Procedures

Various aspects of the way an organisation manages its finances can have an impact on IT developments. The first is the concept of capital versus revenue expenditure. Most IT developments involve capital expenditure in that they are funded as one-off projects rather than out of continuing expenses. But the payoff for a capital project may be a reduced continuing revenue cost somewhere downstream. Depending on the organisation's rules for the 'payback' on capital projects, a capital project cost of, say, £3 million may not be justifiable even if, over a seven-year system life, it could produce revenue savings of 'only' £1 million per annum.

Also, organisations may have only limited funds earmarked for capital projects in a given year but have reasonably generous revenue budgets for ongoing work. In these circumstances it may be sensible to propose a limited initial capital expenditure for a core system, with enhancements and additions being made gradually as funds permit.

The analyst needs to consider who actually holds the purse strings for a particular development and what it is that will convince that person of the worth of the proposed development. Let us suppose, by way of example, that we are to examine the requirements for a new payroll system in an organisation. The paymaster could be the payroll manager, who wants a fully comprehensive system that will enable him or her to offer new services and perhaps even take over the functions of the corporate personnel system, or it could be the IT director, who is developing a strategy of packaged systems running on 'open' architectures, or the finance director, who wants a system that will cut the number of staff, and hence the costs, in the payroll department. The objectives of each of these managers are rather different, and if the analyst is to get a solution adopted, it must be geared to the needs of the person, or people, who will approve and pay for it.

1.3.4 Security and Privacy

The analyst needs to determine fairly early on which sort of security conditions will be required for the proposed information system. These could include:

- ordinary commercial confidentiality, where the main aim is to ensure that sensitive commercial information such as, for instance, the production cost breakdown of products cannot be stolen by the competition;

- more sensitive systems, such as the Police National Computer, where special considerations apply to the holding of, and access to, data;

- very secure systems, such as those that support the armed services and government agencies.

Clearly, the need for rigorous security control could impose major constraints and development costs on the project.

1.3.5 Legal Considerations

It is becoming increasingly the case that the users of information systems are liable for the consequences of things done, or put in train, by those systems. If there are such liabilities, the analyst must examine them and allow for them in the proposed system. Safety-critical systems are the most obvious example, and if one were examining the requirements for, say, an air traffic control system, safety considerations would constitute one of the main constraints of the proposed solution. Other systems have also fallen foul of the law recently, and it cannot be too long before, for example, a credit-scoring agency is found to be liable for the consequences of wrongly deciding that someone is a bad risk.

So far, too, there has been little legal exploration of the subject of consequential losses arising from the use of information systems, and developers have been able to hide behind contract clauses that limit their liability to the cost of the systems's development or some arbitrary figure. There must be some possibility that this will change in the future, so the analyst, in assessing the risks from some proposed solution, ought at least to think about what might be the consequential losses resulting in a system failure.

The law does already have something to say on the subject of storing information about individuals, in the form of data protection legislation. This has two aspects that particularly concern us. These are ensuring that the data is held only for defined and declared purposes, and enabling those with a statutory right to inspect information held about them to do so. So, if the proposed information system may hold information on individuals, the analyst needs to ensure that the requirements of the legislation can be met.

1.3.6 Audit Requirements

An organisation's internal and external auditors will want access to systems to ensure that they are working properly and that the financial information they produce can be relied upon. They may also require that certain self-checking mechanisms and authorisation procedures be incorporated into systems. In some types of system – those supporting pension funds or banks are obvious examples – the need to check and extract audited information forms a large part of the requirement itself. It is very much better, not to say easier, if these audit requirements can be taken into account at the specification and design stage rather than added after the system is complete, so the analyst must talk to all the relevant authorities and find out their requirements alongside those of the more obvious users of the system.

1.3.7 Fallback and Recovery

Most information systems have some sort of requirement for fallback and recovery. These requirements could include the ability to 'roll back' the system to some point before failure and then to come forward progressively to bring the information up to date, or some back-up means of capturing data while the main system is off-line. Standby systems that normally perform less urgent tasks can take over from 'critical' systems, and, if necessary, full system duplication or even triplication may be provided for critical real-time or command-and-control systems. Provision of back-up, though necessary, is expensive, and so the case for the arrangements provided must be examined in strict business terms and the effects on the business of system failure assessed. 'What would be the costs involved?' and 'How long could the business go without the system?' are two of the more important questions to be answered. Recent terrorist attacks have demonstrated the importance of back-up systems and the speed with which they can be brought on-line after a disaster.

Sometimes the analysis of these consequences can produce truly frightening results. In one case there was an investigation of a system that supported a major undertaking and which had distributed data-capture and centralised control. It was found that, if the central processors went out of action for more than two days, the backlog of data in the distributed processors would be such that the system could never catch up, whereas the failure of one of the distributed machines would not become very serious for several weeks.

So, the analyst must carry out a comprehensive risk analysis in this area, using outside expertise in support if necessary, and must keep the resultant constraints in mind at all times.

1.4 Using IT for Competitive Advantage

In the early days of information systems, their justification seemed straight-forward enough. For the most part the systems were 'number-crunchers' that could carry out routine repetitive tasks, such as the calculation of payrolls, much more quickly and cheaply than an army of clerks. The payoff was thus clearly in staff savings plus perhaps some additions in the form of better or more timely information for management.

There are few, if any, of these first-time applications available now, and many administrative systems are now into their third or fourth incarnations. Justification for the new developments has generally been that:

- The old ones are incompatible with newer technological platforms, resulting perhaps from a switch to 'open' architectures.

- They have become impossible to maintain because of the poor documentation or configuration management of many early systems.

- They need skills and resources to maintain them that are no longer available or are prohibitively expensive.

None of these however are business reasons in the sense that they support some key business objective; rather, they are technical reasons justified only in terms of the inherent nature of IT itself.

As expenditure on IT has risen, so managements have become increasingly keen to ensure that the money spent contributes in some tangible way to the achievement of business objectives. At the same time, some more enlightened boards, and some IT directors with a wider interest than in the technology itself, have become interested in the idea of 'IT for competitive advantage'. The concept is simple enough. If IT can give your company some unique offering, or contribute to providing some unique offering, then it will give you a competitive edge over your competitors and hence contribute directly to increased sales and profits. Two examples may serve to illustrate the idea, which is discussed in more detail later in this section.

Example 1

One of the continuing headaches for retailers is the level of inventory, or stock, they keep in their stores. If it is too high, excess funds are tied up in it, profit margins are depressed by it, and it occupies floorspace that could be more usefully employed to display and sell goods. If inventory is too low, they risk 'stockouts', and customers cannot buy what is not on the shelves. In high-volume operations such as supermarkets, if customers cannot buy what they want immediately, they will go elsewhere, and that particular sale is gone for ever.

How can information systems help? A system is implemented that constantly monitors sales at the checkouts and signals a distribution centre when stocks of items fall below predetermined levels. Replacement stock is loaded onto trucks and, provided the operation has been set up correctly, arrives at the store just as the last item is sold. The stock is unloaded straight onto the display shelves and, without having excessive local storage space, the store is able to avoid customers going away empty-handed. Additionally, the cost savings can be passed on to customers as lower prices, thus attracting more business and improving the market share and profitability of the chain.

Example 2

In the late 1970s, many airlines were interested in seeing how they could tie travel agents and customers to their services and, by the same token, exclude their competitors. Several of them formed consortia with the idea of developing powerful booking systems that they could provide to travel agents. These would make it very much quicker and simpler for the agents to deal with the participating airlines than with their competitors. It is interesting to note that, in the major shake-up of the international airline business that occurred in the 1980s and 1990s, it was the airlines that invested most in this technology that moved to dominant positions in the marketplace.

In a competitive environment organisations grow and prosper through increasing their competitive – or strategic – advantage over their rivals. The best-known analysis of this competitive situation is Michael Porter's five forces model, which shows how competitive forces impact on an organisation. We can use this model to see how IS developments can help to improve the competitive position. First, though, because we are dealing with information systems, we need to understand the difference between data and information, and how information is created and valued.

Data is the raw material, the facts and observations of business life that by themselves have little value or useful purpose. Knowing the number of beefburgers sold today doesn't really help us to manage the burger shop unless we know how many were sold on the same day last week, the resources used in making them, the price at which they were sold, and so on. By contrast, information is data that has been processed in some way to make it useful, valuable and meaningful and a possible basis for taking decisions. In our burger shop we might for example have processed raw sales data to show sales by each hour of the day to help us to determine staffing levels.

So, to get information from data we are:

- Processing or transforming it using a defined process. Multiply the number of burgers sold each day by their price to get the revenue for the day.

- Putting it into a context that gives it meaning. Sales by each hour of the day show the busiest times and predict when most staff will be needed.

- Creating it for a purpose. We may be trying to decide whether to change employee shift patterns.

- Using it to help make better decisions through reducing uncertainty and so eliminate the amount of inefficient trial and error.

It's apparent then that information has value, but how is its value assessed? Intuitively managers often say 'No, don't do that. It's just not worth the effort to get that level of detail', or they ask themselves the question 'What would I do with that information if I had it?' The problem comes when they say 'What I'd really like to know is . . . Because then I could . . . and that would mean . . .', so there is a value in having the new information, and although it is difficult to quantify, it is an economic entity and it does have a value. The benefits that result from using information might be clearly visible – tangible benefits – such as cost savings. Or they might be intangible – soft benefits such as business expansion. Often information takes on value because it generates tangible or intangible benefits. Cost–benefit analysis attempts to identify the expected payoff from an information system by quantifying the cost of producing the information and the value of the information when it's produced.

However the cost benefit works out, information users will be concerned with its quality. Let's look at the characteristics of good quality information:

- *Relevant*. Is the information relevant, bearing in mind how I want to use it? When I'm presented with it, is extra processing needed before it gives me what I need?

- *Accurate*. Wrong or misleading information leads to wrong decisions being made. The information needs to be accurate enough for the purpose; small departments budget items of cost to the nearest £100, larger departments to the nearest £1000.

- *Enough*. Decisions are usually taken in an atmosphere of uncertainty. Getting more information isn't always the answer either as it may be neither timely nor relevant.

- *In time*. Information has much less value if it arrives late! It needs to arrive in sufficient time for thoughtful decisions to be made.

- *Clear*. Is the information presented in a form that makes it easy to understand and use? This sounds simple: we just ask the user how he or she would like it presented, and as long as there's one user with unchanging preferences and needs then we can deliver it. Multiple users with different needs and changing preferences – which is most likely to be the case – cause more difficulty.

A useful way of summarising and remembering the characteristics of good information is shown in Figure 1.1.

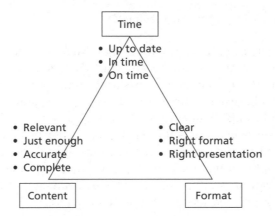

Fig. 1.1 The dimensions of good quality information

What part then does good-quality information play in giving organisations competitive advantage, whether it means more profit, greater market share, getting higher up the government league table, or meeting targets set by an industry regulator? As was said earlier, for organisations to grow and prosper they seek to gain competitive advantage, and they use information systems to develop and sustain this advantage. Here's how Porter's five forces model works. In the centre is the competitive environment, where there is *rivalry* among the existing competitors (Figure 1.2).

Fig. 1.2 The competitive environment

This rivalry can be intense or mild, the result of a growing or contracting market, where one competitor's products are highly differentiated from those of others, or where there are many or few competitors. All organisations in the market are subject to the threat of *new entrants* (Figure 1.3).

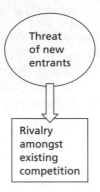

Fig. 1.3 The threat of new entrants

The existing competitors may 'share out' the market in safety if the threat of new entrants is low because the barriers to entry are high. In an extreme case it may be that the capital costs of starting up are very high or it may be necessary to get a licence to operate in the market. If existing customers are very loyal to existing brands, then entry costs may also be high. There may, however, be *substitute products or services* that customers could use instead of the ones currently supplied by the existing organisations. If high prices are being paid to the existing suppliers, who make high profits, then customers may be willing to change. The substitute product may also have advantages of its own – real or perceived – that existing products don't have (Figure 1.4).

Fig. 1.4 The threat of new products or services

So now we have three of the five forces: the competitive rivalry, the threat of new entrants, and the threat from substitute products or services. The remaining two are the *bargaining power of suppliers* and the *bargaining power of customers*. If there are many suppliers then organisations have more choice and more opportunity to negotiate good supply arrangements. Conversely, if supply is concentrated with a few suppliers then the greater power they have. There may also be the costs of switching to a new supplier or being tied to a specific supplier because their product or service has special qualities. For customers, their bargaining power depends on the strength of the brand being bought, product quality, the buyers' concentration versus the sellers' fragmentation and so on. The final model therefore looks as shown in Figure 1.5.

Fig. 1.5 Porter's five forces model

This model of industry competitiveness and the forces in it allows general questions to be asked about the role that IS can play. So we ask whether IS can be used, for example, to

- defend a market position against new entrants;
- reduce the power of suppliers;
- reduce the bargaining power of buyers;
- generate greater market share by winning customers from rivals.

There are reckoned to be three basic strategies that organisations can follow: they can compete on *cost* and try to become the cost leader, they can have very distinctive products and strong brands and compete by being different (a strategy of *differentiation*), or they can compete through *innovation*. Competing on cost means

using IS to reduce production, administration and marketing costs. Increasingly it means working with suppliers and customers as well by making linkages between the systems in the different organisations. The closer customers and suppliers become tied together – through just-in-time supply systems – then the more costly it becomes for customers to switch suppliers. Competing by differentiation means creating a distinction between your products and services and those of your competitors. Information systems are used to offer superior service through order entry and order enquiry systems and total customer care systems. The introduction of customer affinity cards and the associated systems by supermarkets is an attempt to differentiate themselves from their competitors and to make it possible to market special offers to specific groups of customers. Competing through innovation is about finding new ways to deliver customer satisfaction. It could be through the use of IS in research and development or in bringing products and services to the market quickly. This is very much the case now in the financial services industry with the constant introduction of new savings and pension products.

In this section then we've looked at data and information and seen how data needs to be processed or transformed to become valuable information. The characteristics of useful information have been reviewed, and we've seen in outline how information and the use of information systems support the strategy of an organisation. But we need to end with some cautionary notes. Research published in 1998 by the Oxford Institute of Information Management at Templeton College questions some of the generally accepted ideas about IT and competitive advantage. According to this research several questions are being asked, and at least two of them are relevant to us at this point:

- Are claims about IT and competitive advantage overdone?

- Is it beginning to run out of corporate support?

There is general acceptance that IT is being used as a competitive weapon, but now there is doubt about whether marked competitive advantage is being achieved. Arguments are that 'We are different from the well known exemplar cases' and that in any case competitive advantage is short lived: 'We introduced a new product and within weeks someone copied it'. The key issues here are that competitive advantage comes from a detailed analysis of the special forces faced by an organisation and an integrated response over several years. The implementation of IS to support strategic change doesn't deliver immediate knockout blows. Short-lived examples of competitive advantage are well known: supermarket affinity cards are an example. The actions that turn them into sustainable competitive advantage include restricting competitor actions and giving greater access to customers. In the case of supermarket cards these appear to have been absent.

In conclusion, then, information management and the use of IT/IS for competitive is a lively topic. The fact that it now appears in business and computing degree courses as well as in business and computing journals is a good example of its growing importance. We return to it again in Chapter 12.

1.5 Successful Systems

When the new system you've worked on is implemented and running regularly, and you're assigned to another project, how will you know if you did a good job? How will you know if you've helped to produce a successful system? A typical question often used in analysis and design examinations asks:

> You're called in to evaluate the effectiveness of a recently implemented system. What criteria would you use?

Leaving aside project management considerations such as implementation to time, cost and quality you could ask the following questions:

- Does the system achieve the goals set for it? Some of these will be operational running goals concerned with performance, some will be system goals concerned with the production of outputs, and some will be business goals addressing the purpose of the system development.

- How well does the system fit the structure of the business for which it was developed? The new system will no doubt have been developed based on an understanding of the then present structure of the organisation and some appreciation of how it might change in the future. However, it must not be an 'albatross system' that hangs around the organisation's neck limiting its movement and freedom to reorganise. Systems should be designed in a flexible way so that they can be changed to meet changing business conditions.

- Is the new system accurate, secure and reliable? There will be basic requirements for financial control and auditing, but the system should also be robust so as to continue in operation with degraded performance during partial failure. Security from unauthorised access has also now become increasingly important with the growth in the development of tactical and strategic information systems.

- Is the system well documented and easy to understand? Increasingly large proportions of the budget of system development departments are being used in the maintenance and updating of existing systems. The biggest single way of limiting these expenses in the future is to take account of it when we design today the systems of tomorrow.

This 'single-system' view may help to identify the characteristics of successful systems, but it doesn't give a sufficiently wide framework for our analysis. We need to begin with an overview of the organisation as a whole. We can, for example, see the organisation in systems terms, operating within its environment and made up of a series of subsystems. A representation of this that has been widely used is shown in Figure 1.6.

It shows an industrial organisation with subsystems for:

- marketing and purchasing: these are the main links with the environment as represented by customers and suppliers. It's important to recognise, however,

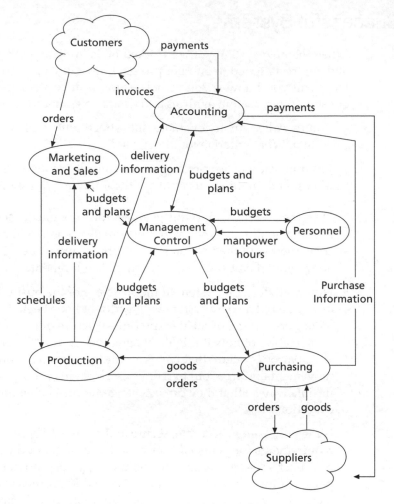

Fig. 1.6 The organisation as a system

that the environment also interacts with the organisation through legislation, social pressures, competitive forces, the education system and political decisions.

- the production system: this is concerned with transforming raw materials into finished products. It applies just as much in service organisations as in traditional manufacturing industry: an architectural drawing office is the equivalent of a motor engine assembly line.

- support systems: these are shown as the accounting, personnel and management control subsystems.

For this organisation to work effectively it has to make good use of information, so the need arises for information systems that collect, store, transform and display information about the business. We can represent this information systems

Fig. 1.7 An hierarchical view of systems

structure in two ways: either in a non-hierarchical way showing each subsystem on the same level, or in an hierarchical way where some systems sit on top of others. This multilevel view is often more helpful as it shows the different levels of control, the different data requirements, and a different view of the organisation of each system. A typical way of representing this structure is as if the systems are arranged in a pyramid as shown in Figure 1.7.

At the top level are strategic systems and decision support systems that *informate* the organisation. Informate is a term that, in brief, means what happens when automated processes yield information that enables new competitive advantage to be gained. At this level systems contribute towards the formulation of corporate policy and direction. These are concerned almost entirely with financial information and other data that show the health of the organisation. Strategic systems use information from lower-level internal systems and externally obtained information about markets, social trends and competitor behaviour.

Underneath strategic systems lie managerial or tactical systems that are concerned with the monitoring and control of business functions. There is therefore a regular supply of data from the day-to-day operational systems, which are manipulated to provide the management information that these systems typically produce. Systems requirements here are for timely, useful and effectively presented reports that enable middle managers to run their departments and divisions effectively. Here also we see the need for systems that can respond to a changing array of ad hoc queries about why the results look the way they do.

The operational systems level is concerned with the routine processing of transactions such as orders, invoices, schedules and statements. They help the organisation to 'do what it does' – make parts, distribute products, manage property. They are not concerned with changing the way the organisation works.

We can now see that the organisation can be viewed as a system, and that the information systems that support it can be strategic, tactical or operational. This is summarised in Box 1.1.

Box 1.1 The three-level systems summary

Strategic systems	Provide information to managers to enable them to make better-informed decisions.
	Support decision-makers in situations that are poorly structured.
	Used to establish plans for the introduction of new business lines or their closure.
	Need greater flexibility to be able to respond to constantly changing requirements.
Tactical systems	Use stored data from operational systems.
	System outputs are well defined as managers can generally identify the factors influencing decisions that they will have to make.
	Usually concerned with the management and control of departments or functions.
Operational systems	Transaction based.
	Handle the routine business activities of organisations.
	Often the first systems to be automated as they provide the raw data for higher-level systems.

There is one more view that we must see before we can leave this topic. It is concerned with the evolution of information systems. A useful model here and one widely used is the Gibson–Nolan four-stage model of:

- initiation;
- expansion;
- formalisation;
- maturity.

Let's consider an organisation moving through this model for the first time. During the *initiation* phase the first computer-based systems to be developed are those best suited to the new technology. These projects are almost always at the bottom of the systems pyramid and involve the repetitive processing of large volumes of transactions. They often begin with accounting systems. Following experience here the organisation enters the *expansion* stage and seeks to apply the new technology to as many applications as possible. This is the honeymoon period for the IS department until one day a halt is called to the ever-growing IS budget and the introduction of development planning and controls signals the start of the *formalisation* stage. It is here that the need for information surpasses the need for data and where the organisation begins to plan its way from a mixture of separate data processing systems towards a more coordinated and integrated approach. Corporate recognition of the need for integrated systems is the characteristic of the *maturity* stage. Here we see the use of open system architectures, database environments and comprehensive systems planning.

There is a final complication. Organisations don't go through this model once. There is no final nirvana of maturity, of fully integrated systems all talking to each other and producing exactly the strategic information needed by top management. The organisation or its component parts can be at different stages in the model at the same time. Having arrived at the *formalisation* stage with large mainframe computers, many organisations were plunged back into *initiation* and *expansion* with the arrival of personal computers. New technology, the development of new applications software packages or significant price reductions in either hardware or software all throw organisations back into the initiation stage.

At the beginning of this section we asked a question about evaluating the effectiveness of a recently implemented system. We conclude with some general ideas on wider aspects of this topic. Surveys in the late 1990s have shown that the issue of measuring the benefits of IT investment has been one of the main concerns of senior IT/IS management. It also appears that, although attention was given to cost–benefit analysis at the beginning of the project, much less attention was given to post-implementation review, and there was consequent loss of opportunity to learn from past project success or failure. Consequently there has been some new work done on sample projects to evaluate the outcomes throughout the lifecycle to give a better understanding of how best to manage projects to achieve the desired results.

Taking this together with some of the earlier comments about the use of IS/IT to deliver and sustain competitive advantage, perhaps the best that can be said at the moment is that the jury is still out.

1.6 The Role of the Analyst and Designer

Earlier in this chapter we said that systems analysts and designers change the world. In discussing the role of the analyst and designer we should therefore begin with a consideration of this change-making initiative. We have a problem, however, in that analysts and designers are not always the same person. This is illustrated by a diagram produced by G.M. Weinburg (Figure 1.8).

It shows very clearly down the centre what he regarded as the analyst's role. The designers and implementers do quite different things, which are not specified, and the analyst is the only link with the users. We also see the difference in recruitment specifications, where those for analysts ask for applications and business experience and those for designers specify software environment and hardware architectures. Life is complicated further by the many sorts of analyst and designer titles, such as business analyst, applications analyst, database designer, network designer, database administrator, infrastructure manager and systems manager. They all draw on the skills that were once the exclusive territory of the

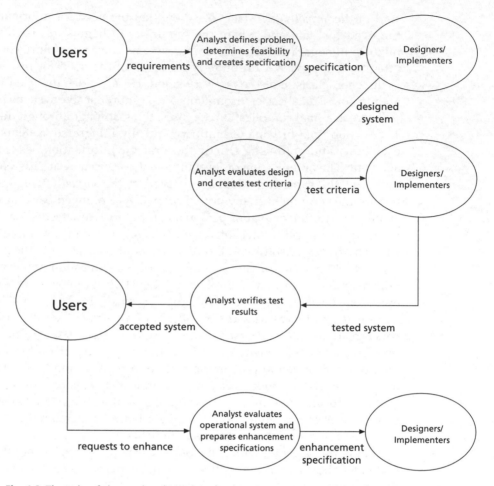

Fig. 1.8 The role of the analyst (Weinburg)

systems analyst. Let us therefore take a step up from this detailed picture that prevents us from seeing 'the wood for the trees'. We can recognise a set of attributes at a general level that all analysts or designers should possess, whatever their job title. As a minimum we should expect our analysts or designers:

- to uncover the fundamental issues of a problem. These might be the bottlenecks in a business system or the logic of a file-processing module;

- to be able to prepare sound plans and appreciate the effect that new data will have on them, and replan appropriately;

- to be perceptive but not jump to conclusions, to be persistent to overcome difficulties and obstacles and maintain a planned course of action to achieve results;

- to exhibit stamina, strength of character and a sense of purpose essential in a professional specialist;

- to have a broad flexible outlook, an orderly mind and a disciplined approach, as the job will frequently require working without direct supervision;

- to possess higher-than-average social skills so as to work well with others, and the ability to express thoughts, ideas, suggestions and proposals clearly, both orally and in writing.

Many designers with very special technical skills and knowledge have in the past sought refuge in their specialisms from the need to exhibit many of the skills and attributes in this list, but in our view the complete list has validity for all analysts and designers whatever their job title.

Finally, in this section are two more light-hearted views about the role of the systems analyst. The first is an American view based on Modell's *A Professional's Guide to Systems Analysis*, in which he lists the many roles of the analyst, some of which are:

- *Detective*. A detective, whether private or official, is one whose primary task is to uncover the facts of an event and to determine responsibility for the event.

- *Puzzle solver*. The puzzle solver is one who either puts things together from component pieces or determines solutions from clues and hints.

- *Indian scout*. An Indian scout is one who is usually the first on the scene and who looks for hidden dangers or for the correct path through the wilderness (of the corporate environment). The Indian scout may also be the first one to find hidden dangers, and may draw the first fire.

Other roles he proposes include artist, sculptor, diagnostician and reporter. Perhaps he was intending to entertain as well as inform his students when he prepared his list. Someone who clearly believes in doing both is Roy Tallis, a longtime friend and fellow trainer, who used to offer his students some Alexander Pope (1688–1744) with their systems analysis when he described the analyst as 'Correct with spirit, eloquent with ease, intent to reason, or polite to please'.

1.7 Ethical Considerations

Mostly in this book we are concerned with getting the job done, with the practicalities of analysis and design. In this section we'll consider some of the ethical considerations of working as a systems analyst. We suggest that you need to consider three issues:

- morality;
- ethics;
- professionalism.

Morality is not about hacking or computer fraud or the misuse of computers. There is legislation to cover these criminal acts. They may or not be immoral, but they are illegal. In the UK the Computer Misuse Act legislates against unauthorised access or modification of computer-held information. Morality is about right and wrong. It's concerned with the goodness and badness of character or disposition. It is therefore a personal thing: it's about your personal beliefs of right and wrong. Macaulay said that there was no 'spectacle so ridiculous as the British public in one of its periodical fits of morality', and no doubt this could be said of other peoples too. He suggested that different ideas about right and wrong might arise at different times to reflect changes in society. This may be so. Because it may be so, professional bodies and employers set out statements of their view of right and wrong, and these govern the way all of us work.

If morality is an individual or personal view of right and wrong, then *ethics* are statements or descriptions that we can use, in the absence of a clear shared morality, to guide our behaviour. In modern management-speak they are often now referred to as *value statements*. They are connected with moral codes, of course, as people formulate them based on what they believe, and they describe how you and I or any other person should behave. If the values are all about honesty, openness and integrity – popular words in value statements – then the organisation believes that employees should behave honestly, openly and with integrity.

Professionalism is a much-misunderstood word. In sport, where commentators talk about the 'professional foul', they are merely describing the qualities or typical features of a profession. Nor should we get hung up about 'professions'; they are described in the Oxford dictionary as a 'vocation or calling, especially one that involves some branch of advanced learning or science'. So professionalism can be described as behaviour that meets the currently acceptable standards of the profession – whatever they are!

As an analyst you'll find yourself – or you should find yourself – constrained by issues of morality, ethics and professionalism. Folk hero Dilbert often finds himself in this situation where he is faced with juggling a variety of constraints that impact his work. Some of the ones you might find are illustrated in Figure 1.9. Without wanting to raise ethical issues to the top of the list of the

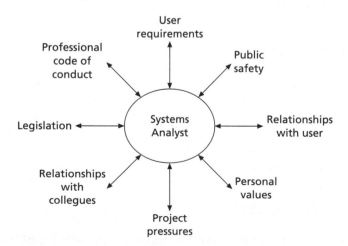

Fig. 1.9 The ethical dilemma

analyst's concerns, it is important to think about the ethical issues of your work. To help you to do just this, the British Computer Society (BCS) has published a code of conduct applicable to its thousands of members. Even if you're not one of them it is worth reviewing how well you measure up against it. The full code is available through the BCS website, and you'll find the address at the end of the box below. In summary though it is in four parts – see Box 1.2 – and deals with

- the public interest;
- relationships with your employer and your customers;
- the profession;
- professional competence.

Box 1.2 An outline of the British Computer Society Code of Conduct

The Public Interest

This section deals with members' responsibility for public health and safety issues, the protection of the environment and the safeguarding of basic human rights. Members are to ensure that they have knowledge and understanding of relevant legislation and that they comply with it.

Employers and Clients

Members are expected to work with due care and diligence and deliver work on time and to budget and to report on any likely overruns as soon as practicable. If their professional judgement is overruled they are to point out the likely consequences. Members are expected to observe the highest standards of financial probity and to respect client and employer confidentiality. There should be no misrepresentation of the capability of products or services.

The Profession

This section of the Code requires members to uphold the reputation of the profession, to work to professional standards and to avoid any action that will adversely affect the good standing of the Profession. There is a responsibility to represent the Profession in public in an honest and balanced way and to act with integrity towards fellow members and members of other professions. Members are expected to encourage and support fellow members in their professional development.

Professional Competence and Integrity

Members shall continue to develop their professional competence and seek to conform to good practice. They must offer to do only that work that is in their area of competence and to accept professional responsibility for it and for the work of their subordinates.

For the full code see www.bcs.org.uk

In the United States the Association for Computing Machinery (ACM) also has a *Code of Ethics and Professional Conduct* covering a similar wide area, and you can find a snappy *Ten Commandments of Computer Ethics* published by the Brookings Computer Ethics Institute of Washington. See the web references at the end of the book.

1.8 Summary

In this chapter we've tried to establish some foundations for the rest of the book. These can be summarised as follows:

- Systems analysis and design is an exciting, challenging, difficult and rewarding trade. It is constantly changing; new solutions are discovered every day. If we had the opportunity to rework systems produced three, five, ten years ago, not only would the solutions be very different but so would the problems.

- The customer is very important. Make sure that you know the customer, and what kind of solution is needed.

- There is no such thing in practice as a perfect system. There are successful systems. Understand the customer's criteria for a successful system. What will produce that wonderful phrase 'Well done, you've done a good job'?

- Systems development is difficult. Take all the help you can in finding better ways to do things. Today's panacea is the use of structured methods. They work and they improve the quality of the delivered system. These methods will change. They may be replaced.

- New systems should be developed only when there is a clear linkage to the organisation's business goals. This means that analysts will need a broad mixture of all-round business understanding as well as a technical competence.

- Systems development takes place in an environment bounded by constraints that change over time as business needs and technology change.

- Ethical issues are important, and should be seen not as constraints but as a foundation for the way in which work is done.

Finally, enjoy this book. All of it works some of the time. That's the best you can expect. Life is imperfect. You have to work with the book's content, apply it and make it work for you. Good luck.

Case Study: System Telecom

Introduction

Throughout this book, we have included examples of how principles are put into practice. The applications used to illustrate the practice include hospital systems, customer systems of various kinds, a library system, student enrolment in a college and others. This diversity also serves to emphasise the wide application knowledge often required of systems analysts. As a contrast we have included a case example so that there can be a more comprehensive treatment of one application.

The example we have chosen is the customer services function from a European telecommunications company. It's not a real company of course, but it is rooted in practicality, with data and ideas drawn from several telecommunications companies and the experience of analysts working in this business area. The material here is some narrative describing the company, some of the dataflow diagrams for the required system, and a data model. There are exercises based on this case study at the end of most of the chapters.

Company Background

System Telecom is a large European telecommunications business with a turnover in excess of £4000m making profits before taxation of just over 20%. It has maintained a record of continuously rising profits since it was established. Its latest annual report says that System Telecom is positioned to achieve above-average levels of growth. It is in one of the world's fastest-growing industries, where the pace of change is likely to accelerate. It believes that it is now where the motor industry was in the 1930s, with many decades of growth and opportunity to come. To perform strongly in the future, however, it will need to implement a continuing programme of new business development, and from the range of opportunities presented to it, it must select those that give it the optimum return. System Telecom is in a capital-intensive business, and always has to balance the income from existing businesses with investment in new businesses. Reducing the investment in new business enables profit to be maximised in the short term, but to the detriment of future growth. Over-investment will reduce immediate profits and cash flow for the benefit of the long term. The shareholders in System Telecom pay particular attention to this balance and to investment in research and development, and new technologies. The company spends between 2% and 3% of its turnover on R&D. It believes that the introduction of new services based on technological as well as market research gives it a competitive edge. It views new systems in the same way, and expects new computer-based information systems to support business goals and generate competitive advantage.

The shareholders in System Telecom are unusual. Unlike most European telecommunications operations, which are state run, recently privatised or on the way to privatisation, System Telecom was set up deliberately to take advantage of the opening up of the European telecommunications market. This followed highly controversial and bitterly contested legislation introduced by the European Commission aimed at breaking down the protective and nationalistic stances of many EU members. System Telecom's shareholders have pledged long-term funding to establish an aggressive and highly competitive technologically based business that will generate a growing profits stream as their own original businesses plateau or decline.

Strategically, System Telecom intends to be the European leader in three core sectors: premium and business services, mobile communications, and basic telecommunications. Central to its premium and business services is EUROCAB, a transnational data highway linking together Europe's major business centres. Services offered through EUROCAB include Bandswitch, the world's first variable-bandwidth data transmission network. This allows companies to transmit high volumes of data at great speed to many distant sites without the cost of permanently leasing large amounts of transmission capacity. Also offered to major companies is the equivalent of a private network and, for individual customers, an international charge card that allows customers to make domestic and international calls from anywhere on the System Telecom network and have the cost of the call billed to a single account.

Future products under consideration include personal numbering, a service already available in parts of the USA, which allows users to redirect their calls from home to office or to wherever they are at particular times of the day.

System Telecom's innovative and entrepreneurial approach has led to a number of highly publicised and commercially successful ventures outside the European Union. It has joined with four substantial Japanese corporations to offer premium services in Japan, with the intention of linking these to Hong Kong and Singapore. In the former Soviet Union it has set up several joint venture companies, including one with Intertelecom, the leading local carrier, to provide international telecommunications as the countries of the former Eastern bloc move towards commercial, market-led economies.

The mobile communications business is still largely confined to the UK and Germany, where it is experiencing rapid growth in subscribers and number of calls. In the UK the service operates mainly within the M25 ring. A new service has just been launched in Germany in the industrialised areas along the Rhine corridor.

Like most 'hi-tech' companies, System Telecom relies enormously on the skills of its people, and places great emphasis on motivating, training and developing people in an international context. It has founded System Telecom University to be the focal point for development and training in technological and business skills.

Although the company has a hard and aggressive business profile it prides itself on being a responsible corporate citizen, and it supports a wide range of charitable, community and cultural projects across Europe.

Systems Background

The System Telecom Board recognises that the success of its business strategy is largely dependent upon its procedures and systems. The effective use of IT systems will be critical in giving the company a competitive edge. A strategic study was commissioned, and the study report identified specific functional areas where automated systems are essential to the efficient running of the organisations. These functional areas are:

- customer services;
- management information;

- personnel;
- payroll/pensions.

The *customer services* function is the area to be considered here. This function provides the administrative basis for the services offered by the company, and will be fundamental in achieving business success. The main task areas within this function are:

- customer registration;
- call logging and charging;
- billing;
- payment recording;
- number maintenance;
- pricing policy.

Customer registration   Customers may be from the commercial or domestic sectors, and are accepted subject to various credit checks. Customer identification details are held and maintained by the system.

Once customers are registered they may subscribe to services, such as fax and telephone, and may have numbers allocated for their use of those services. They then become responsible for payment for all calls logged to those numbers. They may request new numbers or cancel existing numbers as required. Customers who have cancelled all of their numbers continue to be maintained on the system for two years. This widens the customer base for mailshots regarding new services, promotions, etc.

Call logging and charging   Calls are logged by three factors: duration, distance, and timing. Various combinations of bands within those categories are used to calculate the cost of each call. System Telecom operates a number of tariff and subscription schemes that provide financially advantageous facilities for both commercial and domestic customers. The applicable tariff plans are taken into account when calculating charges. System Telecom aims to provide an efficient service at the lowest possible cost to the consumer, and therefore customers are constantly reviewed for inclusion in suitable pricing schemes.

Billing   Bills are issued on a periodic basis. This is usually quarterly but may be monthly, half-yearly or yearly, subject to negotiation with the customer. The bills itemise all charges, both for service subscriptions and for call charges. Tariff plan discounts are also shown. Reminder bills are issued a fortnight after billing, and payment must be made within one month of the issue of this bill or the services are automatically disconnected following issue of a disconnection notice. Payment must be made in full, plus the reconnection charge, prior to the resumption of services. Customers are not eligible for reconnection following a second disconnection. Bad debts are passed to the debt collection department on issue of the disconnection notice.

There is also a set payment scheme whereby customers make regular fixed payments that are offset against their bills. These payments are shown on the bills. Any credit/debit is carried forward to the year-end reconciliation, when a final bill is issued.

Payment recording   Payments may be made in various ways:

- by cash/cheque at specified outlets;
- by standing order;
- by automatic deduction from credit/debit cards;
- by direct debit.

Payments are made subsequent to bills being issued. The method is recorded for each customer.

Number maintenance   Numbers are held on the system and are either allocated to customers or available for allocation. New numbers are specified periodically and set up so that they may be allocated when required.

Pricing policy   The company has several approaches to pricing and uses a number of tariff plans. These are regularly reviewed and updated in order to ensure their continuing competitiveness. Customers subscribe to services via tariff plan agreements.

Additional information about System Telecom is shown on the following charts and diagrams and in the accompanying narrative.

Data Flow Diagrams (DFDs)

The Level 1 DFD shows the required system – that is, the areas of processing that are intended to be automated. The system will support the customer services function within System Telecom, and the DFD identifies six distinct areas of processing within this function. These areas are defined as the following:

1 Maintain Customers.
2 Record Calls.
3 Issue Bills.
4 Record Payments.
5 Maintain Rates.
6 Maintain Customer Facilities.

Process 5 Maintain Rates is shown with an * in the bottom right-hand corner: this indicates that there is no decomposition of this process into smaller areas of processing. Processes marked in this way are explained instead by an Elementary Process Description, which is a textual explanation of the process. Every other process on the Level 1 DFD would be further decomposed by a Level 2 DFD, and they are therefore not marked with an asterisk. Examples of Level 2 DFDs are provided for processes 1 and 4.

There are seven sequentially numbered datastores. Each datastore represents a grouping of stored data items. The same datastore may be shown more than once on the diagram if doing this makes the DFD easier to read. An additional line at the left-hand side of the datastore box indicates where this has occurred and that the datastore appears more than once.

There are nine External Entities shown on the diagram: each one represents a source and/or destination of data. An additional line across the top left-hand corner of the external entity box shows that they have been included on the diagram more than once, just as with datastores.

The arrows on the diagram represent the flow of data. Data may be

- entered by an external entity – a Customer provides Payment/Bank details to Process 4;

- read from a datastore by a process – Process 3 reads Tariff amounts from datastore d3;

- written to a datastore – Process 1 writes customer details to datastore d1;

- output to an external entity – Process 3 informs the Debt Collection Department of bad debtors;

- output to one process from another – the Level 2 DFD for Maintain Customers shows Process 1.1 sending details of an accepted customer to Process 1.2.

The Level 2 DFDs are enclosed by a boundary box. This separates the processes from the interfaces to the external entities and the logical data stores.

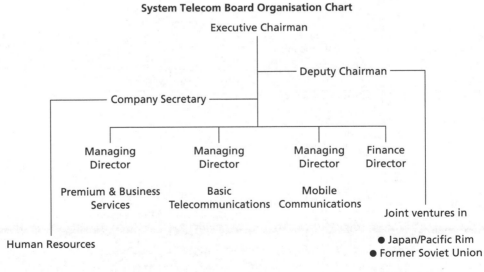

System Telecom Board Organisation Chart

System Telecom Level 1 DFD – Required System

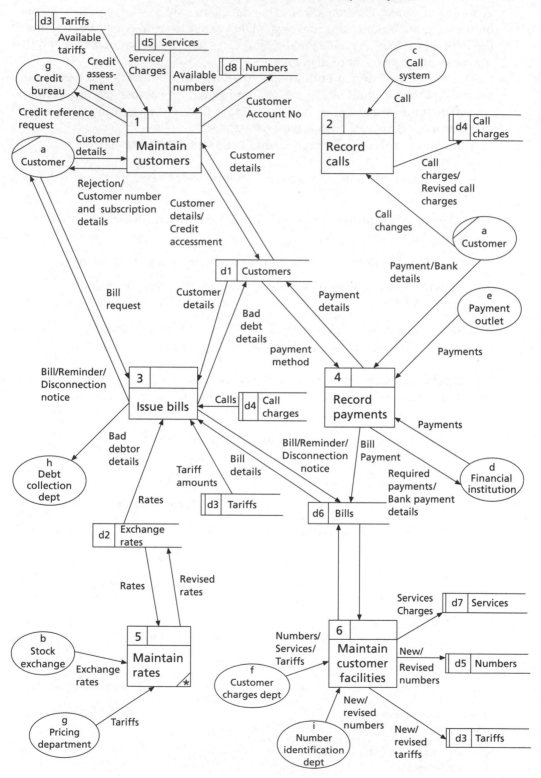

Level 2 DFD – Maintain Customers

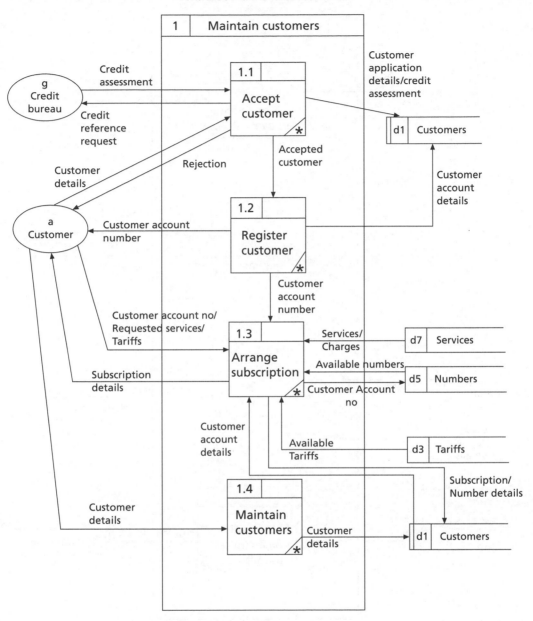

The DFD defines the processing that the system will carry out but not how the system will work. There is no sequence implied in the numbers allocated to the processes or the datastores; they are merely labels. In essence the DFD shows the means of triggering an area of processing and the data that is input, updated and output while the process is carried out.

Level 2 DFD – Record Payments

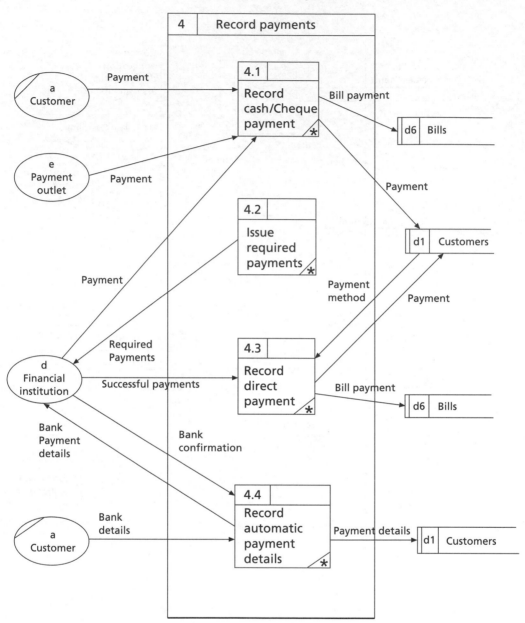

Exercises

1.1 Bearing in mind:

- what you know about System Telecom and the reasons for setting it up;
- its style of operation; and
- the information in this chapter about business;

what do you think would be a reasonable set of business objectives for Systems Telecom for the next three years? What might be the critical success factors for these objectives?

1.2 Having identified some critical success factors, suggest ways in which new computer-based systems in System Telecom might help to achieve them.

1.3 Using the LozCo case study, draw a physical DFD.

Case Study: LozCo Ltd

LozCo is a manufacturer of pastilles and lozenges that are supplied mainly to chemists' shops. They are a small company with a range of products, all of which have medical purposes.

Their production process uses 300 different raw materials, and they hold the details of the ingredients and quantities used in their production process in a product specification file kept by the works manager.

On a weekly basis the directors hold a meeting where they agree the requirements for the next week's production run, and these are typed up as a works order. This order is given to the works manager, but the managing director's secretary retains a copy. The works order contains a number of products to be made that week, and one product may be found on several works orders.

The works manager uses the product specification file to work out the raw material quantities required, and these quantities are deducted from the stock records that he keeps in his office. These records are held manually in loose-leaf files with a section for each of the 300 raw materials that LozCo hold in stock. If this causes an ingredient to go below its reorder level then the works manager will arrange for a purchase order to be sent to the supplier. A copy of this order is retained in the purchase order file. Lozco have several suppliers for almost all of their ingredients.

LozCo manufacture lozenges using a number of similar mixing machines. Particular care is taken to ensure that the mentholated lozenges are always mixed on the same machines.

The machine shop supervisor receives a copy of the works order and allocates the machines to meet the required production run. Details of these allocations are stored in a word-processed file held on a PC in his office. When the week's production is completed he notes the actual weights produced on the works order, and it is returned to the sales director.

LozCo's products all use a number of simple ingredients. In some cases a product's specification may include another product as an ingredient. The ingredients are all purchased from a number of different suppliers, and each ingredient is available from more than one supplier. Each particular lozenge is produced using only one machine, and certain machines are reserved for making particular products.

2 Approaches to Analysis and Design

2.1 Introduction

In this chapter we'll look at some of the alternative approaches to the analysis and design of information systems. Alternative approaches, or methods as they are usually called, are an essential aspect of systems analysis, and they have evolved in parallel with the development of computer technology. We've proposed a framework within which these approaches can be seen in order to simplify the comparisons between them, and in reviewing their differences we attempt to identify the suitability of particular methods for particular types of development. We've selected a number of methods that are either generally well known in the world of software development or are valuable as an insight into the way systems development has evolved in line with the development of technology. We compare structured methods, SSADM in particular, with the object-oriented approach to development, taking these two methods as the dominant ones at this time. We look briefly at the antecedents of these methods to identify some underlying themes in systems development, and we use these to define a framework for understanding different methods. We'll also look at DSDM and RAD approaches and include a brief review of Merise, Euromethod and Workflow modelling.

2.2 A Framework for Analysis and Design Methods

The framework we've adopted identifies three distinct categories of systems model that can be found in a development method. These categories of model are defined as

- the *business system* model;
- the *data structure* model;
- the *dynamic behaviour* model.

This framework for analysis and design methods can be mapped onto some of the earliest approaches to systems development. These early methods were extended in the 1970s with the development of structured methods, and the framework usefully classifies the models used in this approach. The framework is also applied to the object-oriented approach with a degree of success. Other approaches described in the text fit less well, and from this we are able to suggest their suitability for particular types of application development.

Developers in the 1960s placed a heavy emphasis on programming skills, and logic or flowcharts were one of the principal planning tools in application development. As applications became more complex, and management information systems demanded greater and greater amounts of systems integration, the need for a higher level of systems planning was identified. This led to the first analysis and design method to be formally defined, being known as the *NCC (National Computing Centre) method*. The principle models or techniques in this approach were:

- *The systems flowchart* (Figure 2.1). This was a columnar chart showing the procedures in the business departments and the computer department, tracing the flow of items of business documentation through the organisation. This provided the *business systems model* referred to above. The modelling technique matched the departmentalised structure of many organisations,

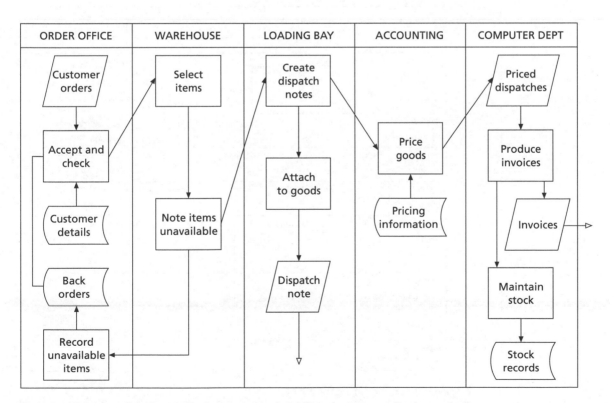

Fig. 2.1 The systems flowchart: a business system model for a departmentalised organisation

Computer File Specification	File description *Outstanding Orders*		System *MSOP*	Document *4.4*	Name *OUTORD*	Sheet *1*

N C C

File type
Input ☐   Master ☑
Output ☐   Transfer ☐

File organisation

Strong medium			Single ☐	Retention period *3 DAYS*	Number of generations *3*	Number of copies *1*
Meg. tops ☑ Disk ☐		☐	Multiple ☑			

Recovery procedure

See operations manual SOP CF1

Keys

PRODUCT CODE (OSORD7) within ORDER NO. (OSORDH) within CUSTOMER REF

Labels

Standard

Level	Record name/ref.	Size	Unit	Format	Occurrence
GA	OSORD				3560–11323
B	OSORDH	24	W	F	1 (PER ORDER)
B	OSORD7	5	W	F	Av 9. (PER ITEM)

Block/batch size		Unit of storage		Number of blocks	
Actual, for fixed length	Maximum, for variable length *Unblocked*	Records ☑	Average	Maximum	
		Words ☐	–	–	
Block/batch size		Bytes ☐	Growth rate		
Average *80,928*	Maximum *105,113*	Characters ☐ Cards ☐	*10% per ANNUM* or determining factor		

MAG: TAPE ONLY	Tracks 7 ☐ 9 ☐	Recording density	Speed	Length *MAX*

DIRECT ACCESS ONLY	Addressing accessing Method	Packing density %	Frequency/condition of re-organisation
	Level	Type of overflow	Size of overflow areas

Notes

Orders remain on file until despatched or altered

S 42

Author *AV*	Issue *A* Date *10/12/84*

Fig. 2.2 File definition form from the 1970s

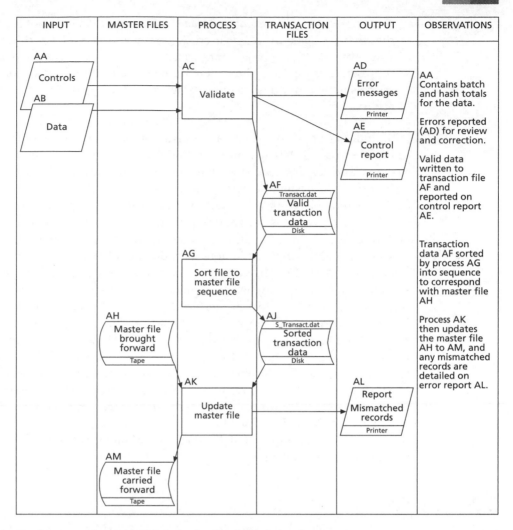

Fig. 2.3 A run chart: dynamic behaviour model for a batch processing

and the separation of the data processing functions from the business functions was typical of the approach to business computing at that time.

- *File definition* (Figure 2.2). The data used in batch processing systems was held primarily in sequential files, often on magnetic tape. The structure of this data was made up of records and fields, and a definition of the content of these was sufficient for the purpose of development. This file definition document represented the first of the *data structure models* that were to evolve rapidly to represent databases and later encapsulated objects as technology improved. The model is predominantly a physical one describing the access method and the medium (tape or disk) used to hold the data.

- *The computer run chart* (Figure 2.3). This was another columnar chart, this time showing the computer programs and files used to process a batch of data. This chart presented the *dynamic behaviour* of the system in terms of the records and files that the batch processes used. A more detailed model of this behaviour was provided by the program flowchart, and the use of two models to represent this aspect of the system foretold the proliferation of behaviour models now found in structured systems methods and in object-oriented approaches.

Although now passed over as an application development method, the impact of this approach is felt when integrating present-day developments with legacy systems, and for this reason we have included illustrations of these models and techniques. The system flowchart shown as Figure 2.1 presents the business view of the system, showing the organisation as a series of functional areas through which a transaction passes. The computing department is shown as an independent functional area providing a batch-processing service. The data structure model is provided by the file definition document (Figure 2.2), which describes the fields in a flat file. The system behaviour is shown in the form of a computer run chart in Figure 2.3, where a sequence of programs is used to validate input transactions, sort them to a masterfile sequence and update the masterfile, creating a new version in the process. Although this method of processing was adopted out of necessity rather than choice, developers should take note of the high degree of security that the approach provides and take advantage of this when appropriate. The problems involved in adapting batch-processing systems to work in an on-line, distributed manner preoccupied developers during the 1980s and 1990s. Windows-based, event-driven systems developed using software such as Visual Basic or MS-Access have now eliminated many of these difficulties. Constructing the batch-processing elements of these new systems has become the new challenge.

2.3 SSADM

The models and techniques used by SSADM fit easily into the structure of the business, data and dynamic models described above:

- Dataflow diagrams and business activity models show the business view of the system, just as the data structure model is shown with a logical data structure diagram and through the use of normalisation.

- Dynamic system behaviour is represented by a number of models, of which the entity life history model is the best recognised. System behaviour is also shown from the perspective of the user with hierarchical task models and, from a file processing perspective, with a model of the access paths through the database and a model of the impact of events on different entities with the effect correspondence diagram (ECD).

The architecture of SSADM is often described as a three-schema architecture in which models are classified as internal, external or conceptual. This three-schema classification provides a useful way of grouping the wide range of models and techniques available in SSADM, and, although some correlation exists between SSADM's three schemas and the business, data structure and dynamic classification, the mapping is not exact. The three-schema architecture can, however, offer a route to incremental development allowing the developer to create parts of the database and selected functions early in the development lifecycle.

2.4 Object-Orientation

The basic principles of object-oriented systems are simple enough, but the problems arise from how such systems are to be developed, and the methods that will be needed to build them.

An *object* is a 'thing' of interest to the system and consists of both data and the logic about itself. Thus it is rather different from a conventional entity, which contains only data. An object belongs to a *class* and, for each class, there is a set of *methods* that defines the behaviour of objects of that class. The behaviour is invoked when the object receives a valid message: this message could come from outside the system, triggered by a real-world business event, or from another object. Finally, objects *inherit* data and methods from their classes and can pass these on to their sub-objects; the subordinate object or sub-object can either behave as its superior would or it can have different methods defined for it. Thus an object-oriented system is a network of interconnected objects. Each object is self-contained, with its own data and logic, and the total system is the total of all objects. When it comes to physical implementation, the objects can be stored as tables of information, rather like a relational database. It is common to read about object-oriented databases and object-oriented programming but, in a true object-oriented system, the two would be one and the same thing.

The models and techniques used in the object-oriented approach map easily on to the business, data and dynamic model classification and reveal a similarity to the SSADM models with a proliferation of behaviour models:

- The use case diagram provides a business-oriented view of the system, with an emphasis on the roles adopted by the user rather than the more general external entity found in the dataflow diagram. In this way the object-oriented approach introduces a user perspective similar to that found in later versions of SSADM with the creation of the User Catalogue and the User Roles. The use case diagram identifies the roles or actors who interact with the system and shows the functions that the system performs for these users. It does not attempt to convert a current system to a logical system and then add new functionality, as is done in structured systems analysis and design, but relies on the intuitive ability of the developer to identify and define the functions required by the user.

- The data structure model used with the object-oriented approach introduces new concepts in the design of data structures, some of which contradict the principles of design advocated by the structured approach. The object-oriented structure model is known as a *class diagram*, and is used to define objects in class hierarchies where the properties of the higher-class members are inherited by the lower members whose individuality is defined by attributes and actions or methods that are peculiar to them alone. The class diagram emphasises the advantages of reusability of functions, and, by establishing generalised methods for performing common functions on similar items of data, not only economises on the effort of developing programs, but also introduces standardised ways of performing basically similar functions on the data, irrespective of the application being served.

2.5 Traditional Approaches

The techniques used by a particular method of analysis and design combine with a life cycle to control the progress of the development project.

Generally, a traditional approach will involve the application of analysis and design skills by competent practitioners. They will use their experience and knowledge of the business being studied, and of the technical environment, to devise and propose a system that meets the users' needs as they understand them. Usually, the consideration of business issues – what the system is supposed to do – will go side by side with the technical evaluation – how the system might work – with no explicit boundary between the two.

By the very nature of the traditional approach, it is not possible to define a sequence that will summarise its use in all projects. However, the following sequence expanded in Figure 2.4 is reasonably typical, and it can be contrasted with that for the structured approach, which follows later.

1 *Analysis of requirements.* The analysts examine the current system, if there is one, and discuss with the users the problems with that system and the requirements for a new one. Generally, no attempt is made to separate functional requirements, such as provision of on-line transactions, from non-functional requirements, such as system response times. Usually, the analysis documentation will not be delivered to the users, and will only be used by the analysts in devising their specifications. Therefore the users will not necessarily review analysis documentation unless specifically asked, for example to check the completeness of interview notes.

2 *Specification of requirements.* The analysts now sift through their documentation and produce a specification of requirements for the new system. This will include functional and non-functional requirements, and will often include a description of the proposed hardware and software as well as the users' business requirements. Very often, layouts for on-line screens and printed reports will be included in the specification. The specification must usually be approved by the users before the project continues, but the degree to which users examine this document carefully varies greatly, depending on the knowledge and interest of individual users, how much time they have available, and on the importance they attach to the project. It is also very likely that the specification will be mainly in text, perhaps illustrated with some

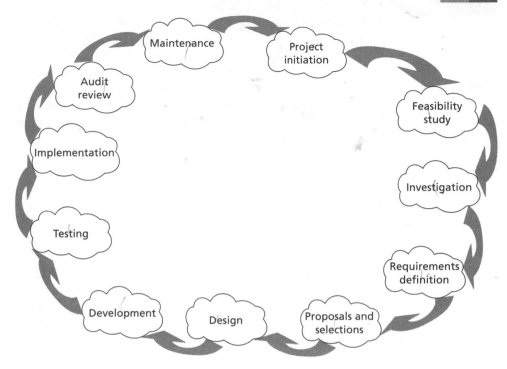

Fig. 2.4 The traditional systems life cycle

flowcharts or other diagrams. For a big system this could result in a very large quantity of text, which, again, will act as a barrier to the users reviewing the specification properly.

3 *High-level design*. Once the requirements specification has been approved, the designers take over and produce a high-level design for the system. This will include the database design and the general structure of menus, on-line enquiries and reports. Individual program specifications will usually be produced later, during detailed design.

Now it will be seen from this outline that the traditional approach does not *mandate* the involvement of the system's users to any great degree. Of course, good analysts have always worked hard to involve their users, to get their views on ideas as they emerge, and to review important analysis and design documents, such as interview notes for example. But the users only *have* to be involved when they are presented with the system specification to review and approve. The result is that analysis and design come to be seen as the province of the technician – of the analyst and designer – rather than as a partnership between developers and users.

The most obvious advantage of the traditional approach is, of course, that it is quite familiar to analysts and that the general methods of working are well understood. There is a lot of experience of traditional methods, and most of those concerned – analysts, project managers and also users – know roughly how the project will proceed. As a result, there is generally no specific, and possibly expensive, training required, although there has always been a need for analysts to be trained in the basic fact-finding techniques, such as interviewing. The documentation resulting from traditional methods is a big, mainly textual, document. As we shall suggest later, there are several problems with this, but at least those who need to review the documentation, either IT professionals or users, will possess the basic skill – reading – even if they lack time to examine everything that is presented to them.

In considering the problems inherent in traditional analysis and design techniques, we need to face up to the fact that the history of IT development is littered with a large number of projects that were either started and never finished or which, even if completed, failed to provide the users with what they wanted or needed. In addition, developers have often laboured to provide areas of functionality that, for one reason or another, the users have never got round to using. In this respect, a large proportion of the money spent on information systems must be regarded as having been wasted. There is more about this in Chapter 4. In considering this depressing state of affairs, it became apparent that problems were generally created during the analysis phase. It was concluded that traditional methods had the following defects:

- Large quantities of written documentation act as a barrier, rather than as an aid, to communication between users and developers.

- There is a lack of continuity between the various stages of analysis and between analysis and design, so that requirements get lost in the process.

- There was no way to ensure that the analysis and design work was complete because it was difficult to cross-check the findings from the analysis stage.

- Systems developed traditionally lack flexibility and are therefore difficult, and also expensive, to operate, maintain and adapt to changing circumstances.

- Traditional development methods tend to assume the use of a particular hardware and/or software platform: this constrains the design so that the users may not get what their business really needs – and the project can be thrown badly off course if the organisation changes platforms during development.

In other words, traditional methods have signally failed to deliver the goods in terms of robust and flexible systems that meet the needs of their users.

2.6 Structured Approaches

Structured approaches were developed in the late 1970s when a number of people in the IT industry began to consider why so many IS developments had gone wrong and failed to live up to their promises. Mostly, they reached a similar conclusion: projects went wrong initially during the analysis phase, and efforts to improve the situation later were usually a waste of time and even more money. Most of these authorities agreed that there was a need for new methods of analysis and design that would offer:

- greater formality of approach that would bring systems development nearer to the scientific method or to an engineering discipline than had been common in IS projects;

- more clarity of stated requirements by using graphical representation as well as text;

- less scope for ambiguity and misunderstanding;

- a greater focus on identifying and then satisfying business needs;

- more traceability, to enable a business requirement to be followed through from initial analysis into the business-level specification and finally into the technical design;

- more flexible designs of system, not unduly tied to specific technical platforms;

- much more user involvement at all stages of the development.

All of the structured methods described later in this chapter result from attempts to meet these requirements in one way or another. As a result, there are some features that are common to all structured methods and to the structured approach in general.

Focus on data structures   – structured approach

Most of the methods concentrate heavily on a thorough examination of the data requirements of the proposed information system. The reasons for this concentration on data are twofold:

- It is a fact that, whereas the processing requirements of organisations can change often and may change significantly, the underlying data is relatively stable: therefore the data provides the soundest base for the development process.

- An inflexible data structure can act as a severe constraint on an organisation wishing to change its systems to match changing requirements. Evolving a flexible data structure early during development yields many benefits later on in the life of the system.

With a sound and flexible data structure in place, it is possible to adapt and amend the processing to meet the changing needs of the organisation.

Use of diagrams and structured English

Another common feature of structured methods is their heavy reliance on diagrams to convey information. The reasoning here is that:

- Diagrams are generally easier for people to assimilate than large quantities of text, thereby providing an easier means of communication between users and developers

- It is less easy to commit sins of omission or ambiguity with diagrams: for instance, failure to mention an important dataflow, or an incorrect statement about the direction of flow, may not be noticed in a long written specification but it will be immediately obvious on a dataflow diagram.

Together with diagrams, many methods make use of *structured English*. This aims to reduce the complexity of the language and reduce the written component of the documentation to brief, terse, unambiguous statements. Alongside structured English goes the extensive use of decision tables or similar to show the processing logic.

Concentration on business requirements

Another important feature of structured methods is the separation of the logical and physical aspects of the analysis and design process. This is done so that both analysts and developers focus on the business requirements of the proposed information system, rather than considering too soon the technical details of its implementation. So, with a structured method, the developers will focus for much of the time on the business requirements of the proposed system. They will look at the data needed to support the system and at the kind of processing that the users will want to support their business. Only once these things have been clearly established will they consider how these features may be implemented.

It may be objected that leaving physical implementation considerations so late in the analysis and design process is rather foolish as, if it then proves impossible to provide the services the users require, the only result can be dissatisfaction and disappointment. This is certainly a possibility, but the increasing power, flexibility and availability of the range of hardware/software platforms make this outcome less likely. On the other hand, focusing on the business requirements, rather than on technical considerations, avoids the possibility of the users having to accept what the developers want to deliver, rather than what they really need. Also, if the full business requirements cannot be met because of some technical impediment, it may be better to abandon the project rather than press on and deliver some limited functionality that may not assist the users much in their everyday work.

We can contrast the traditional approach, which was described earlier, with the following sequence of analysis and design in Figure 2.5, which reflects the general structured approach.

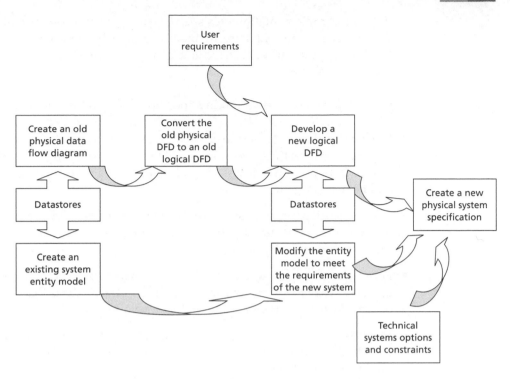

Fig. 2.5 The structured systems life cycle

1 *Analysis of current physical system.* The existing system, if there is one, is studied and documented 'warts and all'. This means that the models will cover all sorts of peculiarities (such as sorting and re-sorting of data) that are purely the result of *how* the system is implemented as distinct from what it is supposed to achieve. The users are required to review and agree the analysis results.

2 *Derivation of current logical system.* By stripping away the physical aspects of the current system, such as the data sorts already mentioned, the analysts form a picture of *what* the system does. This can then be used as a sound basis for the specification of a new and improved system. Again, the users are asked to review and agree the logical system description.

3 *Specification of required logical system.* Further detailed analysis is now carried out to ensure that the requirements of the new system are fully understood. This is then designed, initially at the logical level. Again, this provides a very clear statement of *what* the system is supposed to provide, in business terms uncomplicated by technical implementation considerations. The users are involved throughout this work, and must approve the finished specification before the project can continue.

4 *Specification of required physical system.* Only when all the business requirements have been specified is the design converted into a physical

design for implementation on a specific hardware and software platform. As the issues dealt with here are mainly technical, user involvement will be less than during earlier stages, but user approval must still be obtained for the final specification.

In general, the use of structured methods brings the following benefits:

- We have said already that structured methods concentrate on systems data requirements. As these are more stable than the processing requirements, a system built around a flexible data structure will prove amenable to change and have a longer life.

- The use of diagrams and structured English improves communications between users and developers and increases the chances of the users getting the system they really need.

- Because of the rigour and cross-checking inherent in structured methods, it is relatively easy to spot errors and omissions in the analysis that could otherwise lead to problems later in the development.

- Systems built using structured methods are based on business requirements and should deliver business benefits. Technology is not used for its own sake but in support of business objectives.

- Because technical issues are addressed relatively late in structured development projects, much of the design will be suitable for implementation in a variety of environments. Should the users' hardware or software policy change, it should be possible to go back to the logical documentation and re-develop from there for the new platform.

- A system built using structured methods will have complete, rigorous and consistent documentation, which will help greatly in maintaining and enhancing the system over time. Also, because of the business-level documentation represented in the logical specification, it is possible to evaluate accurately not only the technical, but also the business, consequences of proposed changes to the system.

- It is possible to define precisely the training requirements for the analysts and designers, and for users too. With some methods, qualifications are available that provide some level of confidence in the basic ability of the people carrying out the work.

- Finally, using a recognised structured method means that the users are not tied to any one developer. This means that one could, for instance, commission one firm to carry out the analysis and another to produce the design.

Together with these advantages, however, there are some problems with the use of structured methods, which developers and users need to consider if they are to achieve real success with them. Chief among them are the following:

- Structured approaches tend to shift the balance of effort in an IS project. Traditionally, most of the work went into coding and testing the actual software, with analysis and design forming a lesser component. In part, this resulted from much of the detailed analysis – of processing logic for instance – having to be done by the programmers. With a structured method, however, the balance of work shifts noticeably, and more of the effort is now expended earlier in the project, during analysis and design. There is a commensurate decrease in the programming effort, though not testing effort, and indeed, with some modern development tools, programming may become a relatively trivial task. An obvious problem with this is that the users seem to have to wait for a long time before they actually see any concrete results from the development, such as actual screens or reports. A special responsibility therefore devolves upon the manager of a structured development project to ensure that the users understand that increased work at the beginning of the project will be compensated for later on, and that the higher-quality system that will result will incur lower future maintenance costs.

  It is worth noting that the specifications resulting from many of the structured methods can be fed directly into a code generator for the production of the required programs. This process, in effect, removes the programming phase from the development and means that the actual system can be delivered to the users quite soon after the completion of analysis and design.

- The success of an IS project has always – irrespective of the development method used – depended substantially on the degree of user involvement. With a structured method, user involvement is usually explicitly set out, and the users will be asked to contribute to reviews and approvals at various stages. Once again, the result should be the production of higher-quality systems that meet their users' needs better. The amount of user involvement must, however, be carefully explained at the beginning of the project, and the necessary commitment, to the time and effort involved, must be obtained. In addition, it may be necessary to provide suitable training so that key users can understand fully the documentation being presented to them.

- *Rapid application development* (RAD) has become increasingly popular with the emergence of powerful PC network-based server systems and the use of development languages such as Visual Basic, which provide an easy means of prototyping the development to gain user acceptance. RAD and JAD (*joint application development*) provide one of the most effective development approaches available where project size and location permit the creation of joint development teams, which have the time, authority and breadth of understanding to encompass the project. Projects using remotely located development teams, with widely spread users and managed centrally, require more formally defined stages and deliverables for planning and control purposes, and for this reason the use of structured methods remains popular.

- Some structured methods remain the intellectual property of their designers and developers, who will provide advice, training, consultancy and sometimes support tools for their use. The dangers in this, of course, are that one can get 'locked in' to the single source of supply, and that the high prices charged for the various services may add a considerable extra cost to the development budget.

- *CASE* (*computer-aided software engineering*) tools are becoming more widely used in systems developments, and some of the structured methods become very difficult to use indeed without some form of computerised support. At least one – *information engineering* – is predicated on the basis of an integrated CASE (I-CASE) being available. The reasons for this are the sheer volume of documentation produced, particularly that to support the data modelling techniques, and the need for cross-checking, which computer systems do so well but humans find tedious and time-consuming. The development of CASE tools has not – except where they have been built to support specific proprietary methods – quite kept up with the development of the structured methods themselves. The situation is improving, although setting up the necessary CASE infrastructure can, once again, add to the development budget.

2.7 SSADM

SSADM is the structured method developed by the UK government's Central Computing and Telecommunications Authority (CCTA), and is the preferred method for very large government projects. SSADM has evolved through a number of versions to the point where SSADM version 4+ allows the user to tailor the method to suit the size and type of project under development. The initial versions of the methodology placed an emphasis on conformity to the standard, and this earned SSADM the reputation of being bureaucratic and unsuited to the demands of the commercial developer. Version 4+, however, encourages the developer to customise SSADM, with the requirement that 'the event is preserved as the significant unit of processing specification'.

The main user of the method is, of course, the UK government, and its use is mandatory on many public-sector projects. However, the fact that it is an established and open method, and that SSADM skills are widely available, means that it is becoming a de facto standard method in the wider marketplace. It is also used outside the UK. The Information Systems Examinations Board (ISEB), a subsidiary company of the British Computer Society, provides a recognised qualification in the use of SSADM, and accredits training organisations to run courses leading to its certificate. A tool conformance scheme is in operation for CASE tools that support the method, and there is a large and active international user group.

The method fits the structure defined above with three views of the information system provided by the different modelling techniques:

- *Business system models*. These user-oriented views are provided by the dataflow diagrams and the business activity models.

- *Data structure models*. The logical data structure model and the use of RDA (relational data analysis) model the database.

- *Dynamic behaviour models*. The events that change an entity are modelled with an entity life history diagram that is viewed by most practioners as the fundamental behaviour modelling technique. Effect correspondence diagrams show the data required as input to the event, the entities that are affected by the event, and the operations that are performed on each entity. The enquiry access path diagrams also model the dynamic behaviour of the system.

Extensive cross-checking between these three views provides a high degree of rigour in the analysis and design process.

SSADM is documented in a set of definitive manuals, which describe:

- the structure of an IS project using the method, in terms of the modules, stages, steps and tasks by which the work is tackled;

- a set of analysis and design techniques, to be applied at various stages of the project;

- a series of product definitions, including the quality-control criteria to be applied at each stage;

- 'hooks' so that the method can be coupled with structured approaches to project management, particularly to CCTA's PRINCE method, and to programming, mainly to Jackson Structured Programming (JSP).

The 'life cycle' for SSADM version 4+ consists of seven stages as shown in Figure 2.6. It should be noted that SSADM has nothing to say about the earlier stages of an IS project – a strategy study, for instance – or about the actual development, implementation and maintenance of the system. The outputs from SSADM, however, do fit quite well with, for example, JSP.

The major techniques employed are:

- requirements analysis;
- data flow modelling;
- logical data modelling;
- user/user role modelling;
- function definition;
- entity/event modelling;
- relational data analysis;
- logical database process design;
- logical dialogue design.

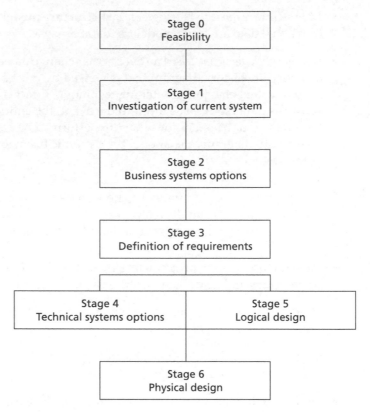

Fig. 2.6 The SSADM structural model

Prototyping can be used, but SSADM confines it to confirming and clarifying requirements, rather than the prototypes being carried forward into the design. In version 4 of SSADM, much use is made of Jackson-like structure diagrams. Some of these – entity life histories, for example – form part of the analysis process but the Update and Enquiry Process Models, in particular, can be implemented directly using some non-procedural programming languages.

As one would expect from an established and widely used method, SSADM has a number of points in its favour. It is a mature method, which has undergone several evolutions to reach its present stage, so it can be used with confidence as a reliable and stable platform for development. Partly because of the support of the UK government, but also because of the decision to make SSADM 'open' – that is, no licence is needed to adopt and use it – the method has become very popular and is used in a wide range of businesses and industries. Skilled staff, therefore, although not exactly plentiful are at least available in reasonable numbers. Because the method is open, many firms offer consultancy, training and CASE tools. This provides a competitive situation, unlike any other comparable method, and makes the cost of adopting SSADM relatively lower. There are also several books available, explaining the method from various perspectives – manager, practitioner and user. Most of the SSADM techniques are developments of methods widely practised elsewhere, so that these are well proven and generally familiar: included here are dataflow diagramming, entity life history analysis, logical data structuring and relational data analysis. The process modelling techniques are less familiar, but do mesh well with Jackson Structured Programming methods. Finally, the method follows the well-established structured route of moving from current physical, through current logical and required logical, to required physical systems specification. There are major user decision points where business systems options (the *what* of the system) and technical system options (the *how*) are considered. User involvement is mandatory and extensive.

There are some disadvantages to the use of SSADM that must be considered, however. The first problem is that of learning the method in the first place. Although most of the SSADM techniques are well established, some are not, and in any case the sheer number of them can pose problems for the student practitioner. The structure is logical, but with five modules, seven stages and dozens of steps and tasks, there is a lot to learn. The ISEB mandates that approved courses should include at least 80 hours of instruction, but experience shows that it takes much longer than this for someone to gain even a basic grasp of SSADM. Many developers feel that SSADM is overly complicated and places too much emphasis on the earlier stages of a project, but this criticism can also be levelled at other structured methods. However, with version 4+, it is certainly assumed that the developer should tailor the application of the method for each project rather than apply it slavishly whatever the circumstances, and this approach may in time help to defuse this criticism.

One problem that does arise with SSADM is that of controlling the large amount of documentation produced. There are difficulties in coordination if large teams are working on a project and the configuration management of documents becomes a major issue. The quality of CASE tools to support SSADM projects has not been too high until recently. Today, there are several competent diagram editors available; many tools provide for various degrees of cross-checking, and some of the better tools offer semi-automatic generation of some SSADM deliverables. Still, there is no fully comprehensive tool on the market. Finally, SSADM becomes rather vague as it moves into the areas of physical design. To some extent, this is understandable as – with the vast range of possible implementation environments that are available – it is impossible to offer detailed prescriptive advice, as can be done for the analysis process. However, some developers find this aspect of the method rather unsatisfactory and not really in accordance with the rigour one might expect from a structured method.

2.8 Yourdon

Edward Yourdon is one of the pioneers of the structured approach to systems development, and his ideas have had a major impact on thinking in this area. Yourdon's approach has evolved over the years, most fundamentally to downplay the need to model the user's current system during the analysis work. The reasoning is that this has proved wasteful of time and effort and has often proved to be very unpopular with users – 'why waste time modelling the current system, when what we want is a new one?' Thus the developer is encouraged to use analysis to build what Yourdon calls the *essential model* – that is, a logical model of the *required* system. This has two components:

- *The environmental model.* This shows the boundary of the required system in the form of a context diagram, an event list and brief description of the reason for having the system.

- *The behavioural model.* This illustrates how the system will work within its boundary, using various diagrams – dataflow diagrams, entity relationship diagrams and state transition diagrams – supported by process descriptions and a data dictionary. Dataflow diagrams show the processes that the system carries out, the various stores of data, and the flows of data between these two; entity relationship diagrams illustrate the data items (entities) that the system uses, and the relationships between them; and state transition diagrams model the time-dependent behaviour of the system, and show the states that the system can be in and the valid connections between different states.

These two component models are *balanced* against each other so that together they form a complete and consistent picture of what the required system is to do. Of course, in developing the essential model developers may well have to study the current system; but this is regarded as a means to an end and not as an end in itself.

The Yourdon approach is not particularly prescriptive in that it does not mandate that the developer must use all of the techniques described. Nor is the use of other techniques excluded if they can contribute to the completeness of the analysis. The emphasis is on choosing and using tools and techniques that are appropriate to the requirements of the individual project.

Once the essential model has been built, it forms the basis for the *user implementation model*. This differs from the essential model in that it takes into account how the system is to be implemented. Options considered here could include, for example, adopting a client–server architecture, using a fourth-generation language of some sort, or seeking a wholly (or partially) packaged solution.

So, major issues considered at this point include:

- the boundary between the computer system and the manual processes;

- the nature and type of the human–computer interface;

- other operational constraints such as response times or system security.

The user implementation model then forms the input into the design process, which Yourdon conceives as the development of further models:

- the *system implementation model*, which shows how the required processing will be allocated to the selected hardware. It has two sub-models concerned with the processor and the tasks to be performed;

- the *program implementation model*, which maps how the individual tasks that make up the system will be developed as program modules.

Yourdon's approach is well proven and based on practical experience. It is suitable for most types of application, real-time as well as commercial applications, and it uses techniques, such as dataflow diagramming, that have now become widely understood. It is, perhaps, less prescriptive than some other methods, which makes it less easy for novices to grasp and apply but more flexible for the experienced developer.

2.9 Jackson

Jackson System Development (JSD) was developed by Michael Jackson and John Cameron. It is fairly widely used in the UK, especially where organisations have already adopted the complementary Jackson Structured Programming (JSP). JSD covers the development life cycle from analysis to maintenance, and works by the composition of processes upwards from an atomic level. It is very concerned with the time dimension of the system, and thus, unlike some of the other structured methods, it is suitable for the development of real-time systems.

JSD proceeds through a sequence of six steps, as follows:

1 *Entity action step.* Here, the developer examines the real world that the IS will model, and describes it in terms of the entities involved and the actions that they will perform or have performed on them.

2 *Entity structure step.* This involves an examination of the time component of the IS. The actions performed by or on each entity are arranged in their time sequence.

3 *Initial model step.* So far, the method has described the real world. Now, a process model is built that simulates, as the IS will simulate, these real-world entities and actions.

4 *Function step.* Functions are now specified that will produce the outputs required from the system. If necessary, additional processes may be identified at this point.

5 *System timing step.* This involves the consideration of process scheduling to ensure that the system's functional outputs are correct and are produced at the right time.

6 *Implementation step.* Finally, the hardware and software required to implement the IS are identified, and the model is transformed into a form suitable for operating in that environment.

It can be seen that JSD relies heavily on the use of models, and this is in fact one of the claimed advantages of the method. By concentrating on the identification of entities, and of the actions that they affect or which are affected by them, the developer avoids building a system that simply provides for existing levels of functionality. Instead, what results from JSD is a very flexible basis for later development, and the resultant system should prove amenable to enhancement and amendment to meet changing business requirements.

Another advantage of JSD is that it does deal very satisfactorily with the time component of systems. Some structured methods are very good at handling commercial applications – payroll, for example – but are less successful when applied in a real-time situation, such as a factory process-control system. JSD, however, is very much concerned with time and the sequencing of events, and so can be used for the development of systems where process is more significant than data.

The major problem with JSD is that it is initially quite difficult to grasp some of its concepts and then to apply them in a real project situation. This, however, is to some extent true of any method, and proper training is, as always, the answer.

2.10 Merise

Merise was designed in France at the beginning of the 1980s and is used widely there and also in Belgium, Spain and Italy. Its use is recommended in many public-sector projects, and it is widely employed for commercial projects as well. A survey in 1989 revealed that more than half the people in France who were using a structured method were using Merise. The control of the method is rather less formalised than, say, for SSADM. There are separate user groups representing the French Computer Society, various companies that use the method, and academics working in the systems field, and these originate and define amendments and enhancements that may be incorporated into the method by the authors of the reference manuals.

Along with SSADM, Merise is one of the major methods used in Europe that have given rise to the idea of the 'Euromethod'.

Merise focuses on the development process required to develop information systems, and addresses the standard life cycle of requirements analysis, specification, design, code production, implementation and maintenance. Like information engineering but unlike, for example, SSADM, the Merise Development Process Model covers the entire range of the development process: that is,

- master plan – of a whole organisation or a major part of it;

- preliminary study – of one or several business areas;

- detailed study – producing a logical model of one or several systems;

- technical study – detailed design of one or several systems;

- code production – for the system(s) designed;

- implementation – of the developed system(s);

- maintenance – of the delivered system(s).

It provides techniques to support the earlier phases of this life cycle – analysis and high-level design – but assumes the use of other methods or techniques – such as Jackson Structured Programming – for the later phases.

Merise's development process model results from three cycles:

- *The life cycle*. This is the conventional idea of representing the creation, life and decommissioning of the system.

- *The decision cycle*. This represents the series of decisions that must be made during the system project.

- *The abstraction cycle*. This is the series of models that are developed to express and document the system.

These three cycles operate in parallel and are interdependent and, between them, determine the shape of the IS project.

Merise produces a number of models of the information system, including:

- A *conceptual data model*, which shows the data entities, their relationships, their attributes and so on. This model is built using a kind of third normal form data analysis.

- A *conceptual process model*, which shows the interaction of events, external or internal to the system, and the operations that the system performs in response to them. This model also incorporates the rules that the system must follow in responding to events.

- A *logical data model*, which can be a representation either of a CODASYL model or of a relational model; there are rules for mapping the conceptual data model onto this logical data model.

- An *organisational process model*, which builds on the conceptual process model but adds detail on where, and how, the various operations take place.

- A *physical data model*, expressed in the data description language of the chosen DBMS.

- An operational process model, consisting of the hardware/software architecture, flowcharts or chain diagrams for batch procedures, and some sort of description – for example a program specification – of how the processing will be implemented.

It can be seen that the development of these models is a sequence moving from conceptual, through logical, to physical implementation.

An obvious strength of Merise is that the method deals with the whole of the systems development life cycle, including construction, implementation and maintenance. Thus unlike, say, SSADM it does not need to be coupled with other methods outside the scope of systems analysis and design. Having said that, Merise is more conceptual than procedural when it comes to the later stages of development.

The conceptual and organisational process models provide a powerful means of modelling the dynamic behaviour of the system. They are probably more accessible to users than the combination of dataflow diagrams and entity life histories that would be required in an SSADM project. The control of the method is rather informal and not as tightly defined as, for example, the Design Authority Board for SSADM. Although all methods tend to be interpreted by individual users, this makes it harder to say what is 'complete' Merise and what is not, although the manuals are generally regarded as the 'orthodox' version of the method. On the other hand, this does make the method more flexible in allowing the immediate introduction of new tools and techniques.

For the English-language practitioner, however, the main problem is that there exists no suitable documentation of the method in English. Apart from the 'official' manuals, there are a number of books available that could be used by someone with a good understanding of technical French.

2.11 Rapid Application Development

Rapid Application Development, commonly referred to as RAD, has become established as a development method suited to applications introduced in short timescales, using software development tools that can quickly generate screen layouts, database tables and reports. A successful RAD development tends to substitute analysis, investigation and specification of user requirements with prototyping and joint application development (JAD) sessions enabling users to agree requirements through a process of incremental development.

The use of stages in a life cycle is contradictory to this method of development, and organisations adopting RAD as an approach to their development frequently differentiate between projects that require a 'waterfall' approach and those that can be developed using RAD. This differentiation, originating in the competition between corporate systems developers working on mainframes computers and IT developers using LAN-based systems, is described more fully in the DMH case study in Appendix 1.

2.11.1 Direct Systems Development Method (DSDM)

DSDM is described as a non-proprietary Rapid Application Development method that is one of the most widely used application development methods in both large and small organisations. The DSDM consortium was formed in 1994 by 16 founding members with the objective of developing and promoting a public domain RAD method. The DSDM approach suggests that traditional approaches to systems development such as the waterfall method can lead to the development team attempting to satisfy inaccurately specified requirements that no longer meet the changing business needs of the organisation. Whereas a traditional project will require varying resources and changing timescales to meet the specified requirements, the DSDM approach recommends changing requirements while maintaining fixed timescales and resources.

2.11.2 Principles of DSDM

DSDM is based upon nine underlying principles that can briefly be summarised as follows:

- *Active user involvement.* Users are seen as part of the development team rather than as recipients of a system imposed on them by management. Joint application development sessions reinforce this feeling, and users are continually aware of the reasons for delays and development changes through their involvement in the decision-making process.

- *Development team empowerment.* The development team, which includes users as well as analysts, must be empowered to make decisions about functionality, usability and requirements without frequent recourse to a higher level of management.

- *Frequent delivery of products.* The development team will focus on the delivery of products on a regular basis rather than focusing on deliverable documentation created during the investigation, analysis and design stages.

- *User acceptance.* DSDM recommends a focus on functionality and fitness for purpose rather conformance to a set of documented requirements.

- *Incremental development.* DSDM recognises that rework and iterative development are inherent in software development as users' needs become more refined.

- *Configuration management.* Configuration management figures strongly in DSDM-based projects, as the need to change and to revise changes is readily accepted.

- *High-level requirements.* Scope and high-level requirements for the project should be defined, and should not change significantly throughout the life of the project.

- *Testing.* Testing is an integral part of the life cycle, with the earlier tests focusing on business needs and the later ones leading to total systems operation.

- *Collaboration and cooperation.* Low-level requirements are often loosely defined at the commencement of the project, and the stakeholders must be flexible and able to work collaboratively to accomplish changes.

Although DSDM is contrasted to the traditional waterfall approach, the development is still defined as a five-phase process consisting of:

1 feasibility study;
2 business study;
3 functional model iteration;
4 design and build iteration;
5 implementation.

Functional model iteration focuses on prototyping to establish user requirements, whereas *design and build iteration* aims to develop these prototypes for use in the operational environment. Diagrammatically this life cycle is represented as three main stages, with feasibility and business study grouped as an opening and closing phase to a project. Each of the three main stages is iterative, and it is accepted that the implementation stages may lead to the discovery of new functional areas or to a need for further work in the functional model iteration or in the design and build iteration.

RAD and DSDM are particularly well suited to object-oriented developments, as the encapsulation of data and methods within each object class allows the developer to create new objects that can communicate with those developed earlier. When each object class meets a business need then incremental development of objects occurs naturally with this type of RAD approach.

Using a decision-making process based on JAD and user empowerment will work well where user representation can account for all the business requirements of the system. Systems with high levels of user interaction requiring the development of screen designs and dialogues that match the users' work patterns are equally well suited to the RAD approach. Projects involving the merging of business interests and the creation of new corporate systems often require negotiation and agreement between many different stakeholders, and may involve several development teams working remotely. In these circumstances the formal definition of requirements in a structured way is an essential factor in the ultimate success of the project.

2.12 Workflow Systems

Workflow describes systems that forward and store electronically recorded information that is reviewed by different parts of an organisation to decide on a service or facility that the organisation wishes to offer. Workflow is widely used in insurance and banking, where decisions on policies and on loans and mortgages require input from a number of different sources within the organisation. By forwarding and storing an electronic image of a form or a document to the parties involved in the decision-making process, the error-prone and time-consuming stage of data entry is removed from the processing cycle. Providing an identity for each workflow transaction enables its progress to be tracked and action taken to deal with delays.

The conventions for *modelling workflow systems* have yet to be firmly established. The modelling approaches described so far all focus on processes or on object behaviour, whereas the workflow system is typified by the communication of decisions between different parties. If we match the workflow problem domain to our classification of business system model, data structure model and behaviour model, then the model needs to show the interaction of the decision-makers, the data that they exchange, and the way in which these two aspects of the system interact.

The most common modelling approach that can be identified for workflow systems is offered by vendor-specific CASE tools that model the aspects mentioned above in different ways. Action Works Process Builder shows the business system model, identifying the flows between the parties involved and how they

Custom Order Workflow

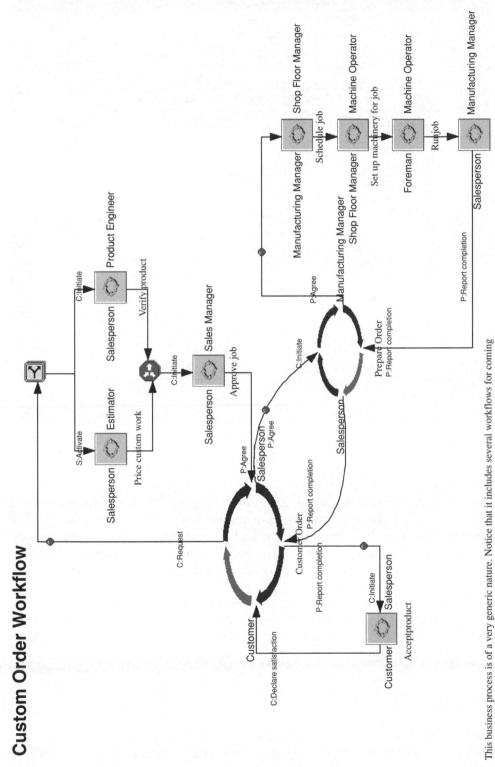

This business process is of a very generic nature. Notice that it includes several workflows for coming to agreement as to how the work is to be performed, several workflows to do the work, and finally two workflows to satisfy both the customer and the salesperson.

This template can be found in most custom manufacturing, and in almost all service businesses.

Fig. 2.7 A workflow model: the business system model

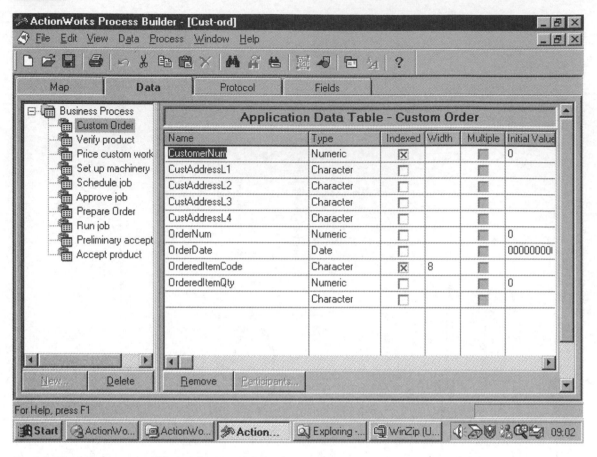

Fig. 2.8 The data items used by each business process

interact, and provides a dictionary facility to define data items found in each flow. Figure 2.7 shows a process map drawn with the ActionWorks Process Builder. The map identifies primary and secondary workflows. The *primary workflow* is the overall goal for the process – in this case to satisfy a customer's order – and the *secondary workflows* are all the tasks that must be done by people for the work to move ahead.

The workflow system is concerned primarily with intercommunication and decision-making, and accordingly the data structure modelling features of the Action Works tool provide a data dictionary feature (shown in Figure 2.8) to identify the data attributes involved in each workflow.

2.13 Summary

Systems analysis and design has evolved in its 40-year existence from a set of documentation standards intended primarily to define the input, output, processing and file structures of computer programs to a methodology offering the well-defined approaches outlined in this chapter. Predominantly, the theme that provides structure to each of these methods is one that recognises the need to model the business system as a whole, to model the data structure and to model the behaviour of the system as it responds to events. A method's emphasis often falls more within one of these three aspects than in the other two, and the professional analyst will recognise the need to select the method best suited to the problem domain under scrutiny.

The large corporate development with a geographically distributed team may best be served by the tight formal definition of stages and deliverables specified in SSADM. Similarly, Merise has become associated with large-scale projects using databases, and, though less rigorous in its definition of stages than SSADM, the flow diagram, conceptual data model and process model correspond to our theme but put more emphasis on all stages of the development from strategy through to maintenance. Jackson System Development emphasises the behavioural aspects of the system and so favours developments with a real-time or engineering bias. The object-oriented approaches serve the analyst well when the development is distributed and involves a number of autonomous interacting bodies. Internet systems and banking applications using automated teller machines are good examples of developments that respond well to object-oriented approaches. Small-scale projects with high levels of user involvement favour the DSDM and RAD approaches, which often incorporate the modelling techniques found in the more formal methods.

Commitment to a single development method is no longer appropriate when systems are required to exploit new technology, or to re-engineer some business processes while joining seamlessly with other legacy systems. In this varied environment the analyst must be ready to match the method to the problem and to use the full range of tools offered by analysis and design methodology.

Exercises

2.1 System Telecom has chosen to use SSADM, and the data flow diagrams and data models are drawn using SSADM conventions. If you had been responsible for choosing a structured method for System Telecom, which would you have chosen? What would be the reasons for making your choice? There is no reason to assume that, just because SSADM has been chosen in the book, it is necessarily the method that a European-based telecommunications company would have chosen. A survey of European methodologies shows that there are several widely used methods available.

2.2 People are sometimes critical of structured development methods because they say that these methods increase the time and cost of the early stages of development. Do you think that this is true compared with traditional development methods?

Equally, it is asserted that structured methods reduce the costs of implementation and maintenance so that system lifetime costs are reduced overall. Do you agree with this? What examples could you suggest to show how structured methods have the potential to reduce system lifetime costs?

2.3 Structured methods are said to improve communications between system developers and their customers (the users). Do you think that this is the case? Can you suggest ways in which this improvement is achieved?

3 Communicating with People

3.1 Introduction

In this chapter we shall be looking at how people communicate: that is, at how they convey facts, ideas and feelings to one another. This is an important skill for all analysts. Much of your time will be spent trying to identify the needs, wants and expectations of your clients. Much of your success as an analyst will depend on how well you understand those around you and on how well they understand you. To be an effective analyst, you will need to know exactly what you want to achieve when you communicate with your customers. It may be that you want to know how or why customers carry out a particular task in a particular way, or it may be that you want to influence them to accept your idea of how the system needs to be organised. But, whatever your purpose, you need to have it clear in your mind at the start. Ask yourself these two questions when you communicate:

- How are you trying to affect the people who are on the receiving end of your communication?

- What words or actions on their part will convince you that you have communicated successfully?

If you don't know the effect you want to have on the other person, and you have no clear idea of what you intend as an end result, you won't know when you have been successful.

Effective communication is more than just telling someone something and noticing whether or not they seem to be listening. It happens when facts, ideas and feelings are conveyed accurately and understood accurately, but it's not complete until we know that this has happened. We need to see some confirmation that our attempt at communication has been successful.

When we tell someone something, the communication model looks like this:

You may think that another word for Target here could be Receiver, but that assumes too much. After all, the target of your message may not even notice it, let alone receive it or respond to it. As a responsible sender, however, you will want to do what you can to turn your target into a receiver. For example, you will take into account what you know about the target, so that if your target speaks French only, you won't speak in English. And if you are to know whether your target has understood what you are saying, and how he or she responds to it, you will need some feedback. With feedback, our model looks as follows. Notice that the target is now the receiver: because we get feedback, we know that the message has been received.

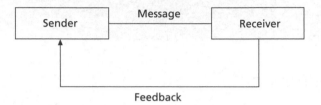

For an analyst, though, this is not a complete model of communication. It is not enough to be able to tell your client what you think, and get some feedback about their views; it is even more important that you both understand each other. In other words, you will each be both sender and receiver. A full model of effective communication will therefore look like this:

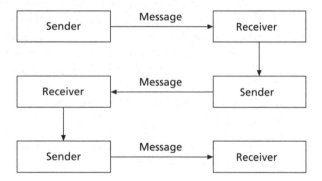

In this model, both you and the person you are communicating to are senders and receivers and will alternate roles. As soon as you have sent, you are ready to receive; having received, it is again your turn to send. Neither of you is merely acknowledging the other's ideas or feelings but is using them as a cue to express your own thoughts, feelings and understanding of each other's point of view.

3.2 Types of Communication

Our communication model works in a number of situations. Although we may think of face-to-face communication in meetings and interviews, there are other forms of communication, and in this section we distinguish between written and spoken communication and consider each from the point of view of both the sender and the receiver. As it is important that appropriate body language backs up the verbal message, we also consider non-verbal communication.

The main forms of verbal communication include meetings (both formal and informal), interviews, presentations and telephone conversations. Written communications include letters, memos, emails, meeting minutes and reports. Some communication is even in a mixture of two forms, as in meetings where agendas are sent out first and minutes taken during the meeting. Each of these types of communication has its own perils and pitfalls, but in all of them we are trying to communicate with the receiver in a form that can be readily understood and accepted.

When choosing the most appropriate form of communication for your purpose, some questions you should ask yourself are:

- Which one of these types of communication would best enable me to get the information I need?

- Which one of these situations would best enable me to influence the potential receiver(s)?

- In which one of these situations would I get the best feedback?

To answer these questions, there are three things to consider: the purpose of the communication, the target audience, and their level of understanding in the area.

- *Purpose.* In thinking about types of communication, remember that you are looking for the best type of communication to suit your purpose. If your purpose is to tell 30 people some information that you know will not need any discussion, it would not be sensible to arrange to meet each one of them separately. A memo, email or report would probably be a good choice here.

- *Target audience.* Here you need to take account of the needs, expectations and feelings of the target audience. If you know that the customer expects you to meet each senior manager at least once, then you will have to have some compelling reason not to do so, but if one particular person is very difficult to meet, you may have to resort to written communication, on the grounds that a memo is better than nothing.

- *Level of understanding.* It is very important to gauge the level of understanding of your intended receivers. If you don't do this, you run the risk of using over-simplified explanations and perhaps being seen as patronising or, alternatively, of using complex technical jargon with someone who doesn't understand it. It is clearly important to communicate at the right level in order to create your intended impression, but how can you do this? The answer is thorough preparation. When preparing to communicate, whether for an interview, a meeting, a presentation or in writing, you must always prepare your ground, to ensure that you are not wasting your time.

Having chosen the most appropriate form of communication, it is useful then to consider good ways of ensuring that you achieve your purpose. Let's look at the advantages of spoken, written and non-verbal communication, from the point of view of the sender first and then from the point of view of the receiver.

One of the strongest reasons for an analyst to use spoken communication is that people tend to feel more personally involved in the work of analysis if they have participated in an active way. Another major advantage is that it allows you to tailor your information, remarks or questions to the responses of the person or people you are talking to. This will mean that you will be able to get your points across more effectively and understand theirs better. If there are strong feelings about the subject under discussion, you are much more likely to find this out in a meeting than at any other time, because people are more likely to talk of their feelings as well as hard, plain facts. Finally, it will enable you to use non-verbal communication. When we communicate with people who are physically present, we read their body language constantly, looking at their expression and their gestures, and evaluating their tone of voice. Since we do this constantly, it is possible to take for granted the skill that we all have in reading others. If communication breaks down, however, we are most likely to notice this through body language. For example, if someone tries to avoid talking about something with you, you are most likely to notice that something is going on through their body language first, then through their tone of voice, and lastly, a long way behind the other two, through the actual words they speak.

Many of the same advantages apply to the receiver as to the sender. When you're a receiver, however, the main advantage is that you can tell the sender straightaway if there is something in what is being said that you don't like. So if you don't understand something, you can ask for further details, and if the sender has got something wrong or is missing something out, you can say so straight away. This means that any of your concerns can be dealt with directly. Being able to change role between sender and receiver is the greatest benefit for both sides as it enables greater clarity and agreement in the communication.

When writing, you will be better able to choose your words more carefully than when speaking. This means that you will be able to change and edit what you write until you are satisfied that it is accurate. Your writing can be used to support your point of view. A piece of writing can prove whether you gave information or your opinion, asked questions of and received answers from a particular person on a particular date. Only something written down can easily prove this. This means that accuracy in written communications cannot be over-emphasised. Communicating in writing can also be cheaper. You can circulate a large number of people with a memo or email much more quickly than you could hope to talk to them all, and this will save everyone's working time.

There is, however, a major problem about communicating in writing: the sender rarely gets immediate feedback from the receiver. This can be for a number of reasons. It could be that the letter, memo, email or report never reached its intended receiver, who is still waiting patiently for it. It could be that the receiver was too busy to read it. It may be that the receiver read the communication hurriedly and failed to see its point. All this time you will have no idea whether you have said the right thing, whether you have written too much or too little, or whether you have put your point clearly. You must bear this potential problem in mind when choosing how to communicate.

One of the greatest benefits of written communication for the receiver is that you can deal with it in your own time. This means that you need not be rushed, and can give due time for thought before giving a response. Another benefit is that you receive someone's best thinking on the subject – the clearest communication they can make on this subject – so, when you keep it, you have the best possible record of their thoughts at that time. This does not mean that their thoughts will always stay the same, but it does mean that you will know if they change in the future.

3.3 Barriers to Communication

You already know that communication isn't always successful. Let's look at some of the barriers that can prevent you from communicating as effectively as you would like.

Sometimes you may not come across clearly. For example, you may not really understand the information you are trying to communicate, or you may not have a clear purpose for your communication. You may not have decided what effect you want to have on your receiver, or you may not know enough about your receiver to be able to judge the impact of your communication. You may not have thought of convincing examples and analogies that would help to back up your case. All of these would indicate that you have not prepared thoroughly enough in advance.

If you are in a meeting, there is a strong probability that you will be able to overcome this problem if you listen carefully. Once you start talking, your receiver might help you by asking for examples, or by asking you to expand on a particular topic. But it is unwise to rely on your receiver's skill to make up for your deficiencies. Your preparation should always be as thorough as you can manage. You may find it useful to make a list of topics you want to cover, points you want to make, and questions to which you need answers. You can then refer to this list in the meeting. There is no harm in letting your receiver know that you have a list to help you; it indicates that you have prepared, not that you don't know what you are doing! Before important presentations – and even some meetings – it is always useful to rehearse exactly how you can make your main points. Some people fear that rehearsing can make them look artificial on the day, because it takes away the spontaneity of the moment. Although it is true that spontaneity is reduced, you will probably feel more relaxed and better able to take advantage of the new ideas that may come to you as you are speaking. It is always better to look practised and competent than it is to appear spontaneously unprepared! Ask yourself the following questions:

- Do I understand the message fully?

- Do I know why I'm communicating it?

- Is the purpose clear?

- Do I understand the receiver's concerns?

- Have I decided when to
  - give information?
  - ask questions?
  - keep quiet?

So far, we have been looking mainly at the message we intend to communicate, but there are other messages we both send and receive over which we don't have so much control. The importance of non-verbal communication has already been mentioned. We can learn a great deal about someone, especially about their feelings, by observing them closely. People are often unaware of what their body language is saying to others, and we often respond on an emotional level without really being aware of what someone else has done that makes us feel the way we do. For example, you may feel alienated by a limp handshake, or by someone who does not look you in the eye or else seems determined to stare at you all the time. If someone stands very close to you, and follows you when you try to move away, you may feel that they are trying to dominate you. Because of this, you may make assumptions about what they are like. You may see the person as 'wet' or a bully, but you may be wrong in your assumption. So you will always find it useful to be aware of how you interpret other people's body language. Whether you know it or not, you will be making judgements about them, and to be of real use to you, those judgements should be explicit, so that you can challenge them, check them out, and even, if appropriate, change them.

Words convey only a small part of the communication on their own; tone of voice backs up the message you are putting across. Suppose you are telling a customer that the changes you suggest will save the company a lot of money. If you say this in an uncertain tone of voice, you may not be believed; but if you sound absolutely confident, there is more chance your suggestion will be taken seriously.

Accent is one of those things that should never be allowed to influence how seriously we treat someone's communication. Unfortunately, many people are affected by another's accent. A strong accent, regardless of where it comes from, can sometimes prevent someone's message being taken seriously if they are working outside of their own region. Similarly, a 'posh' accent can sometimes result in someone being taken more seriously than their communication would deserve. If you have a strong accent, you may not be aware of it. Listening to your voice on a tape will let you know how strong your accent is. You may not be able to change the accent, and you may well not want to, but if you are speaking to someone who is not local to you, avoid any dialect words or unusual local phrases, and perhaps speak more slowly.

The pitch of your voice is often more significant than your accent, because you are even less likely to be aware of it. Youthful voices tend to be higher in pitch than older ones. This can mean that those men with naturally light voices may be seen as less serious and less important than those with naturally deeper voices. Deeper pitches seem to carry more conviction and authority. This seems to be also true for women: Margaret Thatcher, the former British Prime Minister, was trained to lower the pitch of her voice to improve her communication.

If you are communicating in writing, you may be able to spend more time carefully crafting your message to make it wholly complete and utterly clear, but you will lack the feedback that would enable you to rephrase parts that your receiver found difficult or omit parts that your receiver clearly already knew. There are some things you can do that might help to overcome this problem:

- As you write, think all the time of the person who will be reading the communication. It can sometimes help to imagine them peering over your shoulder as you write, and interrupting now and then to ask for clarification of this point or expansion of that point.

- Ask someone else to review your first draft. If possible, make sure that this person is similar to your intended reader. If your piece of writing is to be read by a large number of people, it may be worth asking one or two of them to comment on it before you send it out to everyone.

- After writing, put what you have written away for a time. Even a break of a day will enable you to look at it critically. As you review it, imagine that it was written by someone else. What advice would you give that person in order to make a good piece of writing even better?

It is possible to spoil the whole impact of your communication by poor presentation. If, for example, you wrote a memo because it was a clear, quick, accurate form of communication, but your receiver was upset because he considered it to be cold, impersonal and indicating that you were not interested in his views, then you have presented your communication poorly, regardless of how good the memo was. Even when we choose the correct way of communicating, we may present the information poorly. When speaking, either in a meeting or when giving a presentation, it is important not to speak too quickly. Speaking more slowly will feel unnatural and uncomfortable at first, but it will be a lot easier for your listeners. Your attention must be on making life easier for those who are listening to you, not on making life comfortable for you. When writing, it is essential to make sure that the written output is clear. Unless your handwriting is exceptionally clear, you should always type any important communication. Many people cannot read others' handwriting easily, and so they may not read it at all. For both written and spoken communication, you must organise your information before you start. Even if that means saying to someone, 'I need to get my thoughts in order before I can answer you', it is worth taking a bit of time to know what you mean to say. When answering questions, you will usually find that you need a little time for thought, a breathing space.

Communication sometimes breaks down because the sender and the receiver have different assumptions and are not aware of this. For example, a word or phrase may mean completely different things to each of them. Your customer may ask you to send her a report to present at a meeting on Monday the 18th. You assume that this means you can give her the report on the Monday morning when you have arranged to meet, but on the previous Tuesday she rings you up because you have not yet sent the report. She needs the report on the previous Tuesday because papers presented at the meeting are always sent out three days in advance. Each of you made an assumption, and as a result of that unstated assumption, effective communication broke down.

It is sometimes hard to accept, but there will be times when someone will decide that it is not in their best interests to tell you all you need to know, and they do not communicate fully with you. They may omit something or embellish something, or they may express something ambiguously, hoping that you will misinterpret it. They may even lie, hoping that you will not be able to do anything even if they are found out. Sometimes this will happen because people want to appear more important than they really are, saying something like 'I control everything around here'. Sometimes they do not want others to know what really goes on, saying things like 'We always process every order within one working day'. Because this possibility is always there, never rely on just one person to give you important information. If two people tell you exactly the same, you can be fairly certain that what you now know is accurate, but if they differ in a number of ways, then you know that you have to keep looking for the accurate answer.

3.4 Improving Your Skills

It is difficult to become a successful systems analyst without having good communication skills. However, no one is so good that they don't need to improve! In this section you will find ideas to help you improve your communication skills. Of course, ideas written in a book are all very well; to improve what you actually do, you will need to go out and try things in a new way. We'll look first at getting information, and then at giving information, dealing with meetings and giving presentations.

3.4.1 Getting Information

There are a number of ways in which you can get information. Some information will come from reading, some from listening to people, and some from nonverbal communications.

Every systems analyst has too much to read. You may find that there are reports about what you are doing and about what you propose to do. You will be expected to have some familiarity with them all. There are numbers of books on reading efficiently, and you may well find it useful to go to a bookshop and browse until you find one that you feel comfortable with. In order to use your reading time effectively, you may find it useful to develop a systematic approach, using your concentration well. In order to make best use of your time, you need to give your task your undivided attention. You will know that you have lost concentration when you notice that you have read a sentence or a paragraph or a even a page and have taken nothing in. As soon as this happens, take a break. Few people can concentrate deeply for more than 20 minutes without a brief break, so the odds are that you will need a break every 20 minutes or so.

Analysts spend a large part of their time listening, but listening is not a simple activity: there are many ways of listening. You can listen *for* something: for example, when you are waiting for someone to arrive by car, you listen for the sound of that particular car engine, or the clunk of the car door closing. This is a little like a lawyer in court listening to evidence in order to spot contradictions. Here, the listening is selective, concentrating on one part of the message only. This is part of the listening that you will need to develop as an analyst, and it involves listening only for the essentials, refusing to let yourself be distracted by side issues, even if they sound interesting. Another way of listening is to listen *to* something, when you are actively trying to grasp what it is the other person is trying to communicate, often helping the other person to formulate their views and express them clearly. This is another part of the skill you will need to learn as an analyst, and this time it involves listening to the whole message, not just those parts that you have decided in advance are the ones to concentrate upon.

Fortunately, both of these types of listening can be put together and called *active listening*. We call it 'active' because it is a very long way from settling back and letting someone's words wash over you. This kind of listening works only if the listener takes an active part in the process of communication. It has been said: 'The speaker dominates the conversation: the listener controls the conversation.' Let us explore how a listener can control the flow of conversation.

Active listening starts with the listener's genuine desire to know what the other person is thinking and feeling about something. As an analyst, you must be prepared to listen to people's feelings as well as their thoughts: every new system engages people's emotions as well as their minds. What you do when you listen to someone actively is get inside that person, begin to see things from their point of view, even if it is the opposite from your own. And, more than that, you have to convey that you are seeing things from their point of view. When someone speaks, there are normally two parts to what is said: the *content* and the *feelings behind the content*. Put together, these give us the meaning of what they are saying. If you are listening to someone talking about how incoming mail is dealt with in a complaints department, they might say, 'The man responsible for the mail leaves it in a large box on the table by the window'. This is fairly clear – you get an idea of who brings in the mail and where it is left. If your speaker had said, 'The man responsible for the mail eventually brings it up and then dumps it in a huge box on the table by the window', then the content of the message is the same but the meaning of the message is different.

To be an active listener, you would want to respond to the content, perhaps by indicating the table and checking that you had correctly identified it, but you also need to respond to the feeling behind the content, perhaps by saying something like 'You don't sound too happy about the mail. Is it a problem for your department?' In this way, you indicate both that you have heard the message and that you are prepared to probe to find out the cause of any problem. To be effective as a listener, you need to be able to convey to the other person that you have a sincere interest in them and their views. Your listener will pick up any pretence, consciously or unconsciously, and will no longer speak freely. Remember:

- Active listening.
- Listening for.
- Listening to.
- Content and feelings.
- Genuine interest.

3.4.2 Giving Information

Analysts have to communicate ideas, instructions, information and enquiries in writing in an effective way, accurately, briefly and clearly. Your writing style must conform to the normal rules of spelling and punctuation, you need a style that is neither too terse nor too wordy, and you have to organise your ideas in a way that makes them clear to the reader. Let's look at some guidelines for good writing.

Many people feel that they should be able to sit at a keyboard or a piece of paper and produce expert, clear prose. When they can't do this, they feel that there is some skill that others have which eludes them. The truth is that few people write well at first attempt – the best writers make many attempts until they are satisfied. It is useful to think of structuring your time and effort into three parts:

- prewriting, when you prepare to write;

- writing, when you do the 'real' work;

- rewriting, when you edit what you have written into something that others will enjoy reading.

The first stage is to find out why you are doing the piece of writing. Ask yourself why you have been asked to write something and what you expect to gain as a result of writing it. To write something that is effective, you need to know what you want your reader to do as a result of reading it. It's not enough that the reader now knows something new, or is made aware of something new; what do you want the reader to do as a result of this new awareness or knowledge? Different people react differently. In order to be able to identify what we want our reader to do, we must have a clear idea of what our reader is like. Will the readers have specialist understanding of the main subject of the report? Will you have to remind or tell them why the report was commissioned? Is the subject already important to them? And, if it is, do they know that it is? What do they expect the report to say? What do they want to read – as distinct from what they expect to read? Having considered both your potential reader and your purpose in writing, you then need to gather all the relevant information and organise it to suit the reader and achieve the purpose.

Having done all the prewriting, we are now at a good place to go on to write whatever it is we need to write. What we want to produce is writing that is clear, concise, correct and appealing to read. Accurate spelling and punctuation add clarity as well as correctness to a report.

So far, when looking at prewriting, we have been looking from the perspective of the writer. Let's look at writing from the other perspective. As a reader, you are more likely to read something if it looks interesting. Also, many people who have to read a lot of reports read only parts of them.

Most reports will contain a title page, a management summary, a conclusions/ recommendations section, a main body and perhaps some appendices. Of these, the most important parts to make interesting and clear are the summary and the conclusions/recommendations. Many senior managers read only these parts consistently and rely on their staff to know the detail. Clear, interesting writing usually has few cliches, little jargon and is active, not passive. Most readers prefer such writing, but many writers rely on jargon, cliches and the passive, mistakenly believing that they are writing the correct, accepted style. Nothing could be further from the truth.

Finally, there is the rewriting stage, when you polish what you have already written. At this stage you need to know the mistakes you commonly make, so that you can correct them. You will probably have to write a lot of reports in your job as an analyst. If you follow the *prewrite, write, rewrite* plan, you will produce an accurate, clear document. Let's look at one or two factors that can help to make that document more readable.

The order of sentences in a paragraph of a report can make a considerable difference to the reader's understanding of that document. Paragraphs are easiest to follow if they start with a flag sentence that tells the reader what the topic of the paragraph will be. This paragraph, for example, deals with the order of information in paragraphs. As you are told this in the first sentence, fast readers will be able to scan the topic of the paragraph quickly and then decide whether to read the rest or not. All paragraphs should start with the key idea first, then with a logical sequence of sentences all relating to that key idea.

Word order in sentences should follow the same principle. The most important word or words should come first, like a flag to attract the reader's attention. For example, key words and phrases such as 'in conclusion' and 'to summarise' should always be at the start of the sentence, not hidden in the middle, where they could be easily missed.

If you want people to agree with your conclusions as well as follow your argument, it is a good idea to start with the weakest argument and progress to the strongest. So, if there are a number of possibilities for a new system, all of which have some merit, your report should start with the weakest possibility, explaining why this is the weakest, and progressing on through the others with explanations as to why they should not be chosen, ending with the strongest, together with reasons as to why this one should be chosen.

3.4.3 Meetings

If you ask people to describe what makes them effective at meetings, the chances are they will list:

- careful preparation;
- well-structured information;
- clear presentation of the ideas.

It follows, then, that if you are to be effective in meetings, you should consider these three topics.

Most meetings circulate something to the participants in advance. This may include an agenda, minutes of the last meeting, briefing papers, proposals, or reports. As a participant, you have to decide what is important in this mass of paper. A properly prepared agenda will help you to do this. It will give you titles of the topics to be discussed and an idea of what will be required of the participants – a decision, a briefing, for information only, and so on. You should also be given an idea of how long the topic is expected to last. In this way you can devote your preparation to those topics that require some action by the group and which are expected to take some time. Beware of the meeting where nothing is circulated beforehand – it probably means that most people will do no preparation and that the meeting will be ineffective.

In order to be able to contribute well in the meeting, you will want to ensure that you know what you intend to say. Some written notes can be valuable, particularly if you take time to think of what could persuade others to your point of view. You need to ensure that your notes contain information that is accurate and not open to argument. If you have one previously undetected error in what you say, you may well find that people pick on that error and so lose the whole point of your argument. Also, if you have a good clear case with one or two supporting examples, you can make your point. If you were to bring in other arguments in support of your position, you could fail. Some listeners pick on the weakest of the arguments and dismiss it, and with it the whole position. People are more interested in people and specific cases than in abstractions, so use examples, illustrations and case histories, especially if you can use information known to your listeners where you can be certain they will agree with your conclusions. Write your notes in a way you can easily understand and then refer to them when you need to. Many people don't use notes for meetings, and you may feel that you will look inexperienced if you do so, but it is better to look inexperienced and thoroughly prepared than to look inexperienced and totally confused! Even though you have your notes, listen to what others are saying, and be prepared to modify your views. Finally, don't over-prepare. Come with an open mind, not just a series of answers and conclusions that you have come to without hearing the other points of view.

You will have noticed that a large part of careful preparation is about ensuring that the information you present at the meeting is well structured. There are, however, some other things you can do to ensure that you make a good impression at meetings. If you will be making a proposal at the meeting, one good thing to do is to lobby other attendees beforehand. It is especially useful to see the most influential people before the meeting and try the proposal out on them. If they agree with you, you will have an influential ally; if they disagree with you, you can find out why and still have time to do something about it before the meeting. You could adjust your proposal so that you do have support; you could marshall your arguments so that you can convince others; or you could drop the proposal, at least for the moment, if it is clear you will not succeed. But whatever happens, you will have lost nothing.

As an analyst, one of the areas you will be talking about in meetings is change. If you expect opposition to what you will be saying, the best plan is to anticipate what others may say, and then prepare counter-arguments. You may not know the details of what the others will say, but if you are proposing a change, the two most common counter-arguments are that it's too expensive and that it won't work. If you can anticipate these attacks and have your position already prepared (and backed up with facts and figures), you are more likely to have your point of view accepted.

If you disagree with what someone says in a meeting, there are some things you can do to make your point have more chance of being accepted.

- Having established that it is the idea you are criticising, not the person proposing it, hesitate before you disagree. There is a fair chance you have not understood clearly what the person meant. It is often a good idea to restate succinctly in your own words what it is you think you heard. In this way, the speaker can clarify for you what was meant. Either there will be no disagreement, or the disagreement will become more sharply focused.

- If the person putting forward the idea is speaking in the abstract, it is usually a good idea to ask for a specific example. Someone may say, 'All senior management is interested in is cutting costs, not in making this a better system'. This may or may not be true, but if you disagree with the abstract statement, you could generate conflict. A better approach would be to ask for supporting evidence or to wait until the person gives the evidence. Then you have something concrete to work with.

- Agree with anything you can of the other person's point of view, making statements such as, 'I agree that there will be a significant cost saving if we adopt this plan, but there will also be the possibility of generating more business, and that possibility is what I think we should be discussing here.'

- One of the best ways to avoid an argument is to ask questions rather than attack someone's views. So you could say, 'Geoff, you said a number of times now that you think this proposal would never work here. What makes you think this?' rather than 'Of course this proposal would work here'.

- Once you know why the person holds a particular view in opposition to yours, you may find that you both have the same objectives and differ only in your preferred ways of achieving them. In this case, you should concentrate on the similarities between your views before you go on to disagree. In this way, you have taken some of the sting out of the opposition, and stand more chance of winning the other person round to your viewpoint.

3.4.4 Presentations

Most analysts will have to speak in public. You may sometimes look at good public speakers and envy them their natural ability, but while it is true that some people do have exceptional natural ability, most good speakers work hard to develop their skill. It is important to be as thorough as you can about preparation. Doing so allows you to deal with some of the essentials before you stand up to face your audience. If you know you are well prepared, you can then turn your attention to the task in hand – making a good impression on your listeners. When you first hear that you will have to give a presentation, there are four areas you need to concentrate on:

- your audience;
- your purpose;
- your material;
- your intended location.

The first two of these will have an enormous impact on your material, and the last one will have an impact on how you will deliver your material.

The first area to look at is your audience. This will come first because the first questions you need to ask are about the audience. As when you write, you have to tailor everything about your presentation to your audience. Even if you think you know nothing about them, there are bound to be things that you can find out. You can call their secretaries, or you can talk to other people who have experience of speaking to such an audience so that you can have a clear idea of what is expected from you. You will need to know, in particular, how much they already know about the subject you'll be presenting. In addition to this, there are always a number of things that you already know about every audience you will be presenting to. First of all, in some ways, each member of that audience will be a bit like you. So if you consider when you have felt uncomfortable during others' presentations, you will have some ideas about what to avoid during your own presentations. Also, if you remember what you have enjoyed about others' presentations, you can use this as a guide for what could be effective for you.

Once you have decided what your audience is likely to need from you, you can then turn your attention to the material. This time the first question to be answered is: 'Why have they chosen me to make this presentation?' You need to be clear in your own mind about why you have been chosen. Do you have a particular skill or ability that others lack? Or were you the one member of the team with adequate time to prepare? Whatever the reason, knowing why you have been chosen will help you to meet the purpose of the presentation.

The next question to be answered is 'Why am I giving a talk?' People are often asked to make presentations without knowing the reason. If you have no idea why a talk is needed, rather than a letter, report, article in a journal or a series of telephone conversations, then you will not be able to do a good job.

Finally you need to find out the answer to the question 'What is my purpose?' When you present, you may be trying to do a number of things, but you need to have the purpose in your mind. Are you trying to persuade? Or to inform? Or to train? Or to sell? Do you want to give background information or detail? Once you know this, you can move on to decide what your material should be and how you can structure it to achieve your objective.

When preparing your ideas, research your topic and, when you know all you need, write down your ideas in any order. Collect everything you may need for the topic at this stage. You can prune your ideas later. At this stage, collect even information that you find dull or boring – your audience may need it or may find it interesting. And do it as early as you can, as your thinking will mature with time. Then review your collected material after a little time. Decide what to include and what to leave out. Include only material that will have the impact you intend upon your particular audience. Consider a structure that will enable you to get your message across. This will not only help you with your preparation, it will also help your audience to follow where you are during your talk. Then prepare your notes to help you keep to your prepared structure. These can be as full or minimal as you prefer, but make sure that you pay extra attention to the start and the end of your presentation, as these are the two areas where your audience will particularly notice your performance. Your notes will give you the best chance of remembering what you want to say and help you prevent you from either getting lost or drying up.

Very few people present without any notes at all. Even fewer do it well. Some guidelines for notes are:

- Once you have made them, use them to help keep you on track. Beware of the last-minute inspiration as you stand up, as you have no idea of how it will affect your timing or the balance of your talk.

- Write them yourself. A surprising number of people give talks using notes written by someone else who was originally scheduled to give the talk but now can't. At the very least, if you have to use someone else's notes, ensure that you understand them thoroughly, and rewrite them for your own use.

- Use only one side of the paper, and number all of your pages.

- Consider using index cards. They are easier to handle and less obtrusive than paper pages.

- Use colour to highlight important points, headings, new topics and optional parts to be included if there is time.

There is a continuum from 'no notes at all' to a 'full script'. You should choose the place on the continuum where you think you will feel the most comfortable, and try out your notes when you practise.

Comprehensive notes are suitable for most people most of the time and will be quite full, probably with most of the following:

- a sequence of headings and subheadings, each with the first few sentences;

- links from one section to another;

- summaries and conclusions;

- references to visuals;

- prompts to help with any interactive parts;

- examples you intend to use;

- timing notes, to ensure you keep to time.

Simple notes, sometimes called *skeletal notes*, are much briefer and are most suitable if you are familiar with the subject. They would normally consist of:

- key headings;

- key words/phrases to jog your memory;

- prompts to sequence the ideas.

When your notes are complete, you will know exactly what you will be doing during your presentation. Now make a rough version of anything you will need for the presentation. You may need to use visuals, show graphs or distribute a handout. None of these should be left to the last minute. Finally, have a run-through beforehand. This will not only give you the chance to assess your timing and adjust it if necessary, it will also let you experience what it will be like presenting that material. If there is anything you feel uncomfortable with, you can change it before your audience has to experience it. You may want to get some feedback from colleagues, or from a video camera, so that you can get an idea of your impact.

When listening to you, your listeners will not be able to go back and re-read parts they did not understand the first time. You need to do something to ensure that they are unlikely to lose their place, and, if they do, that they can find it again quickly and easily. The best way to give your audience this help is to have a clear and accurate structure. A well-known and frequently used structure is often called the 'Three T's'. It looks like this:

- Tell them what you are going to tell them.

- Tell them.

- Tell them what you told them.

To put it another way, you could have an introduction in which you outline the main sections of your talk, a middle where you present each of these topics, and a conclusion where you sum up what you said previously and ensure that your listeners go away with your message ringing in their ears.

In the introduction, you need to make a good impression at the start. You need to attract the interest of your audience and build on their desire to listen. One way to do this is to look comfortable and happy with presenting. It is an unfortunate fact that in the first two minutes of your talk the audience will be judging how comfortable you are as a presenter, when it is the very time that you are likely to be feeling most nervous. If you have a good introduction that is well rehearsed, you will get through those first few moments more comfortably and make a good impression.

In your introduction, you will need to welcome your audience and introduce yourself and the topic. Because you have prepared thoroughly, you will know why you are presenting, and it may be appropriate to tell this to the audience, to build up your credibility. It will also be useful to define the subject you will be talking about, what you will cover and what you will not, any parts that you will concentrate upon in particular, and so on. You also need to describe the procedure, how long you intend to talk, whether you will give a handout, whether it would be useful for them to take notes, whether they should ask questions as you talk or whether you would prefer them to ask questions at the end, and so on. All of this establishes a comfort zone for you and your audience for that presentation. With everyone comfortable and knowing what is expected from them, you can move on to the main body of your talk.

Within the main body, a good general guide is to work from the known to the unknown. You cannot transfer new knowledge or information to someone in an effective way unless you relate it to something they already know. As well as this, people will accept your ideas and conclusions better if you establish a context for them. Also, you will be talking about a number of related topics. As the ideas are not already linked in the mind of your audience, you need to create this link for them. One way of doing this is to introduce and sum up each topic, ensuring that there are adequate signposts for your audience to be able to see where they are going, where they are and where they have been. Another structure you could use for a persuasive or sales presentation is the 'Four P's'. These stand for:

- Position (the audience should already know this).

- Problem (they should know this too).

- Possibilities.

- Proposal (your recommendation).

An example might be that our *position* is that we all want to go out together tonight. The *problem* is that the car we were intending to use has broken down. There are a number of *possibilities*: we could call a rescue organisation, we could take a taxi, we could take a train, or we could take a bus. I *propose* that we take a bus to the station then go by train, as that way we will all be able to have a drink. It is a logical structure, which can be expanded well beyond a few sentences.

A structure that is rarely extended beyond a few sentences is that of the 'sound bite', the mnemonic for which is PREP. This stands for:

- Position.
- Reason.
- Example.
- Position.

Once you are aware of this structure, you will notice a number of politicians use it in answer to questions. It goes like this:

My position on this matter is . . . My reason for this is . . . Let me give you an example . . . So, I firmly believe that (and the position is restated) . . .

It is an ideal structure for sounding expert and authoritative in a few words.

At the end, your audience will probably appreciate being reminded of your main messages. If something you have said was important, consolidate by restating it. This is your last chance to get your message across – your last chance to make a good impression on your audience. Many poor presenters falter into silence, shuffle their notes and then sit down looking apologetic. You do not have to be stunningly original, but you do need to be memorable in those last few moments. Ensure that you finish on a high note, where you convey your enthusiasm for your subject. You will do this only if you plan it well before you stand up.

Many a good presentation has been spoilt because the presenter failed to check the venue in advance. You need to know about the audiovisual equipment. Try to visit the room and use the equipment beforehand. That way you will get a feel for the place, which will help you in your final preparation of the material. You'll be able to check out the computer projection equipment and the support that will be available on the day. You will also see how the equipment and furniture are set out. You can then decide whether you like them like this or whether you want to change them.

Having dealt with all the preliminaries beforehand, your time and attention during the presentation are on your delivery. When you present, you want to be your own natural, relaxed self, but just a little larger than life. How can you do this? In order to stand up and be yourself, you need to have controlled your nerves to some extent. You will probably never be free from nerves – many great presenters and actors were racked with stage fright all through their careers – but you can control nerves with some simple techniques. Many people find when they start to speak in public that they cannot quite breathe properly. Sometimes they run out of breath part way through the sentence, leading to a loud first part where the breath was sufficient and a quiet second half where it was not. Sometimes they need to breathe in the middle of sentences, and so create an unnatural pause. Sometimes they breathe very shallowly and sound rather as though they are attempting to run a marathon. You can avoid problems like this, and feel more calm than you did before, by doing some simple breathing exercises.

It is also important to use your body to reinforce your message, not negate it. It will establish you as someone who can be trusted to tell the truth. It will establish you as expert in the subject you are talking about. Because it will be appropriate to the situation, it will vary from time to time, but there are a few things that are constant:

- *Eye contact*. You will only build up rapport with your audience if you look at them. This is particularly true in the first few minutes of your talk. If you avoid their eyes then, you will have to work hard to regain the ground you have lost. Avoid all extremes, so do not stare at anyone either. You need to distribute a calm, even gaze throughout your whole audience, particularly to those people who look less than delighted. If someone is smiling and nodding, they are already on your side, so give them just enough attention to keep them happy while spending more attention on converting the doubters.

- *Open posture*. If your body position is closed, with arms folded and shoulders hunched, you will not look relaxed. If you look defensive, which is how a closed body posture is often interpreted, your audience may believe that you do not know what you are talking about.

- *Avoid mannerisms.* You will have seen presenters with mannerisms: they jingle coins or keys in their pockets, play with pens, stand still like a stuffed dummy or march like a soldier up and down. No doubt you could add other mannerisms to this list. Regardless of what the mannerism is, it conveys to your audience that you are uncomfortable in some way. This discomfort is catching, and they will feel it too. But that is not all: these distractions will stop the audience from focusing on the message you are conveying.

- *Be yourself.* However uncomfortable you may feel, you should be presenting yourself as well as the content of what you say. There will be a way you want to present, a way you want to sound and look: whatever it is, it should reflect you, the person, not someone else. Enhancing your own personal style means that you will be presenting yourself a little larger than life.

One thing that will help you achieve the effect you want is to focus your attention where it should be during your talk: on your audience, not on your state of mind. Your audience is listening to you because they need something from you. This something they need will depend on what your purpose is: to persuade, sell, inform, and so on. But if you focus on them and their needs, you will take some of your attention away from yourself and your nerves. You will know when you are achieving the effect you want if you read your audience. Look to see what you think their state of mind is. Are they confused? Or sceptical? Or bewildered? Or happy? You will get this information from making eye contact with them. If you also have some brief pauses in what you present, you can allow your audience to catch up with you, and you will give yourself time to look at them all and see how you think they are feeling. If they ask questions, you can judge their tone of voice as well as the content of the question.

Whatever you think their state of mind to be, do not leave it there. You need to check that you have received the right message from them, so reflect back what you have assessed to see if you are accurate, saying something like: 'I seem to have confused you here.' This gives them the chance to reply: 'I am confused. You described what you were going to do and that's not what you've done.' As the source of confusion is now out in the open, you can clear it up. If you do not clear it up, that person could leave your presentation confused and lacking support for your ideas. By handling the confusion, you have gained an ally.

It is not always appropriate to invite questions, but presenters generally do so. Communication is two-way, so most presenters feel that question time will allow the audience to have their say. At the same time, many presenters worry a lot about such questions. However you decide to handle questions in your presentation, you must tell your audience what you expect from them. There are a number of ways you can structure the time for questions:

- spontaneously: ask them as they occur to you;

- interim: you ask 'Are there any questions?' at times when you feel there may be;

- at the end of the talk;

- written questions presented in advance, at the end or after a short break.

Whenever they occur, here is a model for answering questions effectively:

- *Listen.* There are presenters, some politicians among them, who do not answer the question they have been asked. Sometimes this is because they prefer to answer another question, but sometimes it is because they have not heard the question. If you are not sure you have heard it accurately, ask the speaker to repeat it.

- *Pause.* This gives you a little time for thought and gives the audience time to assimilate the question.

- *Repeat/clarify.* Often, people in the audience do not hear the question the speaker has been asked. By repeating it, they get to hear it for the first time. But this is not all; by repeating it in your own words, you are checking back that you have understood the question, so clarifying your understanding. An extra bonus is that you get an extra moment to think of the answer.

- *Respond.* This may seem too obvious to state, but answer the question. Do not answer one you would have preferred to have been asked; do not waffle around the subject because you cannot answer the question; never lie; do not make this the opportunity to put in those points of your talk that you forgot to give at the time.

- *Check back with the questioner.* It is courteous to check that you have dealt with the topic to the questioner's satisfaction. Doing so will also ensure that you can clear up any lingering queries.

This model will help you deal with almost any type of question and help to keep the audience thinking of you in a positive way. Whatever method you choose, ensure that it is appropriate to you and your talk, and that you have told your audience, preferably in your introduction, when and in what format they should ask questions.

3.5 Summary

This chapter has presented a model for effective communication, where the communicators alternate between sending and receiving. Such a model works in a number of situations: face-to-face communication, meetings and interviews, written communication such as reports, and non-verbal communication. Whatever the situation in which you are communicating, there are three things you always need to know in order to ensure that you are successful: the purpose of your communication, the nature of your intended audience, and their expertise in your subject. We looked at barriers to effective communication: not coming across clearly, not listening effectively, poor presentation, different assumptions or someone not communicating fully. There were also guidelines for coming across effectively, for improving your listening skills, your writing skills, your contributions in meetings and your presentation skills.

People spend a lot of their time communicating, sometimes well but sometimes badly. It's worth spending time to improve your skills, as the payoff can be huge, not just in your job but in your life as a whole. Communication is an area where many of us are complacent, so reading this chapter every six months or so is a good way of keeping the ideas in mind and ensuring that you make the most of what you have learned.

Exercises

3.1 A particular application in System Telecom is giving cause for concern because of the increasing number of programming errors being found during its early operational life. Herr Norbert Rothaas has asked you to chair a meeting that will clearly state the problem and recommend appropriate action. He then wants you to give him a short verbal summary of the main issues and back this up with a report. How would you plan for this assignment?

Think first of all about the implications of the assignment. You need to:

- find out who can contribute towards resolving this issue and bring them together in a constructive environment;

- organise an effective meeting;

- investigate the problem and identify solutions;

- make a brief presentation to him;

- write an accurate and comprehensive report.

Each of these is a systems task in itself. Three of them have been covered in this chapter, but you will have to be creative to work out how to complete the first task of bringing the appropriate people together.

3.2 Assume now that you have completed the assignment. You've made your presentation to him and submitted your report, which he has accepted. You are now required to present to the user department manager and senior staff, and the application development team for this system. Your presentation will be different. What will be the structure of the presentation and the headings you will use? This event is likely to be a more emotionally charged event. How will you handle this?

4 Building Better Systems

4.1 Introduction

In March 1988, at an annual meeting in Gleneagles, the Computer Services Association of Great Britain announced the results of a study undertaken by Price Waterhouse which revealed that £500 million a year were wasted by users and suppliers in the United Kingdom as a result of quality defects in software. An earlier United States Government Accounting Office report had investigated a number of federal software projects costing a total of $6.3 million. Out of these, half were delivered but never used; a quarter were paid for but not delivered; and only $300,000 worth was actually used as delivered, or after some changes had been made. The rest was used for a while, then either abandoned or radically reworked. In 1989, the British Computer Society advised the Department of Trade and Industry that losses due to poor-quality software were costing the UK £2,000 million per year.

Reports and studies such as those described above have highlighted the problems associated with quality failures in systems development and have led to moves towards building better systems that meet the needs of the user, are cost-effective, and are produced on time and within budget. Developers of software products and information systems are being encouraged to adopt definite policies and practices that are carried through from requirements analysis to maintenance and user support phases. For example, in Britain, the Department of Trade and Industry is sponsoring a quality management certification initiative, called TickIT, the aim of which is to achieve improvements in the quality of software products and information systems throughout the whole field of IT supply, including in-house development work.

In this chapter we shall turn our attention to this important area of quality, looking first at some definitions and then at the contribution made by a number of 'gurus' to our understanding of quality. We shall discuss quality management, including the standard ISO 9000, and then go on to describe techniques for building quality into systems analysis and design and into all parts of the software development process.

4.2 Quality Concepts

The term 'quality' means different things to different people, depending on their perspective. To some it means 'finding the errors' or 'making sure it's correct', and involves checking the deliverables of a system. For others it is about the process of production, and means 'doing it right first time', 'achieving the standard' or 'getting the job done in the best possible way.' Actually these definitions point to the fact that there are a number of dimensions to the concept of quality, which we shall examine. In this book, our working definition of quality is:

conforming to the customer's requirements

where 'customer' can be either an external customer (a client) or an internal customer (a colleague), and 'requirements' relate to both the product and the service delivered.

Customers

The concept of an internal customer, and an internal supplier, is important to an appreciation that our definition of quality goes beyond the interface between the software supplier and the client to include all our working relationships. The roles of internal customer and internal supplier are constantly changing. For example, consider the situation when an analyst hands a report to a secretary to be typed. Before handing it over, the analyst (the supplier) will have checked with the secretary (the customer) the form in which the secretary would like to receive the written draft (for example, with pages numbered, paragraphs clearly marked, written legibly etc.). When handing back the typed document, the secretary becomes the supplier, and will ensure that the requirements of the customer (the analyst) have been met, for example completed on time, in the required format and with spellings checked.

In both internal and external customer–supplier relationships, the supplier must first talk to the customer to ensure they fully understand the customer's requirements, if a quality product or service is to be delivered. The requirement will include details of:

- what is required;

- the most appropriate way of producing or delivering it;

- the involvement and contribution expected from each party during the process.

Product and service quality

The deliverable to the customer – the thing they see or experience – is a product or a service, or both. Product quality can be defined as the degree to which a product meets the customer's requirements. According to this definition, what the customer thinks about the quality of the product is all that counts. One can speak of better product quality only if the customer *perceives* the product to be better, no matter what the experts may consider to be objective, factual improvements. Service quality can be defined as the degree to which a service meets the recipient's requirements. The quality of service can be described as having two components: *'hard'*, the tangible content of the service such as the number of times the phone rings before it is answered, the user guide, the number of post office counter staff available at lunch time, the comfort of the aircraft seat; and *'soft'*, the emotional content of the service, the friendliness, flexibility, helpfulness of the service provider, the atmosphere of the premises, the treatment of complaints. Studies conducted in the United States show that the human factor has a crucial bearing on the customer's perception of the service quality. 'Soft' service is therefore often more important than 'hard' service in a customer's perception of quality.

All too often, suppliers concentrate all their effort on investigating the customer's product requirements, but in order to deliver a quality package to internal as well as external customers, their service requirements (hard and soft) must also be investigated.

4.3 Quality Gurus

In this section we'll look at the work of three influential 'quality gurus' – W. Edwards Deming, Joseph Juran and Philip Crosby – in order to understand the origin of current approaches to the subject. There have been three 'generations' of quality gurus. First there were the Americans such as Deming, who developed the philosophy and took the idea to the Japanese to help them rebuild their economy after the Second World War. The second generation were Japanese gurus who built on the original ideas and introduced techniques such as quality circles and fishbone diagrams. Finally came the third wave, typified by Tom Peters and Philip Crosby, who, influenced by the Japanese, have developed new ways of thinking about quality in the West.

W. Edwards Deming

The origin of the Japanese ideas of quality management can be traced back to an American named W. Edwards Deming. Deming found that managers in postwar Japan were much more receptive to his concepts than their Western counterparts – whose perception was that quality increased the cost of the product and adversely affected productivity. Under Deming's guidance Japanese companies took a number of important actions:

- They invited customers into their organisation and worked with them to improve quality.

- They removed responsibility for quality from a separate department and ensured that all line managers worked to their own clear quality objectives.

- Responsibility for quality was delegated to all levels of staff within an organisation.

Deming was trained as a statistician, and his ideas are based on *statistical process control* (SPC), a method that focuses on problems of variability in manufacture and their causes, using statistical process control charts to identify and separate off 'special' causes of production variability from 'common' causes. The special causes would then be analysed and problem-solving methods applied. He proposed a systematic, rigorous approach to quality and problem-solving, and encouraged senior managers to become actively involved in their company's quality improvement programmes. Deming's philosophy was described in 14 points addressed to all levels of management. The key messages were:

- Create a sense of common purpose throughout the organisation.
- Build quality into the product.
- Buy from the best supplier rather than the cheapest.
- Establish a programme of continuous training.
- Improve communications within the company and with customers.
- Drive out fear – encourage people to work together.

Deming argued that emphasis should be placed on controlling the production process rather than concentrating on the end product, and that a higher quality of product results in reduced costs.

Joseph Juran

Joseph Juran, another American writer who was also very influential in Japan in the early 1950s, began his career as an engineer. His message is aimed primarily at management, who he claims are responsible for at least 85% of the failures within companies. He believes that quality control should be conducted as an integral part of management control, and that quality does not happen by accident but has to be planned. Juran's central idea is that management should adopt a structured approach to company-wide quality planning, and that this should be part of the *quality trilogy* of quality planning, quality control and quality improvement. This would mean:

- identifying customers and their needs,
- establishing optimal quality goals, and
- creating measurements of quality

in order to produce continuing results in improved market share, premium prices and a reduction in error rates.

Philip Crosby

Philip Crosby is another influential writer and speaker on quality, whose book *Quality is Free*, published in 1979, became a best-seller. He developed the concepts of 'do it right first time' and 'zero defects'. Recognising the role management and employees play in the framework of an appropriate quality culture, he defined the four absolutes of quality management:

- Quality is defined as conformance to the customer's requirements, not as 'goodness' or 'elegance'.

- The system for implementing quality is prevention, not appraisal.

- The performance standard must be zero defects, not 'that's close enough'.

- The measurement of quality is the price of non-conformance.

According to Crosby, the price of non-conformance – the cost of doing it wrong and then having to put it right or do it again – is about 20% of revenue for manufacturing companies and up to 35% for service companies.

All three of the gurus described above agree that quality is a continuous process for an organisation; that building quality into the production process – prevention – is more effective than just testing or checking the product at the end of the process – inspection; that management is the agent of change; and that training and education should be continuous processes at all levels.

What are the implications of these ideas for software developers? Four main points seem to result from these ideas about quality:

- There needs to be a greater investment of time and effort in the early stages of system development, if the cost of correcting errors at the end is to be reduced. This is consistent with the message that prevention is more effective than inspection. Research conducted by IBM has shown that 75% of software development costs are associated with testing, debugging and maintaining software, and if this figure is analysed, over 80% of the testing, debugging and maintenance cost can be traced back to problems introduced during analysis. A more systematic approach to analysis could make a dramatic difference to these figures, and this is the purpose of the structured methods described in this book.

- The cost of correcting an error during implementation is many times greater than the cost of putting it right during analysis. For every hour spent tracing a bug at the analysis stage, it takes 60 hours to find it at the testing stage. The use of reviews and walkthroughs at every stage of development would help with the early detection of errors. This supports the idea, put forward by the 'gurus', that quality is a continuous process. There is sometimes a fear that quality assurance will only delay a project, but if managers don't invest the necessary time and resources to build reviews into the development process, they are putting themselves in a similar position to a frog placed in boiling water. If you put a frog in cold water and gradually turn the heat up, the frog will not notice that the water is boiling until it is too late. If problems are not detected early, during formal reviews, management may not be aware of them until too late, when the cost of putting these problems right can be huge.

- Clients who have been questioned about their satisfaction with the product and service delivered by software suppliers have identified that one cause of dissatisfaction is their discovery that project personnel do not have the level of experience or expertise that they were led to expect. By investing in the training and development of its staff, not only will a company be supporting one of the main recommendations of the gurus for ensuring quality, but it will be raising its chances of doing the job right first time and also building the client's confidence. Philip Crosby has said that before you can expect people to do it right first time, you need to tell them what 'it' is, and show them what doing it right looks like. Crosby describes this as investing in prevention, an idea we shall explore further in the next section.

- The gurus agree that management is the agent of change. Managers on software projects must take the lead in making quality an intrinsic part of the development process. Often software development project managers don't give the projects a chance to achieve this because they focus on only two issues: 'Is the project running according to budget?' and 'Is it on schedule?', rather than first asking the key question 'Are we meeting the customer's needs?'. Once this has been addressed, the other questions about schedule and budget can then be asked.

4.4 The Cost of Poor Quality

It is sometimes claimed that there is no real way of measuring quality. This is not true, however. It can be measured by calculating the total costs incurred by a company not doing the job right first time. This measure is called the cost of poor quality, or the price of non-conformance, and includes the following types of cost:

- prevention;
- appraisal;
- internal failure;
- external failure.

Prevention

The cost of prevention is the amount spent to ensure that the work will be done correctly. It includes risk reduction and error prevention, for example ensuring the design is right before beginning production. Examples of prevention costs are supplier evaluations and the training and development of staff.

Appraisal

Appraisal costs are those associated with inspection and testing of both the company's own products and products received from suppliers. On software projects, appraisal costs might be associated with testing, walkthroughs, Fagan

The Appraisal System

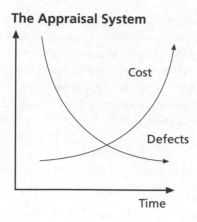

The Prevention System

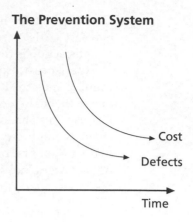

Fig. 4.1 The costs of appraisal and prevention

inspections (described in section 4.7) and design reviews. The idea of appraisal is to spot the defects as early as possible in the process so they can be fixed, saving additional costs later. Figure 4.1 shows a comparison between appraisal and prevention costs. As the cost of appraisal within a company rises, because of more resources being devoted to inspecting and testing, the number of product defects is reduced significantly. For example, the more design reviews carried out during system development, which involves an increased investment in appraisal, the greater the chance of spotting and correcting defects.

With prevention, on the other hand, the costs fall as the number of defects falls. If, for example, everyone on a software project is trained in the use of a structured development method, the only additional training required would be for new people joining the project, and so the cost of training – the prevention cost – would fall.

Internal failure

The cost of internal failure is the cost of rectifying everything that is discovered to be wrong while the product or service is still in the company's possession or under its control. An example would be part of a software system having to be scrapped, and then designed and coded again, as a result of a major problem being unearthed during integration testing. In other words, thinking back to the discussion about customers earlier in this chapter, internal failure costs are incurred in putting right problems with the product or service before it is delivered to the external customer because the requirements of the internal customers have not been met.

Some companies spend a lot of time inspecting their products and fixing defects, without attempting to prevent the problem that originally caused the defects. This has been described as scraping burnt toast, based on the premise that if your electric toaster is burning the toast, you can either fix the problem – the toaster – or deal with the symptoms of the problem – scrape the burnt parts off the toast. This phenomenon is illustrated in Figure 4.2, where an automated

Fig. 4.2 'Scraping burnt toast' (reprinted with permission from *The Team Handbook* by Peter Scholtes)

system has been developed to enable the symptoms of the problem to be put right, while the real problem remains unresolved.

External failure

External failure costs are incurred by a company because defects are not detected before the product or service is delivered to the external customer. Examples of these are the cost of fixing software or hardware problems during the warranty period, and the cost of handling customer complaints. They also include the cost to the business of an external customer cancelling or withholding repeat business as a result of poor service.

If quality costs within an organisation are examined, internal and external failures will typically account for a third to a half of the total cost of poor quality. A similar proportion of the cost of poor quality will relate to appraisal and only a small percentage to prevention.

This is shown in Figure 4.3, which represents the effect on a company's quality costs, expressed as a percentage of total operating cost, of implementing a quality improvement program over a 5–7 year period. The total cost of quality, which initially is 25–40% of total cost, drops to a figure between 5% and 15%. Of the final figure, over 50% is spent on prevention measures rather than on appraisal or on correcting failures. The margin between the initial and final cost of quality is measured in savings to the company.

In addition to the direct, measurable costs, there are the indirect costs of poor quality, which are very difficult to measure. The following story illustrates this point. A manufacturer produces bicycles for children. Stabilising wheels are provided as an optional extra and are held on by the use of nuts and bolts that are an integral part of the bicycle. The stabilisers are produced separately from the bicycles. The manufacturer is made aware of a problem when bicycles start coming back in under guarantee because the stabilisers break off owing to the weakness of the bolt.

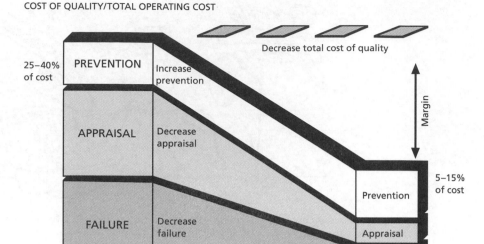

COST OF QUALITY/TOTAL OPERATING COST

Fig. 4.3 The effect of quality improvement on the cost of poor quality

This is an example of external failure. The direct cost of this quality failure to the manufacturer is incurred in supplying new, stronger bolts and distributing these to retailers and to customers who have complained. However, consider the child who is given the bicycle as a present on Christmas Day and, because of the broken bolt, can't ride it. The indirect cost of poor quality will include the petrol used in taking the stabilising wheels and the broken bolt back to the shop where the bicycle was purchased, and the time wasted by the child's parents in sorting out the problem, not to mention the fact that their Christmas has been spoilt because the child was so unhappy about the broken bike. Then there is the loss of repeat business from the customer and the loss of potential future business when the parents tell their friends and colleagues about the problem. On average it costs five times more to win a new customer than to keep an existing one, and, according to one survey, if you buy a product and are pleased with the purchase, you tell, on average, eight other people about it and how happy you are with it. But if you are unhappy with the product you have bought you will make your dissatisfaction known to 22 other people. Add all this together and you begin to get an idea of how great the indirect costs of quality failure are – and much of this will be invisible to the manufacturer.

So how can a software developer ensure that quality is taken seriously so that better systems can be built? One answer to this question is to measure the cost of poor quality in their organisation, by developing metrics that give them numbers that indicate where problems exist, and enable improvement to be monitored. Another answer is to introduce a quality management system in which measurement may play a part, and this is the subject of the next section.

4.5 Quality Management

To ensure that quality is maintained when developing software so that products and services are delivered that conform to the customer's requirement, three concepts are important – quality control, quality assurance and quality management.

Quality control is the task of ensuring that a product has been developed correctly – to requirements and to standard – and that the procedure identified for its development is effective and has been followed. Quality control is done best by the person or team who did the work, but it should include an independent contribution from a peer – someone who could have done the work, but who didn't. This might be provided by an equivalent member of a different team. For instance, a completed system design document should be reviewed not just by the person who has written it, but also by an independent person. It is surprising how many previously unseen errors and problems can come to light when the author 'walks through' a document with someone else, or examines a product against its requirements and relevant standards. Quality control also covers the procedures and methods used for the work. These must be identified beforehand, even if they are the usual ones, in a *quality plan*, and any deviation from them must be explained and assessed. It is important to maintain records to show that quality control has been carried out, and to indicate on the product or, if this is not possible, on an associated record, that it has been reviewed successfully. Quality control is the responsibility of everyone in the organisation.

Quality assurance is the responsibility of a smaller group of people. Someone independent of the work area or project checks that quality control has been performed, that it has been effective, and that the products are complete and suitable for delivery or for further use by someone else within the project. A formal audit of a software project is an example of quality assurance in action. The principal aim of quality assurance is to achieve confidence that the job or product will be acceptable to the external customer or to those involved in the next stage of development – the internal customers. Usually, this is done by the supplier – preferably by someone in an independent quality assurance role – and the evidence is recorded and made available to the customer. In effect, quality assurance is a check on quality practice in terms of the performance and effectiveness of the quality plan.

Increasingly, there is recognition that, in addition to quality control and quality assurance, a further level of monitoring is necessary, which can be described as *quality management*. This describes the establishment and maintenance of a quality system within the organisation, the company, the division or the project, and is usually the responsibility of senior people in that area. The hierarchical relationship between quality control, quality assurance and quality management is illustrated in Figure 4.4 – the quality pyramid.

The foundation of an organisation's *quality management system* (QMS) is a statement of its objectives and policy for quality, which should of course correspond to the type and scope of product or service being offered. There must be a description of the responsibilities and the internal organisation for the QMS, to ensure that quality control and quality assurance practices are understood and are operated effectively. A major reason for doing this is to allow an external

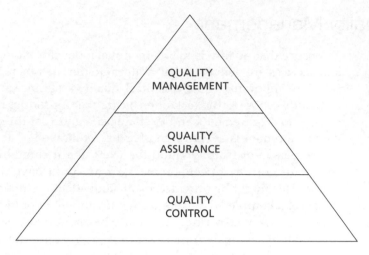

Fig. 4.4 The quality pyramid

customer to assess the supplier's attitude and approach to quality, both before work is placed with the supplier, and throughout the progress of the work. The QMS is a company's framework, within which all work is performed, using only procedures and methods that are defined, checked and visible.

Standards

A QMS will specify the standards to be used for tasks carried out within the organisation. Standards are needed to help people do the job right first time, as a means of communication, making it easier for teams to work together and ensuring that products developed will be compatible and contribute to producing consistent maintainable systems.

As an encapsulation of expert knowledge, standards can help newcomers and save time by preventing the need for different individuals and teams to have to 'reinvent the wheel'. They play an important part in quality control, enabling individuals to check that they have done what they should have done, and usually cover technical, administrative and managerial procedures within a company. Although standards are supposed to make life easier, their effectiveness is reduced if they are seen as inappropriate, out of date, not helpful, ambiguous, long winded, too detailed or too vague. In order to deliver the benefits described above and be seen as important and useful on projects, they must be living documents. In other words, they must be owned by somebody. The owner must be willing to listen to feedback, both positive and negative, about the standard and be prepared to make changes – or recommend that a new standard is created to fill the gap. To enable this to happen, a QMS must include:

- procedures for the regular – at least annual – review of every standard;
- mechanisms to allow users of the document to direct comments about the standard to the owner;

- a catalogue listing all the standards in the system and a central keeper of the latest version of each standard.

It is also the responsibility of each individual in the organisation to make the standards system work by giving feedback to the owner of the standard and by ensuring at the start of a piece of work that the standard being used is the latest version.

A lot of time and effort is usually expended in introducing a quality management system to an organisation. Is all the work justified? In a report published in 1991, which contains the findings of an NCC survey of IT companies who had introduced a formal QMS, the benefits to the organisations concerned were summarised by responses such as these:

- 'It helps to identify the company.'
- 'It helps to ensure repeat business.'
- 'It makes our practices coherent' (gives a 'house style').
- 'It helps new joiners settle in more easily.'
- 'You realise that all processes are QA' (everything contributes to quality).
- 'Now we know what we do and how we do it.'
- 'It has brought greater confidence in our ability to deliver.'
- 'Our products now have the stamp of quality.'
- 'It has brought us closer to the customer.'

The survey also pointed to the fact that businesses became more professional in their approach, that a sense of ownership was created within the organisations, and that a quality culture attracted quality people to work for the company.

A *quality manager* will usually have day-to-day responsibility for the QMS, although this may not need to be a full-time role once the quality system is established and running effectively. The QMS is documented in a *quality manual*, which also includes or refers to descriptions of the methods and procedures used on work tasks. This manual also becomes a valuable marketing and selling aid, as it provides evidence to the outside world of the means by which a supplier achieves quality of work and product, and is part of the basis on which the quality system can be assessed.

The current approach in forward-looking companies is for quality managers to assist, advise and support quality initiatives but not to take direct responsibility for them. This allows for the development of TQM (*total quality management*). TQM can be defined as 'implementing a cost-effective system for integrating the continuous improvement efforts of people at all levels in an organisation to deliver products and services that ensure customer satisfaction'. TQM requires a stable and defined QMS and a company-wide commitment to continuous improvement, which involves everyone in the organisation working together towards a common goal. In addition, to be effective, TQM needs two other important components to work together:

- *Tools and techniques.* To enable every employee to be involved in continuous improvement, common tools and techniques must be adopted throughout the organisation, and individuals and groups should all be trained in the use of these tools.

- *Human factors.* It is vital that everyone is motivated to take part in the process and that their contribution is recognised. The culture of the organisation must encourage cooperation and team work. Leadership styles must be appropriate to enable this to happen.

TQM represents a fundamental shift from what has gone before. Quality control and quality assurance remain important, but the focus is on a process of habitual improvement, where control is embedded within and is driven by the culture of the organisation. Senior management's role is to provide leadership and support, the main drive for improvement coming from those people engaged in product and service delivery. The task of implementing TQM can be so difficult that many organisations never get started. This has been called TQP – total quality paralysis! Understanding and commitment are vital first steps that form the foundation of the whole TQM structure, and these must be converted into plans and actions. Implementation begins with the drawing up of a quality policy statement, and the establishment of the appropriate organisational structure, both for managing and for encouraging involvement in quality. Collecting information about the operation of the business, including the costs of poor quality, helps to identify those areas in which improvements will have the greatest impact, after which the planning stage begins. Once the plans have been put into place, the need for continued education, training, and communication becomes paramount.

In summary

- *Quality control* (QC) involves ensuring that a task has been done correctly.

- *Quality assurance* (QA) is the process of checking that QC has been carried out satisfactorily so that products are complete and suitable for delivery to the customer.

- A *quality management system* (QMS) is concerned with implementing the quality policy of an organisation. It includes the management of QC and QA, the keeping of records, the maintenance of standards, and the identification of individuals responsible for the various tasks.

- The *quality manual* documents the quality management system adopted within an organisation.

- *Total quality management* (TQM) goes beyond the QMS and refers to a scenario in which quality lies at the centre of an organisation's business, permeates every area of activity, and involves everyone in the company in a process of continuous improvement.

Clients are becoming more assertive in demanding that software suppliers can demonstrate that quality underpins the development of computer systems.

A formal way of demonstrating that a working quality system is in place is certification to the international standard for quality management, ISO 9000 – also known as BS 5750 or EN 29000 – and clients are now making certification to this standard a prerequisite for suppliers wishing to bid for their work. Because of the importance of ISO 9000 to software developers, the next section of this chapter summarises the requirements of the standard.

4.6 ISO 9000

ISO 9000 is really a family of standards for software quality, and the two important members of the family to mention here are ISO 9001:2000 and ISO 9004:2000, which are shown schematically in Figure 4.5. These two standards have been formatted as a consistent pair to make them easy to use, and to relate to other management systems such as environmental standards, and the sector-specific requirements such as ISO/TS/16949 in the automotive industry and TL 9000 in the telecommunications sector.

The ISO requirements for a quality management system are for all organisations that need to demonstrate their ability to consistently provide products that meet customer (and applicable regulatory) requirements, and aim to improve customer satisfaction. It has been organised in a relatively user-friendly format with terms that are easily recognised by all business sectors. The standard is used for certification/registration and contractual purposes by organisations seeking recognition of their quality management systems.

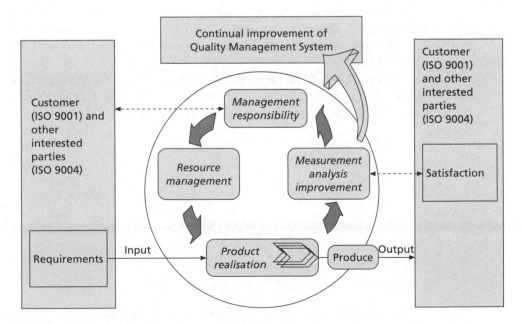

Fig. 4.5 The ISO 9001:2000 quality management system

ISO 9001:2000 is used if you are seeking to establish a management system that provides confidence in the conformance of your product to established or specified requirements. It is now the only standard in the ISO 9000 family against whose requirements your quality system can be certified by an external agency. The standard recognises that the word 'product' applies to services, processed material, hardware and software intended for, or required by, your customer.

There are five sections in the standard that specify activities that need to be considered when you implement your system. You will describe the activities you use to supply your products and may exclude the parts of the *product realisation* section that are not applicable to your operations. The requirements in the other four sections – *quality management system, management responsibility, resource management and measurement, analysis and improvement* – apply to all organisations, and you will have to demonstrate how you apply them to your organisation in your quality manual or other documentation.

Together, the five sections of ISO 9001:2000 define what you should do consistently to provide product that meets customer and applicable statutory or regulatory requirements. In addition, you will seek to enhance customer satisfaction by improving your quality management system.

ISO 9004:2000 is used to extend the benefits obtained from ISO 9001:2000 to all parties that are interested in or affected by your business operations, and interested parties in this case include your employees, owners, suppliers and society in general.

ISO 9001:2000 and ISO 9004:2000 are harmonised in structure and terminology to assist you to move smoothly from one to the other. Both standards apply a process approach. Processes are recognised as consisting of one or more linked activities that require resources and must be managed to achieve predetermined output. The output of one process may directly form the input to the next process, and the final product is often the result of a network or system of processes. The eight quality management principles stated in ISO 9000:2000 and ISO 9004:2000 provide the basis for the performance improvement outlined in ISO 9004:2000.

These eight principles are defined in ISO 9000:2000, *Quality management systems: Fundamentals and vocabulary*, and in ISO 9004:2000, *Quality management systems: Guidelines for performance improvements*. They are:

1 Customer focus.

2 Leadership.

3 Involvement of people.

4 Process approach.

5 System approach to management.

6 Continual improvement.

7 Factual approach to decision-making.

8 Mutually beneficial supplier relationships.

The nature of your business and the specific demands you have will determine how you apply the standards to achieve your objectives.

4.6.1 The TickIT Initiative

TickIT is about improving the quality of software and its application. We've already seen that almost every business depends on the correct manipulation of information by computer systems. Software is the key to the successful operation of these systems: poor-quality software can severely affect efficiency and competitiveness.

So to meet customers' quality expectations, software suppliers – including in-house developers – need to define and implement a quality system that covers all the essential business processes in the product life cycle, and TickIT guides the developer to achieve this objective within the framework of ISO 9000.

An important purpose of TickIT, which is supported by the UK and Swedish software industries, has been to stimulate software system developers to think about:

- what quality really is in the context of the processes of software development;
- how quality may be achieved;
- how quality management systems may be continuously improved.

Although certification of compliance to ISO 9001 is a contractual requirement for software suppliers in certain market areas, it should be a by-product of the more fundamental aims of quality achievement and improvement, and the delivery of customer satisfaction.

With regard to certification itself, the objectives are to:

- improve market confidence in third-party quality management system certification through accredited certification bodies for the software sector;
- improve professional practice amongst quality management system auditors in the software sector;
- publish authoritative guidance material (the TickIT Guide) for all stakeholders.

TickIT procedures relate directly to the requirements set out in ISO 9001:2000 and to the guidance contained in the Issue 5.0 TickIT Guide.

4.7 Quality in the Structured Life Cycle

In the traditional approach to developing an information system, there was little or no quality checking at each stage of the development process. There was ample testing of programs, interfaces, subsystems and finally the complete system, which ensured that when the system went 'live' it worked. However, the quality system did not ensure that the working system satisfied the requirements of the customer who had asked for it.

If testing is properly designed and planned, it can be very effective at locating defects. However, it can never be completely comprehensive. Checking every path through even a simple program can take a large amount of time. It is particularly difficult to trap defects introduced in the earliest stages of analysis and design, or facilities that have been 'lost' between one stage of development and the next. Such defects are often the ones that cause the most concern. Another drawback of relying on testing is that it can be done only in the later stages of development as it actually exercises code. Various studies show that, at the testing phase, the cost of correction may be 60 times greater than a correction made before the coding begins, and that the correction of a defect in an operational system can be 100 times greater. As a result, the cost of defect correction for large products can be over half of the total development cost.

With the introduction of structured approaches to system development, each stage of the project became a *milestone*, the deliverables of which had to be signed off by the developer and the customer before the next stage began. This ensures not only that the system does work when it finally goes live, but also that the client is in full agreement with the interpretation of the requirements – from the earliest stage to final implementation. A procedure for agreeing and signing off milestones, which is part of many structured methods, is the *structured walkthrough*, and a more formal technique that is also used on software development projects is the *Fagan inspection*. In this section we shall describe these two review techniques.

4.7.1 Structured Walkthroughs

A *structured walkthrough* is the review of products at the end of a stage in the development of a system by a group of relevant and competent persons. The prime objective of the walkthrough is to identify problems and initiate the necessary corrective action. There are two types of walkthrough – formal and informal. A formal walkthrough is a full review of all the work done in one stage of structured development, and involves the client. An informal walkthrough, on the other hand, is internal to the development project and reviews each step of the development within a stage. User involvement is optional in an informal walkthrough. In any walkthrough there are at least three people, but the recommended maximum is seven. The roles played by the attendees of the walkthrough are as follows:

- *Presenter*. The person who has done the work and is now submitting the relevant documentation for quality assurance.

- *Chairperson*. The person responsible for circulating the documentation prior to the meeting, choosing the time and the location, and chairing the meeting. The chairperson must also be familiar with the appropriate standards.

- *Secretary*. The person responsible for documenting the problems raised and then reading them back at the end of the meeting so that priorities can be assigned and follow-up action agreed.

- *Reviewer*. A person from the same project as the presenter.

In formal walkthroughs there will be extra reviewers:

- a *user representative* – mandatory for the formal agreement and signing-off of a development stage;

- an *extra observer* from the same project;

- an *unbiased observer* from another project, an optional role which can be useful in providing objectivity.

A walkthrough is divided into three stages: preparation, the walkthrough meeting itself, and the follow-up. Preparation takes place at least three days before the walkthrough and involves the *presenter* preparing the documentation on the product to be reviewed and passing this to the *chairperson*, who then distributes the documentation and notifies the reviewers of the time and location of the walkthrough meeting. The walkthrough meeting should be kept short – between 60 and 90 minutes – and is a meeting in which the *presenter* walks the *reviewers* through the product. The prime objective of this session is to ensure that a product meets the requirement and conforms to the appropriate standards, and that any defects are identified. An additional benefit of a walkthrough is the spread of information, knowledge, ideas and new approaches. A number of follow-up actions are available to the walkthrough team:

- Accept and sign-off the product.

- Recommend minor revisions with no need for a further review.

- Recommend major revisions, and schedule another walkthrough to review the revised product. In this case the person creating the product will have a written record of the identified problems, produced by the secretary, and the actions required. The necessary corrections are then made for resubmission in the next walkthrough.

Problems associated with walkthroughs

The problems with walkthroughs that often arise are: inadequate preparation by the reviewers; too much time spent discussing solutions rather than identifying defects; the author being defensive about his or her work; the walkthrough rambling on for too long. It is the chairperson's responsibility to avoid these problems by enforcing a time limit, ensuring walkthrough standards are adhered to, and reminding attendees, before the meeting, of the purpose of the walkthrough and the importance of preparation.

4.7.2 Fagan Inspections

A *Fagan inspection* is a formal review technique developed by Michael Fagan, a British engineer who worked for IBM. It was based on established review methods such as the structured walkthrough, but was designed to eliminate the problems associated with walkthroughs described above. An inspection can be

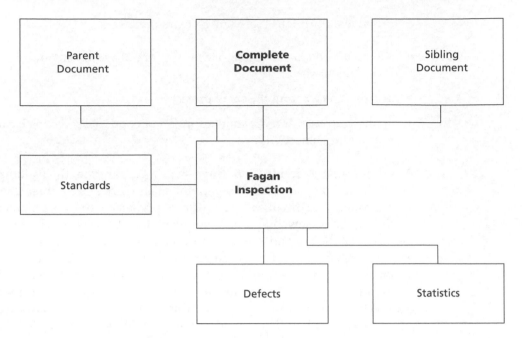

Fig. 4.6 The inspection process

defined as a formal examination of an item, against a previously produced item, by a group of people led by an independent chairperson, with the objectives of finding and recording defects, using standardised checklists and techniques; initiating rework as necessary; monitoring the rework; accepting the work, based on stated exit criteria; and adding to and utilising a base of historical defect data.

The technique has been continually refined in the light of experience and is applicable to all types of document, including functional specifications, program designs, code listings and test output. The inspection process involves checking a completed document for conformance to documents at a higher level – parent – and at the same level – sibling – and to relevant standards. Each non-conformance – defect – identified is recorded and used in the rework of the document, and statistics are collected to monitor the efficiency of both the software development and the inspection process. This process is illustrated in Figure 4.6.

The objectives of Fagan inspections are to identify and correct as many defects as possible early in the development process, so that the next stage can proceed with confidence, and to minimise the number of defects in the final system so that maintenance costs are reduced. The inspection process consists of a number of fixed stages: *planning*, during which the inspection team is appointed and any administration is performed; *overview*, the purpose of which is to ensure that those inspecting the document understand how it fits into the system as a whole; *preparation*, during which each member of the team takes time to become familiar with the item to be inspected and all related items; *the inspection meeting*, the most visible part of a Fagan inspection, at which the document is formally examined; *rework*, the task of correcting all defects found, performed by the author of the inspected item; *follow-up*, checking that the rework has been performed adequately.

The optimum number of attendees at the inspection meeting is between three and six. A number of roles have been defined for attendees, and these are summarised in Figure 4.7.

At the meeting the document is paraphrased aloud by the reader in segments agreed with the moderator. To ensure that everybody can hear the reader, the reader sits at the furthest point from the moderator, and if the moderator can hear distinctly, it is assumed that everyone else can. A suggested seating plan is shown in Figure 4.8. After each segment has been paraphrased, the moderator asks each inspector in turn for their comments on that part of the document. Comments are expected to be constructive criticisms about aspects of the document. All comments made are termed 'defects' and are recorded by the scribe. Any discussion of comments is restricted to ensuring that the nature of the defect is clearly understood. The meeting is intended only to bring defects to light, not to discuss solutions to any problems raised, nor to criticise the author. At the end of the meeting the moderator appoints one of the inspectors as reviewer of the rework, and makes a preliminary decision on whether or not the work needs to be reinspected. After a maximum of two hours, the meeting ends. After the meeting, during the so-called 'third hour', possible solutions to issues raised during the inspection meeting may be discussed informally by the attendees.

The moderator ensures, after the meeting, that the rework is completed, reviews the decision about whether another Fagan inspection of the reworked document is required, and ensures that all relevant statistics have been recorded.

4.8 Summary

In trying to give you an idea of the scope and diversity of quality issues, we have covered a lot of ground, from quality concepts to methods and techniques for ensuring quality in systems development.

We began by introducing our working definition of quality, 'conforming to the customer's requirements', and the key ideas of product and service requirements, and internal and external customers. The ideas of the quality gurus Deming, Juran and Crosby (and others) have caused people to question the way quality is managed in organisations, and have led to a move from inspecting deliverables for defects to building quality into the process of production. We have discussed the implications of these ideas for systems developers, and for business in general, describing the difference between the control, assurance and management of quality, and explaining the meaning of the acronyms QC, QA, QMS and TQM. The content of the international standard for quality management, ISO 9000, which has become increasingly important to our industry in recent years, has been described, and we have discussed how it can be applied to software development.

The last section of the chapter has introduced techniques for building quality into systems analysis and design – the structured walkthrough, which is an integral part of a structured approach to systems development, and the more formal Fagan inspection.

THE MODERATOR

The Moderator is specifically trained for this role and, to provide objectivity, should be drafted from outside the Author's project team.

The Moderator will be familiar with the type of document being inspected and should:

- check that the entry criteria have been met;
- appoint Inspectors, detailing special roles;
- liaise with the Project Manager to set up the Inspection;
- send out details of the meeting, the document to be inspected and other relevant material;
- plan the Inspection process;
- chair the meeting;
- record the effort spent on preparation, inspection, rework and review;
- ensure that the Author understands the rework required;
- follow up the rework;
- decide whether reinspection is necessary;
- collate and distribute statistics.

THE INSPECTOR

Inspectors prepare for the meeting by reading the document, checking for understanding of the document contents and for any specific points requested by the Moderator (e.g. checking against a specific higher level document, looking at a specific interface, checking against project standards). At the meeting, each Inspector should:

- contribute to the defect detection process;
- avoid introducing any distraction to the meeting (e.g. alternative methods of achieving the same result).

THE SCRIBE

The Scribe records all defects found. Each defect is normally given a unique number and its location marked on a clean copy of the document.

THE READER

The Reader is responsible for guiding the inspection team through the material during the meeting by paraphrasing the content of the inspected item in portions agreed with the Moderator. The Author may not be the Reader as the object of reading the item is to ensure that the contents are not open to misinterpretation. The Reader should:

- liaise with the Moderator to establish a reading pattern (and NOT ask the Author for clarification);
- prepare the document for paraphrasing;
- read the document as planned (focus and pace are vital, in doing this);
- contribute to the defect detection process.

THE AUTHOR

The Author attends the meeting as a reference source and as a validator. The Author should:

- liaise with the Moderator only;
- supply the Moderator with documents;
- act as a reference source or validator in the meeting, and NOT to volunteer information;
- take copious notes during the meeting so that the reason and source of all logged defects is known at rework time;
- understand the defects found and their knockon effect;
- provide estimates for rework within 24 hours;
- rework the inspected item, assigning a category and severity to each defect.

Fig. 4.7 Roles in a Fagan inspection meeting

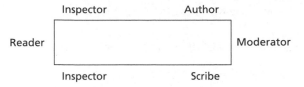

Fig. 4.8 Seating plan for a Fagan inspection meeting

We should like to conclude by bringing together a number of ideas presented in this chapter in a model to help you, either as part of an analysis or design team or as an individual, to build quality into your work. This model is represented graphically as Figure 4.9.

The job of an individual or a team can be thought of as a series of tasks, each with its own input and output. For example, a task could be carrying out a fact-finding interview, presenting system proposals to a client, developing a data model of the system, or writing a report. The *outputs* of the task are the products or services supplied to the customer. This could be an internal customer or an external customer. The *inputs* describe everything that is needed to produce the outputs, and the *task* is the process that transforms the inputs. Once the task is completed, an *evaluation* must be carried out to review how well the task was achieved, and to provide information for improvements in the future.

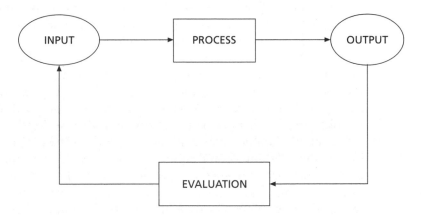

Fig. 4.9 A model for building quality into your work

4.8.1 Inputs

Often the way in which quality is assessed on projects is by looking at the deliverables – the products or services supplied to the customer. However, while it might be valid to inspect these deliverables, find any defects and then trace them back to where they occurred, building quality into a task means going even further back in the process and examining the inputs before beginning the work.

There are four inputs to any task:

- a statement of the customer's requirement;

- a method for completing the task;

- the resources available;

- the individual's ability, attitude and working standards.

To build quality into the task it is important to ensure that all of the inputs to the task have been reviewed and are appropriate.

To be clear about exactly what the customer – external or internal – wants, you need a statement of the customer's requirement. This should include an explanation of why the product or service is required, and the detailed requirements as specified by the customer – including their 'soft service' requirements, which will always include the need to feel valued and to be treated with courtesy and respect. The list of requirements should be agreed formally or informally with the customer, who should be notified if there are problems in meeting their requirements: for example if you can't complete a report by the agreed time.

It's important to establish early on whether there is an approved method for carrying out the task, and whether standards or guidelines exist. As part of the quality improvement process, questions should be asked: is this the best method, the most efficient, most cost-effective, fastest, safest, or could it be improved?

Before beginning the task, you need to check what resources – materials and people – are available. Equipment should be adequate, appropriate, safe to use, in good working condition and properly maintained. It is not easy to do a task properly if the correct equipment is not provided. Any materials needed to do the task must be correct for the task and of the appropriate quality. Last, but not least, you will need to check who is available to assist with the task, to support, to guide, to provide information or supply specialist skills.

The ability, attitude and working standards of the person or people doing the job are the most important input to consider when building quality into a task. People must have the ability to do the job properly, and must receive the appropriate training. A positive attitude makes the job more satisfying, and decreases the incidence of human error, while the standard of performance the individuals set for themselves will be critical to the overall quality of the work done.

The combination of an individual's attitude, ability and working standard can also be described as *personal quality*. Personal quality depends on a number of factors, such as self-perception, state of mind, motivation, and awareness of the customer's requirements. The scope for improving personal quality can be determined by comparing your actual performance – what you achieve here and now – with your ideal performance – your expectations, requirements and goals. Personal quality is important for the team as well as for the individual. The sum of everyone's scope for improvement is a measure of the overall scope for development of a project team, a business group or a department. It can be argued that personal quality is at the root of all other quality within an organisation.

4.8.2 Outputs

In addition to the product or hard service that you hand over to the internal or external customer, it is worth emphasising here that the output also includes the soft service. In a meeting with the client, for example, this means making them feel valued, treating them with courtesy, giving them your full attention, and not showing any signs of negative opinions you may have formed.

4.8.3 Evaluation

Assuming that we have built quality into the task by getting the inputs right, and ensuring that output meets the customer's requirements, a further question needs to be asked: 'How well did we do?' For example, was the system delivered on time and within budget? Was the information provided during fact-finding interviews accurate and complete? Did we treat the customer with courtesy and helpfulness at every stage of the development? Did we, individually and as a team, live up to our own working standards? This process, called *evaluation*, is often left out on projects, but it is important that it is done in order to 'close the loop' and build quality into future tasks. If the answer to any of the questions asked above is 'no', the failure must be analysed (What went wrong? Why did it go wrong? Which inputs need to be improved?). It is only by the evaluation of success or failure that improvement can be a continuous process.

Exercises

4.1 System Telecom has a policy of developing and using computer-based systems to give it commercial advantage. One of the consequences is that new systems need to be 'developed on time, within the budgeted cost, and to quality'. What does 'to quality' mean in this context?

4.2 It is said that the use of structured methods improves the quality of the developed system. Bearing in mind your understanding of 'quality', •explain how structured methods contribute towards achieving it.

4.3 Would it be useful for System Telecom to apply for ISO 9000 certification? What are the internal and external benefits that might come from certification, and what would be the cost of a successful application for certification?

4.4 System Telecom has decided to buy an application package for its personnel system. There are several available to choose from and no particular advantage to be gained from developing a new system in house. The most appropriate package appears to be a relatively new one with, as yet, few users. It is therefore particularly important to make a rigorous assessment of the quality of the package. You are assigned to assess the techniques used by the supplier to ensure software quality. What techniques would you expect to find being used?

5 Project Management

5.1 Introduction

In this chapter, we look at project management for the analysis and design of information systems. Because of the increasing need for formality and structure, we have used examples from the UK government's PRINCE2 (PRojects IN Controlled Environments) method. Its general approach is a codified form of the procedures that successful project managers have always used, and it therefore has widespread applicability.

Analysis and design are part of a process of development that leads towards an operational information system: before analysis starts, there may have been strategic and feasibility studies; after design finishes will come the coding, testing and installation of computer programs.

Unfortunately, in systems development – as in many other fields – different people have adopted different names for the same things; or the same names for different things. The terms here are those widely used in the IT industry, but if you are used to different terms, don't worry – the meaning will be clear from the context.

5.2 Stages of System Development

5.2.1 Before Analysis and Design

Ideally, the need for information systems will grow from the development of business strategy, as explained in Chapter 1 (section 1.2). This strategy may have been developed internally, by the business's own senior management, or may be the result of the work of management consultants. In either event, it forms the starting point for IS projects. Once the business knows where it is going, it is possible to sketch an IS strategy that will support it on its journey. Management consultants may have been involved here, too, or the business's IT director may have developed a strategy for the approval of the board. An IS strategy will typically cover the overall scope of information systems in the business. It may also include a general hardware policy, for example the organisation's preference for hardware, proprietary or open systems and so on, and some commitment to specific development methods and tools.

New systems projects usually begin with a feasibility study. Its purpose is to examine the proposed development at a high level and to make preliminary business decisions on whether to commit funds to it. In carrying out a feasibility study, the major analysis techniques will be employed but not, this time, to produce a detailed specification of the requirement. Instead, the analysts will be trying to define:

- the overall scope of the proposed system;

- an idea of the system's probable size;

- the general development approach to be used, for example bespoke versus packaged, in-house versus bought-in;

- the costs and benefits that will flow from the development;

- the impact that the new system will have on the business, particularly on areas outside the system's scope;

- the resources and timescales that will be required for the full development.

One objective of carrying out a feasibility study is to define the *triple constraint* within which the project should operate. This concept, fundamental to project management, is illustrated in Figure 5.1.

What the triple constraint says is that any project is defined by the timescale for its completion, the budget available, and a specification of what exactly is to be produced, to what standard. To some extent, these three elements can be traded off against each other: one may, for example, be able to finish earlier if some part of the functionality is sacrificed; or the highest possible quality may be attained if the timescale can be extended or the budget increased. The precise balance will vary from project to project so that, for instance, an air traffic control system project will tend to favour the quality constraint whereas projects to deal with the introduction of the euro were heavily constrained by time.

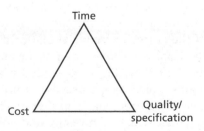

Fig. 5.1 The triple constraint

5.2.2 Analysis and Design

Analysis and design begins with requirements analysis. If there is already an existing computer system, then analysis can start there. In particular, the analysts will be looking for problems with the existing system, or additional requirements that the replacement must have. Some effort must be made to categorise these into, for example, vital, useful and 'nice to have' so that decisions can be made later on which features to include in, or leave out of, the new system. A particular challenge for the analysts in this stage is to think about 'what' the existing systems are doing, rather than how they do it – in other words to look at the business needs rather than the technical implementation.

It is unusual nowadays to find a requirement for a computer system where there has been none previously, but it can happen. For example, many organisations are grappling with how to embrace e-commerce. Although the solution (often not very satisfactory) is to bolt a web-based front end onto an existing sales order processing system, the best solutions seem to be those that have rethought the whole way they do business in the Internet age – or which have started from scratch with no 'legacy' systems with which they need to interface.

At some stage during requirements analysis, decisions must be taken on precisely what is to be included in the new system. Some of the requirements will turn out to be vital, others less so, and there will always be a trade-off between functionality and cost. It is crucial that these decisions are made by the system's users or by their senior management, and that the implications of these decisions are carefully evaluated.

Once the requirements for the new system have been properly documented, it must be specified in sufficient detail to form a basis for development. This specification must include:

- a specification of business requirements, and
- a specification of a technical platform and development path.

In general, it is desirable to keep these two aspects as separate as possible, otherwise the business requirement gets confused with the technical means used to meet it. This can have adverse consequences later during the maintenance of the system or if it is desired to change it to some other technical environment.

Business needs must be documented in such a way that they can be reviewed by, commented on and accepted by the system's users. It has generally been found that the diagrammatic approach favoured in structured methods has definite advantages here over the more traditional narrative approach. The implications of the choice of technical platform must also be spelled out and brought to the attention of the users. Whatever means of specification is employed, it is very important that the users formally agree the requirement before system design begins. This is not to prevent future changes – pretending that there won't be changes in requirements is to defy reality – but so that the developers have a baseline against which to measure and control change. Finally, looking forward to delivery of the final system, the requirements specification should provide the criteria against which the users will ultimately test and accept the system. Ideally, these acceptance criteria should be in the requirements specification itself. Making sure of the acceptance criteria at this point will save a lot of time, trouble and argument for both developers and users later on in the project.

Armed with a comprehensive requirements specification, the developers can now set about designing a system that will meet the users' needs. The design will include:

- database or files required to support the new system;

- update facilities, as online screens or batch programs, to be available to the users;

- range of reports and enquiries to be provided;

- detailed processes to be invoked when invalid or incompatible data are encountered;

- procedures for fallback and recovery after a system failure.

Design is a more purely technical process than analysis, and the users will be less involved in the detail. However, the users must see and approve such things as screen or report layouts – after all, they will have to work with them. Their consent may also have to be gained if it appears from the technical design that the defined performance criteria cannot be met – if, for example, an online response time looks like being longer than expected.

There is, of course, an alternative way of providing a new computer system than developing one and that is to look for a *COTS* (commercial off the shelf) system – in other words a package of some sort. This is particularly likely for 'bread and butter' applications such as payroll or accounting, where there is unlikely to be any commercial advantage to be gained by developing a system to meet the requirements. A package offers the potential advantages of shared development costs, shorter implementation timescales, a readily available support infrastructure, and upgrades to meet changing legislative and other requirements. As against that, a package may not in fact be a particularly good fit with the business requirements and may involve either unacceptable changes to working practices or high costs of customisation or tailoring – which may destroy the benefits of using a packaged solution in the first place.

This means that the desire to find a packaged solution does not invalidate the need for a proper analysis of the requirements, but it may alter the emphasis of the analysis work. The analysts will need to focus on *what* the new system is designed to achieve in business terms but be more careful about *how* it should work, as potential package solutions may achieve the same business results via a different route. Only if the 'how' is crucial – and sometimes this is the way in which commercial organisations differentiate themselves from their competitors – should it be included in the requirements specification and, later, in the invitations to tender issued to potential suppliers.

Even if a packaged solution is the required outcome, the analysts ought to specify the requirements in enough detail so that, should no package prove suitable, the project can revert to developing a solution. In addition, sometimes the answer is to buy a package to provide core functionality and then to build around that core the facilities that are needed to meet the complete business requirement, in which case full analysis of the requirements will be needed in order to specify the additions and enhancements.

5.2.3 After Analysis and Design

The design is now transformed into an actual computer system through the development and testing of programs. *Program testing*, or *unit testing* as it is also called, is carried out by the programmers, who check that each program meets its own design specification. Once it has been established that each individual program works on its own, it is necessary to integrate the programs and to check that they work together as a system. Generally, integration testing will be incremental: that is, programs (a) and (b) will be fitted together and tested, and then program (c) will be added. However, in a very large or complex system, it will be necessary to explore a large number of testing threads to ensure that the programs all work correctly in their different combinations.

When all the integration tests are complete, the developers now carry out their own system test to ensure that, as far as they are concerned, the system works together as a whole and meets its design objectives. The system test criteria will be partly technical – derived from the design documentation – but will also relate to the functional and non-functional needs contained in the requirements specification. Once the developers are satisfied that the system operates properly, the users are invited to carry out their acceptance tests. Acceptance criteria should have been derived from the requirements specification. However, the important point is that users should be accepting only against the *expressed and documented requirement*, and not against what they might now think they really want. If the users' requirements have indeed changed then the changes can be discussed and, if agreed, can be implemented. This process must not, however, be allowed to prevent acceptance of the current system if it does really meet its documented objectives.

The accepted system is now installed on the computer on which it will operate, and it is commissioned. At this point, the developers will hand the system and all its associated documentation and test regimes over to those who will operate it. Commissioning may be a progressive affair, with functions being added incrementally. There may also be a need for file creation or data take-on and for progressive changeover from a previous system. All of these activities will require careful planning and management.

Finally, the system starts to operate live and, we hope, to deliver the business benefits for which it has been designed. It is very likely that some sort of support arrangement will be agreed with the users so that problems that arise during live running can be dealt with and also so that the system can be enhanced to meet the users' changing business requirements.

5.3 Project Planning

Two important things should be understood about planning: first, that it is essential for a project's success and, second, that it should be undertaken as early as possible. There is often a reluctance to plan, perhaps stemming from a feeling that this will unduly constrain the development and perhaps also from a fear that the developers will be committed too early to a course of action that later proves untenable. This is understandable, but it does not really make sense. A plan should not be seen as a straitjacket but as a map setting out the route to be followed. The thing to remember is that the plan is not the project; it is only a model of the project. It is created so that the project manager can use it to check progress and adjust the work to changing circumstances.

So what will a good plan look like, and what will it contain? First, a good plan must be a flexible, revisable document. We have already said that any plan can only be regarded as a model, and will have to be modified and revised as the project progresses. So it makes sense to devise a structure that will allow for this revision rather than constrain it.

From this it follows that we shall not want to treat the whole project as one gigantic task. Rather, we shall want to break it down into more manageable sub-tasks that we can modify more easily. There is another reason for this breakdown: when we come on to estimating later in this chapter, it will be clear that much more accurate estimates can be produced for small tasks than for large ones. Alternative methods of achieving this project breakdown are considered in the next section.

Apart from a breakdown of the work involved, a plan will also contain:

- a description of the organisation of the project, showing who the personnel are and their roles and responsibilities;

- descriptions of the products to be produced, with their completion and quality criteria;

- descriptions of the individual work packages for team members;

- an analysis of the interdependence of the various tasks, expressed perhaps as a network diagram;

- an analysis of the risks involved in the project, with the possible counter-measures for each risk.

There is some debate in project management circles as to whether the quality plan should be part of the project plan or a document in its own right. We have adopted the second approach here, but in practice it makes little difference. The important thing is that the quality issues are thought through and the project's approach to them properly documented: this topic is covered later in this chapter.

5.3.1 Stages in Planning

Planning requires a methodical approach. One that has been found to be successful over many projects is described here.

(i) Break the project down

There are two slightly different ways of breaking down the project into smaller components – by work breakdown structure or by product breakdown structure.

With the conventional *work breakdown structure*, we start by considering the overall project and progressively break it down into its component hierarchy of stages, steps and tasks. For systems development projects, an obvious set of stages is:

1 Business strategy.
2 Information systems strategy.
3 Feasibility study.
4 Requirements analysis.
5 Requirements specification.
6 System design.
7 Program development and testing.
8 Integration testing.
9 Acceptance testing.
10 Installation and commissioning.
11 Live operation/support.

These stages are, though, still too big to control properly, so we need to break them down into steps. If we take requirements analysis as an example, we might break it down into these steps:

1 Interview users.
2 Examine document flows.
3 Study rules and regulations.
4 Build a data model.
5 Develop dataflow diagrams.
6 Review results with users.

Finally, we need to decide the individual tasks that make up each of these steps. For 'build a data model', these might be:

1 Identify data entities.
2 Produce entity descriptions.

3 Identify relationships between entities.

4 Carry out normalisation.

5 Validate data model against processing requirements.

6 Complete documentation.

7 Enter information into data dictionary.

Of course, this is not the only way in which we could have approached this breakdown. Suppose, for example, we were going to analyse the requirements for a new system to support a business. At the top level (stages), we could have broken our project down into functional areas such as marketing, production and accounts. Then we might break down each area again into steps, so that 'accounts', for example, could become accounts payable, accounts receivable, and banking. And, finally, we could have the same set of tasks (interviews, data modelling and so on) as the bottom level within each step. The actual method of decomposition will be decided by the project manager, taking into account the nature of the work to be undertaken. The important thing, though, is to create a set of low-level tasks against which we can make our estimates and control our project.

The *product breakdown structure*, which is a feature of the PRINCE2 project management method, approaches this decomposition from a slightly different angle – that of the products that will result from the project. Considering our development project again, we would find some top-level products such as 'delivered system' and 'requirements specification'. We could then break these down so that the requirements specification might be found to consist of:

- Function definitions.
- Dataflow models.
- Logical data model.
- User descriptions.

Each of these would have component products: the data model, for example, would consist of a diagram plus entity and relationship descriptions.

These are all what PRINCE2 calls *specialist products* – that is, they are the things that the project is explicitly set up to develop. But PRINCE2 also recognises other types of product: management products, such as the plans and reports that the project will generate; and quality products, such as quality definitions and review sign-offs. The point to grasp about PRINCE2's use of products is that this approach forces the developers to focus their attention on the *deliverables* from the project – what is going to result from it. Each PRINCE2 product will have a description and a set of completion criteria that will be used to determine whether it has been properly developed and tested.

With the product breakdown structure approach, we ultimately consider what work has to be done to develop each product – and thus, by a different route, we get back to a list of the fundamental tasks that need to be undertaken to complete the project.

(ii) Estimate durations

With the tasks clearly defined, it is now possible to estimate the duration of each task. The first thing to remember is that there is a difference between the amount of work needed to complete a task – the *effort* – and the actual time it will take – the *elapsed time*. This is because, however hard people work, they can never spend 100% of their time on project-related activities. People have holidays, they become sick, they go on training courses, and they have to spend time on non-project work such as attending management meetings.

When planning a project, therefore, it is necessary to make allowances for all these time-stealers, and a common way of doing this is to assume that only four days in each week are available for productive project work. In other words, if the effort to complete a task is estimated as four days, then allow an elapsed time of five days and remember to record both calculations.

(iii) Calculate dependences

In planning project work, it is important to know which tasks are dependent on other tasks. In many cases, dependences will be fairly obvious – one cannot test a program until it has been written, for example. Let us assume that we have a task called 'collate and print requirements specification'. Clearly, we can carry out this task only when all the component materials of the specification have been completed. So, this task might have three dependences:

- on the completion of the function descriptions;
- on the completion of the data model;
- on the completion of the dataflow models.

If these three tasks have different durations, then the 'collate and print' task can begin only when the *longest* of the three has been completed.

For the moment, we need only to consider all of our tasks carefully and record which ones are dependent on which; we shall consider what we do with this information in the next stage.

(iv) Produce network diagram

The network diagram is one of the most valuable tools for the project manager. In the example here, the diagram consists of a series of boxes representing tasks connected by arrows that show the dependences between the tasks. Each box contains the data, as shown in Figure 5.2. Figure 5.3 illustrates our description of the process of creating a network diagram.

We begin our time analysis with a forward pass through the model to calculate, by addition from the start date, the earliest start and finish dates for each task. We then complete a backward pass to calculate, by subtraction from the end date, the latest start and finish dates for each task. The difference between the earliest and latest finish dates for each task represents its *float* – a useful planning resource – and those tasks that possess no float are said to be on the *critical path*.

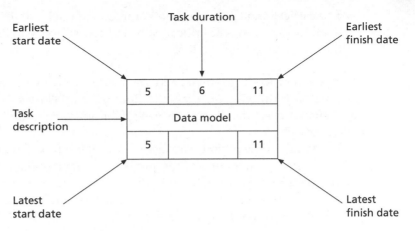

Fig. 5.2 Network diagram task box

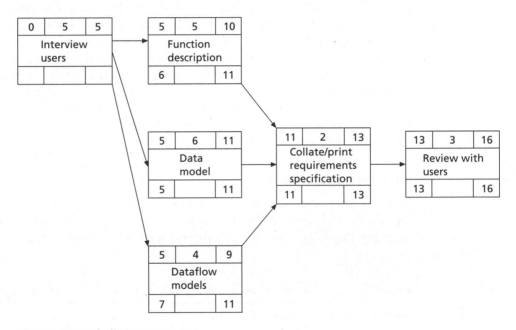

Fig. 5.3 Network diagram process

We said earlier that three tasks were prerequisites for the task 'collate/print requirements specification'. If we look at Figure 5.3, we learn these things about the three tasks:

• The earliest finish date for 'function description' is day 10, but the latest finish date is day 11: so there is one day's float in that task.

• The earliest finish date for 'dataflow models' is day 9, and the latest finish date is day 11: so there is two days' float in that task.

- The earliest and latest finish dates for 'data model' are the same: so there is no float, the task is on the critical path, and any slippage in this task will cause the whole project to slip too.

This is a very trivial example, and you could probably see which was the critical task without drawing the diagram. But you can also see that, on a large project with many tasks, the diagram is essential to understanding the interdependence of the tasks.

The value to the project manager of working out which are the critical tasks is obvious. If, in our example, the project manager finds out that the task 'data model' is going to run late, then the manager knows that the project will be delayed. So it might make sense to switch resources from 'dataflow models', which has two days' float, to 'data model' to bring the project back on course.

(v) Barcharts

Barcharts provide a highly visual way of showing when each project task will be tackled and its duration. A typical barchart lists the tasks vertically, and the duration of each is indicated by the length of horizontal bar.

Figure 5.4 shows our same sequence of analysis activities, and you will notice that the fact that 'function definitions' and 'dataflow models' are not on the critical path is clear because 'collate/print' does not start immediately they finish.

When drawing up the barchart, the project manager will take the dependences into account and juggle tasks between team members so as to achieve the optimum staffing plan.

(vi) Individual work plans

Each team member should be provided with an individual work plan showing the task/s they are to work on and how long they should take. A common way of doing this is to provide each person with a personal barchart containing a

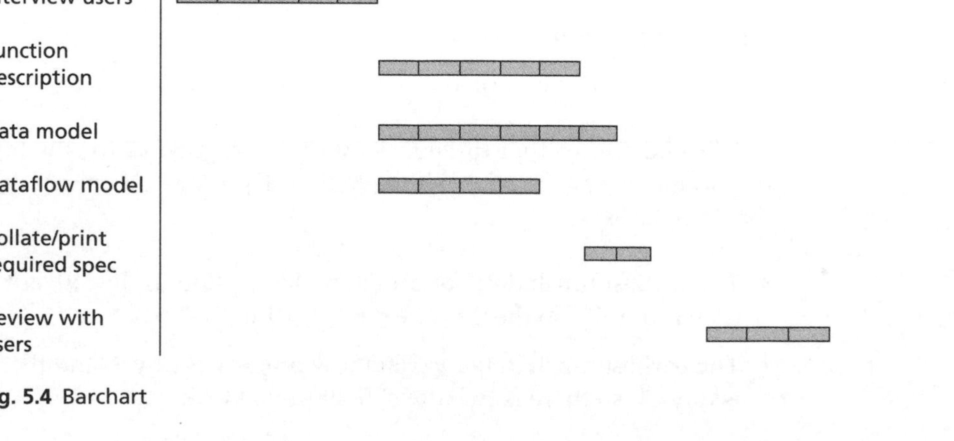

Activity	01 02 03 04 05 06 07 08 09 10 11 12 13 14 15 16 17 18 19 20
Interview users	
Function description	
Data model	
Dataflow model	
Collate/print required spec	
Review with users	

Fig. 5.4 Barchart

subset of the tasks shown on the overall plan. Individual work plans should also contain the following:

- descriptions of the products to be produced;
- definitions of the completion criteria that will be applied;
- information on the methods and standards to be used.

(vii) Review/reappraise/revise

Plans are not static documents. Things go wrong on the best-organised project, delays and problems are encountered and even, on some rare occasions, tasks take less time and effort than expected. The project manager must, therefore, constantly review the plans, reappraise where the project has got to and revise the plans as necessary. Whenever plans are revised, everyone concerned should be informed of the changes, and this is particularly important where changed work plans need to be issued to individuals.

5.3.2 Planning for Quality

If a project is to be completed to the correct level of quality – which we can define as meeting its stated requirement – this will not happen by itself. Quality must be planned for, like all other activities (as explained in Chapter 4), and a good way of doing this is to produce a quality plan.

The quality plan may be part of the project plan, or it may be a document in its own right. This does not matter too much, but what is important is what is included. A quality plan should cover, at least, the following topics:

- a description of the technical methods to be used during the project;
- details of the standards to which the work will be performed – either by including the standards in the quality plan or, more usually, by cross-referencing;
- an outline of the means, both how and when, by which quality will be checked during the project, for example by reviews or structured walkthroughs;
- an analysis of the risks to project quality and how these can best be met.

As with the main project plan, it may be necessary to carry out quality planning in outline only at the start of the project and to fill in the details as they become available.

5.4 Estimating

It has to be said at the outset that estimating for software projects does not have a very good track record. The reasons for this are many and various but they include:

- the difficulty of defining precisely enough the scope of software projects;

- the fact that most projects involve a degree of innovation, so there is little history to go on;

- a lack of experience in estimating in the people carrying it out;

- the general lack of suitable metrics.

To these should be added something we might call 'political bias', where the estimator is trying to produce a result it is thought that the boss wants to hear, rather than an accurate one.

Of these difficulties, though, the most common are the lack of scope definition and the lack of metrics. If we compare software production with, say, a mature industry such as civil engineering, we find that in the latter:

- Nearly all projects, no matter how apparently innovative, can be broken down into elementary tasks that have been done before – such as laying a course of bricks.

- There are abundant metrics available, in the form of standard reference works with tables on, for example, the time to produce so many square metres of concrete flooring.

- Civil engineering estimates are produced once the design is known – once the architect has drawn the plans – not *before* design commences.

The morals for software engineers are therefore twofold:

- Only estimate firmly on the basis of a clear programme of work.
- Collect and use metrics.

5.4.1 Estimating for Analysis and Design Work

The main problem with estimating for the analysis phase of a project is that, by definition, the developers do not know the scope, size or complexity of the system until they start to do the analysis work. The first thing to do, then, is to get some overall idea of the scope of the system to be studied. A sensible approach is to carry out a high-level analysis to find out where the departmental boundaries are, how many people are involved, and some broad measure of the volumes of data handled. For example, if examining a sales order processing system, the numbers of invoices produced per week would be a very useful metric.

This high-level information will enable some important basic questions to be answered. For example:

- How many people must be interviewed?

- How complex are the procedures we need to study and document?

- Are there outside parties, such as auditors, whose views must be taken into account?

- Are there existing computer systems to be studied, and, if so, is there business-level documentation available or only program listings to work from?

Any assumptions on which the estimates are based should be included with the estimates and stated in the contract for the analysis work. Then if, for example, it turns out that more interviews are needed than planned, the developer has a good case for asking the customer for more time and money to complete the analysis. If the work is being done by an internal IT department, an informal 'contract' with the users should still be created so that all parties agree the basis on which the analysis has been planned. Remember as well that, even though there is high-level commitment to a project, to the users themselves the analysts will initially be a nuisance, and interviews will have to be fitted in around their 'real' work. So, without building undue slack into the estimates, a realistic view must be taken of how many interviews can be fitted into each day, and how often the same user can be revisited.

To some extent, estimating for the design work is rather easier than for analysis, as at least the scope of the system should now be agreed, and its dimensions and complexity will be understood. However, the designers must plan to take the users along with them as their design proceeds, and adequate provision must be made for this. Design is essentially the process of taking the documented requirements and translating them into an implementable computer system.

The estimates for design can therefore be based upon the various components of the design, for example:

- logical data design;
- the design of physical files;
- process design;
- the human–computer interface;
- security and control requirements.

As with analysis estimates, any assumptions should be fully documented. So, if you are planning to design for one of the fourth generation languages, you may not intend to produce full program specifications; but if you switch to, say, COBOL, these may be required after all and you will have to revise your design estimate.

5.4.2 Advantages of the Structured Approach

We have already seen that one of the problems of estimating is trying to decide the tasks that need to be accomplished. In this area, the very obvious advantage is that the structured method is well defined and therefore provides a detailed list of the tasks involved. However, care must be exercised even here, as there may be implicit or unstated tasks that a given method does not cover. In SSADM, for example, the first three substantive steps in requirements analysis are:

- Step 120 – Investigate and Define Requirements.
- Step 130 – Investigate Current Processing.
- Step 140 – Investigate Current Data.

It is likely that suitable metrics will be available from previous projects. As the same approach is used on each, it is only necessary to make allowances for scope and complexity to be able to use data from one project to produce estimates for another. Of course, this is rather a simplification and does depend on the collection of the metrics in the first place but, even without these, a project manager with previous experience of the method can make more realistic estimates for the new work.

We have already said that systems development is bedevilled by a lack of metrics. To rectify this will take time and effort, but it is important that project managers collect metrics to assist them and others on later projects. To be of value, the metrics must:

- be collected accurately and honestly, even if this shows up shortcomings in the estimates;

- have qualifications attached, so that project peculiarities can be taken into account when reusing the statistics;

- be collected on a consistent, like for like, basis.

5.4.3 Using Function Point Analysis

Function point analysis is a method for estimating systems development time. Unlike other estimation methods, Mark II function point analysis uses the products of structured systems analysis and design as the basis for estimation, and was originally developed by the UK government in 1990. Other development estimation methods such as Cocomo and Delphi are based upon estimates of the number of lines of code (LOC) that the development will need. Although this can be a useful and an accurate method of estimation, it relies on the estimator having a good understanding of the system under development. It can be difficult to apply to new systems when they are in the analysis and design stage.

Function points are calculated from the inputs, outputs and entities visited by a system, and you must decide what part of the system you are measuring. You might take the processes on the level 1 DFD, or those on each level 2 DFD, and the lower the level you go to, the more detailed it becomes and generally the number of function points goes up. The recommended level therefore for development estimates is to look at each logical transaction that is triggered by a unique event of interest in the external world, or a request for information which, when wholly complete, leaves the application in a self-consistent state in relation to the unique event.

We begin with step 1, where we count the input attribute types. If a type of attribute occurs more than once in input it is only counted as one. We count the number of output attribute types and we count the number of entities that are visited. Counting attributes and entities visited probably sounds straightforward, but this is not always the case, and the Function Point User Group has a counting practices manual at www.uksma.co.uk that provides a more detailed viewpoint. Briefly, however, an entity is counted as an entity visit if it is updated. If the program reads a number of entities, such as base tables, for reference purposes, then these are called the *system entity* and the entity count is increased by one in total. If the entity is an interface between the application you are estimating and another application that reads it then not only is the entity count increased by one, but the attribute types should also be included in the output attribute count if they are formatted for the receiving process.

Step 1: Count the function points

First, we calculate the unadjusted function points (UFPs) using the average industry weightings of:

Input attribute types $= N1 \times 0.58$
Output attribute types $= N2 \times 0.26$
Entities visited $= N3 \times 1.66$

Step 2: Calculate system size from technical complexity factor

We then calculate the size of the system by multiplying the UFPs by a technical complexity factor (TCF). This varies from 0.65 for systems built by experienced developers to 1 if the software is totally new to them.

$S = TCF \times UFP$

Step 3: Calculate weeks (elapsed time) to build the system

Knowing now the size of the system, S, we can calculate the weeks needed to develop it by multiplying the square root of S by 2.22. This gives the total development time for the whole life cycle.

Development time in weeks $= 2.22 \times \sqrt{S}$

Step 4: Calculate the effort

The effort needed to develop the system is calculated by using a productivity factor, P, which is determined according to the programming environment and is taken from a table or from organisation-held data.

If the system is a batch system the effort should be increased by 50%. Table 5.1 shows some values of P for systems of varying size.

Step 5: Calculate the number of people needed to complete the project

The number of people required to complete the development is calculated by dividing the effort multiplied by 0.044 by the weeks calculated above. Don't be

Table 5.1 Some productivity values for 3GL and 4GL developments

System size, S	3GL productivity, P	4GL productivity, P
50	0.099	0.158
100	0.106	0.169
150	0.111	0.178
200	0.116	0.185
250	0.118	0.189
300	0.119	0.191
350	0.119	0.190
400	0.117	0.187
450	0.113	0.181
500	0.109	0.174
600	0.098	0.156
700	0.085	0.137
800	0.074	0.118
900	0.065	0.104
1000	0.058	0.093
1100	0.055	0.088
1200	0.054	0.087

surprised if the result is less then a whole person. It simply means that that task would take only a percentage of a person's time over the elapsed weeks.

Effort for on-line = S/P
Effort for batch = $1.5S/P$

Step 6 Allocate the time and effort over the whole life cycle

The elapsed time and effort must be spread over the entire life cycle, and the proportions are shown in Table 5.2.

This has been an abbreviated account of Mk II function point analysis, which can be used as an introduction to the technique. When used professionally, technical complexity factors and productivity factors are calculated for the environment in which the analysis is being used. Care must be taken when counting function points to establish the boundaries of each transaction, to identify those attributes that cross the boundary. Although the practice is open to criticism, developers have little else to fall back on when estimating system development time. Although there are other well-known estimating methods used by software engineers, COCOMO and Wideband Delphi in particular, these methods start with an estimated number of lines of code, a figure that the systems analyst can only guess at. Using the products of structured systems analysis, the analyst can

Table 5.2 Elapsed time and effort percentages

	Effort (%)	Elapsed time (%)
Requirements analysis	11	20
Requirements specification	11	15
Logical system specification	5	5
Physical design	10	10
Code and unit test	46	25
System test	12	15
Implementation	5	10

quantify the system at an early stage in the life cycle and start to draw estimates from these figures.

5.5 Project Monitoring and Control

The plan is only a model, an idealisation, of what you want to happen on your project. It is vital to check constantly that the planned things are happening, that your ideas are working out in practice. This requires the project manager to be rigorously honest in measuring progress and facing up squarely to the problems that will surely arise. Only on the basis of accurate information can proper decisions be made to keep the project on course. Work must be checked using some regular and systematic method. Typically, this will involve project staff completing activity logs or timesheets and the holding of regular progress meetings.

Team members should report regularly – usually weekly – on:

- the tasks they have been involved in during the week;
- the effort spent on each task;
- the effort they estimate will be required to complete each task and the likely completion date;
- any problems encountered.

It is much better for estimates of 'time to complete' to be made as objectively as possible, even if the result is a shock to the project manager. Corrective action can then be taken to keep the project on track.

It has been observed that it is not the underestimated tasks that usually sink projects; rather it is tasks that were not suspected at all. We might also add that growth in the scope of work is another factor that leads projects into disaster. So, the project manager must be vigilant to spot additional tasks creeping in and the boundaries of the project expanding. However small these changes may seem at the time, they can have a considerable impact on the final outcome of the project. It should also be remembered that input – effort – is not the only thing that needs monitoring. Output – the quality of delivered work and products – must also be kept under constant review and, again, rigorous honesty is required if the project is to deliver acceptable products at the end. The monitoring and control process can be reduced to a convenient five-stage model that provides a standardised approach:

1 *Measure* – what progress has been made.

2 *Compare* – the measured work is compared with the work planned.

3 *Evaluate* – are we on plan, ahead or behind? What corrective action can we take?

4 *Predict* – the result of each possible corrective action, or of no action.

5 *Act* – tackle the problem now.

5.5.1 The Control of Quality

The quality control procedures will have been documented in the quality plan. There are three elements to quality control:

- *what* you are going to control;
- *when* you are going to apply quality control; and
- *how* you are going to do it – the methods you will use.

In general, all finished technical products – as defined in the project plan – should be the subject of quality control (QC), but you may also want to apply QC to interim products. You may also want to apply QC during production, to make sure that the team is on the right track. The project manager must devise a review regime that keeps the products under constant review but without actually proving a hindrance to doing the work.

As to QC methods, some of the most used, and most effective, have proved to be:

- *Management review*, whereby the project manager or team leader examines the work of the team members and provides feedback and criticism: this does require that the manager shares the same discipline as the team members, which may not always be the case.

- *Peer review*, which is similar to management review except that analysts, say, review and criticise each others' work. This method is useful when the project manager does not have the right background or the time to examine all of the work personally.

- *Structured walkthrough*, whereby a piece of work is examined more or less line by line by a team of reviewers (see Chapter 4).

The Fagan inspection has proved very effective and is becoming more widespread (again, see Chapter 4).

When carrying out reviews, remember that the purpose is to discover defects and inconsistencies – not to find solutions. The problem should be documented, perhaps with an assessment of its severity, and the rectifications remitted to its author or another nominated person.

5.5.2 Documentation Control

Every project needs a proper system to control the documentation it will produce. The documentation standards to be used on a particular project may be imposed on a supplier by the customer, may be determined by existing installation standards, or may be procedures devised by the project manager; more likely they will be a composite of all three. Whatever standards are adopted, it is crucial that they are clearly set out – probably in the quality plan – and are understood by everyone concerned.

In systems development work, and especially where the developers are working to a quality system such as BS 5750/ISO 9001, the issue of traceability is very important. That is, it is necessary not only that things are done as planned but that this can be proved to be so. Thus it is vital that important decisions are recorded and can be located and referred to later. Quite often, important points of detail in analysis are resolved in telephone conversations with users. Where this is the case, it is a good policy to reflect back the decision in a written note to the user or, at the least, to make a note of the content of the call with the date, time and participants. Finally, an idea that has been used with success on some projects is the concept of a *project log*. Progress is recorded on a day-to-day basis, and also notes can be made of any significant issues that crop up.

5.5.3 Change Control

Change is an inevitable fact of project life. As IT projects tend to take a long time, the users' requirements are almost bound to change, and their business itself may undergo major restructuring. The old idea that one can 'freeze' a specification and then work to it is obviously useless; what would be the point of delivering to the users a system that reflected how they *used* to work?

If change is inevitable, methods must be evolved to manage it. It is the lack of these methods that usually leads to problems. The methods needed to control change will depend to some extent on whether the work is being done in-house or by an external contractor, and, in the latter case, on whether the contract is for a fixed price or not. However, in all cases, some general rules should be followed:

- No change should ever be accepted without thorough investigation of its consequences.

- All requests for change should be logged and then examined to decide whether they are feasible, how much more effort will be involved, how much it will cost, and what the consequences are.

- Both user and developer must agree and accept the change, in the full knowledge of what it will mean for each of them.

With an internal development, changes will have an impact on the project's budget, and this must be approved by whoever controls the finances. For an external project, the developer may not be too concerned if the work is being done on a time-and-materials contract as the change will probably involve more work and hence more revenue. So the customer must be careful that the costs do not jump alarmingly. If the contract is for a fixed price, the developer must protect the profit margin and hence will resist all changes unless the customer agrees to pay for them.

5.5.4 Configuration Management

Configuration management is the process of controlling the development and issue of the products of a development. On all projects it is an important matter, but on large projects configuration management can be a major and central task of project administration. Configuration management includes:

* establishing 'baselines' for each product, so that when it is changed the new version can be clearly identified from its predecessor;

* ensuring that information is readily available on which versions of each product are compatible with which versions of other products;

* ensuring that changes in a late-stage deliverable are reflected back properly into its prerequisites.

Configuration management and change control are often confused, but the two, though related, are clearly different. Change control consists of managing the alteration of the stage of a project from its initiation until its implementation, whereas configuration management is concerned with documentation and control of the changed products.

5.6 PRINCE2

We have made various mentions of PRINCE2 in this chapter, so it is worth saying a little more about this project management method. It was originally developed for use in IT projects within the UK government, but it has now been extended to cover all types of project and all sorts of organisation. Essentially, PRINCE2 is codified good practice, bringing together the hard-won experience of a lot of project managers to provide guidance on the most effective conduct of projects.
PRINCE2 has three main elements:

* *Components*. The method defines the essential components necessary for the success of a project, such as planning, change control and configuration management, all discussed earlier. A very important component is identified as a suitable organisation structure, and PRINCE2 proposes a project board where the often-conflicting objectives of the various project stakeholders can be discussed and reconciled.

- *Processes*. PRINCE2 has a series of process models that illustrate how, for example, to initiate a project or manage the delivery of products. These process models provide guidance that can be adapted for use on a variety of projects of different sizes and complexity.

- *Techniques*. The method has guidance on a number of techniques, although it recognises that the type of project will dictate many of the techniques used by project managers. However, one of the most important techniques is product-based planning, to which we have referred earlier in this chapter.

Although PRINCE2, considered as a whole, can seem somewhat daunting, it does provide an excellent framework that can be tailored to meet the specific requirements of almost any project, and using something like PRINCE2 avoids the tendency to 'reinvent the wheel' for each new project.

5.7 Summary

Planning is crucial to the success of systems development projects and should be begun as early as possible. The project plan will describe what is to be done, by whom, and when, and the quality plan will define the methods and standards to be used. Estimating for analysis will be, to some extent, provisional until the scope of the project has been pinned down, but design can be estimated with more accuracy once this has been done. All plans must be treated as provisional and must be refined and remade in the light of more information and actual project experience. So the project manager must put in place suitable mechanisms to monitor progress, and must act decisively on what is thereby discovered. Change is inevitable in projects, and procedures must be used to ensure that it is controlled properly. Similarly, a proper configuration management system is required to ensure that the products of the project are properly documented and controlled.

Exercises

5.1   As part of its expansion programme, System Telecom has brought forward the plan to develop a new system, and is setting up a temporary development team for it. The team will be disbanded once the system has been implemented, and as a consequence everyone except the project manager is either a contractor or employed on a fixed-term contract. What particular problems will this give the project manager?

5.2   What techniques could be used during the systems development life cycle to ensure that the developed system meets its objectives?

5.3   It is said that user involvement during systems analysis and design is very important. Describe how users can be involved in analysis and design, and in the management of the project.

5.4   System Telecom supports a number of social benefit and charitable activities in the countries in which it operates. It has decided for the first time to support La Societé du Troisième Age (STA) in France. This charity helps old, single people who live in their own accommodation, and issues them with a System Telecom pager/panic transmitter. Local branches of STA will raise funds for local people so that pagers can be purchased. System Telecom wants to help these local activities to be organised efficiently. It has therefore offered to help by providing guidelines about fundraising activities. You have been asked to prepare a work breakdown structure for local car boot sales. This will then be given to local organisers to help them in organising such fund raising events. Prepare this work breakdown structure.

5.5   If you were the chairman of a local STA committee how would you monitor and control the progress of your committee's projects?

6

Systems Analysis: Concepts

6.1 Introduction

Taking a simple view, we can model systems development as shown in Figure 6.1 where analysis is represented as a discrete stage, which fits neatly between feasibility and design. The model indicates the relative position of the stages in the development process, but systems analysis cannot always be so easily compartmentalised, and there is frequently an overlap between analysis and feasibility and between analysis and design. Indeed, the time on a project at which analysis ends and design starts can often be identified only because it says so in the project plan! High-level analysis begins during feasibility, high-level design begins during analysis, and analysis continues as part of the design process. On small projects, analysis and design may be carried out by the same team of people, who have the job title analyst/designer or simply system developer.

Although it's important to appreciate this overlap between the stages of system development, for the purposes of this book we are treating analysis and design as separate processes. In this chapter we shall answer the question 'What is systems analysis?', consider a structured approach to analysis, and examine systems development life cycles.

Fig. 6.1 Stages in system development

6.2 What Is Systems Analysis?

The Oxford Dictionary defines *analysis* as follows:

> separation of a substance into parts for study and interpretation; detailed examination.

In the case of systems analysis, the 'substance' is the business system under investigation, and the parts are the various subsystems that work together to support the business. Before designing a computer system that will satisfy the information requirements of a company, it is important that the nature of the business and the way it currently operates are clearly understood. The detailed examination will then provide the design team with the specific data they require in order to ensure that all the client's requirements are fully met.

The investigation or study conducted during the analysis phase may build on the results of an initial feasibility study, and will result in the production of a document that specifies the requirements for a new system. This document is usually called the requirements specification or functional specification, and it is described it as a *target document* because it establishes goals for the rest of the project and says what the project will have to deliver in order to be considered a success. In this book, we are defining systems analysis as that part of the process of systems development that begins with the feasibility study and ends with the production of this target document.

A systems analyst will be required to perform a number of different tasks in carrying out the analysis phase of a development project. As a result of discussions with practising analysts, five areas have been identified into which these tasks can be grouped, and these are represented in Figure 6.2.

- *Investigation*. This group of tasks consists of all the fact-finding activities that an analyst may have to undertake. At the heart of these activities is the key skill of asking questions, orally or on paper, which will yield the required information. However, observing others and searching through documents can also be important tasks in gathering information.

- *Communication with customers*. Many analysts regard this as the single most important factor in ensuring a successful outcome to the analysis and producing an accurate specification of the client's requirements. It will include all the tasks that involve communicating ideas in writing, over the phone or face to face. This communication can be formal – presentations, meetings,

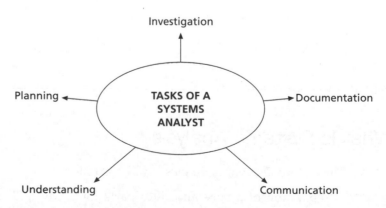

Fig. 6.2 The tasks of a systems analyst

walkthroughs and reports – or informal, but it does need to be regular and as open as possible. It may include giving explanations, providing reassurance and dealing with concerns expressed, as well as exchanging factual information. In addition this group of tasks will also include regular communication with others on the analysis team and their internal customers.

- *Documentation.* The production of documentation, like communicating with the customer, is a broad heading that encompasses many tasks. The writing of meeting minutes and interview records, the drawing of data models, the compiling of lists or catalogues of requirements and the reviewing of documents produced by others would all be included in this group. To be useful to the author and to the rest of the analysis team, any documents produced must be complete, accurate and easily accessible to those who need them. The involvement of the users in checking these documents is a useful way of ensuring accuracy, and has the added advantage of contributing to the building of a good working relationship.

- *Understanding.* This is a heading that really includes all the others, because at the heart of the analyst's job is the desire to understand the information collected, so that they can pass on this understanding to others on the project. The tasks in this group will include checking facts with the person who initially supplied them, cross-checking them where possible with others, and recording them as precisely as possible. It also involves a number of interpersonal skills, especially listening, if *real* needs are to be documented and problems are to be understood from the *users'* point of view.

- *Preparation and planning.* This group of tasks will include the planning of analysis activities, estimating how long these activities will take, and scheduling them to fit in with the project plan. Also included are the management of time and other resources, detailed preparation for interviews, and the work involved in putting together presentations and walkthroughs. Analysts agree that these activities can be time consuming, but are essential if the analysis is to proceed smoothly.

We talked in Chapter 1 about the role of the analyst. In thinking about the tasks the analyst has to perform, we can add the following guidelines, which have been identified by practising analysts:

- Check and agree the terms of reference before beginning your work.

- Involve the client as much as possible, both formally and informally, in developing your understanding of the system.

- Don't take information at face value.

- Be prepared for some resistance. The analyst is concerned with change, and this is uncomfortable for many people.

- Be aware of political issues in the client's organisation, but don't get involved.

- Remember that ownership of the system must always stay with the users.

6.3 Development Life Cycles

The model in Figure 6.1 shows analysis occurring just once in the life of a project, and then the next phases of the project follow on from this. As we suggested, this is not really true; and there are several other lifecycle models to consider. The first of these, the *b-model* of system development – devised by Birrell and Ould – shows in Figure 6.3 the whole life cycle of a system. Development is represented as a vertical straight line – similar to the horizontal path in our original model – and this leads into a maintenance cycle at the bottom. Each stage of the model is important, and no stage is independent of the others. Analysts need to be aware of all the other stages in the life cycle and not just their part of it.

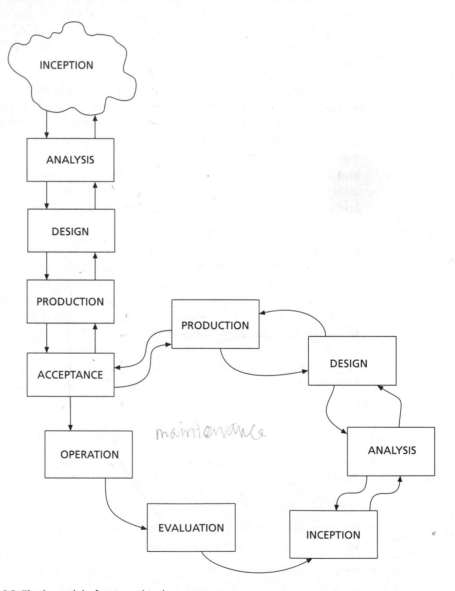

Fig. 6.3 The b-model of system development

The b-model life cycle begins with *inception*, the identification of the need for a new computer system. This leads to the *analysis* stage, the objectives of which are to define the problem, to create a detailed specification of what the system has to do, and to agree with the customer the level of service and performance required. This stage on the b-model also includes the feasibility study – an initial investigation to enable a properly informed decision to be made about whether to commit resources to the project. The next phase is *design*. The objectives of design are to define the structure and content of the system and specify how the system will be implemented. Within this phase, interfaces, dialogues, inputs and outputs are designed, and program and file or database specifications are produced as deliverables.

Once the design is complete, the *production* of the system can begin. During this phase program code is created and tested, supporting manuals and documentation are produced, and work proceeds according to the agreed development schedule. In parallel with this activity, data may be converted into a form that can be used by the new system, and training courses may be designed and implemented in preparation for handover. *Acceptance* marks the point at which the system is installed, handed over and paid for by the client. Any testing at this stage is usually conducted by the client to make sure the system does what they requested. Acceptance of the system by the client is a contractual issue and a project milestone.

Once development is complete, the system 'goes live' and is used by the client to meet the needs of the business. This is the *operation* phase. During the operation phase, there will be an *evaluation* of the system by the users, which may lead to the *inception* of ideas for changes and improvements, and the beginning of the maintenance cycle. During the maintenance cycle, the system may be modified a number of times. For each modification, there will be another analysis phase where the problems associated with the current system and the requirements for changes would need to be investigated and understood. Although this might be a much smaller piece of work than the initial analysis phase of the development project, the same principles will apply, and the same types of task will need to be completed. Maintenance may account for the bulk of the total work done on the system, and more than one change may be moving through the cycle at the same time. While a major change is moving slowly round the maintenance cycle, several smaller changes may move round it quickly.

You will notice in Figure 6.3 that there are two-way arrows between most of the boxes; it is sometimes necessary to go back a step if there is a change in the requirement or if an error introduced earlier in the development shows up only in a later phase.

Next there is the *waterfall model*, which was originally published in 1970 by Royce. In this model, system development is broken down into a number of sequential sections or stages represented by boxes, with each stage being completed before work starts on the following one. The outputs from one stage are used as inputs to the next. This is illustrated by the 'flow' from one stage to the next. For example, using Figure 6.4, the product design products are completed and accepted before being used as inputs to the work of the next stage, detailed design, and so on.

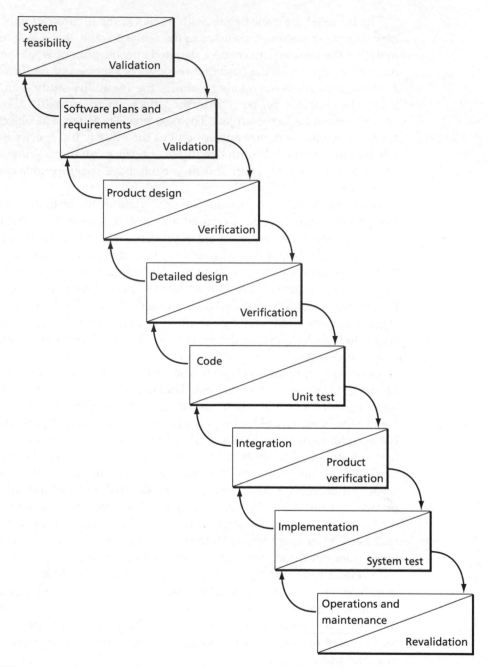

Fig. 6.4 The waterfall model

Each stage is divided into two parts: the first part covers the actual work being carried out in the stage, and the second part covers the 'verification and validation' of that work. *Verification* is taken to mean establishing the correspondence between a product and its specification – in other words, are we building the product in the right way? *Validation*, on the other hand, is concerned with whether the product is fit for its operational mission – in other words, are we building the right product? Typically, there is a degree of iteration of work and products within a stage, but very little between stages. Rework, where necessary, is carried out in succeeding stages, and the original stage in which the product was produced is not revisited. For example, if a new requirement is identified during the detailed design stage, the project will not return to the software plans and specification stage but will incorporate the reworking within the current stage. This may mean that some of the previously delivered products need to be amended however.

Nowadays, the waterfall model is generally taken to mean any sequential model divided into consecutive stages and having the attributes of the original model. The identification and naming of the stages are not fixed, and can be modified to suit particular project characteristics.

Ads →

The model has a number of good points. Apart from the sequencing of activities, it addresses elements of quality management through verification and validation, and configuration management by baselining products at the end of the stage. It does not have explicit means for exercising management control on a project, however, and planning, control and risk management are not covered. Nevertheless, the stage-by-stage nature of the waterfall model and the completion of products for the end of each stage lend themselves well to project management planning and control techniques and assist in the process of change control. Many projects still use versions of the waterfall model, generally with some of the shortcomings of the original one addressed, and the model is used as the basis for many structured methods such as SSADM. Waterfall models work best when the level of reworking of products is kept to a minimum and the products remain unchanged after completion of their 'stage'. In situations where the requirements are well understood and the business area in general is not likely to undergo significant business change, the waterfall model works well. In situations where the business requirements are not well understood and where the system is likely to undergo radical change, a different approach from that suggested by the waterfall model may be more appropriate.

A variation on the waterfall model is the 'V' model, in which the successive stages are shown in a 'V' formation as in Figure 6.5. In the diagram, the left, downward leg of the V shows the progress from analysis to design to programming and the increasing breakdown of the system components. The right, upward leg shows the progressive assembly and testing, culminating in the delivered product. The important feature of this model is that it shows correspondence between the different stages in the project. For instance, the individual programs or modules are tested against the individual module designs, the integrated set of software is system-tested against the system design, and the final system is user acceptance-tested against the requirements specification. This model demonstrates elements of quality assurance (QA) in its treatment of this correspondence.

In contrast to the waterfall approach, the *spiral model* introduces an evolutionary or iterative approach to systems development. The waterfall model concentrates on a stage-by-stage process, with the end products from one stage being finalised before the next stage is begun. This works reasonably well where the requirements of the system are well understood by the users and the

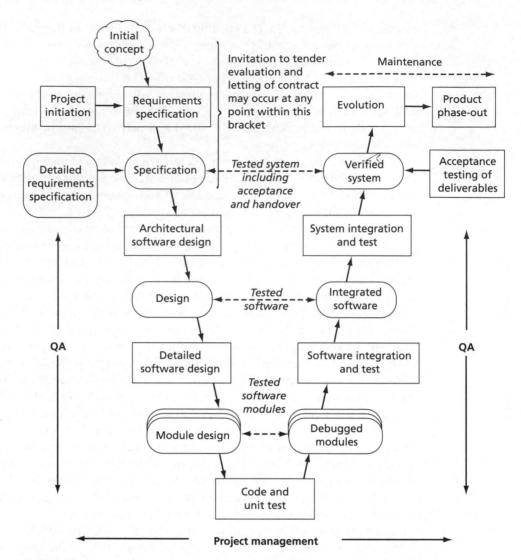

Fig. 6.5 The 'V' model (reproduced with permission of the National Computing Centre Limited from the *STARTS Guide* 1987, which was supported by the Department of Trade and Industry)

environment is stable. There are often occasions where the requirements are not well formed or understood by the users, where it is difficult to specify the requirements, or where it is difficult to determine how a proposed solution will perform in practice. In this situation, an evolutionary approach may be appropriate. This involves carrying out the same activities over a number of cycles in order to clarify the requirements, issues and solutions, and in effect amounts to repeating the development life cycle several times.

The original spiral model was developed by Barry Boehm, and it is shown in Figure 6.6. The project starts at the centre of the spiral and progresses outwards.

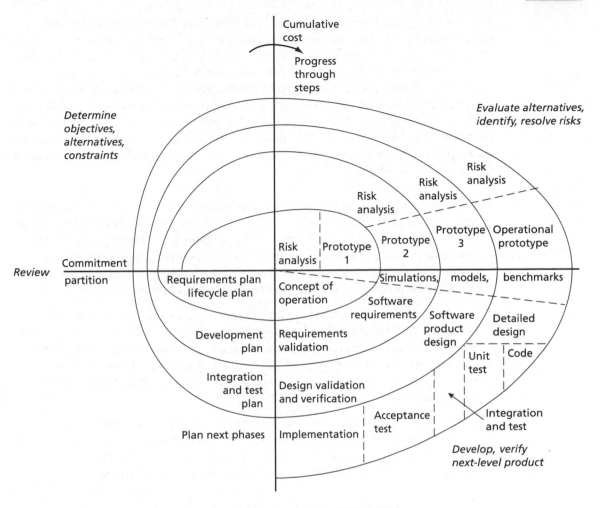

Fig. 6.6 Boehm's spiral model (*Computer*, May 1988, © IEEE)

At the centre, the requirements will be poorly understood, and they will be successively refined with each rotation around the spiral. The total cost of the project will increase as the length of the spiral increases. The model is divided into four quadrants:

- The top-left quadrant is where the objectives are determined and the alternatives and constraints identified.

- The top-right quadrant is where the alternatives are evaluated and the various risks are identified and resolved.

- The bottom-right quadrant is where the development takes place. This in effect covers the same area as the more conventional waterfall model.

- The bottom-left quadrant is where the next phase or iteration is planned.

The Boehm spiral introduces the important concepts of objective setting, risk management and planning into the overall cycle. These are all very desirable from a project management point of view as they apply explicitly to factors that may affect the timely delivery of the system within its defined constraints.

In the *traditional approach* to systems development, 'traditional' tends to mean unstructured and somewhat non-specific, and most traditional approaches are based on variations of the waterfall model. Although the overall picture will probably be familiar, the actual methods of developing the systems are almost as numerous as the projects themselves. In a typical traditional approach, three of the stages are as follows:

- *Analyse requirements.* In this stage the analyst considers the current system and investigates any problems associated with it. The users are also interviewed to obtain their views of the problems and to get their ideas for improvements. Other sources of information about the system and the new requirements would also be investigated at this time. The output from this stage would probably be no more than a set of notes put together by the analyst.

- *Specify requirements.* In this stage the analyst considers the information that has been accumulated, and produces a requirements document. This is likely to be a mix of business requirements, functional and non-functional requirements and an overview of the proposed hardware and software. Elements of the physical specification in terms of screens and printed output reports might also be included.

- *Produce high-level design.* The designer would consider the requirements document and, on that basis, produce a high-level design for the system setting out the database design, the input and output specifications, the menu structure and the overall program design and breakdown.

6.4 A Structured Approach

Analysis can be considered to be a four-stage process, as illustrated in Figure 6.7. This process begins with the analyst investigating and understanding the *current physical system*. This will involve fact-finding activities and the recording of information about how the current system operates. As part of this process, the analyst will also be constructing models to show the data and processing within the system, as well as documenting problems and requirements described by users of the system.

The next stage requires the analyst to move away from the constraints that determine how the current system is physically implemented, and to put together a clear picture of the logical functions carried out by the system – in other words, to state exactly what the system is doing rather than how it is doing it. This view is described as the *current logical system*. To move to the *required logical system*, the customer's requirements for a new information system must be mapped onto the current logical system. This will state what the new system will do. By discussing the requirements with the users who

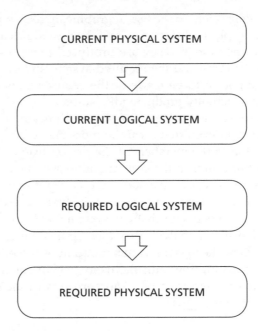

Fig. 6.7 A structured approach to systems analysis

specified them, priorities can be assigned and a number of alternative versions of the required logical system can be developed. These alternative versions can be presented to the client as part of the system proposal.

Finally, when the client has given the go-ahead to the system proposal, the *required physical system* can be developed. This involves specifying in detail exactly how the new system will work, and begins during analysis, with the high-level design included in the functional specification, and continues during the design phase of the project.

In traditional approaches to system development there was a tendency to move from a description of the current physical system to a specification of the required physical system without considering the underlying logical view. Structured techniques such as data flow diagrams and data models support the four-stage model described above and ensure continuity between analysis and design, by developing logical views of the system.

6.4.1 Structured Systems Analysis

Structured systems analysis, which is based on the four-stage model described above, also has associated with it three general principles:

- modelling;
- partitioning;
- iteration.

Modelling refers to the use of graphic models, which are employed wherever possible, in place of narrative text, to provide clear and unambiguous information about the system. They are produced to represent both the current system and data structure and the required system and data structure. They enable detailed investigation to be made of the requirements and the design before money is spent in actually producing the system.

Partitioning describes a method of breaking the system down into a number of smaller parts so that it can be more easily understood, and so that work can be allocated to the members of the project team. The system is first considered as a whole to establish the system boundaries. Once these have been agreed with the users, the system is partitioned, on a top-down basis.

Iteration: As it is unlikely that the first representation of the current system and the requirements for the new system will be completely accurate first time, structured systems analysis provides opportunities for revisiting and amending the models of the system. If this iteration of the process of analysis is carried out in close consultation with the users, it will ensure that our understanding of the existing system is correct and agreed with the client before development of the new system begins.

6.5 The PARIS Model

We have divided the process of analysis into five stages, each of which will be described in detail in subsequent chapters. The first letters of each step form the five-letter word PARIS, which is a useful mnemonic to help you remember the steps. The five steps are:

1 Planning the approach

This is the vital first stage in the PARIS model, and the success of the systems analysis phase of a project will depend on the thoroughness and care with which planning is carried out. During planning, objectives are set, constraints identified, terms of reference agreed, and preparations made for fact finding. Planning is described in Chapter 7, which also includes a section on the feasibility study.

2 Asking questions and collecting data

This includes all the fact-finding activities carried out as part of the analysis. The key technique here is interviewing, which applies many of the principles introduced in Chapter 3 on communication. Interviewing is described in detail in Chapter 8 under three headings – planning, conducting, and recording the interview – and there is also a section on difficult interviews. Other fact-finding methods described in Chapter 8 include observation, designing and sending out questionnaires, document analysis and record searching.

3 Recording the information

The third stage in the model is about recording information. The fact-finding methods, used during stage 2, yield many facts and details about the current and required systems. This information must then be recorded in a clear and unambiguous way. In structured systems analysis, a series of diagrams – or models – are drawn to represent the system, and these can be interpreted and built on by the analysis team, and may also be reviewed by the user to check that the information gathered by the analyst is complete and correct. Chapter 9 introduces two important models that are used to document the current system: the *data flow diagram* and the *data model*. Both are part of all structured methods, but we shall be concentrating on the way they are implemented in SSADM to explain how they are constructed and interpreted.

4 Interpreting the information collected

Having documented the current physical system, we need to understand the underlying logical system, and then consider how the client's requirements can be built in. Again, diagrams can be used to help analysts through this stage of the PARIS model, and Chapter 11 describes some techniques that can be used.

5 Specifying the requirement

The final stage in the model, *specifying the requirement*, is described in detail in Chapter 12. This involves the analyst in preparing a number of options, based on the models constructed earlier, for the development of the new system. These options are discussed with the client, costed, and then presented in a way that emphasises the benefits they will bring to the client's business. The analyst, during this stage, will usually be involved in writing a report, and in preparing and delivering a presentation. Once a decision has been made by the client on the way forward, a detailed functional specification will be prepared so that the designers will know exactly what the system has to do to meet the requirements.

6.6 Summary

This chapter has introduced the process of systems analysis, illustrated this with models, and explained where analysis fits into the development and maintenance life cycle. The PARIS model, which divides the job of analysis into five stages, provides the structure for five of the following chapters, and each stage of the model will now be described in detail. *Planning the approach* is described in Chapter 7; *Asking questions and collecting data* in Chapter 8; *Recording the information* in Chapter 9; *Modelling systems behaviour* in Chapter 11; and *Specifying the business requirements* in Chapter 12.

7 Systems Analysis: Planning the Approach

7.1 Introduction

One of the main causes of project failure is inadequate understanding of the requirements, and one of the main causes of inadequate understanding of the requirements is poor planning of system analysis. In this chapter we examine the first of the five stages of systems analysis described in Chapter 6 – *planning the approach* – and highlight the contribution that careful planning makes to the successful outcome of a project.

There are a number of starting points for the systems analyst. Feasibility studies or technical design studies may have been carried out, or a high-level analysis may have been completed. Whatever the starting point, the first step taken by the systems analyst should be to plan the approach carefully, bearing in mind the old adage that 'failure to prepare is to prepare to fail!'

Before beginning the detailed work of collecting, recording and interpreting data, the analyst will need to stand back, recall the objectives of the project, and consider the following three points:

- What type of information is required?
- What are the constraints on the investigation?
- What are the potential problems that may make the task more difficult?

Having taken time to do this, the analyst is then in a position to plan the actions needed to take him successfully through the process. Let's consider an example to illustrate the importance of doing this. Imagine that you work for a computer services company based in the UK. Your company has just won the following contract with *The Instant Image Corporation* (TIIC). The contract covers:

- analysis of TIIC's current warehousing, stock control and manufacturing systems and the integration of these systems;

- an investigation of TIIC's current problems and of future strategic plans in this area;

- production of a report outlining your company's proposals for meeting TIIC's future systems requirements in warehousing, stock control and manufacturing systems.

The Instant Image Corporation is a multinational company, based in the United States, with a presence in most countries throughout the world. It is world famous for the manufacture of photographic products, especially film and paper. They used to manufacture small, cheap cameras, but these products are less popular now and the Japanese make most of the new popular compact 35 mm models. A new manufacturing unit for digital cameras has recently been set up in Korea to supply all TIIC units worldwide. The company is split into a number of country-based organisations, with the largest in the United States. *Instant Image UK* manufactures most of the products required by the UK, apart from digital cameras, but imports additional products from sites in France, Germany and Spain. Increasingly the smaller countries' organisations cannot compete with the US organisation in terms of productivity and profitability. The parent company in the United States has decided to split the worldwide operation into three divisions – America, Europe and Asia/Pacific.

Each division will act as an integrated whole, servicing all the product needs of its marketplace. This will mean closing down or modifying some production sites and radically changing the warehousing function in each country. There is no intention to integrate computer systems across all the European companies at this point.

Instant Image UK has four manufacturing sites. Cameras are manufactured in Luton, photographic paper in St Albans, 35 mm film in Birmingham, and special products in Croydon. There are warehouses at each manufacturing site; the head office and distribution centre are both located in Croydon.

Against this background think about how you would plan this investigation. You may find it helpful to think about the following:

- critical information you require before the investigation starts;

- how you will get this information;

- the fact-finding techniques that will be appropriate;

- the danger areas for the project and for your company.

In producing your plan, you will have made a list of questions that, as an analyst on the project, you would need to ask before beginning your work. Questions covering the scope of the investigation – the resources available, the budget, the timescale, the key TIIC people to speak to, and any restrictions on carrying out the analysis; questions about the business and the company's organisation; questions, as well, about the objectives and expectations of the client. Standing back from the task and identifying key questions is the first stage of the planning process and, as we shall see, is critical in giving the best chance of success later on.

As part of the planning process, analysts must ensure that:

- they understand the objectives and terms of reference agreed with the client;

- they are aware of constraints that affect the analysis process;

- they plan the research, initial contact and other tasks to be completed during the investigation and manage time appropriately.

In this chapter we shall be discussing each of these areas. We shall also turn our attention to the feasibility study, describing what constitutes such a study and considering its value as a piece of analysis in its own right.

7.2 Objectives and Terms of Reference

To understand more about the client's expectations, you need to ask a number of key questions at the beginning of the analysis phase of the project:

- Who initiated the project?
- What is their role in the organisation?
- What are their objectives for the project?
- What are the company objectives?

Once you know the answers to these questions, you can begin to understand the context in which the analysis is to be carried out. A project will usually originate to meet the needs of one or more parts of an organisation. For example:

- Senior management may need earlier and more accurate information to improve their control over the business and enable strategic planning to be carried out.

- Line managers may need a new system, or enhancements to an existing system, to better support the activities of the company.

- The IT department may have identified a more cost-effective or efficient solution to a problem as a result of new technologies or methods becoming available.

Whatever the source of the initiative, the senior management of the organisation will expect to see measurable benefits resulting from their investment in the project. Benefits such as:

- increased profitability;
- improved cash flow;
- more effective utilisation of resources, including people;

- improved customer service (resulting in higher levels of customer satisfaction);

- faster access to management information;

- better management control.

If you understand which of these objectives are the most important to the person, or people, who initiated the project, you are in a better position to address these areas when planning the analysis and also when presenting system proposals at the end of the analysis phase.

The stated objectives of the client will usually be recorded in the terms of reference. These will have been agreed with the client before the start of analysis, and should define the scope of the investigation about to be undertaken. Indeed, the word SCOPE provides a useful mnemonic, which we can use to summarise the main areas included in the terms of reference.

- *System boundary*. This will define the area of the organisation under investigation and may also specify the limit of any new system implemented as a result of the project.

- *Constraints*. Factors, including budget, timescale and technology, which may restrict the study, or the solution, in some way. These constraints will be considered in more detail later in this chapter.

- *Objectives*. An unambiguous statement of the expectations of those in the client's organisation who have initiated the project. These may be broken down by function or department. Well-defined objectives are clear and measurable.

- *Permission*. This will indicate who in the client's organisation is responsible for the supervision of the project and, if permission needs to be granted – for example to extend the scope of the analysis – who has the authority to do so. Points of contact and the appropriate reporting structure may also be defined.

- *End products*. A description of the deliverable or end products of the investigation. This will usually take the form of a written report and a supporting presentation to managers of the client organisation.

As we pointed out earlier, it is important that the terms of reference, once they have been agreed with the client, are clearly understood by everyone in the analysis team. They are useful not only in the planning stage of systems analysis, but also later on during recording and interpretation to resolve disputes that might arise about, for example, the system boundary. If no written terms of reference exist, the analysis team would be well advised to prepare a draft based on their understanding and present it to the client for agreement.

For example, the terms of reference for the analysis team doing the investigation into The Instant Image Corporation could be as follows:

The suppliers' team will:

1 Investigate the existing warehousing, stock control and manufacturing systems in TIIC at the Luton, St Albans Birmingham and Croydon sites.

2 Document these systems and identify the characteristics, deficiencies and problems in these systems using the same analysis and documentation techniques as will be used for the equivalent studies in France, Germany and Spain.

3 Working with the teams in France, Germany and Spain propose new systems for the UK operation that will meet the UK's requirements for a central warehousing function and create opportunities for the use of common systems across Europe.

4 Produce a written report of the findings of the analysis for the new European Board by .... This is to be followed by a presentation and workshop by .... and subsequent system proposals by ....

In these terms of reference, the system boundary is clear (warehousing, stock control and manufacturing at the four UK sites), some constraints have been identified (a timescale and the need for common analysis and documentation methods), and four objectives are stated. The issue of permissions has been resolved as the sponsoring body appears to be the new European Board, and the end products are clear.

But what about the things that remain unclear? It seems as though there is a target organisation structure for the new European division, but is it clear how this will be translated into physical locations and facilities? Is the central warehousing function to serve only the UK? Will there be European plants for manufacturing or will each country keep its own? And what are the implications of considering the use of common systems across Europe? The first thing that the analysis team will therefore need will be a statement of TIIC's intentions.

7.3 Constraints

Terms of reference have been agreed with the client. The objectives of the analysis phase are clear. Now it is essential that all constraints on the analysis are understood early in order to help with planning and to avoid problems arising during detailed analysis. Some constraints may have been set by the customer, which will limit the options that can be presented as part of the system proposals. They are illustrated in Figure 7.1.

These constraints will probably be included in the terms of reference, and cover:

- *Technology*. The customer may be committed to a particular hardware or software solution. Indeed, there may be a corporate strategy in this area. For example, they may require any new system to run on their present mainframe computer, or to be developed using specified software such as Oracle – in order that it can be integrated with existing systems.

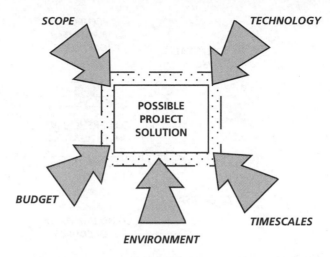

Fig. 7.1 Constraints on the possible solution

- *Environment*. The system may have to work in exceptional conditions, for example in a missile, in a submarine, on a factory floor or on a customer's doorstep. The system may be used by skilled or unskilled operators, perhaps by operators wearing protective clothing.

- *Timescales*. Project delivery times based on the customer's immovable timescales may also be specified. These could in turn be determined by the introduction of new government legislation or by a key date in the business cycle of the client's organisation.

- *Budget*. If the work is to be done by a systems house, the contract may well be a fixed-price one. This poses real problems for the analysts on the development team. How much resource is committed to the analysis phase? What other budget constraints exist? For example, how much money is available for the purchase of new hardware or software, and are there any limitations on the annual operation budget?

- *Scope*. What is the area under investigation in this project? What is the boundary of the system? Which parts of the organisation are off limits?

All of these factors will constrain any solution presented by the analysis team. But there is also another set of constraints that need to be identified by the analyst early on, because these will limit the way in which the investigation is conducted. These will include the areas shown in Figure 7.2.

These constraints, which are listed below, will enable the analysis team to determine which fact-finding methods are most appropriate, as well as help them to put together a detailed plan for the investigation.

- *The project resources available during the analysis*. How much support will be available to the analysis team? For example, will CASE tools be available for producing documentation? Will there be administrative support from the

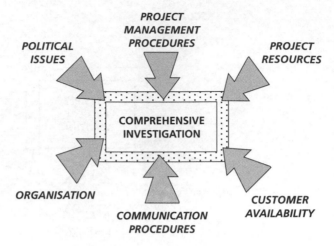

Fig. 7.2 Constraints on the investigation

project office? Are there colleagues who have worked with the client before who would be available to give advice to the team?

- *The availability of customer contacts.* It is important to know whether appropriate staff will be available for discussion and to review analysis products. For example, an organisation might require that all interviewees be given three days' notice, or that review meetings involving client staff cannot be held on any Monday or Friday.

- *The political issues important in the customer's organisation.* There may be politically sensitive issues in the organisation that an analyst should be aware of before embarking on the investigation. For example, the introduction of a new computer system might mean that fewer employees are needed to do the work, or that one department will have to close down. In this case, the analyst should be clear about whether the staff to be interviewed are aware of the implications of the change, and what line should be taken if difficult questions are asked.

- *The complexity and size of the organisation.* This will influence the choice of fact-finding techniques, and could mean that sampling methods have to be used. If, as part of an investigation you are undertaking, you need to collect information from all parts of a large organisation, a number of options are available, including:

  - interviewing everyone;
  - sending out questionnaires;
  - interviewing a representative sample.

  It is important that the implications, costs and benefits of the alternatives are understood and discussed with the client.

- *The project management procedures used by the project team.* An analyst will need to be aware of the expectations of the client organisation with regard to the management of the analysis phase of the project. It might be, for example, that the client organisation uses a structured approach to project management such as PRINCE2, or the client may require the team to give detailed information about the planning and monitoring techniques to be used during the analysis phase of the project.

- *Communication procedures.* It is important that the analyst is aware of, and follows, the communication procedures set up within the project team and between the project team and the client. This may involve agreement on appropriate channels of communication and the identification of named individuals as 'contacts'.

Business analysis techniques – described in Chapter 12 – offer some tools for dealing with these issues.

7.4 Preparing for Detailed Analysis

In order for analysts to be well prepared for the later stages of systems analysis, and to increase their credibility in interviews with client staff, the time they spend on research during the planning stage represents a good investment. This will mean that, in addition to reading and understanding the terms of reference, the contract should be studied, as well as any background documents, such as preliminary studies, which put the current work into perspective. Researching the client's organisation will involve reading the annual report of the company, obtaining organisation charts showing departments involved, personnel and job responsibilities, and building up a list of any special terminology used together with definitions. By talking to people in your own organisation who have had dealings with the client in the past, you can gather valuable 'off the record' information about working relationships. In addition your organisation might have information about similar work that has been done for other clients, for example previous studies and their outcome together with user decisions.

Having completed the initial research described above, you can begin to identify the types of information you will need to collect during your investigation. To help in this process, a list of the areas to explore should be prepared. Obviously this will vary according to the business of the client and the nature of the project, but the following are examples of topics that the analyst may wish to investigate:

- *Growth.* What plans does the organisation have for future growth, and what would be the information requirements to support this growth?

- *Functionality.* What are the major areas of the business – the functions – that will be investigated during the system, and what are the client's requirements for the functionality of the system?

- *Procedures.* What procedures, standards and guidelines govern the way in which the organisation conducts its business – and are they written down somewhere?

- *Volumes.* What are the volumes of data that pass through the system? For example, how many orders are processed by the sales department in a week? How many amendments are made to customer records each month?

- *Fluctuations.* What bottlenecks or hold-ups are there in the system, as well as 'peaks' and 'troughs' (busy and slack periods) in the operation? Where and when do these occur in the current system? What steps are taken to deal with these?

- *Information required.* What information is currently required by the business in order to carry out its functions effectively, and what are the sources of this information? What information, if it were available, would bring significant benefits to the organisation?

- *Environment.* In what type of environment is the business conducted, and how does this affect the way in which information is exchanged?

- *Problems.* In the view of users, what are the main problems with the system, what are the implications of these problems, and how might they be overcome?

In planning the approach to analysis, an important area to consider is the first face-to-face contact with the client. This initial contact should be formal and at the highest level possible. In addition to any fact-finding objectives, a key aim of this contact will be to build a good relationship with the client and to establish the analyst's credibility. In this meeting, and indeed in all subsequent meetings with users, the following guidelines represent good practice.

- Focus on confidentiality, integrity, respect and confidence-building.
- Recognise expertise in the users and welcome their input.
- Have as a key objective the need to build the client's confidence.
- Keep everybody informed. This includes client contacts and project staff.
- Be discreet and diplomatic.
- Double-check any information gathered.

There are many tasks to complete during systems analysis; time is limited, and often different stages of the analysis process will be taking place at the same time. One other area, therefore, for the analyst to consider when putting together the plan for detailed analysis is the management of time. Time is a resource to be budgeted, managed and used. To help you manage your time as effectively as possible, here are some guidelines:

- *List objectives and set priorities.* Decide what you are really trying to achieve during the analysis, list your objectives, and, having done this, decide on the priorities of each. The temptation is to start with the small, trivial jobs to get the desk clear, so that the difficult, involved tasks can be dealt with later. But interruptions, telephone calls, visitors and distractions can mean that 'later' never comes!

- *Make a daily 'to do' list.* Daily, as a routine, at the same time (whenever best suits you), make a list of the things you actually want to do today to move a step – even a short one – towards your objectives. Some people find it helpful to prepare their 'to do' list in advance, at the end of the previous day.

- *Handle paper only once.* Once you have picked up a piece of paper, don't put it down until you have taken some action on it. 'Pending' should mean 'awaiting the completion of some action I've already initiated' – not 'too difficult today'.

- *Set and keep deadlines.* With our own jobs, and with those we delegate to others, the work expands to fill the time available. So setting deadlines at the outset is a good discipline. A long, complicated job, such as the analysis of a system, can be split up into steps or stages, with a planned deadline for each stage. And don't forget to build in some contingency when budgeting time to allow for the unexpected.

- *Ask yourself frequently 'What's the best use of my time right now?'* You must train yourself to take frequent breaks, to come out of the trees to take a look at the wood.

- *Always carry a notebook.* To collect information or ideas as they occur, a useful idea is to carry some type of notebook rather than collect numerous little scraps of paper, which can get lost.

- *Do it now.* In other words, avoid procrastination!

7.5 The Feasibility Study

A feasibility study is really a small-scale systems analysis. It differs from a full analysis only in its level of detail. The study involves analysts in most of the tasks of a full systems analysis but with a narrower focus and more limited time. The results of the study help the user to decide whether to proceed, amend, postpone or cancel the project – particularly important when the project is large, complex and costly. However, a feasibility study is no substitute for a full, detailed and thorough analysis of the client's system. Different people can provide different parts of the answers in a feasibility study: those who initiated the study, the technical experts, and those who will have to use the new system. The job of the analyst is to pull all this information together and present it to the client in the form of a coherent report. Detailed investigation of operational and procedural activities during a feasibility study is very limited. Analysts should concentrate on providing the answers to four key questions:

- *How much?* The cost of the new system.
- *What?* The objectives of the new system.
- *When?* The delivery timescale.
- *How?* The means and procedures used to produce the new system.

During the feasibility study, a number of structured techniques can be used to record the findings in an effective way, and later to present data in a graphical form. These techniques are described in more detail in Chapters 9 and 11. At the end of the study a report is prepared for the client.

The feasibility study report has to address three levels of feasibility:

- *Technical feasibility*. Is it going to work?

- *Business feasibility*. Are cost and timescales right for the business, and will potential returns justify the initial outlay?

- *Functional feasibility*. Will the solution satisfy the end users?

If, for example, you were building a house, it wouldn't be enough just for the house to stand up (technical feasibility) and for the price to be right (business feasibility). You'd have to want to live there as well (functional feasibility).

Figure 7.3 illustrates the main sections of a feasibility report. The contents of these sections could be as follows:

Background

- Terms of reference.
- Reasons for the study.

This section will outline the background to the project and the way it relates to the stated objectives of the organisation.

The current situation

- Overview of current situation.
- Problems and requirements identified.

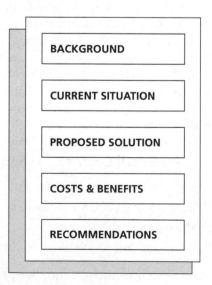

Fig. 7.3 The feasibility report

Proposed solution

A description of the requirements of a new system along with a number of options explaining how this solution might be implemented. Each option will address:

- Technical implications – how it meets the requirements, the hardware and software needed.

- Operational implications – the impact the solution will have on the business in terms of human, organisational and political aspects.

- Cost implications – both initial (capital) and continuing (operational). There are a number of methods of assessing the costs of solutions. In the feasibility report, the analyst should use the cost assessment method specified by the client.

Cost–benefits analysis

- A comparison of costs and benefits prepared using whatever evaluation technique is favoured by the organisation.

Recommendations

- Summary of the previous sections of the report.
- Recommendations as to how the client should proceed.

Three distinct types of recommendation can be made in a feasibility report:

- Advising the client to progress with the full detailed analysis. If this is the case, a plan would also be included for this phase of the project.

- Advising the client to review the terms of reference or the scope of the study before proceeding further or making any judgement on feasibility.

- Advising the client to scrap the project as it is not feasible; the resources could be better spent elsewhere.

Once the feasibility report has been delivered, and assuming that the recommendation made by the author(s) is to proceed, the detailed systems analysis phase can begin, and any preliminary work done as part of the feasibility study will be valuable in planning and carrying out the later stages.

7.6 Summary

In this chapter we have looked at planning the approach to analysis. In the past this stage has often been rushed or omitted, and this has led to costly problems later on, but by careful planning many of these problems can be avoided.

We have discussed the importance of understanding the client's objectives and agreeing terms of reference that reflect the SCOPE (System boundary, Constraints, Objectives, Permission and End products) of the investigation. We have considered constraints that need to be identified as early as possible by the analyst. These may limit the possible solutions to, or the investigation of, the client's problems. Stages in preparing for detailed analysis have also been described in this chapter, beginning with research and moving on to planning the initial contact with the users. Time management, another skill needed by an effective analyst, has also been discussed.

We looked finally at the feasibility study and feasibility report. The existence of a feasibility study does not mean that detailed analysis is not required – a full and comprehensive analysis is the only way to provide a thorough understanding of the user's requirements. However, a feasibility study does provide a useful starting point for a full analysis.

The overall message behind all the sections in this chapter has been this: by taking time, standing back from the problem and carefully planning your approach to analysis, you give yourself the best chance of success.

Exercises

7.1 Imagine that you are the Personnel Director of System Telecom. Prepare the terms of reference for a project to develop a new personnel system.

7.2 Using the example of The Instant Image Corporation, how would you plan the approach to the systems analysis needed for the contract won by your computer services company? Take account of the apparently imperfect terms of reference suggested and identify the direction of your approach and how you would begin.

7.3 This chapter talks about face-to-face contact with the client and the need to build a good credible relationship. If you were an analyst meeting the System Telecom Personnel Director for the first time to discuss the terms of reference mentioned in question 7.1, how would you begin to build this relationship? Be as specific as you can.

Systems Analysis: Asking Questions and Collecting Data

8.1 Introduction

Fact-finding takes place from the start of the project – during the feasibility study – right through to the final implementation and review. Although progressively lower levels of detail are required by analysts during the logical design, physical design and implementation phases, the main fact-finding activity is during analysis. This fact-finding establishes what the existing system does and what the problems are, and leads to a definition of a set of options from which the users may choose their required system. In this chapter we consider the second stage of our systems analysis model – *asking questions and collecting data*. Fact-finding interviewing, an important technique used by analysts during their investigation, is described in detail, and a number of other methods used to collect data are also described.

In the last chapter we discussed the importance of planning and of preparing thoroughly before embarking on detailed analysis. If this has been done, you will already have collected quite a lot of background information about the project and the client's organisation. You may also have been involved in carrying out a feasibility study. You will have some facts about the current system: these may include details of staff and equipment resources, manual and computer procedures, and an outline of current problems. This background information should be checked carefully before beginning the detailed fact-finding task. You should now be ready to begin asking questions, and, as a result of your planning, these questions will be relevant, focused and appropriate.

In carrying out your investigation you will be collecting information about the current system, and, by recording the problems and requirements described by users of the current system, building up a picture of the required system. The facts gathered from each part of the client's organisation will be concerned primarily with the current system and how it operates, and will include some or all of the following: details of inputs to and outputs from the system; how information is stored; volumes and frequencies of data; any trends that can be identified; and specific problems, with examples if possible, that are experienced by users. In addition, you may also be able to gather useful information about:

- departmental objectives;
- decisions made and the facts upon which they are based;
- what is done, to what purpose, who does it, where it is done and the reason why;
- critical factors affecting the business;
- staff and equipment costs.

In order to collect this data and related information, a range of fact-finding methods can be used. Those most commonly used include interviewing, questionnaires, observation, searching records and document analysis. Each of these methods is described in this chapter, but it is important to remember that they are not mutually exclusive. More than one method may be used during a fact-finding session: for example, during a fact-finding interview a questionnaire may be completed, records inspected and documents analysed.

8.2 Fact-finding Interviews

An interview can be defined as 'a conversation with a specific purpose'. This purpose could be selection in a recruitment interview, counselling in a performance appraisal interview, or collecting information in a fact-finding interview. An interview is a form of two-way communication that requires a range of interpersonal skills to be used by the interviewer to ensure that the purpose is achieved. The interviewer will need to be a good listener, to be skilful in the use of questions so that the conversation flows smoothly, and to be able to control the interview while building and maintaining rapport with the interviewee. In a fact-finding interview these skills are needed to collect and record information in order to build up a picture of the current system, and to catalogue the requirements for a new one. In describing this fact-finding technique we shall look at three stages: planning, conducting and recording the interview.

8.2.1 Planning the Interview

When planning a fact-finding interview, you are trying to answer five questions:

1 What do I wish to achieve as a result of these interviews?
2 Who should be interviewed?
3 How will these interviews be conducted?
4 What topics will be covered during the interviews?
5 Where will the interviews take place?

The answer to question 1 helps you to identify a set of objectives; question 2 leads you to a list of interviewees and to a sequence in which they will be interviewed; the answer to question 3 gives you a format or structure for the interview; in answering question 4 you are putting together an agenda; and there are implications for both interviewer and the interviewee depending on the answer to question 5 with regard to location. We shall consider each of these issues in turn.

The first stage in planning the interview is to set clear, specific and measurable objectives. If such objectives are set, not only will you understand what you are trying to achieve, but there will also be some criteria for measuring the success of the interview when it has been completed. An objective is written in the form:

> By the end of the interview, the analyst will have put together a list of the major problems encountered by Pat Clarke when using the current system.

This contains a time (by the end of the interview), an action (putting together a list), and a deliverable (a list of the major problems encountered by Pat Clarke when using the current system). This can be used to evaluate the success of the interview, because the question 'Has the analyst achieved this objective?' can be answered with either a 'yes' or a 'no'.

An objective can be defined as either passive or active. Passive objectives are concerned with collecting information from the interviewee, whereas active objectives are about decisions or actions that you require the interviewee to take. An example of a passive objective is

> By the end of the interview, the analyst will have identified the interfaces between bookings and sales and collected copies of any forms that pass between the two departments.

An example of an active objective, on the other hand, would be

> By the end of the interview, the interviewee will have agreed to contact the managers who report to her to enable further fact-finding interviews to be set up.

In putting together an interviewing plan, you will identify who in the client organisation you wish to see and the order in which you wish to see them. Key people and decision-makers will need to be interviewed first. Often they will not be able to provide the detailed information, being removed from the day-to-day operation of the business. However, they can provide you with a high-level view of the current system and a strategic view of the business, as well as information about their requirements for the new system. They will also be able to suggest the best people to fill in the detail. When planning a logical sequence for the individual interviews, it is helpful to tie this in with the structure of the system under investigation. This should enable you to gradually build up the whole picture, while also giving the opportunity to hear the views of a range of users of the system.

Most fact-finding interviews follow a similar structure, which is shown in diagrammatic form in Figure 8.1. This consists of four stages – social chat, overview, questions and answers, and closing. The length of each stage will vary, depending on the individual being interviewed and the amount of detail required, but the percentages shown in Figure 8.1 represent a typical breakdown of the total time available.

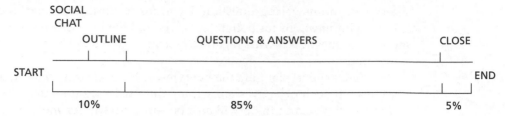

Fig. 8.1 The structure of a fact-finding interview

Social chat

An interview begins with a casual, friendly opening to create a relaxed atmosphere and put interviewees at their ease. This is an opportunity to reassure the interviewee, who might be feeling nervous, as well as calming any nerves of your own. During this stage you can give the interviewee some background information about the reasons for the investigation and answer any questions they have. The early minutes of an interview are critical in building rapport with the interviewee and making it feel more like a conversation and less like an interrogation.

Overview

Having created a relaxed atmosphere in the first stage of the interview, you now move on to outline what will happen next. In effect you are 'signposting' the various parts of the interview, and it is usually helpful at this point to have the agenda visible to both parties. During this overview you can also explain the objectives of the interview, the time you will need, and the main topics to be covered, as well as asking for the interviewee's permission to take notes.

Questions and answers

This is the fact-finding part of the interview. In this stage you ask questions to find out as much as possible about the interviewee and their role in the organisation. By listening carefully to the answers, making notes and checking understanding of the information collected, a lot of useful information can be gathered. It is important to keep control and direct the interview during this stage to ensure your objectives – both active and passive – are met. It is also important to maintain the rapport, remembering that you are not there to evaluate the interviewee but to hear their views.

A useful model for structuring the questions and answers stage of the interview is shown in Figure 8.2. As you can see, there are four steps in this questioning model, designed to guide the analyst through the fact-finding process and provide information about the user's problems and requirements.

In conducting an interview, the questions should initially be at a high level so information is gathered about the background and work environment of the interviewee (user) within the organisation. These are called *context questions*, and often contain the words 'tell', 'explain' or 'describe'. For example:

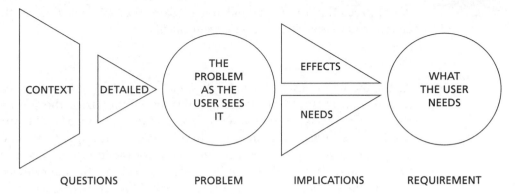

Fig. 8.2 The questioning model

'Can you describe your main responsibilities as sales manager?' 'Take me through a typical day in this office.' 'Will you explain this department's role in the organisation?' 'Tell me about the main stages in the bookings cycle.'

The context questions are followed by a set of *detailed questions*, which enable you to obtain specific information about the areas explored in step one. This information will usually include facts and figures that indicate volumes as well as operational peaks and troughs. For example:

'You mentioned a problem that occurred last February – can you say more about that?' 'On average, how may invoices would be processed each month?' 'You said that the current procedures cause difficulties for your staff – what sort of difficulties?' 'Which months in the year are the busiest for you?' 'Do you have examples of the documents you're describing?'

The context and detailed questions should help you to understand the current system and enable you to identify the nature and cause of specific *problems*.

Once problems have been identified, you should ask further questions to find out what *effects* the interviewee believes each problem has on the organisation and, more specifically, on their area of responsibility:

'So what effect does this problem have on your work?' 'Can you give me examples of the sort of comments that members of staff in your area have made about the current purchasing system?' '. . . and when the orders are held up in Keith Smith's section, what is the impact of that in your section?'

The fourth step, which can take place alongside step three, is to explore the user's views about the solution to a problem and to find out what the user *needs* to correct the problem. It is important during fact-finding to discover what the user's *real* needs are, so that any solution developed will be efficient and effective:

'In your opinion, what steps could be taken to solve this problem?' 'If you had a free hand to make changes, how would you improve the system?' 'Which of the requirements you've described is the most important for the business at the moment?' 'What is the single most important change that would make life easier in this department?'

An appreciation of effects and needs, from the point of view of the user, will enable you to identify the user's *requirements*.

Closing

As the model indicates, time should be left at the end of the interview to bring it to a formal close. In closing the interview, summarise the points discussed, checking key facts with the interviewee, and describe what will happen next as a result of the information obtained. In most cases it is appropriate to offer to send a copy of the formal record of the interview for the interviewee to check and confirm. Finally, arrangements can be made to re-contact the interviewee if there are any problems, thereby 'leaving the door open' for future discussion.

The content of the interview must also be carefully considered during the planning phase and an agenda produced. The starting point for this task is the list of objectives prepared earlier. Using the objectives – especially the passive ones – the information to be collected can be prioritised as follows:

1 Facts that you *must* find out in order to develop the new system. This relates to the key objective, or objectives.

2 Facts that you *should* find out to add flesh to the bare bones of the system.

3 Details that, given the time, you could find out to add the final polish to the system.

Prioritising your fact-finding according to these three headings provides an outline to guide you through the interview. This approach can be represented as a tree (Figure 8.3).

The key fact-finding objectives – 'must find out' – form the *trunk* of the tree. From these, an agenda can be prepared listing these areas as main headings. We can leave the trunk and go down the *branches* to get supporting information – 'should find out' – which will provide additional information about the key areas. The *leaves* provide the final level of questioning – 'could find out' – representing detailed questions about specific areas within the list of objectives. Having travelled out to the leaves to collect the detail, we can return to our main objectives on the trunk of the tree, and so avoid the danger of 'falling off' the tree by getting lost in details and losing sight of the main purpose of the interview. The *saw* in the diagram is a reminder that the agenda might have to be pruned if the available time is used up. Such pruning should enable the interview to be properly closed and a second interview to be arranged.

A final point to consider when planning the interview is where it will take place. There is usually a choice of location – either on the client's premises or at the analyst's office. Both choices have associated advantages and disadvantages, which are summarised in Table 8.1.

As can be seen from the table, the analyst's offices have many advantages for the interviewer, whereas on the other hand there are clearly good reasons – in terms of access to information – for travelling to the client's premises. A midway point, which is often the most satisfactory, would be a dedicated office on the

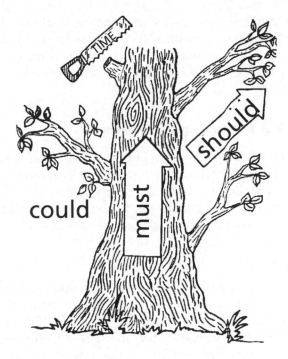

Fig. 8.3 Fact-finding: the tree structure

Table 8.1 Comparing possible interview locations

Client premises	Analyst's office
Advantages	*Advantages*
Little inconvenience for client – no travel	Interviewer in control
Client will be relaxed	Interviewer more relaxed
Client will have information to hand	Client away from day-to-day pressures
Other client staff are available	Fewer interruptions, and privacy guaranteed
	Interviewer has information to hand
	Interviewer lays out room
Disadvantages	*Disadvantages*
Possible interruptions, e.g. phone, people or intercom	Other client staff are not readily available
Privacy not always possible, e.g. open plan	Client may not have all information to hand
Layout not always acceptable	Client may not feel relaxed
Analyst has no access to own information	More inconvenient for the client
Not as easy for interviewer to control	

client's premises in which the analyst would conduct the interviews. This would be a private area, with a layout decided by the analyst, where client staff could be interviewed without such distractions as telephone calls. All the interviewee's information would be readily available, and in addition other staff would be nearby.

8.2.2 Conducting the Interview

Having emphasised the importance of careful planning to make sure that the time spent conducting a fact-finding interview is used effectively, we now turn our attention to the interview itself to consider how the work done during the planning phase may be put to good effect. In this section, we'll discuss two key skills – listening and questioning – as well as the important issue of control.

Listening

As we pointed out in Chapter 3, listening is an essential component of any effective face-to-face communication. It is at the heart of the process of interviewing, and the quality of the information gathered by analysts depends to a large extent on the effectiveness of their listening. An effective listener will not only encourage the interviewee to provide them with clear and accurate information, but will also understand much more of what they hear. This said, listening is not a well-developed skill for most people. Although we are taught in school to read and write, few of us have been formally taught to listen. Being an effective listener means: not being switched off just because the other person is not clear or concise; not reacting emotionally; not letting the other person's mannerisms distract you; keeping an open mind until the other person has completely finished; being patient with slow and ponderous speakers; and trying not to interrupt.

To be effective listeners, analysts need to work on developing their skills in this area as well as on adopting an open, receptive attitude when engaged in listening. We shall deal first with the skills, described in Chapter 3 as *active listening*, and then go on to discuss attitude and the blocks to effective listening.

'Active' listening has been defined as a set of techniques through which one person can obtain information from another. It involves the listener communicating their interest and their understanding to the speaker, encouraging them to continue, and giving them the opportunity to talk without constant interruption. Active listening also enables the interviewer to better control the flow and direction of the interview. There are both non-verbal and verbal signals that demonstrate that active listening is taking place.

Non-verbal signals

You can communicate that you are actively listening by showing that you are paying full attention. This involves:

- looking at the person;
- maintaining eye contact, but not staring;

- nodding your head from time to time;
- appropriate facial expressions, especially smiling;
- attentive body posture, which is often shown by a listener leaning forward.

Verbal signals

There are a number of ways that will indicate clearly that you are not only listening but also interested in what the other person has to say.

- repeating in your own words, e.g. 'So what you are saying is . . .';
- summarising key points;
- encouraging the speaker to continue, e.g. 'That's interesting, tell me more';
- asking questions to obtain further information or clarification;
- making encouraging noises.

Attitude and blocks

Perhaps the chief requirement for effective listening is to have 'room' for others. It is not sufficient just to develop appropriate verbal and non-verbal listening skills. We have all seen politicians on television who have been coached to display the skills associated with active listening but who demonstrate from their subsequent remarks that an open attitude was not present behind their behaviour. If we are preoccupied with our own thoughts, ideas and views we are not mentally 'available' to listen effectively. When listening it is helpful to really try to understand the other person's view without superimposing one's own views or judgements prematurely – a major block to effective listening.

Other blocks to effective listening include:

- listening for an opportunity to interrupt to talk about your own experience;
- listening for agreement rather than understanding;
- assuming you know, and understand, what the person is going to say;
- rehearsing your response to something the speaker has said;
- preparing in your mind the next question you are going to ask.

With all of these blocks, the listener is moving concentration away from the speaker and onto personal issues. Once this happens, the listener is in danger of missing not only the words being spoken, but also, and perhaps more importantly, the subtle non-verbal messages being communicated in the tone of voice and body language of the interviewee.

Questioning

The other key interpersonal skill that needs to be put into practice by the analyst during fact-finding interviewing is questioning. Asking the appropriate question to obtain the information required is a technique that has many other applications and which is central to fact-finding interviewing. As we shall see later, it is also an important technique to use when designing questionnaires, another means of collecting data during systems analysis.

Different types of question elicit different types of response and are, therefore, used for different purposes. A selection of question types are described below:

- *Closed questions*. Closed questions close down the conversation. They produce a definite 'yes' or 'no', or sometimes 'perhaps', and can help to control the talkative interviewee. They are also useful for checking and clarifying facts. For example, 'can you . . . ?', 'will you . . . ?', 'have you . . . ?', 'is it . . . ?'.

- *Open questions*. Open questions, on the other hand, open up the conversation. They are used to obtain information, provide insight into a client's feelings and motivations, and encourage the quiet interviewee to relax and be more forthcoming. For example, 'tell me . . .', 'please explain . . .', 'could you describe . . . ?', 'how is your purchasing organised?', 'what is your opinion of . . . ?'

- *Probing questions*. As the name suggests, these questions are used to obtain more detail to probe further when a previous question has not yielded sufficient information. For example, 'why?', 'please could you tell me more about . . . ?'

- *Probing techniques*. These include planned pauses, periods of silence, or an unfinished sentence. These are more subtle, and often more powerful, ways of probing, which can be used instead of, or in conjunction with, probing questions.

- *Reflective questions*. This involves repeating a key word or phrase to encourage the speaker to say more about it. For example, 'difficulties?', 'a significant number?' Used as described, reflective questions act as probes to elicit more information. They can also be used to demonstrate active listening when they reflect not a key word but an unspoken message or feeling. For example, 'it sounds like the new system is really causing you a problem', 'you seem very pleased about that . . .'.

- *Limited-choice questions*. The objective here is to direct the other person's attention to a range of options, while leaving them with the final choice of answer. For example: 'Which of these three courses of action is most suitable . . . ?' 'Is your busiest time in April or in September?'

- *Leading questions*. Leading questions imply the correct answer. Examples: 'Would you agree that . . . ?', 'Don't you feel that . . . ?, 'So all your problems result from the introduction of these new procedures?' They can be useful in confirming information, but the danger is that the interviewee will agree because this is the easiest option. They should be used sparingly, if at all, and are usually better framed as a different question. Another danger, if they are used too often, is that the interviewer can appear pushy and irritating.

- *Link questions*. For example: 'In view of what you have just said about the importance of credit terms, how important are delivery times?', 'The point you've just made about customers leads me to another question: how do new customers appear on the system?' Link questions like these are excellent for steering the discussion from one topic to another while allowing the other person to do most of the talking.

Putting questions together to take the interviewee through a particular area is another part of interviewing that the analyst should address. The sequence of questions asked during an interview can be critical in the successful achievement of objectives. One useful model in building a sequence of questions is the funnel that is illustrated in Figure 8.4. In this model, the interview begins with open questions at the wide end of the funnel, followed by probing questions to focus on specific points raised in response to the open questions. These are followed by closed questions to obtain factual data and lastly by summarising to check that the facts collected are correct.

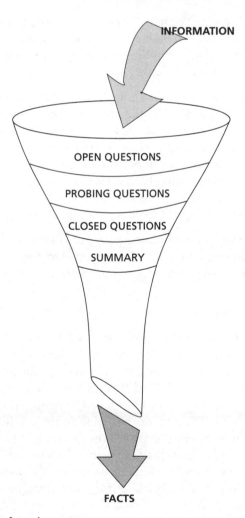

Fig. 8.4 The fact-finding funnel

Control

It is important to remember that, however much you open up the interview during questioning, you, as the interviewer, must always be in control of the process. Guiding conversations by using the right questions is one way of maintaining this control. Other controlling techniques include:

- *Signposting*. Giving the interviewee an idea of the path you are planning to take and therefore the reason for your questions. An agenda is very useful, and can be used to bring the interview back on course if control begins to slip away.

- *Confirming*. Restating or repeating the interviewee's statement to ensure that you have clearly and correctly received their message.

- *Summarising*. Consolidating what has been covered in the discussion; clarifying and checking for understanding.

- *Note-taking*. Memory is fallible; recorded notes are less so. It is a compliment to the client to demonstrate a desire to be accurate, and note-taking can also be useful in controlling the interview by giving the analyst some thinking time during the interview.

- *Listening*. As well as being a useful skill in its own right, listening is one of the best methods of maintaining control of the interview. By showing that you are involved and interested in the discussion, through the correct use of eyes, body, head and voice, you are confirming to the interviewee that he or she is the most important person to you at that moment. If, in addition to this, you are concentrating hard on what is being said, it is much easier to find a point at which to enter the discussion and then move it on to the next 'branch' of the 'tree' – the next topic on your agenda – without antagonising the interviewee.

- *Pausing*. A well-placed pause or silence is a good way of keeping control and allowing you to decide the next step. Silence will also often encourage a quiet person to provide more information.

Recording the interview

Having looked at planning and conducting a fact-finding interview, we now turn to the subject of how to record it. This is an area that is particularly important when asking questions, as the record of the answers given will form the basis for constructing models of the system. No matter how skilled the interviewer, or how good their questioning and listening, the interview is likely to be less than successful if the recording techniques are incomplete or inappropriate. Often interviewers comment on how difficult it is to develop a recording technique that is easy to use, unobtrusive during the interview, non-threatening to the interviewee, and understandable after the interview.

Some general guidelines for note-taking include the following:

- Always ask for permission to take notes.

- Ensure that you use an 'open' note-taking style, and don't hide what you are writing from the interviewee.

- Pause during the interview while recording important information; don't try to listen and take notes at the same time.

- Check with the interviewee that the information recorded is correct, and make sure that any actions required by either party are accurately recorded.

Many fact-finding interviews result in the interviewee describing a lot of complex procedural details, and it can be difficult to capture this information unambiguously. A graphical technique can simplify the capture of this sort of information, but to be effective it must be simple and quick to use, and be easily understood by the interviewee so it can be checked for accuracy. For example, a mind map can be used to record information. This consists of a central idea, or topic, enclosed in a circle with related topics radiating out from the circle. The data flow diagram, which provides a pictorial view of how data moves around an information system, is another recording technique that has been used effectively by many analysts. It is described in the next chapter.

In order to take reliable information away from a fact-finding interview, the time immediately following the interview is critical. It is essential to read through your notes and ensure they make sense. Complete any unfinished sentences, tidy up any parts which are difficult to read, and fill in any gaps while the information is still fresh in your memory. If this task is left too long – and overnight is often too long – you will not be able to remember all the important points, or what you intended by the hieroglyphics on the page! At the same time as carrying out this check you can add any additional comments to your notes, such as informal comments or feelings that might be useful in subsequent interviews or which may help other members of the team.

The other recording task after the interview, although this one is not so urgent, is to prepare a formal record of it. This serves at least two purposes: it is the official record of the interview, which can be accessed by others on the project, and it is a document that can be checked by the interviewee to make sure it is accurate. The NCC Interview Report provides the headings required for a formal record of this kind. Figure 8.5 is a formal interview record based on the NCC form. This is a comprehensive form, and the amount of detail may not be appropriate in every case. However, a formal record should contain the following information as a minimum:

- the date, location and duration of the interview;
- the names of the attendees;
- the agenda or objectives;
- the main points discussed;
- any conclusions;
- any actions;
- the date of next meeting if appropriate.

Title		System	Document	Name		Sheet
Interview record		BBS	2.1	CTS/IR 14		1 of 2

Participants Pat Clarke, CTS Bookings	Date
Manager	5th January 2003

Objectives/Agenda	Location
To understand Pat Clarke's role, including details of procedures; to determine the problems encountered when using the current system; and to establish his requirements for a new system	CTS offices
	Duration
	10.00am – 11.15am

Results	Cross-reference
1. BACKGROUND	
Pat Clarke has worked for Computer Training Services (CTS) since it was set up by the parent company, Industrial Services Ltd, in 1986.	
She is responsible for maintaining the booking system in CTS. Customers book courses, and PC keeps a record of these (on the bookings board), sends acknowledgements and joining instructions, deals with enquiries and cancellations, supervises resourcing of courses and prepares a monthly report for the Training Director.	
PC reports to the Training Director and has an assistant, Sandy Southgate, who is responsible for providing resources for scheduled courses.	Doc. IR 14/1 Organisation Chart
PC's role is central to CTS's booking and billing system and as the company has grown, so have Pat's responsibilities.	
2. DETAILED PROCEDURES	
2.1 Bookings	
	Doc. IR 14/2 Booking form
Customers may book courses on the official CTS booking form and this is treated as a confirmed booking. Any other booking is described as provisional. These may be telephoned bookings, memos or letters from customers, or memos from the sales department.	
PC phones customers who have booked provisional places, five weeks before the course to gain confirmation. Customers may confirm in writing at any time. If a provisional booking is confirmed, it is marked with a tick on the bookings board to indicate a confirmed booking.	
2.2 Cancellations	
If a customer cancels up to five weeks before the course, they will not be charged. If they cancel less than five weeks before the course, they will be charged the full amount.	
2.3 Under subscribed courses	
If there are still places on a course five weeks before it runs, PC notifies Chris Hislop in Sales who will try to fill the remaining places. If the course does not reach the minimum number of delegates, CH and the Training Director will decide whether this course should run, and PC is informed (in writing) of their decision.	

Fig. 8.5 A formal interview record

Difficult interviews

The interviewing techniques described are based on good practice, and have been successfully used in numerous fact-finding interviews. However, there will be times when you find yourself in a situation where, even before you ask the first question, you realise that, because of the attitude of the interviewee, the interview is going to be difficult. It might be that the interviewee is very talkative, and begins to explain at high speed – and not very well – the procedures in their job. In this case, the control techniques outlined earlier would be appropriate. However, an interviewee who appears quiet and defensive is often more challenging, and an aggressive interviewee is, for many analysts, the most difficult of all. In both of the latter situations it would first be necessary to attempt to build rapport with the interviewee if the interview is to be effective. This is because real communication takes place at an emotional level as well as at a logical, verbal level. Building rapport means finding connections between yourself and the interviewee and developing these 'bridges' by:

- involving the interviewee in discussion;
- listening to and understanding their point of view;
- gaining their trust.

It takes time and energy to develop empathy by trying to see the situation from the interviewee's point of view, but if the interviewer is able to do this, the interviewee will be less likely to defend or justify their position. They may even look at their own point of view more objectively.

The analyst contributes to the building of rapport by:

- *Demonstrating personal warmth* – by smiling and showing interest.

- *Removing barriers*. Communication consists of one person – the sender – sending a message and another person – the receiver – receiving and understanding it and then responding in some way. In effective communication there will also be some degree of rapport between the sender and the receiver. Barriers can block this communication, as shown in Figure 8.6. These barriers may be *physical*, involving furniture arrangements, noise, or interruptions. They may be *semantic*, concerning the choice of words and how they are said – for example being too technical, using jargon, oversimplifying or engaging in sarcasm. The barriers might also be to do with *body language*: either the inappropriate use of body language by the interviewer or a failure to 'read' the body language of the interviewee. On this last point, the interviewer should be on the look-out for any significant change in the body language of the interviewer that suggests the interview is moving into a difficult area – for example turning away, avoiding eye contact, leaning back in the chair. Another signal to look out for is body language that doesn't match what is being said.

We have already discussed the key role of active listening in the fact-finding interview. In addition to listening, two other approaches to building rapport are:

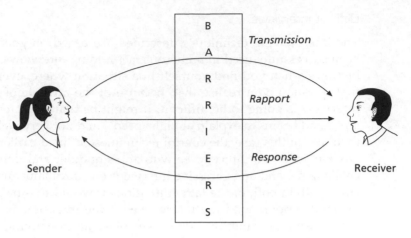

Fig. 8.6 Barriers to effective communication

- *Involving the interviewee.* We can involve the interviewee by asking for information or investigating their opinion. This can often *draw out* the intention, goals and position of others. For example: 'I'd be interested to hear your suggestions about how to deal with these problems.'

  The interviewer can also *encourage* the interviewee by giving credit to their contribution. For example: 'That's a very interesting point you have raised. Could you explain how that might work?'

  By being *responsive* to the interviewee's questions and concerns, the interviewer is building an atmosphere of trust. For example: 'I can understand your concern about your job, but at present this investigation only covers the current situation.'

- *Openness.* By being open about their motives and intentions, interviewers help to create that same behaviour in the interviewee. Disclosing information is one way to achieve openness. For example: 'If you are concerned about the recommendations, it may be possible to give you a copy of the report before it is published.'

  By accepting criticism without being defensive, we can increase our credibility on major points where it really matters with the interviewee. For example: 'You're right. I haven't taken all the points into consideration.'

  Asking for help lets the interviewee know that you need their input to find the solutions to their problems. For example: 'You know, I can't do this without your help.'

  Remember that your objective is always to build trust. As the confidence of the interviewee grows so will their openness and honesty. In situations where the interviewer is met with an aggressive attitude or some other strong emotion, it is important to bear in mind that this feeling is usually directed at the company or the system represented by the analyst rather than at the analyst personally.

8.3 Questionnaires

The use of a questionnaire might seem an attractive idea, as data can be collected from a lot of people without having to visit them all. Although this is true, the method should be used with care, as it is difficult to design a questionnaire that is both simple and comprehensive. Also, unless the questions are kept short and clear, they may be misunderstood by those questioned, making the data collected unreliable.

A questionnaire may be the most effective method of fact-finding to collect a small amount of data from a lot of people: for example, where staff are located over a widely spread geographical area; when data must be collected from a large number of staff; when time is short; and when 100% coverage is not essential. A questionnaire can also be used as a means of verifying data collected using other methods, or as the basis for the question-and-answer section of a fact-finding interview. Another effective use of a questionnaire is to send it out in advance of an interview. This will enable the respondent to assemble the required information before the meeting, which means that the interview can be more productive.

When designing a questionnaire, there are three sections to consider:

- a *heading section*, which describes the purpose of the questionnaire and contains the main references – name, staff identification number, date, etc.;

- a *classification section* for collecting information that can later be used for analysing and summarising the total data, such as age, sex, grade, job title, location;

- a *data section* made up of questions designed to elicit the specific information being sought by the analyst.

These three sections can clearly be observed in the questionnaire in Figure 8.7: the heading section is at the top (name and date), the next line down is for recording classification information (job title, department and section), and the data section is designed to gather information about the duties associated with a particular job.

The questionnaire designer aims to formulate questions in the data section that are not open to misinterpretation, that are unbiased, and which are certain to obtain the exact data required. This is not easy, but the principles of questioning described earlier in this chapter provide a useful guide. A mixture of open and closed questions can be used, although it is useful to restrict the scope of open questions so that the questionnaire focuses on the area under investigation. To ensure that your questions are unambiguous, you will need to test them on a sample of other people, and if the questionnaire is going to be the major fact-finding instrument the whole document will have to be field tested and validated before its widespread use.

One way of avoiding misunderstanding and gaining cooperation is to write a covering letter explaining the purpose of the questionnaire and emphasising the

XYZ CO. LTD – DUTIES LIST		
SURNAME AND INITIALS		DATE FORM COMPLETED
YOUR JOB TITLE	DEPARTMENT	SECTION

Enter each main duty you perform, and indicate how many hours per week it requires–

No.	DESCRIPTION OF DUTY	Approx. hours per week
	Other activities (lunch, tea-breaks, etc.)	
	TOTAL HOURS WORKED PER WEEK	

WHEN COMPLETED HAND THIS FORM TO YOUR SUPERVISOR

Fig. 8.7 Sample questionnaire

date by which the questionnaire should be returned. Even with this explanation, an expectation that all the questionnaires will be completed and returned is not realistic. Some people object to filling in forms, some will forget, and others delay completing them until they are eventually lost!

To conclude, then, a questionnaire can be a useful fact-finding instrument, but care must be taken with the design. A poor design can mean that the form is difficult to complete, which will result in poor-quality information being returned to the analyst.

8.4 Observation

The systems analyst is constantly observing, and observations often provide clues about why the current system is not functioning properly. Observations of the local environment during visits to the client site, as well as very small and unexpected incidents, can all be significant in later analysis, and it is important that they are recorded at the time.

The analyst may also be involved in undertaking planned or conscious observations when it is decided to use this technique for part of the study. This will involve watching an operation for a period to see exactly what happens. Clearly, formal observation should only be used if agreement is given and users are prepared to cooperate. Observation should be done openly, as covert observation can undermine any trust and goodwill the analyst manages to build up. The technique is particularly good for tracing bottlenecks and checking facts that have already been noted.

A checklist, highlighting useful areas for observation, is shown as Figure 8.8.

A related method is called *systematic activity sampling*. This involves making observations of a particular operation at predetermined times. The times are chosen initially by some random device, so that the staff carrying out the operation do not know in advance when they will next be under observation.

Working conditions
    light
    heat
    noise
    interruptions

Layout
    ease of access
    movement possible
    proximity to colleagues, filing systems and telephones

Ergonomics
    workstation arrangements for microcomputing, use of terminals and printers
    furniture layout
    adequacy of furnishings

Supervision
    management style
    availability when needed

Workload
    light, heavy, variable, bottlenecks

Pace and method of working
    peaks and troughs of activity
    procedures and standards

Fig. 8.8 Observation checklist

8.5 Record Searching

Time constraints can prevent systems analysts from making as thorough an investigation of the current system as they might wish. Another approach, which enables conclusions to be drawn from a sample of past and present results of the current system, is called *record searching*. This involves looking through written records to obtain quantitative information, and to confirm or quantify information already supplied by user staff or management. Information can be collected about:

- the volume of file data and transactions, frequencies, and trends;
- the frequency with which files are updated;
- the accuracy of the data held in the system;
- unused forms;
- exceptions and omissions.

Using this information, an assessment of the volatility of the information can be made, and the usefulness of existing information can be questioned if it appears that some file data is merely updated, often inaccurate or little used. All of the information collected by record searching can be used to cross-check information given by users of the system. This doesn't imply that user opinion will be inaccurate, but discrepancies can be evaluated and the reasons for them discussed.

Where there are a large number of documents, statistical sampling can be used. This will involve sampling randomly or systematically to provide the required quantitative and qualitative information. This can be perfectly satisfactory if the analyst understands the concepts behind statistical sampling, but is a very hazardous exercise for the untrained. One particularly common fallacy is to draw conclusions from a non-representative sample. Extra care should be taken in estimating volumes and data field sizes from the evidence of a sample. For instance, a small sample of cash receipts inspected during a mid-month slack period might indicate an average of 40 per day, with a maximum value of £1500 for any one item. Such a sample used indiscriminately for system design might be disastrous if the real-life situation was that the number of receipts ranged from 20 to 2000 per day depending upon the time in the month, and that, exceptionally, cheques for over £100,000 were received. It is therefore recommended that more than one sample is taken and the results compared to ensure consistency.

8.6 Document Analysis

When investigating the data flowing through a system another useful technique is to collect documents that show how this information is organised. Such documents might include reports, forms, organisation charts or formal lists. In order to fully understand the purpose of a document and its importance to the business, the analyst must ask questions about how, where, why and when it is used. This is called *document analysis*, and is another fact-finding technique available. It is particularly powerful when used in combination with one or more of the other techniques described in this chapter.

In the previous edition of this book we showed a Clerical Document Specification originally prepared by the UK National Computing Centre, and it still serves as a good example of what can be used to help with the process of document analysis. A copy of the form is shown as Figure 8.9. Even if the form cannot be fully completed at the first attempt, it will point to those topics that need further investigation.

8.7 Summary

As we have seen, there are a variety of methods that can be used by the systems analyst to gather information. These methods involve asking questions and collecting data.

Asking questions is a key activity, which can be achieved either by interviewing or through the use of a questionnaire. Interviewing is the most widely used fact-finding technique, and is at the heart of systems analysis. To be an effective interviewer, the analyst must work on their interpersonal skills, such as listening and building rapport, as well as developing effective recording techniques. Questionnaires should be used with care, and are only really appropriate when a relatively small amount of information is required from a large number of people or from remote locations.

Data can also be collected by other methods that do not involve asking questions directly, although their use may lead the analyst to further investigation. These methods include observation, record searching and document analysis. Observation can help in understanding where the current system is working well and where problems are being experienced, and can also provide clues as to why this is happening. Searching records enables the analyst to confirm or quantify information that has been provided by the client, whereas document analysis is a systematic approach to asking questions about documents collected during the investigation.

These techniques can be regarded as a tool kit that can be used flexibly by systems analysts during their investigation. They can be used in isolation, or in combination, to gather information about the current system and to understand the requirements for any new system. The way in which the data collected is recorded by the analyst is the subject of the next chapter.

Clerical Document Specification	Document description *Purchase Order*		System *POS*	Document *3*	Name *PUORD*	Sheet *1*
N C C	Stationery ref. *DS 46*		Size *A4*	Number of parts *4*	Method of preparation *Typed*	
	Filing sequence *by order number*			Medium *loose leaf binder*	Prepared/maintained by *HO Admin*	
	Frequency of preparation *as required*			Retention period *3 months after payment*	Location *HO Admin supervisor*	

Monthly VOLUME *S*	Minimum *20*	Maximum *300*	Av/Abs *120*	Growth rate/fluctuations *no growth likely*		

Users/recipients	Purpose	Frequency of use
– *HO Admin*	*Raise order*	*daily*
– *Purchase accounts*	*To check against supplier invoice*	*monthly*
– *Originator of order request*	*To check against delivery & authorise payment*	*weekly*

Ref.	Item	Picture	Occurrence	Value range	Source of data
1	*Supplier name*		*1 per order*		*POR*
2	*Item to be ordered*	*9 (6)*	*5 per order*	*000001–999999*	*POR*
3	*Quantity of item*	*9 (6)*	*as ref 2*	*000001–999999*	*POR*
4	*Est. cost of item*	*£999999.99*	*as ref 2*	*000001–999999*	*POR*
5	*Total order value*	*£999999.99*	*1 per order*	*000001–999999*	*POR*
6	*Delivery address*		*1 per order*		*POR*
7	*Authorised signature*		*1 per order*		*HO Admin*
8	*Date of order*	*99AA99*	*1 per order*	*rec'd date*	*HO Admin*
9	*Order number*	*9 (5)*	*1 per order*	*00000–99999*	*pre printed*

Notes

S 41

Author *DY*	Issue *3* Date *12.8.2002*

Fig. 8.9 NCC clerical document specification

Exercises

8.1 In this chapter, five different methods for the collection of information have been described. They can be used separately or in combination during fact-finding. Choose different circumstances from System Telecom to illustrate the usefulness of these methods.

8.2 Your boss is thinking about writing a book about data processing management. To help her come to a conclusion she has asked you to prepare a report identifying what's involved in writing such a book and what the benefits might be. You will have to interview her and one or two additional authors to gather information. How will you go about:

- preparing for these interviews;
- conducting the interviews;
- analysing the information?

What conclusion will you come to, and how will you tell your boss?

8.3 During the fact-finding stage of a big project, different activities are carried out by different members of the project team: for example, some people may investigate processing requirements while others analyse the data. This may mean that there are many different views about how the existing system works, and the nature of the new requirements. How can you ensure that all of the systems investigation work is consolidated into a coherent whole?

9 Systems Analysis: Recording the Information

9.1 Introduction

Having looked earlier at planning and at the process of asking questions and collecting data, we now look at the third stage of the PARIS model of systems analysis – *Recording the information*. Typically, the analyst collects a considerable amount of information during the investigation phase, which may include interview reports, observation records, sample documents, completed questionnaires and lists of problems and requirements. Some of this relates to the current system, and some to the new system required by the client.

It is important for the systems analyst to record this information in an unambiguous, concise manner that will be clear and accessible to others, and which can be used by other analysts and designers involved in developing the new system. Structured techniques were developed to help system developers to record information in this way, using diagrams and a limited amount of text, and in this chapter we introduce some of the key techniques.

As we saw in Chapter 2, structured analysis and design views information systems principally in two ways: first as data – the information that the system records – and second as processing – what the system does with this data. The most common techniques used for describing these two aspects of systems are data flow diagrams for processing, and entity models – also described as logical data structures or entity relationship diagrams – for data. Neither of these techniques, however, describes the precise order in which the system processes data. A third major view of the system, which describes the order in which external and internal events affect the system and the data, and brings together a view of the processing to complete the description of the system, is described in Chapter 11.

Structured techniques are used to model the existing manual or computer system using information gathered from users. These models are then modified and extended with new user requirements in order to produce models of the new, required, system. The model of the required system is based on the current system because there is usually a core set of processing that will still be required unless there has been a drastic change in the way the enterprise operates. The data held by the existing system is unlikely to change, although in most cases new data will be required.

This chapter introduces the techniques of data flow diagramming and entity modelling, describes how they are used, together with a data dictionary, to record information about the current system, and explains how a requirements catalogue is used to record new requirements. These activities are closely related, and are conducted in parallel during the early stages of requirements analysis.

Before introducing these recording techniques we shall briefly describe data dictionaries and CASE tools, which help the analyst to create and edit diagrams, and to store data in a structured and meaningful way. Without data dictionaries and CASE tools the large-scale application of structured methods would be difficult, if not impossible, to achieve.

9.2 Data Dictionaries and CASE Tools

An essential concept underlying the use of structured methods is that of the *data dictionary*. A data dictionary is used to record all those pieces of information about a system (textual or numeric) that cannot be recorded on diagrams. It is the underlying structure that links the different views of the system presented by different types of diagram. In SSADM, for example, the importance of the data dictionary is recognised in the concepts of *data flow models* (DFMs) and *logical data models* (LDMs), in which diagrams and their associated background documentation are considered as a whole. In effect it is a database that supports analysts and designers in their tasks of analysing, modelling and designing computer systems.

It is possible to use a paper-based data dictionary, but purpose-designed dictionaries based on commercial database management systems (DBMS) are now generally used. This is because they show the relationships between all the different components of the system's models and designs that are constructed in a project using structured methods. This enables the impact of changes in one part of a model to be traced through to other components, making it much easier to keep the models consistent and accurate.

CASE stands for Computer Aided Systems Engineering, and is a term used to describe any software tool designed to make the development of computer systems easier. A data dictionary system can therefore be considered a CASE tool, although the data dictionary concept predates that of CASE. The term is also used to describe drawing tools specifically designed for the production of the types of diagram used in structured methods. These tools make it much easier and quicker to create and change diagrams than using paper and pencil, or even general-purpose computer-based drawing tools. They also produce more professional and readable results than manual methods. CASE tools also incorporate drawing tools and a data dictionary, making it possible to check sets of diagrams for consistency and to see the results of changes. These tools can be used to generate components of the eventual physical system, such as the database design, from the system models produced during analysis, and can partially automate many trivial analysis and design tasks.

9.3 Data Flow Diagrams

Data flow diagrams are the most commonly used way of documenting the processing of current and required systems. As their name suggests, they are a pictorial way of showing the flow of data into, around and out of a system. They can be understood by users, and are less prone to misinterpretation than textual description. A complete set of DFDs provides a compact top-down representation of a system, which makes it easier for users and analysts to envisage the system as a whole.

9.3.1 DFD Components

DFDs are constructed using four major components: external entities, data stores, processes and data flows. Figure 9.1 shows how a DFD would be constructed using SSADM conventions, in which a process is represented by a rectangle, a data store by an open rectangle, a data flow by an arrow and an external entity by an ellipse.

- *External entities* represent the sources of data that enter the system or the recipients of data that leave the system. Examples are clerks who enter data into the system or customers who receive letters produced by the system. In SSADM they are shown as ellipses with a name and a unique identifier consisting of a single lower-case letter.

- *Data stores* represent stores of data within the system. Examples are computer files or databases or, in a manual system, paper files held in filing cabinets. They are drawn as open-ended rectangles with a unique identifier, a box at the closed end and the name of the store in the open section. Manual data stores

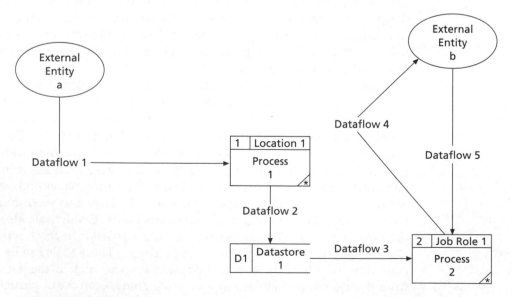

Fig. 9.1 Basic data flow diagram components

are identified by the letter M followed by a number, and identifiers for computerised stores are prefixed by a D. Data stores cannot be directly linked by data flows either to each other or to external entities without an intervening process to transform the data.

- *Processes* represent activities in which data is manipulated by being stored or retrieved or transformed in some way. They are shown as larger rectangles with a numeric identifier in a box at the top left corner. The location where the process takes place or the job role performing it is recorded in a box in the top right corner and is used only in diagrams of the current physical system. The name of the process is recorded in the remaining area at the bottom. Process names should be unambiguous, and should convey as much meaning as possible without being too long. In general, names should take the form of an imperative and its object, as in Open Account. Generalised verbs such as Process or Update are not usually helpful. Some practitioners insist on the use of verb-fronting phrases for process descriptions to ensure that the process is an action performed by the business.

- *Data flows* represent the movement of data between other components, for example a report produced by a process and sent to an external entity. They are shown as named arrows connecting the other components of the diagram. Data flows are generally shown as one-way only. Data flows between external entities are shown as dotted lines.

It may be necessary to draw the same external entity or data store more than once on the same DFD in order to make the diagram clear and to avoid too many crossing lines. An external entity that appears more than once in the same diagram is shown with a diagonal line at the top left. Duplicate data stores are given an additional vertical line on the left side of their reference boxes.

9.3.2 DFD Hierarchies

A system is rarely simple enough to be shown on a single DFD, and so a hierarchical set is produced. This consists of a top-level DFD in which the processes are major system functions described in more detail by one or more associated lower-level DFDs. The process of breaking a higher-level (parent) DFD into its constituent lower-level (child) DFDs is known as *levelling*. There are no particular rules to levelling, the aim being simply to make the diagrams less cluttered and therefore easier to read and understand. As a rule of thumb, however, processes on the lowest level, called *elementary processes*, should correspond to single events or actions affecting the system, for example cashing a cheque in a banking system.

Figure 9.2 shows a level 1 (top level) DFD, and Figure 9.3 shows a DFD from the next level down. The diagrams illustrate a number of additional conventions that have not been described yet.

The first thing to notice is that the child DFD – level 2 – has a box round it. This corresponds to a process box on the level 1 DFD and contains the same identifier. Processes on the child are given identifiers that show that they are

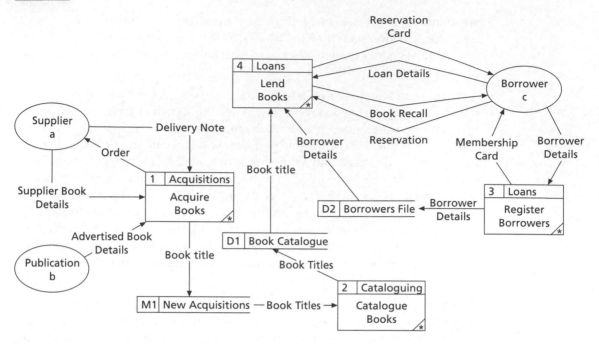

Fig. 9.2 Level 1 DFD for a library system

sub-processes of the one on the parent by adding a number to the identifier of the parent, separated by a point: for example, process 1 on the level 2 DFD for process 4 has the identifier 4.1. The values of these numbers have no significance, as DFDs do not show the sequence of processing, only the flows of data between them. In this they differ from flowcharts, which are specifically intended to show a sequence of actions and decisions. Some of the process boxes on the diagrams are shown with an asterisk enclosed by a diagonal in the bottom right-hand corner. This means that the process concerned is not broken down any further and is therefore an elementary process. These occur in Figures 9.1, 9.2 and 9.3.

External entities, data flows and data stores can also be broken down into more detail on lower-level DFDs. External entities that are components of a parent external entity are distinguished by suffixing numbers to the parent identifier. In a similar way child data stores are referenced by their parent's identifier followed by a lower-case letter. Data store 1 within process 4, for example, has the identifier D4/1. Data flows are not given any reference other than their name, but a data flow shown as a single line on a parent DFD may represent a number of flows on its child. On level 1 DFDs double-headed arrows may be used as a short-hand way of representing two or more flows in opposite directions in lower-level DFDs.

Diagrams alone are not sufficient to convey an understanding of the system being modelled. It is important that DFD components are described in more detail than can be conveyed by the short names they are given in the diagram. For example, data flows consist of a list of data items that must be documented in a data dictionary so that the data items can be related to attributes in the data model. The term *data flow model* (DFM) is used in SSADM to refer to a complete

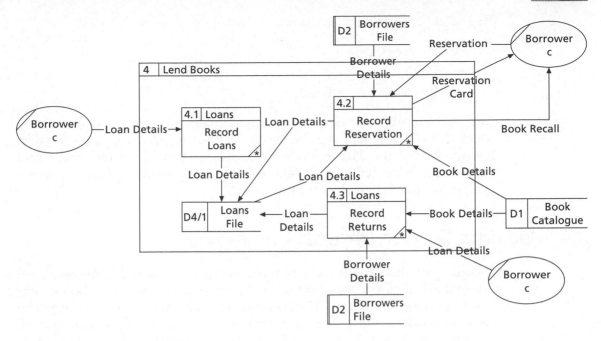

Fig. 9.3 Level 2 DFD for Lend Books

set of DFDs describing a system, plus the necessary data dictionary documentation of objects shown on the diagrams. The extent to which higher-level DFDs are documented may vary, but it is essential that objects at the bottom levels are clearly described in order that the diagrams can be unambiguously understood, and to ensure that information about the system is carried through to later stages of the project.

Generally speaking, only external data flows – data flows into and out of the system – need to be described in detail. These *input/output* (I/O) descriptions contain:

- identifier of the object *from* which the data flows (e.g. the process number);
- identifier of the object *to* which the data flows;
- data flow name;
- description of the data flow.

In a similar way only the bottom level – the elementary processes – need to be described, as this is where the detailed processing occurs. Elementary process descriptions consist of:

- process number;
- process name;
- description of the process – this may be a simple textual description, or may use more rigorous techniques such as structured English or decision tables.

External entity descriptions contain:

- external entity identifier;
- external entity name;
- description of the external entity.

Data stores are initially documented in a similar way, by a text description associated with the data store identifier and name. However, once the data flow model and the data model have become reasonably stable, data stores are documented in terms of the entities that they contain, as this provides a good way of cross-referencing the two models.

9.4 Modelling Current Physical Processing

So far we have described the structure and content of DFDs and DFMs but, given a clean sheet of paper at the beginning of a project, how do you build up your model of the existing system? The basic answer to this question is that you talk to users of the system and, using the techniques already described, gradually work down from a high-level view showing major functional areas by inserting more detailed processing into DFD levels that you create below these as you become more familiar with the system. It is important that this is done with constant feedback from the users to make sure that you have got things right. The identification of functional areas and lower-level processes is subjective, but provided the diagrams are used as a means of communication between analysts and users a realistic consensus view of the system can be agreed.

Two areas may cause difficulty when starting out. One is defining the boundary of the system. What are the parts of the business to be included in the system? And once the system boundary has been defined, what are the boundaries of the top-level functional areas included in the system? Two subsidiary techniques help to answer these questions: context diagrams and document flow diagrams.

A context diagram is similar to a top-level DFD but with the whole system shown as a 'black box'. In other words, external entities and data flows into and out of the system are drawn but no processes or data stores are shown. An example is shown in Figure 9.4. Context diagrams are used early in a project as a means of describing and agreeing the scope or boundary of the system to be developed.

Document flow diagrams may be used as a preliminary to producing DFDs for the current system in the early stages of a project. As their names suggest, they are used to show how documents move round in a manual system. The example in Figure 9.5 shows how documents and the people or departments who handle them are represented. By drawing boundaries around parts of the diagram, different functional areas of the system can be distinguished. Areas of the diagram outside the boundaries are external to the system and will appear as external entities and external data flows on the current system DFDs. The bounded areas will appear as processes on the level 1 DFD.

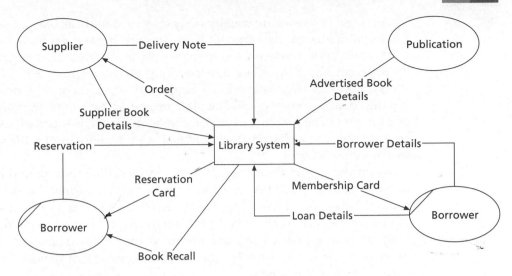

Fig. 9.4 A context diagram

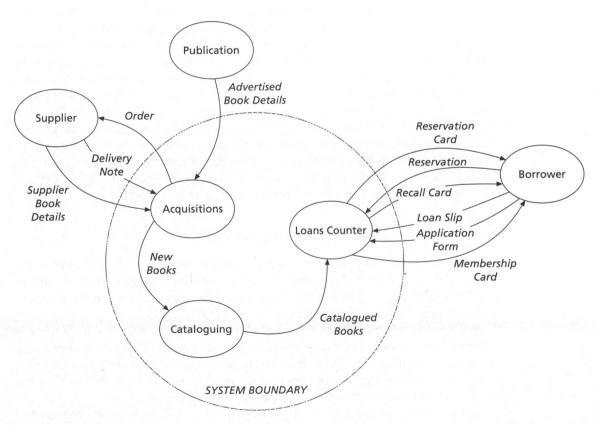

Fig. 9.5 Document flow diagram

Top-level processes are usually fairly easy to identify as they often correspond to departments in the organisation. In our library example Acquisitions, Cataloguing and Loans are likely to be separate sections in a large library, run by different librarians. They indicate the presence of processes called Acquire Books, Catalogue Books and Lend Books. However, these activities may not be organised into sections, and the staff in one section may perform a number of processes. The presence of major data stores such as the book catalogue and the loans file can also indicate different areas of activity even if the work is done by the same section.

When the top-level processes have been identified they should be looked at in more detail to see if they need to be broken down further. Lend Books, in our example, has been broken down into Issue Books, Reserve Books and Recall Books. These may in their turn be broken down still further. Issue Books may be split into Record Book Loan and Record Book Return. The aim is to break the processing down until the bottom-level processes each handle a single event such as the return of a book.

9.5 Entity Models

An entity model represents the network of relationships between classes of things that need to have data recorded about them in the system. The term *entity type* or *entity* is used to describe a 'class of things'. Having drawn an entity model, it is possible to show how the system can use these relationships by following them as paths for obtaining related pieces of data, either for update or for reporting and enquiry purposes. For example, many different transactions may be made on a bank account during a month. In order to print a monthly statement for the account, all the transactions must be found and a relationship between the *entities* 'bank account' and 'transaction' must be present. The general concept of a bank account corresponds to an entity, whereas the bank account for a particular customer is known as an *occurrence* or *instance* of the entity. As this example shows, entities represent not only physical objects but also conceptual objects, such as 'bank account', or events, such as 'transaction'.

9.5.1 The Logical Data Structuring Technique

As we are using SSADM as our example structured method, we'll look at the *logical data structure* (LDS), which is the name given to the entity model in SSADM. LDSs are simpler than DFDs in that they have only two major components – entities and the relationships between them.

Entities, as already described, are classes of things about which data is recorded in a system. An entity is usually represented as a rectangle containing its name, written as a singular noun. It is important that entities are given meaningful names, preferably ones that are used by or will be understood by the users. In SSADM the entity rectangles have rounded corners.

Relationships are shown as lines linking entities. Relationships can be traversed in both directions, and so each end of a relationship is named in order to describe it from the point of view of the entity at that end. Most relationships are between one master entity and many detail entities. This is known as a *one-to-many relationship* and is shown by giving the line a 'crow's foot' at the many or detail end as shown in Figure 9.6, which represents a relationship between one 'bank account' and many 'transactions'. Other methods may use an arrow rather than a crow's foot. Relationships may also be many-to-many or one-to-one. This classification of relationships is known as the *degree of the relationship*. One-to-one relationships are uncommon, as it is usually found that two entities that are linked in this way can be combined to give a single entity. Many-to-many relationships are more common, but it is usual to resolve them by introducing a new 'link' entity that is a detail of the two original entities, as shown in Figure 9.7. In this case the many-to-many relationship between 'book' and 'borrower' is resolved by introducing the entity 'loan', which has a relationship with both 'borrower' and 'book'.

Relationships are also classified in terms of their *optionality*. This describes the situation where the analyst considers whether an entity occurrence at one end of a relationship can ever be present in the system without the presence of a corresponding occurrence of the entity at the other end of the relationship. Figure 9.8 shows the different types of optionality that may occur.

Relationships can be described as *exclusive*. One type of exclusivity occurs if a detail entity has two (or more) masters and an occurrence of the detail may be linked to only one of the masters but not both. The other is the converse situation where a master may be linked to only one of two or more sets of details. Exclusive relationships are shown by drawing an exclusion arc to connect them, as shown in Figure 9.9.

The first diagram shows that an appointment may be made with only one doctor or one nurse or one midwife. An appointment may not be made, for example, with a doctor and a nurse, or with two doctors. The second diagram states that a doctor may have responsibility either for one or more research

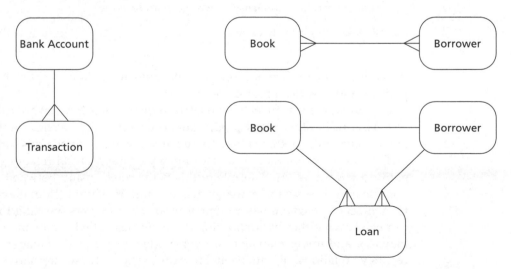

Fig. 9.6 A one-to-many relationship   **Fig. 9.7** Resolving a many-to-many relationship

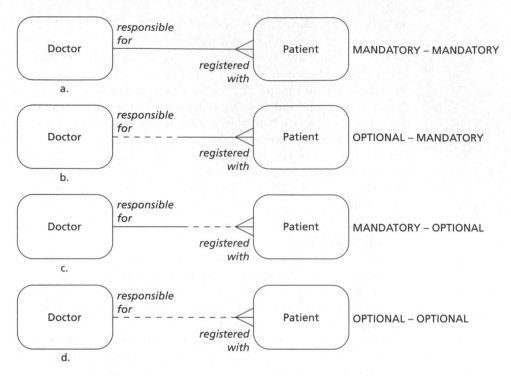

a.   a doctor *must* be responsible for one or more patients and
a patient *must* be registered with one and only one doctor.

b.   a doctor *may* be responsible for one or more patients and
a patient *must* be registered with one and only one doctor
(for instance if some doctors only do research).

c.   a doctor *must* be responsible for one or more patients and
a patient *may* be registered with one and only one doctor
(for instance if temporarily registered patients are not allocated to particular doctors).

d.   a doctor *may* be responsible for one or more patients and
a patient *may* be registered with one and only one doctor.

Fig. 9.8 Optionality in relationships

programmes or for one or more patients, but cannot have responsibility for both
patients and research programmes.

It is possible for entities to be related to themselves in what are called *recursive
relationships*. In other words, individual occurrences of entities can be related to
other occurrences of that entity. There are two ways in which this can happen.

The first is where there is a one-to-many or hierarchical relationship between
entity occurrences. An example of this is the relationship between managers in
a company. The senior manager has a number of middle managers working
for him, each of whom has a number of lower managers working for them. This
can be shown either by identifying three entities called senior manager, middle
manager and lower manager, or by a single entity called manager, which has a
recursive relationship with itself. Figure 9.10 shows these alternative approaches.
Notice that the recursive relationship is optional at both ends. This is because

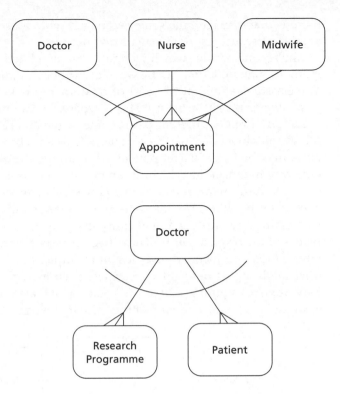

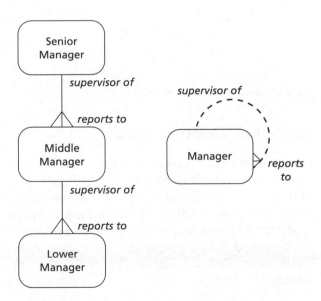

Fig. 9.9 Exclusivity in relationships

Fig. 9.10 Recursive relationships

there is one manager, the senior manager, who does not report to another manager and because junior managers do not supervise other managers.

The second way in which an entity can be related to itself is where there is a many-to-many relationship between occurrences, indicating a network structure. The classic example of this sort of relationship is known as the *bill of materials processing* or BOMP structure. This is where, for example, a piece of machinery is made up of many different parts, some of which are sub-assemblies that themselves contain a range of different parts. This structure is not a hierarchy, as some parts may be listed as components at a number of different levels of assembly. One way in which the structure can be shown is as a single entity linked to itself by a many-to-many relationship. However, a more helpful representation is gained by breaking the many-to-many relationship into two one-to-many relationships and creating a new entity that acts as a link between different occurrences of the original entity. These two representations are shown in Figure 9.11, where food products are used as an example. For instance, jam is a food product made up of other food products such as fruit and sugar. However, jam may appear as an ingredient of a cake, which also has fruit or sugar specified as ingredients independently of their use in the jam.

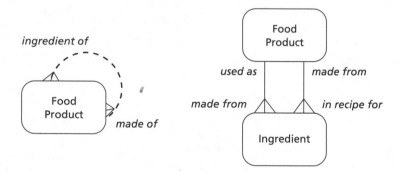

Fig. 9.11 More recursive relationships

9.5.2 The Logical Data Model

As with DFDs, LDS diagrams are not able to carry all the information that analysts need to record about a system. A logical data model (LDM) consists of an LDS diagram and a set of entity descriptions and relationship descriptions, which give more detail about the diagram components.

Relationship are usually documented in both directions. In other words, they are described from the point of view of each of the two entities that make up the relationship. For each relationship 'half', the following information should be recorded:

- first entity name (the entity at this end of the relationship);

- second entity name (the entity at the other end);

- relationship name or phrase shown on the LDS;

- description of the relationship (in business terms);
- degree of the relationship (one to many, many to one, etc.);
- cardinality of the relationship (the number of second entities expected to be linked to each first entity – this may be an average or, better, a distribution);
- optionality of the relationship;
- list of users and their access rights to the relationship (update, read, etc.).

Entity descriptions should contain at least the following information:

- entity name;
- alternative names (synonyms);
- description of the entity;
- the owner (this is the user to whom the data in the entity belongs);
- list of users and their access rights to the entity (update, read, etc.);
- expected number of occurrences of the entity and growth rates;
- rules for archiving and deleting entity occurrences.

One of the things we also need to record about an entity is the list of attributes it contains. An *attribute*, or data item, is a piece of information that the system needs to record about an entity. Attributes may be held by an entity purely as information, or they may play a role in relationships between entities, in which case they are known as *key attributes* or *keys*. Keys are principally of two types: prime keys and foreign keys.

Prime keys are used to identify different occurrences of the same entity. The entity 'bank account' is a generalisation of many different occurrences of individual bank accounts. To extend our previous example, in order to produce a statement for a particular account on demand it must be possible to pick out that account from all the other accounts in the system. The way to do this is to identify, or invent, a piece of information about the account that is unique and distinguishes it from all other accounts. The obvious candidate for this in our example is the account number.

Foreign keys are attributes that are also present as prime keys on other entities. They are another means of indicating that there is a relationship between the two entities. The entity that has the attribute as its prime key is the master of the entity in which it is a foreign key.

It is not always possible to use single attributes as keys. Sometimes a combination of two or more attributes is needed to identify an entity uniquely and act as its prime key. Keys consisting of more than one attribute are known as *compound keys*, whereas keys that contain only one attribute are called *simple keys*.

9.6 Modelling Current Data

Modelling the data in a system is in some ways more difficult than modelling the processes. Most people tend to think of what they do and how they do it. They think about the processing aspect of their job, more than the data or information they handle.

The starting point in developing a logical data structure (LDS) is to identify the entities that must be included. An initial set of the major entities is often fairly easy to develop. When reading documents that are used in or which describe the current system, or when talking to users, certain nouns will crop up over and over again. Frequent repetition of nouns such as 'customer' and 'account' will suggest the need for entities to represent them in a banking system, for example. A bank statement will reinforce the importance of 'account' as an entity by having an item called 'account number' on it. This indicates both an entity and its possible key. The example of a bank statement is also presented as a warning, however. It might appear at first sight that an entity 'statement' should also be present on the LDS. This would only be so, however, if information about the bank statement itself needed to be held on the system. Virtually all the information on a statement belongs to some other entity such as 'customer', 'account' or 'transaction'. Probably the only information about the statement itself is the date it was produced, and so the only reason for having a 'statement' entity would be if a chronological record of when statements were sent to customers was required.

Once an initial list of entities has been identified, a first attempt at an LDS can be made by considering the relationships between them. Some relationships may seem fairly obvious. For example, a customer may have many accounts and, at first sight, one might think that an account might only be held by one customer. This would be represented by a one-to-many relationship between 'customer' and 'account' on the LDS. However, all possible relationships between entities should be examined and decisions made on whether they are required or not. Drawing a matrix that cross-references entities to each other may help here. The exact rules for each relationship must then be established by questioning the users. It may turn out, in our example, that joint accounts are allowed and that the correct relationship is many-to-many. In early versions of the LDS produced by the analyst, many-to-many relationships can be left on the diagram, and they will normally be resolved into two one-to-many relationships with a new 'link' entity at a future stage. In our example this might be called 'account holder'. This example shows how some, less obvious, entities may be identified in the course of examining the relationships between the major entities.

An example of a simple LDS for a library system is shown in Figure 9.12. This should be compared with Figure 9.7 to show how additional entities and more complex relationships may be discovered by investigating data requirements in more detail.

An LDS should be clearly laid out, with as few crossing lines as possible. The convention is normally to have masters positioned above details so that entities with the least number of occurrences tend to be at the top of the page and those with most at the bottom. This often means that the major entities appear in the top half of the diagram and lesser entities in the bottom half. An LDS is likely to need amending and/or extending many times before it reaches its final state, and so the use of a purpose-designed CASE tool is recommended to reduce the amount of time this takes and to give the most readable results.

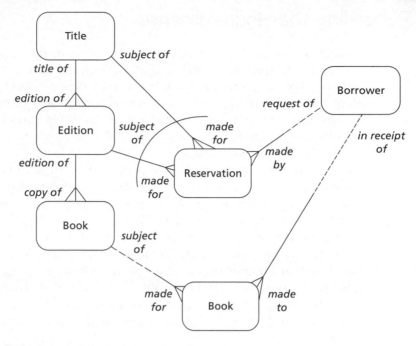

Fig. 9.12 Simple logical data structure for a library system

9.7 The Data Catalogue

As its name suggests, the data catalogue is a list of all the data items or attributes that have been identified as being required in the system. Attributes are the individual items of data that are used to describe entities in the logical data model and which travel along data flows in DFMs, where they are listed on the I/O descriptions. The data catalogue is in fact a subset of the data dictionary and is concerned with individual data items and the values they may take.

The information that should be recorded about attributes includes:

- attribute name;
- alternative names (synonyms);
- description of the attribute;
- attribute location (entity or data flow);
- relationships to other attributes;
- format (including units and length);
- values (or ranges of values) the attribute is allowed to have;
- rules for deriving the value of attribute occurrences;
- optionality of the attribute;
- the owner, i.e. the user to whom the data in the attribute belongs;
- list of users and their access rights to the attribute (update, read, etc.).

9.8 Recording the Requirements

Requirements for the new system are recorded in the requirements catalogue together with the source of each requirement, the user or user area to which it belongs, how important it is, and how it is to be satisfied by the new system. Requirements should also be cross-referenced to any processes in the current system DFM that carry out related processing. This makes it easier to map the requirements onto the current system DFM in order to develop the required system DFM later in the project.

The requirements catalogue is begun early in a project, as soon as any information has been gathered, but entries are developed and refined throughout the analysis and design stages as more is learned of the system and as the views of users and developers crystallise.

A requirement is commonly documented as a functional requirement – what the system must do in business terms – and one or more associated non-functional requirements that specify measures of how the system is to deliver the functionality. For example, a functional requirement might be to print library membership cards. An associated non-functional requirement might be that the cards should be printed within 30 seconds of confirming membership details.

The information that should be recorded for each requirement consists of:

- requirement identifier;
- source of the requirement (the person who raised it);
- the owner of the requirement (the person or department to which it applies);
- priority or importance of the requirement;
- description of the functional requirement;
- list of the associated non-functional requirements and their values or measures;
- benefits of satisfying the requirement;
- possible solutions to the requirement;
- cross-references to related documents and requirements.

9.9 Summary

This chapter has introduced logical data modelling for recording data and data flow modelling for processing. These techniques are central to virtually all structured analysis methods. The techniques use diagrams to make it easier to visualise the system as a whole and the way the components fit together. They also record background information that cannot be shown on diagrams. This detail is recorded in a data dictionary or CASE tool that enables it to be structured in a way that ties in with the diagrams.

In the early stages of a project the techniques are used to describe the workings of the system that is to be replaced. This system is usually a mixture of manual and computer processing. The reason for modelling the current system is that it is rare for the underlying data and core processing to need to change radically. The aim is usually to improve and extend the system model and to take advantage of more modern hardware and software to provide better performance and facilities. The current system model therefore provides a starting point for developing the new system model.

At the same time that the current system model is being developed, requirements for the new system are captured and recorded in a requirements catalogue. The new data and processing requirements are then applied to the current system model to produce a data flow model and a logical data model for the new system. The way in which this is done is described in Chapter 11.

Exercises

9.1 The case study information you have shows a level 1 DFD and two level 2 DFDs for System Telecom. Using the level 2 DFDs as models, and the other case study information, draw a level 2 DFD for the process 'Issue Bills'.

9.2 Having drawn the level 2 DFD for 'Issue Bills' write the elementary process description for one of the process boxes.

9.3 Using the level 1 DFD for System Telecom and other case study information, what are the major entities of the Customer Services System? There are more entities than this, so how have you chosen to identify the major ones? A good place to start is to list the criteria for identifying entities.

9.4 Having identified the major entities from the Customer Services System, choose one of them and identify the data items that make up that entity.

9.5 Read the Shark Loan Company case example and prepare a single level data flow diagram from it.

9.6 From the Ravenelli Ice Cream case example construct an entity model to support the ordering, accounting, manufacturing and purchasing of materials.

9.7 From the LozCo case example in Chapter 1, p. 33, construct a logical data structure diagram of the activities of LozCo.

9.8 From the LozCo case example construct a physical DFD.

Case Study: The Shark Loan Company

The Shark Loan Company provides finance for car purchasers who are buying second-hand cars. The company is in contact with a large number of dealers in the UK and offers a low interest rate loan scheme for selected purchasers. Dealers will use different loan companies depending on the status of their purchaser. When a purchaser requires finance the dealer sends a credit application on behalf of the purchaser to the local Shark office. The local office enters these details on to a client file and sends them to a credit-checking agency in London. When the agency replies by post, the reply is recorded in the client file by the local office. The client file is processed daily by the regional office, which takes the client details from the file and produces a set of finance documents, which are then sent to the dealer when a client's application has been approved by the checking agency in London. The regional office updates the client file when this happens. The dealer then obtains the purchaser's signature on the finance documents and sends these back to the loans department in the Shark regional office. The client file is updated to show the loan start date, and the Loans Department passes the finance documents to the Payments Office, which either sends a standing order to the appropriate bank or sends a payment book to the client.

Shark maintains a strict check on its debts, and wants to hold a record of the payments received from its clients throughout the period of the loan. It is considering introducing at least two more methods of payment in addition to the standing orders and payment books. Shark will allow a client to have more than one loan provided each loan has received credit approval.

Case Study: Ravenelli Ice Cream

Ravenelli Ice Cream supplies owner-drivers with ice cream products for direct sale to the public. Each owner-driver gives Ravenelli an order for the supplies they need showing the van – identified by the registration number – and the driver's name. Each driver brings in one form per day for his or her own stock. The forms cover a number of items such as cones, wafers, choc ices, chocolate bars, 99s, and many different types of ice lolly. In addition to their own van sales the vans have a number of institutional and wholesale customers to whom they deliver, and they submit an order form for each customer showing that customer's code number, name and address. Ravenelli invoice these customers directly and pay commission to the van drivers for obtaining and delivering the order.

Ravenelli themselves buy many of their products from wholesalers, and they have accounts with over 500 different suppliers, who supply them with a range of products. Most products can usually be obtained from more than one supplier.

Ravenelli also supply ice cream directly to bulk trade outlets such as supermarkets, hotels and hospitals. These outlets send purchase orders to Ravenelli on a regular basis. Some of the items that Ravenelli supply are made up from basic ingredients on the premises. Ice cream, for example, is usually made from milk, cream, emulsifier, palm nut oil and a number of vitamins, colourings and other synthetic ingredients. Ravenelli have always wanted to be able to automatically calculate the additional raw material ingredients they will require when they work out the total amount of ice cream they are going to have to supply in a day.

Ice cream is manufactured by a fairly simple mixing process that uses uniquely numbered and identified confectionery-mixing machines to ensure that certain flavours and types of ice cream are mixed only in certain machines. Ravenelli have over 300 ice cream recipes, and each machine will accept only certain ones. All machines are capable of mixing at least five different recipes. A code number identifies every recipe, and this code number is the same number that is used to identify the finished products that are supplied to the various outlets.

All products have a product code that identifies them uniquely. Some products are made up from other products. A Whipperoo Special, for example (product code WS1200), uses basic ice cream, which is made from the above ingredients, together with chocolate chips, raspberry sauce and several other ingredients. Ravenelli hold stock of all the ingredients they use, and treat the 'made-up' items such as the basic ice cream mix as another stock item, as they create it in bulk on a weekly basis.

10 Object-Oriented Methods

10.1 Introduction

Object-oriented (OO) methods allow the developer to exploit the technology of distributed computing environments, Internet-based systems and communications software and tools. The structured methods approach, emerging in an age of corporate systems development and centralised database software, was often found to be unsuited to the development of networked, graphically interfaced systems, particularly when those systems were developed incrementally using distributed computing.

Distributed computing encourages the development of small, free-standing systems that are capable of providing user benefits they require very rapidly. These systems will tend to encapsulate the data and the application it serves on a PC or a small network of PCs and communicate with other systems using messages or with file transfers. Whereas the structured systems approach seeks to partition the system by processes and to lead to large corporate databases, the OO approach identifies real-world objects, and, by modelling their behaviour, uses these as the discrete building blocks of the new system. The free-standing PC with its single application supporting a specific function, maintaining details of customers or suppliers, for example, is physically the forerunner of the OO-designed system, where the customer is a class of object with methods associated with it to maintain its currency and validity.

The OO approach originated in software engineering, and it is commonplace to find coded examples of objects in texts that describe OO from the software engineer's perspective. As the method has become more widely understood, it has been applied to the analysis and design of systems and has thus become more acceptable as a tool for the systems analyst. Introducing an OO approach where the legacy systems have been developed using structured methods can involve major redevelopment of both software and organisational structures. The term *business process re-engineering* is often applied to this type of development, and the experienced system analyst will approach such projects with caution.

10.2 Principles of OO

There are a number of principles that are associated with OO methods, and it is difficult to rank these in importance. Three terms most frequently cited in this respect, however, are *inheritance*, *encapsulation* and *polymorphism*.

10.2.1 Inheritance

Inheritance is derived from the idea of objects forming classes. In simple terms, an object can be defined at a high or *superclass* level with certain characteristics and certain procedures that are then inherited as properties by the lower or *sub-classes* of the object. For example, an employee in a company has a name and an address, and there is a procedure for acquiring, checking and changing these data items. Employees may, more specifically, belong to particular employment categories – machine operators paid according to their technical grade or salespersons paid according to their bonus status. Each of these lower-level classes will have their own procedures or methods and their own unique items of data. Inheritance, however, allows the developer to structure the system so that the procedures created at a general level can be reused or *inherited* at the lower level. In addition to the economies in development costs generated by this reuse of software, the generalisation, inherent in the approach, leads to a more uniform and consistent user interface. The employee is a *class* of object and the machine operator is a *subclass* of it. The salesperson is another *subclass* of the object employee.

Objects and object classes are fundamental building blocks in the OO approach. They provide the structure model for the system in the same way that the entity model does for the structured methods approach. Identifying classes is both an analysis and a design activity, and the designer must make decisions about the level of generalisation to be applied to the system. The definition of an entity in structured systems is often given as 'something the system wishes to hold data about'. A formal definition of an object, first set out in Coad and Yourdon (1990) is 'An abstraction of something in a problem domain, reflecting the capabilities of the system to keep information about it, interact with it, or both'. This is more difficult to envisage, so we cling to the shorter explanation of 'something the system wishes to hold data about'. Objects can initially be identified by the use of nouns in a requirement's definition. A banking system might have a high-level requirement specified as 'to provide cash to customers using cash cards from cash points and from service counters in banks, maintaining customer accounts'. The objects that can be identified from this requirement would be a cash point or a service counter or a customer or a bank or a cash card. Here the analyst is using the concept of the object as an analytical tool to help understand the problem domain. In the design phase the concept will be reapplied to develop the necessary software.

The analyst must identify abstractions in the objects to be able to define the superclasses. The cash point and the service counter both perform a similar function, and the data items they use and the operations they perform may lead to a superclass being defined. An attribute of the superclass might be 'cash available' and the operation might be 'reduce available cash'. At the terminal and the service counter level each of these subclasses will have specific attributes and operations. The terminal subclass might have attributes of cash point identifier and cash point location, and these attributes might have operations such as 'Store location ID' specifically associated with the terminal subclass. The service counter subclass might have attributes such as bank teller's name and branch address associated with it, and recording these attributes might be an operation linked to them. The attributes used by these objects are said to be 'encapsulated' within the object, and as such they cannot be accessed directly by another object. When another object wishes to obtain the location id of the automated terminal then it does so by sending a message to the terminal object asking it to use its own retrieval method to obtain the terminal id and to transmit it to the requesting object. In software terms, this communication facility is performed by programs sometimes referred to as *middleware* or more correctly as an *object request broker*. Where the software system is supplied by a single supplier such as Microsoft, the object request broker facility is transparent to the users, and hence linked and embedded objects have become a familiar concept to users operating in this environment. Microsoft users are familiar with the facility, which allows them to retrieve data from an Access database and use it in a spreadsheet or to reference a Word file from the database. When the development seeks to associate objects encapsulated by different software systems then the passing of messages becomes more complex, and protocols such as that for open database connectivity (ODBC) are required to allow the exchange of data.

10.2.2 Encapsulation

Encapsulation is an essential characteristic of OO development. The development of relational database systems set a goal of separating processes from data so that changes to the data structure could be made without necessitating changes to the processes that manipulate this data. In OO the development goal is set differently. The data held by the object can be accessed, read or updated only by the operations that are defined for that object. A message has to be sent to the object requesting it to perform the appropriate operation and to return the value requested. In the database approach the read instruction and the attributes to be read can be specified by the enquiry process using an SQL statement. The object-oriented method requires software to pass the request from one object to another object so that the operations can be performed by each object in their own way. An analogy could be drawn by imagining that each object, its operations and data are held on separate PCs using incompatible software. One might use a program written in Pascal and another might use a program written using MS-Access. In terms of the case study included as Appendix 1, Denton Motor Holdings, an object called Customers might be held on the first of these machines and an object called FinancialTransactions might be held on the second machine. To associate a financial transaction with a customer, the OO system would require a message-passing facility to ask the Pascal-based system to read its customer file using the appropriate read commands and to ask the MS-Access based system to locate a particular financial transaction for that customer. The software used to pass these messages is the *object request broker*. Microsoft's Windows implements many of the requirements of an object request broker transparently by facilitating the linking of objects manipulated by its own software products such as MS Word, MS Access and MS PowerPoint. Although this is not always theoretically satisfying to the OO specialist, and the use of Microsoft's specific proprietary standard can impede communication with other objects, the facility is extremely productive for many application areas.

10.2.3 Polymorphism

The term *polymorphism* first occurred in the English language in 1839, and was defined as 'the occurrence of something in several different forms'. It has been adopted in OO to encourage designers to use common operations to do similar things. Although the operations required to close an object such as a spreadsheet may be completely different from those used to close a text file, both operations are known as *close*. When an object issues a message to another object to perform an operation it does not need to know how that operation is performed, or even what class of object the request is being passed to. The message *jump* will convey different meanings to a horse at a fence, a paratrooper in an airplane and a person in a burning building, yet each of these classes of object understands the message and performs the operations that are appropriate to their class. In a company accounting system, a budget object might want a total commitment value from a number of other objects to calculate an overall expenditure figure. A message requesting these objects to 'calculate total to date' might be executed in many different ways by objects such as an employee, an inventory item, a sub-contractor, or an expense claim. Polymorphism encourages the designer to identify similarities between the ways objects perform and to define them in abstract terms. This abstraction makes systems less interdependent, and so makes it easier to modify subsystems independently. Polymorphism is a development that can be compared to the term *data independence*, which was coined in the 1970s to refer to the separation of data structure from program structure provided by database management software. The availability of cheap processing power has led to distributed processing as users develop their own systems independently, and polymorphism has become the new goal. The principles expressed in the OO approach define the way these developments can occur within a framework that allows different systems to interact successfully without the need for bespoke communication and linking software to create an MIS system.

10.3 Object-Oriented Models

In Chapter 2 we defined a meta-model for a systems methodology as being made up of three model types. These three types were defined as:

- business system models;
- static structure models;
- dynamic behaviour models.

OO fits this meta-model well. The business systems model is supplied by the use case diagram, the static structure models by the class inheritance diagrams and class responsibility collaboration cards, and the dynamic behaviour models have state transition diagrams, collaboration diagrams and sequence diagrams. Let's look at each of these. We've based them on Rumbaugh and Booch and used the Rational Rose drawing tool.

10.3.1 Use Case Diagrams

A use case diagram is constructed to show the required functionality of the system in the analysis phase and to specify the actual behaviour of the system in the design phase. An ellipse with a description of the transaction or events taking place represents the use case (Figure 10.1).

The use case is said to be *associated* with an *actor*, often represented by a matchstick man. The term 'association' has no precise meaning in this context; it is represented by a single solid line, sometimes with an open-ended arrow at the end of the line, and can be named to indicate its purpose. The actor may be using the use case or passing a message to it or initiating a process with it, as shown in Figure 10.2. The actor indicates the boundary of the system and represents the system users. Semantically, this is the weakest type of association in OO. CASE tools such as Rational Rose hold details of an actor's specification in the same way as the specification of an object is held.

A relationship can exist between use cases, and this is known as a *generalise* relationship. A use case may use or extend another use case. When a function is required by a number of use cases, for example a function to locate a specific instance of an object, then each of the use cases can be said to *use* it. A use case can *extend* another use case when it is invoked by the first use case to provide some additional functionality. An actor named `SalesClerk` might be associated with a use case `CheckDealerCredit`. This use case might use the general case `FindDealer` and be extended by the case `PrintCurrentStatement`. The extended relationship is shown with the arrowhead pointing towards the use case that invokes the extension, whereas the *uses* relationship shows the arrowhead pointing from the using case to the case being used.

Fig. 10.1 The 'use case' icon

Fig. 10.2 An actor and a use case

In Figure 10.3, use case A *uses* B, whereas it is *extended* by C. C will have associations with other actors and can be used independently. *Extends* is defined as a generalisation that is used to express optional behavior for a use case. The *uses* generalisation is defined as one that describes common behaviour between two or more use cases.

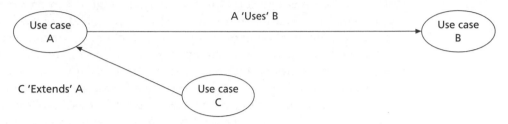

Fig. 10.3 Two types of relationship: *uses* and *extends*

The use case diagram is a business model for an OO specification. It can used for analysis purposes, to record system requirements and enable the analyst to understand how the current system works, or for design purposes, to show the system behaviour and the meaning of a particular set of procedures. The diagram is usually backed up by a description that may briefly state what the use case does. In some circumstances it is preferable to use a more detailed breakdown of the actions performed by the user or actor and the responses from the system. The use case specification is then shown as a dialogue between the actor and the system response, as in Table 10.1. CASE tools supporting OO

Table 10.1 Use case descriptions

`ProcessTransaction`

Actor and Event	System Response
The `PurchaseClerk` enters an item to be re-ordered	The system retrieves the `Supplier` details
The `PurchaseClerk` enters the quantity to be re-ordered	The system issues the purchase order

`CheckStockAvailability`

Actor and Event	System Response
The `WarehouseMan` enters the number of the item which has been requested	The system displays the quantity in stock
extended by;	uses;
The `WarehouseMan` enters the customers name	The system finds the customer's details
The `WarehouseMan` confirms the order request	The system prints a dispatch note

`AcceptOrder`

Actor and Event	System Response
	uses;
The `SalesClerk` enters the customers name	The system finds the customer's details
The `SalesClerk` confirms the order request	The system prints a dispatch note

developments provide facilities both for the diagram and for the dictionary description of theses actions and responses. Figure 10.4 is a use case diagram showing the way in which purchase orders and despatches are handled in the DMH case study.

Each use case is triggered by an event and involves an actor and a response. When a use case is developed in the analysis stage it can be compared to the logical dataflow diagram, and it is sometimes described as an *essential* use case. The use case description avoids any technical elements. It can be adapted later to describe how the use case will operate, including references to the database tables to be accessed and the characteristics of the GUI to be used. The use case descriptions in Table 10.1 extend the warehousing example in Figure 10.4, describing the actor, the event and the system response as a series of steps for three use cases. The first use case is named 'ProcessTransaction' and deals with the interaction between the purchasing clerk and the suppliers. The second and third use cases – CheckStockAvailability and AcceptOrder – deal with the receipt of an order and its processing. CheckStockAvailability shows both the *extends* and the *uses* association.

10.3.2 Class Inheritance Diagrams

Class inheritance diagrams are the static structure models of OO developments. Objects are said to belong to *classes*. Objects are things such as a person, a transaction, a machine, or anything that can have attributes and can exist in different states. Objects are often similar to entities in structured systems analysis, although an object is an abstraction of anything within the domain of the system. Entities are limited to 'things you wish to hold data about' such as customers, orders and invoices. In a banking system a cash dispenser might be an object, just as a machine tool might be an object in a manufacturing system. Objects are an abstraction of a thing found in the real world, and they are said to have a state, attributes

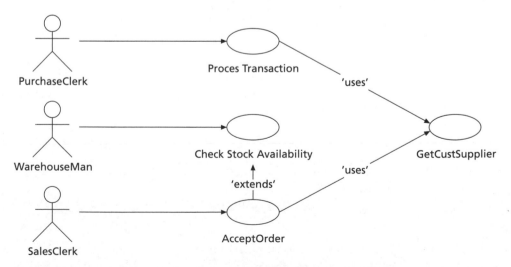

Fig. 10.4 A use case diagram for processing purchase orders and picking stock

and behaviour. When the analyst first attempts to identify the objects relevant to the system being investigated, one approach that can be taken is to identify the nouns used in the description of the system, and to ask for each of them:

- How is it identified?
- What does it do?
- What data is there about it?

Identifying objects is often the first stage in OO analysis, and initially the analyst can safely include anything as an object that seems relevant to the system. These will be refined as the model is developed, and may disappear from the class diagram altogether if they are found to be irrelevant.

Objects are fitted into classes by establishing their similarities. A class defines a set of objects; an occurrence of a single object is known as an *instance* of a class. An invoice might be a class of object, and sales invoice number 1234 might be an attribute of an instance of this class. The analyst would notice the similarities between sales invoices issued by a company and the purchase invoices that it receives. This might lead to the definition of the abstract class 'transaction' which has attributes and methods common to both purchase and sales invoices. These might be attributes such as date, reference number and value with methods, used by both purchase and sales invoice processing, such as 'accept new invoice' or 'modify existing invoice'. Methods specific to each SalesTransaction subclass type, or a PurchaseTransaction, are specified at a lower level. Figure 10.5 illustrates this with an output from the Rational Rose CASE tool.

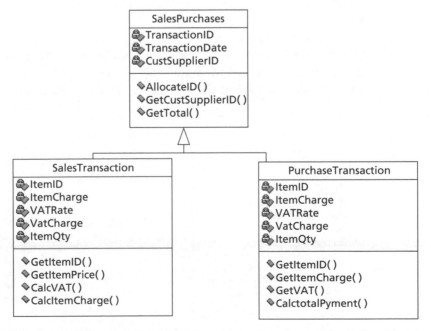

Fig. 10.5 A class hierarchy for sales and purchase transactions drawn using Rational Rose's CASE tool

Abstract and concrete classes

Object classes are defined as being abstract or concrete. An *abstract* class is found at the top of a hierarchy representing the general characteristics of the objects being modelled. It does not actually exist in real life; the instances of the class occur lower down the hierarchy. The term *superclass* is used to define this type of object, and in the Unified Modelling Language (UML) the term *stereotype* is similarly used. Modelling the transactions that are processed by an accounting system, we might identify the superclass `Transaction`, which has a date, a value, a source, and methods to receive, store and delete it. Figure 10.5 shows this with the superclass `SalesPurchases`. Instances of this class of object occur only in the form of actual sales and actual purchases, defined at the next level of the object hierarchy. At this level they are said to be *concrete*. The term *instantiate* is frequently applied in OO modelling, and the concrete class is an example of an *instantiated* class of object. When an object is instantiated, what we are saying is that we have obtained a real example of that object. As the superclass objects referred to above are abstractions, we are never going to encounter any actual occurrences of them in the real world.

Modelling object hierarchies is done by identifying the general characteristics of the information used by the system and building the hierarchy to exploit these generalisations. One benefit that is derived from these generalisations is the reuse of their components when developing new software that meets the changing needs of the organisation.

Classes of object interact. These interactions are represented by a line connecting the two objects, named to signify the association. The association is given a meaningful name that is indicative of its purpose. In the example in Figure 10.6 the association between the `Customer` and the `StockItem` is named `PlacesOrderFor`.

An association can have *attributes*. This is similar to the many-to-many relationship found in data modelling. In data modelling the many-to-many relationship is eliminated in favour of two one-to-many relationships linked to the 'intersection' data. In an OO model we use an 'association' class to perform the

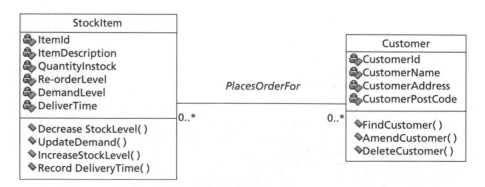

Fig. 10.6 The association between the `StockItem` object class and the `Customer` object class using the Rational Rose CASE tool

same service. Our model above now has the additional class of ItemsOrdered linked to the association between customer and item (Figure 10.7).

When we model objects such as customers and invoices we can miss the significance of the OO approach as the models appear very similar to those produced by the data modeller in structured systems analysis. Many organisations, having developed accounting and stock control systems based on relational database technology, can see no benefit in changing to an object-oriented system. Their organisational structure will be based upon a functionally decomposed model with departments such as accounts, order processing, sales and purchasing. Moving to an OO-based system could entail radical changes to their organisation as its structure becomes based on the behaviour of the classes of the objects that they use. Although relational databases dominate the market for accounting and administrative systems there are some business areas that they are not suited to, and the developer must look to OO databases to meet requirements. An engineering drawing office circulating and developing designs is not well served by a traditional database management system, and indeed any area of activity in which the main component of work is a visual image or a diagram will be better served by an OO approach and an OO database. The commercial transactions found in life assurance and insurance involve the exchange of documents for decision-making and authorisation. These systems often use *image and workflow* software for this purpose. The 3NF (third normal form) structures used by a relational database system do not support a system where a scanned image of incoming documents is created and circulated electronically to the different parties involved in processing the information on the document. This replication

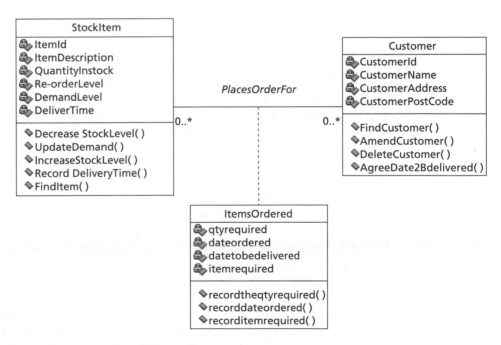

Fig. 10.7 The association class ItemsOrdered

of the information allows simultaneous decision-making to take place and reduces the throughput time for the transaction. Integrating this type of application with applications using the formatted data structures found in a relational database system forces the analyst to apply OO principles alongside the normalisation and entity modelling approach used by the data modeller.

10.3.3 OO Behaviour Models

OO methods represent system behaviour in three different ways. Just as SSADM uses entity life histories and effect correspondence diagrams to show how the database changes as events occur, so OO shows the interaction between objects and their changing characteristics through the use of three diagramming conventions. The changing characteristics of a single object are shown with a *state transition diagram*; the order in which the objects become active and service a particular use case is shown with a *sequence diagram*; and the logic of the way the objects collaborate and pass messages to each other is represented by a *collaboration diagram*.

State transition diagrams

Early OO developers used a diagram known as a state transition diagram to show the characteristics of the object's behaviour, to assist the program design. Many of the principles behind OO originated from a programming background where the work of James Rumbaugh and Grady Booch had broken new ground in the 1990s. The state transition diagram or *statechart*, as it has become known in UML terminology, can be equated to the entity life history in SSADM.

Objects have a state. This is a finite, non-instantaneous period of time in which the object fulfils a condition. A house purchase contract might be 'awaiting completion' or a numerical machine tool might be 'repositioning a machining tool'. These are states that are initiated and completed by some event. It is the event that causes the object to move from one state to the next. Certain classes of object will change their state more frequently than others. A student class of object in a university might pass through several states as he or she moves from an applicant through to being a graduate or postgraduate, having passed a number of stage assessments. Each stage assessment moves the student to the next level if they are successful. Starting as a level 1 fresher, they progress through the stages of academic examinations and industrial placement until their final transition is achieved by graduation. In the same system domain the object 'Module' – an object used to maintain information relating to a taught subject – might simply be a current or withdrawn module with no other associated state changes.

The statechart diagram has a start state represented by a solid circle and a final state represented by a solid circle with a surrounding ring. Each state change is annotated with the change event that causes it to happen. In Figure 10.8 we see a class diagram for an abstract superclass CollegePerson with the real-world object classes Student and Lecturer inheriting the identifier and name attributes and the assignment operations that go with them. We define these first before looking at the state changes they will encounter.

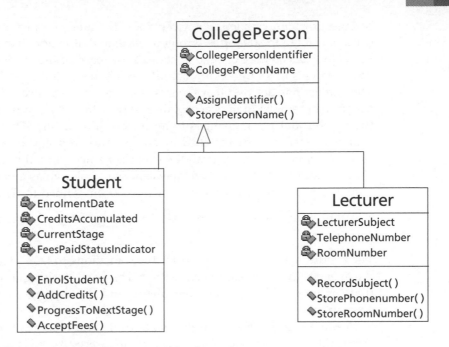

Fig. 10.8 A Student and Lecturer object hierarchy

Having defined these object classes we now require to model their behaviour, and this can be done using the state transition diagram. Figure 10.9 shows the events that cause state changes to the student object. The changes to the student object are very similar to the changes that would be seen if this was modelled as an entity for a relational database. However, the event that causes a change in state to the student object will be matched by an operation that has been specified as a method for this class of object. The student object moves from the state of being a conditional applicant to an enrolled student when the university

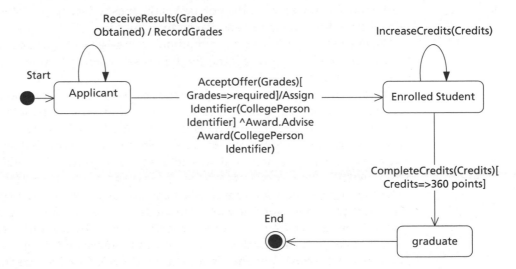

Fig. 10.9 A state transition diagram for the object Student

receives the student's letter of acceptance. The analyst must decide which events cause a change in state. It is wrong to assume that every change in the data held by the object causes a change in state. In the case of the student, the conditional offer changes to an unconditional offer when the A-level grades are announced. The analyst has decided that the state change from applicant to enrolled student occurs when the student's acceptance of the offered place is received, not when the conditional place changes to an unconditional one. The event causing the change of state will be matched by an operation that has been specified for this class of object. On the diagram the event is named, and any data that is used by the operation that the event triggers can also be shown as a parameter list. Event naming can be done to a syntax, which has been defined for UML as

```
event (arguments) [condition] / action ^ target.SendEvent
(arguments)
```

The conditions must be satisfied for the transitions to take place. The action, like the event, may have parameters with it. The SendEvent denotes a type of event that sends a message to another object, and this too may be accompanied by parameters.

In the example above the first state transition changes the student from an applicant to an enrolled student when the offered place is accepted. The event is defined as AcceptOffer, and the parameters or arguments with this are Grades. A guard condition is set with this state change to ensure that it occurs only when the applicant's grades are equal to or greater than those specified.

The transition to from applicant to enrolled student can be specified in the UML notation as:

```
AcceptOffer(Grades)[Grades=>Required]
/AssignIdentifier(CollegePersonIdentifier
^Award.AdviseAward(CollegePersonIdentifier)
```

We have the event name and the guard condition followed by the action and its argument. The final part of the notation is the message sent to another object, the Award class, with the argument that accompanies it.

The event AcceptOffer has a condition [Grades=>Required]. In this case the condition would be true if the conditions set when the student was offered a place have now been met.

The operation that issues the student registration is defined at the superclass level as AssignIdentifier, and the attribute is named CollegePersonIdentifier. This is all included in the syntax specifying the state change. A message is sent to the Award object to show that a place on this award has been accepted, and this message is accompanied with parameter StudentID.

In OO design, the user interface is a class of object in its own right, and the statechart provides a useful way of modelling its behaviour. A particular use case will be serviced by a window or form, or even by a set of forms, and the state changes that the windows undergo can be modelled using the statechart. The user interface will be first in a loading state, then an active state; perhaps it will be suspended while some other object is active, and it will finally be unloaded. Similarly, the controls within the window may benefit from being modelled. A list box control may be loaded, populated, used in a selection process and finally unloaded. The value of each model will be based on the complexity of the state transitions that it undergoes, and the developer will have to decide the level of detail that is needed for the application. As the interface itself is a class of object, it will be modelled using a hierarchical class diagram. This hierarchy of window objects and controls has, however, been extensively modelled and implemented in languages such as Visual Basic, and we view these classes as components available for reuse in our development.

The state transition diagram shown in Figure 10.10 models the changes that occur in a single class of object and provides the software engineer with a detailed specification of the way the methods associated with an object are integrated to create the desired software system.

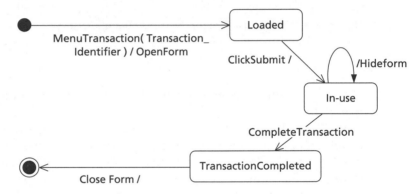

Fig. 10.10 A user interface modelled using a state transition diagram

Objects interact to form complete systems. The behaviour of object interaction is shown with the *sequence diagram*, which shows the exchange of messages between different objects in a time sequence. The sequence diagram provides a detailed expansion of a use case in the same way that a 'mini spec' or process description describes the processing logic of the lowest-level process box in a data flow diagram. The sequence diagram is drawn with the objects across the top of the page and a 'lifeline' from each object extending down the page. In our warehousing case study we have Customer, StockItem and ItemOrdered objects, and a sequence diagram showing the interaction of these objects would be created as shown in Figure 10.11. Messages flowing between the objects are

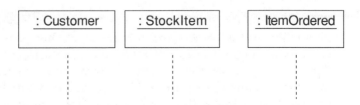

Fig. 10.11 The objects that will interact for the use case AcceptOrder

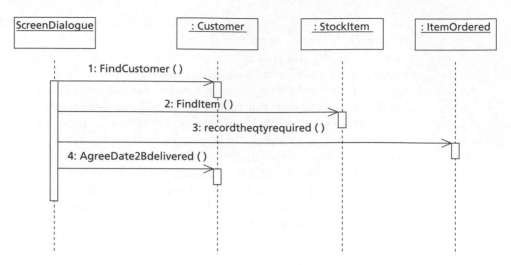

Fig. 10.12 A sequence diagram for the warehousing case study

now added with horizontal arrows that show how control is passed from object to object.

In Figure 10.12 we also have the addition of a screen dialogue object. In OO development the screen dialogue is identified as a class of object known as an *interface object*. We have seen how this object can be modelled using the state transition diagram in Figure 10.10, and it now participates in the sequence of message passing in the sequence diagram. In OO development it is common to differentiate between classes of objects. Objects can belong to a business class, a human interaction class or a data management class. When the sequence diagram is constructed from the use case view it will show the interaction of the business or application classes. The dialogue object is classed as a human–computer interaction object; the Customer and StockItem objects are part of the business or application logic. The storage and retrieval of classes can be handled by a special data management class, which will permit the business classes to be reused with different file management systems. The ScreenDialogue object sends a message to the customer object first; then to the stockItem object. Message 3 is sent to the ItemOrdered object to record the quantity ordered and message 4 to the customer object to agree the delivery date.

Collaboration diagrams

The collaboration diagram is similar to the sequence diagram as it shows the interaction of the objects and the messages that pass between them. The collaboration diagram does not show the time sequence of the interactions. In Figure 10.13 we see the sequence diagram created from the AcceptOrders use case as shown in Figure 10.12 converted to a collaboration diagram. As this is a reorganisation of the model rather than a new design this process can be performed automatically by the OO CASE tool.

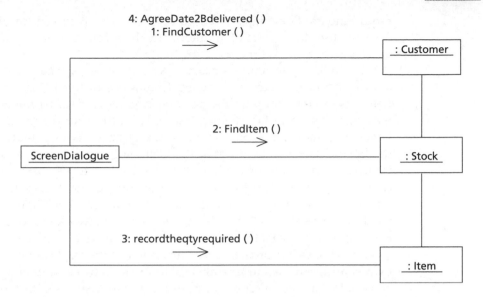

Fig. 10.13 A collaboration diagram produced from the `AcceptOrders` sequence diagram

10.4 Summary

Techniques alone do not provide a development methodology, and the way that the OO techniques interact needs to be specified if they are to be effective. In Figure 10.14 we see how the user requirements drive the development of the use cases and the class diagrams. These are developed in the analysis phase of the project. Each use case will give rise to an interaction diagram in the design phase: this will usually be a sequence diagram. As these are developed, the class diagram may be adapted to develop additional classes to meet the processing

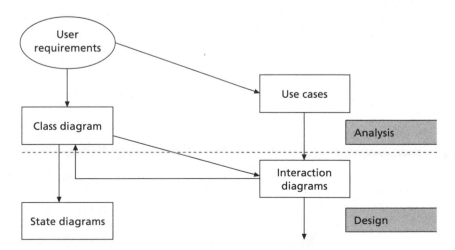

Fig. 10.14 The interaction of the OO techniques

requirements. Sometimes it becomes necessary to introduce an intermediate class to store the results of an interaction between two classes, and HCI classes are developed at this time.

OO modelling techniques provide what may be regarded as the most important extension to systems modeling techniques in the 1990s. Some practioners will argue that OO approaches are a replacement for earlier methods in the same way that any scientific advance can replace an earlier theory. Systems analysts have recognised for a long time that the essence of good analysis is to look at the business system, and not at the technology that it uses, and this may well influence our choice of method. When selecting an OO approach it is significant to recognise that the interaction of the objects that we see in the OO behaviour models is curiously reminiscent of the database navigation that developers used in the 1970s and 1980s using the codasyl networked model. When a business system can benefit from a distribution of its activities over a number of locations the OO approach is recommended. If the application is better serviced by a centralised system it is likely that the structured system approach will be chosen. Promoting either of these approaches for reasons of fashion or familiarity is the route to failure.

11 Systems Analysis: Modelling Systems Behaviour

11.1 Introduction

At this point in the process, the analyst has collected information about the current system by asking questions, gathering documents and recording details about the current system using diagrams and text. It is now important to make sense of the data, to draw out the underlying logic of the system and to map out the requirements for the new system. This involves checking details with the user, amending existing models, and constructing new ones.

In Chapter 9 we described two structured techniques – data flow modelling and entity modelling – and showed how they are used to describe the existing manual or computer system. This chapter explains how the models created using these techniques are extended to incorporate the new requirements, and it introduces new techniques that are used to model the required system in more detail and which form the basis of logical design. The most important of these new techniques adds the dimension of time to the picture of the system we have developed so far. It does this by modelling the sequence in which internal and external events trigger processes that change the data. The *entity life history* shows the way in which business events cause changes to the entities held in the database. The *state transition diagram* shows how, in an OO-modelled system, an object moves from one state to another when certain events occur. Input and output data streams consist of patterns of data that can be modelled using *input/output structure diagrams*, and the order in which a database is processed can be shown with an *effect correspondence diagram*. Detailed behaviour models that show the logic of a complicated process can be represented with decision tables, flowcharts or structured English.

Throughout the chapter we will refer to SSADM, although similar techniques are used in other structured methodologies.

11.2 Creating a Logical Model of Current Processing

Three different data flow models (DFMs) are produced during a project: the current physical DFM, which represents the current system 'warts and all'; the logical DFM, which is produced by removing any duplicated or redundant processing or data from the current physical DFM; and the required system DFM, which shows how the new processing and data required by the users are incorporated into the logical model. Existing systems are often badly structured because they were not designed from first principles but were simply developed over time. As a result they can include inefficiencies, such as the same data being held in more than one file, or the same processing being performed more than once by different programs. In addition to this being a waste of effort, it also increases the likelihood of error. Structured methods aim to increase efficiency and reduce error by creating systems in which common data and processing are shared wherever possible. One of the ways this is done is by rationalising or *logicalising* the current system DFM before incorporating the requirements for the new system.

What does logicalisation mean in this context? Put simply, it is a tidying-up process. We create a DFM that shows the existing system with all its inefficiencies and duplications removed. This results in a well-organised and clear picture of the system as it should be rather than the way it actually is. By adding the new requirements to a logical DFM we do not perpetuate all the things that were wrong with the old system.

The major tasks in turning a physical DFD into a logical DFD include rationalising data stores and processes. Let's see how this is done.

An existing system may store customer information in more than one place, for instance paper records in one department and a PC database in another. These are combined into a single logical data store called Customer, which includes the data from both physical data stores. In the library system introduced in Chapter 9, the New Acquisitions and Book Catalogue data stores would be merged into a Books data store. Sometimes we also need to split physical data stores if they contain two completely separate types of data, such as Customer information and Product information.

In addition to the main logical data stores there may be a need for transient or temporary data stores. These are common in physical systems, and many of them are not logically necessary and will be removed in the logical model. However, there may, for example, be a need for a batch of data to be entered into the system by one process and then checked and authorised by a manager using another process before the main data store is updated. Data in transient stores is always deleted by the process that reads it, as the data is either accepted for inclusion in the main data stores or rejected.

Bottom-level processes are merged, either because they are duplicates of each other or because they represent a sequence of small tasks that can be combined into one larger task. Duplicate processes often occur because two or more files contain the same information, and the information is entered into each file by a separate process. We can combine these processes so that the data only has to be entered once.

Processes are removed if they do not update the information in the system but only reorganise it – for instance by sorting it – or output it in reports or enquiries. In the latter case the processes are not removed altogether but are simply moved to the requirements catalogue in order to make it easier to see the essential update processes on the DFDs.

When we are satisfied with the new sets of logical processes and data stores, they need to be put together to form the new set of logical DFDs. The elementary processes are grouped to form higher-level processes or functions if they use closely related data or if they are used by the same external entities. Processes may also be grouped if they have similar timing requirements, such as year-end processes.

It is important that the logical DFM is checked against the current physical DFM to make sure that nothing essential has been lost and nothing added during logicalisation. It is also important that the model fits together and makes sense, and that it ties in with the logical data model. This latter activity is aided by producing a logical data store/entity cross-reference table, which shows which entities are contained in each logical data store. In the logical model an entity is allowed to appear in only one data store, and cannot be split across different data stores.

11.3 Modelling the Required System

Having created logical models of the current system, the requirements for the new system, documented during the analyst's investigation, can be added to these models.

Existing processes that are to be automated in the new system are carried over from the logical DFM to the required system DFM, making sure that changes resulting from the new requirements are included. Existing processes that are to remain manual tasks are removed, along with any associated data stores, data flows and external entities that are not used by the remaining processes. New processes are modelled based on the information contained in the requirements catalogue, and added to the DFDs at the appropriate points with any new data flows, data stores and external entities that are needed. For instance, a Record Fines process could be added to the set of processes included in the library system.

In a similar way, entities and their relationships are carried over, added or removed to create the required entity model, and the data dictionary is updated to reflect the changes to the models.

Once the new models are fully documented in the data dictionary they are re-viewed and checked against each other and against the requirements catalogue. Every requirement in the catalogue must have a cross-reference to the process or processes that are intended to satisfy it. To make sure that data requirements are satisfied, the contents of the data stores in the process model are checked against the contents of entities in the entity model using the updated logical data store/entity cross-reference.

There is also an additional technique that can be used to validate the entity model. Entity models are produced by a top-down approach, identifying the 'things' about which a system must hold data and then defining the relationships between them. The attributes of the entities – the items of data they contain – are identified and described in the data catalogue. An alternative, bottom-up, method is to identify the individual data items that the system must hold independently, and then to build data models by identifying the relationships between the items and grouping them according to these relationships. This technique is known as *relational data analysis,* and is described fully in Chapter 17. It can be used to build a model of the data, which can then be compared with the required system entity model. If there is a difference between the models then the necessary corrections can be made.

11.4 Adding the Time Dimension

We now come to the third major view of the system, one that will enable us to define the order in which processes update the data. This view models the events that affect the system, and is important in structured methods – particularly in SSADM, where it forms the basis of detailed process modelling and analysis. A number of different techniques have been devised to model this sort of information, such as state transition diagrams and Petri nets, but we shall continue to use SSADM to illustrate the structured approach, by describing two techniques: *entity life histories*, which provide a data-oriented view, and *effect correspondence diagrams*, which provide a process-oriented view.

An event is something that happens – an occurrence. It is useful for the analyst to distinguish between real-world events, business events and system events. Real-world events cause business events, which in turn cause system events. In the earlier stages of analysis the distinction between the last two may be difficult to make, as it will not yet be clear which parts of the business are to be computerised. An example of a common real-world event is that when a person moves house. This has an impact on businesses for whom that person is a customer – a business event – and will require the details held on a database by that business to be updated – a system event.

Analysts and users often speak in terms of the business event when they mean the corresponding system event, and vice versa. For an analyst, it is important that the effects of a system event are clearly defined to help with the process of logical design specification. A system event acts as a trigger for a process or set of processes to update a defined set of data.

An initial set of system events can therefore be identified by picking out all the data flows entering data stores in bottom-level DFDs in the required system DFM and tracing them back to an initial trigger either inside or outside the system. We could for example trace a data flow into a 'Customer' data store back to a 'Maintain customer' process and thence back to a 'Customer address change' data flow that crosses the system boundary from a 'Records clerk' external entity. This data flow suggests an event 'Customer change of address recorded', but another data flow 'New customer details' could suggest another event, 'New customer recorded'. Draw this out for yourself to see it fully. Not all events will be obvious from the DFDs. In this example other events can be envisaged, such as 'Customer change of name recorded', even though there is no data flow corresponding to it. So it is important to carry this task out critically rather than treat it as a purely mechanical exercise. The process of reviewing the DFM to identify events may uncover omissions from the model, particularly if the user's help is enlisted, as it should be.

The type of event we have been discussing so far is described as an *externally triggered event*, as it requires data to enter the system from an external entity. The data flow represents the trigger for the processing associated with the event. There are also two other types of event, both of which originate from within the system rather than outside it. These are the *time-based event* and the *system-recognised event*. They are both likely to be handled by batch processes, as they do not have input from an external entity. The presence of all three types of event may be deduced by considering Figure 11.1. 'Loan recorded', 'reservation recorded' and 'return recorded' are all externally triggered events. 'Recall issued' may be either a time-based event or a system-recognised event.

Time-based events are triggered by the arrival of a specified date or time, or by the passage of a specified period of time following another event. This type of event is quite common, an example being 'Year end' for financial and accounting systems. In Figure 11.1 'recall details' may be triggered by a loan becoming overdue a specified number of days after it was made.

System-recognised events are caused by the system recognising a change in its state caused by a piece of data it holds being changed to a specified value. The system monitors itself for this change and triggers a process when the change is detected. For example, in Figure 11.1 'recall details' could also be triggered when the system detects that a reservation has been made for a book title.

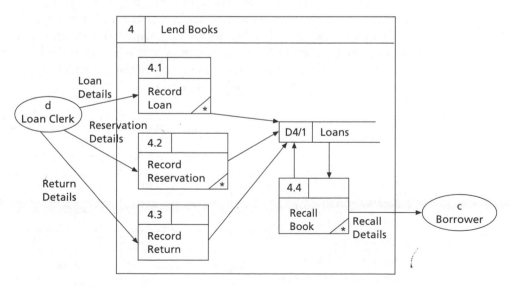

Fig. 11.1 Event recognition

11.5 Modelling the Effects of System Events

The activities described in this section define the effects that system events may have on entities and the order in which these effects are allowed to occur, and provide the basic framework around which detailed models of individual update processes can be built. In SSADM, these techniques are known as *entity–event modelling*.

Two types of model are produced in entity–event modelling.

- *Entity life histories* (ELHs) are diagrams that show which events affect particular entities and in what order.

- *Effect correspondence diagrams* (ECDs) show all the entities that may be affected by a single event plus any entities that may need to be read for navigation or reference purposes.

ELHs in particular are an important analysis tool, as their production requires a detailed understanding of the business rules that control updates to the database. Close user involvement is needed in their production, and this frequently highlights anomalies and omissions in the DFM or the LDM.

The first step in entity–event modelling is to create a matrix that cross-refers entities to the events that affect them. The list of entities that forms one axis of the matrix is taken from the required system entity model. The list of events for the other axis will come from the definitions of system functions. For every entity in the matrix, determine which events create it, which modify it and which delete it, and letter them C, M or D as appropriate (see Figure 11.2).

When the entity–event matrix is thought to be complete it should be checked to make sure there are no empty rows or columns, as this would imply redundant entities or events. The matrix should also be checked to make sure that every entity is created by an event and, preferably, is also modified and deleted by one or more events. Once we are satisfied that the matrix is as complete as it can be, work on ELHs and ECDs can begin. The starting point for creating an ELH is the column for the relevant entity, whereas an ECD is constructed by taking all the entities that appear in its row in the matrix and putting them in the correct order, as shown below in section 11.9.

Entity	Title	Edition	Book	Loan	Reservation	Borrower
Event						
Book Acquired	C	C	C			
Book Catalogued			M			
Book Borrowed				C	D	M
Book Reserved				M	C	
Book Returned				D	M	M
Borrower Registered						C
Membership Terminated			M	D	D	D

Fig. 11.2 Part of an entity–event matrix

11.6 Entity Life Histories

An entity life history (ELH) is a diagrammatic way of representing the different types of event that may affect an entity, the order in which they may occur, and the effects that they may have. ELHs effectively summarise all the different life paths that occurrences of an entity may take between their creation on the system and their deletion.

The ELH technique is based on concepts developed by Michael Jackson for structured program design. The essential idea is that all data processing can be described in terms of sequence (order), selection (choice) and iteration (repetition) of processing components, which are derived from the data structures. In an ELH these ideas are used by analogy to model sequences, selections and iterations of events affecting an entity.

An example of a simple ELH is shown in Figure 11.3. This ELH looks very much like a Jackson structure diagram and contains examples of sequence, selection and iteration. It shows, in a simple library example, that a borrower entity is created when a borrower first registers with a library, and that no more changes may be made to the entity after the borrower closes membership. In between these 'birth' and 'death' events there may be a number of 'life' events. Jackson rules are observed in that the diagram shows that it is possible for there to be no changes between creation and end of life for a particular instance of Borrower, as an iteration may occur zero, one or many times.

Figure 11.4 shows some of the other conventions which are used, in a completed ELH for Borrower. The additional features are parallel lives, quits and resumes, operations and state indicators.

Parallel lives are used when there are two (or more) independent sets of events that can affect an entity. As events from the two sets are not dependent on each other, but only on events from their own set, they cannot be ordered together in a predictable way. In Figure 11.4, for instance, change of address or of name are

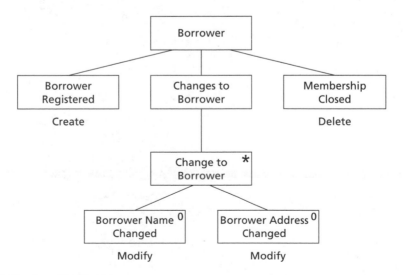

Fig. 11.3 Simple entity life history

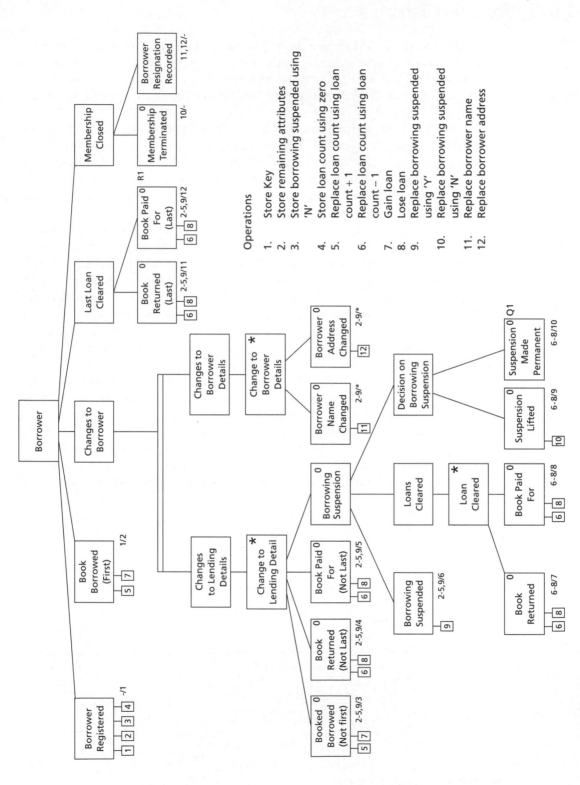

Operations

1. Store Key
2. Store remaining attributes
3. Store borrowing suspended using 'N'
4. Store loan count using zero
5. Replace loan count using loan count + 1
6. Replace loan count using loan count – 1
7. Gain loan
8. Lose loan
9. Replace borrowing suspended using 'Y'
10. Replace borrowing suspended using 'N'
11. Replace borrower name
12. Replace borrower address

Fig. 11.4 Completed entity life history

events that can happen to people quite independently of the way they conduct their borrowing activities, and therefore they have no direct relationship to events that are specific to their roles as borrowers. The diagram illustrates the convention whereby events that *are* specific to the system under consideration are treated as part of a primary life and are shown on the first branch of the parallel bar. The less application-specific events are shown as an alternative or secondary life on a second branch.

Quits and *resumes* are a means of jumping from one part of the diagram to another in order to cope with exceptional or unusual events. If used indiscriminately they can undermine the apparent structure of the diagram and make it more difficult to understand. Analysts should therefore use a quit and resume only when they are sure that there is no sensible way in which they can use normal Jackson structures to show what they want. Another reason for avoiding them if possible is that there is some controversy about exactly how they should be used. For example, should a quit be mandatory or should it only come into effect if certain conditions are true? It is safer to make them mandatory and to annotate them to this effect, but other analysts may not make it clear how they are using them so interpret with caution! Figure 11.4 shows a quit (Q1) from the Suspension Made Permanent event to a resume (R1) at the Membership Terminated event. This means that, if a borrowing suspension is not lifted because the borrower does not return overdue books or pay for lost books, then the system will allow librarians to terminate membership.

Operations are attached to the events to describe what update effects they have on the entity. An operation appears as a small box, in which a number provides the key to a corresponding entry on a separate list of operations. SSADM provides a standard set of operations such as 'store', 'replace' and 'read', which are qualified by relevant attribute or entity names or by expressions such as 'replace balance using balance + transaction amount'.

State indicators are added to each event in order to provide a label for the state in which an occurrence of that event will leave the entity. These states may correspond to values of existing attributes or may require creation of a new 'entity status' attribute. The value of the state indicator on an entity occurrence shows the point it has reached in its life cycle and therefore what events are allowed to affect it next. State indicators are attached to each event on an ELH, and valid before and after states for that event are shown, separated by an oblique. For example 2-5,9/3 means that the event to which this is attached puts the entity into state 3 and that the entity must be in states 2, 3, 4, 5 or 9 before this event is allowed to take effect. A state indicator consisting of a hyphen means no state: that is, the entity does not exist (e.g. -/1 or 11,12/-). The purpose of state indicators is to indicate error processing that will be needed in the required system. Errors that result from allowing an event process to update data that is in the incorrect state are called *data integrity errors*. Where there is a parallel life a separate set of state indicators is needed to label the states in the second life. This is because there are no dependences between events in the two lives and therefore no connection between the entity states that result from their effects.

A final point about ELHs is that there is not necessarily a 1:1 correspondence between events and their effect on entities. It is not unknown for a single occurrence of an event to affect two different occurrences of an entity in different ways. An example would be an account transfer event that involves the closure of one account and the opening of a new one. The account entity acts in two different roles in this situation, and so the ELH shows entity roles as different effect boxes for the same event, with the role that the entity takes in each case shown in square brackets after the event name (see Figure 11.5). It is also possible for separate occurrences of an event to affect the same entity occurrence in different ways. An example is an account closure request event. This event may have different effects depending on whether the account is in credit or in debit. In other words, the effect of the event is qualified, depending on the state of the entity. Qualified effects are shown with the effect qualifier in round brackets after the event name. An example in Figure 11.4 is the Book Borrowed event, which has different effects depending on whether it is the first loan or a subsequent loan.

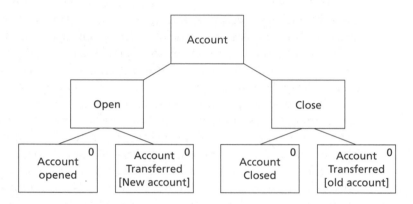

Fig. 11.5 Entity roles

11.7 Producing Entity Life Histories

The power of the ELH technique is in its precision. In trying to describe *exactly* what should happen as a result of a given event, questions may be raised not only about the accuracy of the DFM and the LDM but also about the way the business is conducted in the real world.

A set of ELHs is usually created by making two passes through the LDS. The first pass works from the bottom of the LDS with those entities that do not act as masters in any relationship but only as details, and gradually moves up the diagram until all entities have been modelled. The reason for working from the bottom of the LDS upwards is that events that affect a detail entity may also have effects on its master, and this is more easily seen by starting at the detail end of relationships. An example of this is where a balance attribute is held on an account entity. Whenever a new transaction entity is created for an account the balance on the account entity is modified by the transaction amount. The aim in this pass is to produce first-cut ELHs showing the 'typical' life of each entity. In the second pass the ELHs are reviewed, starting with entities at the top of the

LDS and working down to those at the bottom. This time all the less common or less obvious effects are searched out and the ELH structures are modified to include them.

When developing an initial set of ELHs the entity–event matrix is used as a guide. For each entity, pick out its creation event from the entity–event matrix and draw it on the left of the diagram. If there are more than one represent them as a selection. Next look at the events that modify or update the entity and work out in what sequence they are allowed. Add them to the diagram after the creation events using a Jackson-like structure with sequence, selection and iteration as appropriate. This is usually the most complex part of the diagram, and may need a lot of thought and consultation with the users in order to determine precisely what the rules are. Consideration of the detailed effects, in terms of operations, attributes updated and so on, should make the order clearer. In some cases the introduction of quits and resumes or parallel structures may be necessary, as described in the previous section. Lastly, deletion events must be added to the right of the diagram. The structure is not usually very complex, but there may be selection between different events, as with creation.

When first-cut ELHs have been produced for all entities they are reviewed, starting with entities that have no masters, in order to incorporate less common or exceptional events. Situations that may need to be considered are:

- interactions between entities;
- reversions;
- random events.

Interactions between entities often centre round death events. An example of how an event affecting a detail entity may also affect its master is where a bank account cannot be closed until all loans related to it have been paid off. Conversely, detail entities may be affected by events belonging to their masters. For instance, an application for a bank account that is outstanding when a customer dies will not go through its normal life but will be terminated early as a result of the death of the customer. This is also an example of a *random event*, the position of which on an ELH cannot be predicted. Random or unpredictable events are represented either by using the parallel life construct or by a special variant of quit and resume in which the quit is from anywhere on the ELH to a single resume event. Figure 11.6 shows a random event that could

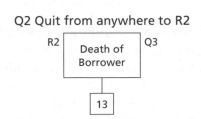

Fig. 11.6 Random event

be added to the ELH in Figure 11.4. This example shows an additional operation for recording the death of the borrower and would need a resume (R3) on the Membership Terminated event. This approach is normally used for exceptional events that lead to the death of the entity, whereas parallel lives are used when the life continues.

Reversions occur when an event results in a return to an earlier point in an entity's life. The quit and resume notation is used, just as in Figure 11.4, but the resume event is earlier in the life history than the quit event.

Once analysts are satisfied that the structures of the ELHs are correct, the processing operations that produce the effects are added, though as already noted it is helpful to consider them in the earlier stages. If this has not been done it is quite likely that their addition will highlight errors in the ELHs.

The final task before going on to produce ECDs is that of adding state indicators to the ELHs. This is a mechanistic task, which is done automatically by some CASE tools, as the sequence of values for state indicators should follow the structure of the diagram.

11.8 Effect Correspondence Diagrams

Effect correspondence diagrams (ECDs) represent an alternative, event-focused, view of some of the information shown in ELHs. An ECD is produced for every event that can affect the system and shows all the entities that may be updated or read by the process corresponding to the event.

ECDs are named after the event they represent, and show 1:1 correspondences between the entities which are updated by the event. If an event updates one occurrence of entity A and one of entity B then a rounded box is drawn for each entity and a double-headed arrow is drawn between them to show the correspondence. A Jackson-like construct is used to show whether more than one occurrence of an entity is updated in the same way. In this case a box representing a set of the entity occurrences is drawn. This is connected by a plain line to a box below it which represents a single occurrence of the entity. This box has an asterisk in the top right corner to show that the effects of the event are repeated (iterated) for each occurrence of the entity.

Effect qualifier and entity roles, described in the previous section, are also shown and are called *optional effects* and *simultaneous effects* respectively. If the effect an event has may be qualified by the state of the entity, this is shown using a Jackson-like selection or option structure. The entity is shown as a rounded box with two (or more) boxes below it, each connected to the entity box by a plain line and each containing the name of one of the possible effects and a circle in the top right corner to show that it is one of a selection. Entity roles mean that the event has simultaneous effects on different occurrences of the entity. This is shown by drawing a box for each occurrence affected, with its role in square brackets, and an outer box representing the entity type.

Two effect correspondence diagrams showing these conventions are given in Figures 11.7 and 11.8.

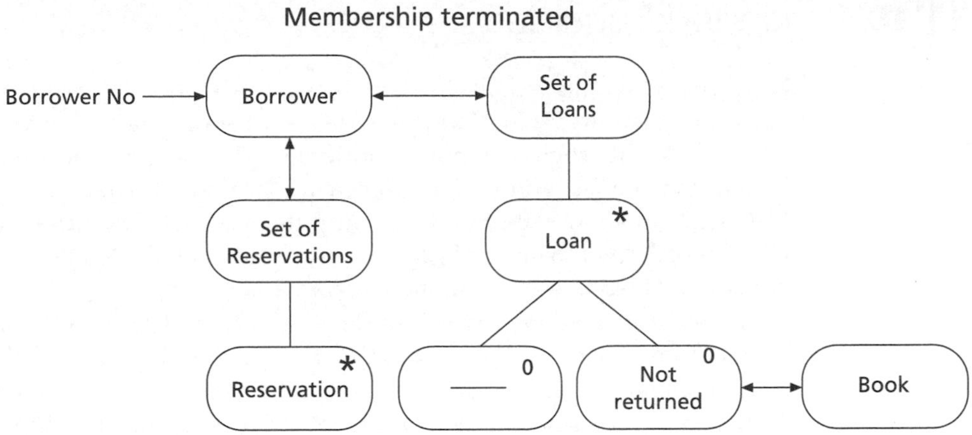

Membership terminated

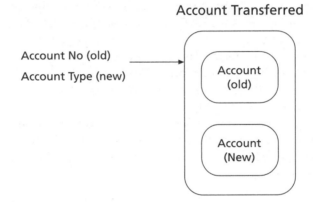

Fig. 11.7 Effect correspondence diagram

Account Transferred

Fig. 11.8 Effect correspondence diagram: simultaneous effects

11.9 Producing Effect Correspondence Diagrams

A starting point for producing an ECD is gained by reading along the corresponding event row of the event–entity matrix in order to get a list of the entities that it affects. Then draw a box for each entity, drawing the boxes in roughly the same position to each other as they appear on the LDS. Add simultaneous, optional and iterated effects as described above. Next draw in all the 1:1 correspondences. The input data for the event must then be added. This comprises a list of attributes that usually includes the primary key of an entity that acts as the entry point of the process triggered by the event. A single-headed arrow is drawn from the attribute list to the entity to indicate that it is the entry point. Lastly, entities that are not updated but which provide reference data for the process or which must be read in order that other entities may be read (i.e. for navigation) are added to the structure.

The completed diagram shows all the entities that must be accessed by processing triggered by the event.

11.10 Modelling Enquiries

Not all processing results in data being updated. The principal purpose of most information systems is to provide a source of data for screen enquiries and printed outputs such as reports and letters. Requests for information from the system are in effect non-update events, and are called *enquiry triggers* in SSADM. It is usual to show only the major outputs of a system on the required system DFM in order not to clutter it up with too much detail. Details of other enquiries are documented in the requirements catalogue.

An *enquiry access path* (EAP) is the equivalent of an ECD where processing does not involve the update of entities. EAPs show the access path or navigation route through the LDM for enquiries and reports. For each enquiry or report an EAP with the same name is produced. EAPs are used as input to both data design and process design. They can be used to derive an output structure for use in logical design of the equivalent enquiry process. They also show data access points that must be built into the data design.

In appearance EAPs are very similar to ECDs, but instead of double-headed arrows being used to show 1:1 correspondences between entities single-headed arrows are used. These access correspondences indicate the order in which entities need to be read in order to perform the enquiry. As with ECDs, selections and iterations are shown using Jackson's conventions. An example of an EAP is shown in Figure 11.9.

The basic approach to developing EAPs is to draw a view of the LDS showing the required entities. The entities can be identified by looking up the attributes in the enquiry function I/O structures in the data catalogue. Master to detail

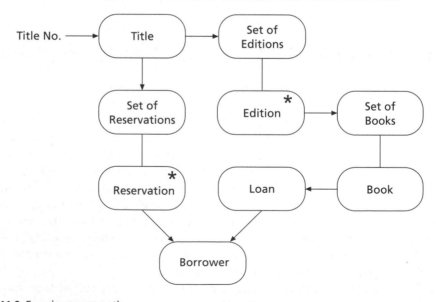

Fig. 11.9 Enquiry access path

accesses are drawn vertically and detail master accesses horizontally. Relationship (crow's foot) lines are then replaced by arrowhead lines showing the direction of access. Where more than one occurrence of an entity may be accessed it is replaced by two boxes, one representing the set and below it, connected by a plain line, an asterisked box representing a single occurrence, as in ECDs. Selections are added where required, also in the same way as in ECDs. Lastly, the entry point for the enquiry is shown by listing the input attributes required to trigger the enquiry and connecting the list to the first entity to be accessed. As with ECDs it may be necessary to add entities purely for navigation purposes. For instance, if the attribute triggering the enquiry is the prime key of an entity that does not have data output from the enquiry, but which is the master of detail entities which *do* provide output data, then it may need to be added to provide the entry point for the enquiry.

Each EAP must be validated by checking that the accesses shown are supported by the LDM. It must be possible to read entities either directly by reading a master from its detail or by reading the next detail for a master. If not then either the LDM must be changed to support the access or a processing solution (such as a sort) must be found. The EAP must also be consistent with access rights granted to users of the function, if these have been defined.

11.11 Defining the User View of Processing

The techniques we have been describing up to now model the *internal* processing and data needed for the required system. However, we also need to look at how the system is organised from an *external* viewpoint: how access to data and processes is organised to suit the users.

Detailed models of processing are at the event level in SSADM because events correspond to the smallest unit of update processing that can be performed while preserving the integrity of the data. However, different events or enquiries may be related to each other functionally or may need to be processed together for business reasons, and so SSADM also has the concept of the *function*. Functions are made up of one or more enquiry or event-level update processes that users need to run at the same time or in close succession. In a menu-driven system online functions correspond to the processing available from the lowest levels in the menu hierarchies. An example of an offline function would be an end-of-month batch run, which may serve many different time-based events. A function can provide the processing for one or more events and, conversely, an event may be served by more than one function.

SSADM provides a model of a function in terms of separate input and output (external) and database (internal) processing components. See Figure 11.10.

A typical example of the difference between a function and an event-level process, which also shows the difference between logical and physical events, is that of the credit card bill. The payment slips attached to credit card statements often have change of address forms on the back so that a payment and an address change can be returned on a single piece of paper. Receipt of one of these forms is a single physical event, but it may contain payment data, address data

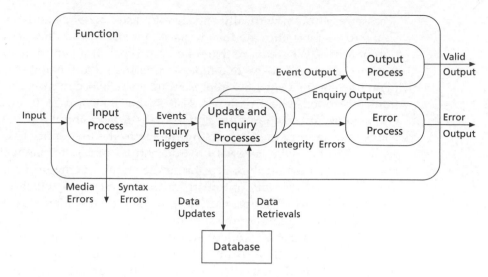

Fig. 11.10 The universal function model

or both. In other words it is able to carry data for two different types of logical event that do not *have* to occur together. Users may nevertheless wish to have a single function that allows the data associated with both events to be entered on the same screen, particularly if changes of address are rarely notified in any other way. This would not prevent them having another function just for change of address if they wanted.

The important point to note about functions is that they package processing in the way that *users* want, in order to fit in with the way they wish to work. Generally speaking, if users often wish to enter data for two or more events at the same time then a single function serving those events will be required, possibly in addition to functions serving some of the individual events. Different types of user may have different requirements for what processing they need packaged together. It is therefore necessary to identify the different user roles needed to run the system and the functions that must be provided for them. SSADM includes a user role–function matrix as one of its products and uses this as a guide or framework for defining menus and the navigation paths allowed between functions. The complete online system can be represented as a menu hierarchy that provides access to functions at its bottom level.

A function can be classified in three ways: as an update or an enquiry, as online or offline, and as system- or user-initiated. These classifications overlap to some extent: for instance, an update function may include some enquiry processing. It may also include both online and offline processing.

The first step in identifying potential update functions has already been described by recognising system-initiated and user-initiated processing on the DFD. Whether functions are online or offline may be a user choice or may need to be finally decided in physical design. The major source of potential enquiry functions is the enquiry requirements document in the requirements catalogue, though some may appear on the DFDs. The final decisions on the grouping of processes into functions should be made in consultation with the users and in the context of how use of the system is intended to fit into the user's overall job.

In SSADM important functions are chosen for prototyping so that the users are given a more concrete means of visualising what they have requested and can modify their detailed requirements if necessary. These prototypes are intended *only* for checking user requirements, and are not intended to be developed as part of the final system.

11.12 Modelling Input and Output Data

The method used to model processing structures for data input to and output from functions is based on Jackson-type structures, as already described for ELHs. The same idea that processing components should be matched to the data structures they act upon applies here. The organisation of input and output data into sequences, selections and iterations in data flows can be used as the basis for modelling the corresponding I/O processes.

Figure 11.11 shows the SSADM I/O structure for an online update function and demonstrates the diagrammatic representation of these ideas. Each leaf on the diagram is known as an I/O structure element, and the data items making up these elements are documented on the I/O structure description that is produced for each I/O structure. The data items in the I/O structure descriptions for up-date functions are taken from the corresponding data flow I/O descriptions in the required system DFM. For enquiry functions the data items have to be determined by discussion with the users. In both cases the structuring of the data needs to be derived from the views of the users. The I/O structures are used to help decide the grouping of data items when developing screen and report layouts during the design phase.

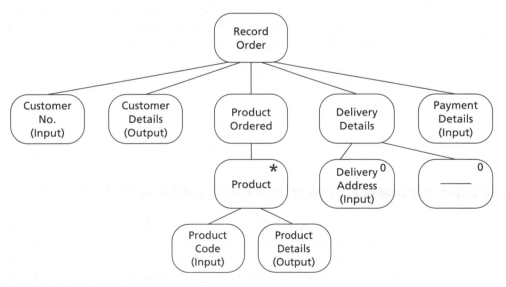

Fig. 11.11 Input/output structure

11.13 Modelling OO System Behaviour

The structured approach treats the business event as the driving force behind the systems behaviour, and in this respect OO and structured systems are similar. It is events that trigger state transition changes in objects, just as events cause changes to the attributes of an entity in an entity life history. The object model is held by some practitioners to be a more realistic representation of the real world, as objects are things that actually exist, whereas databases or entities are abstractions created to meet the needs of the software system. In fact the two abstractions often vary little, and consequentially the behaviour models that manipulate them often look similar. In our library example the structured systems DFD Lend Books shown in Figure 11.1 identifies three externally triggered events that cause a change to the loans data store – Loan Details, Reservation details and Return Details – and one internally produced event. Although the entity life history shows 16 business events that cause changes to the entity borrower, when we look at it as an object and map its state changes we find three main changes. The first of these is when the member registers with the library. The borrower becomes an ActiveBorrower with the loan of the first book, and the borrower ceases to be a borrower when they resign their membership. However, within the ActiveBorrower state a suspension of the borrower's rights can occur if a book is not returned after it has been recalled, and so a *nested transition* is shown dealing with the suspension of the borrower's rights. Modelling system behaviour by mapping state changes of objects is less detailed than the entity life history. The state transition diagram does not provide the completeness check that the ELH provides, as it lists only the events that cause a state change. Other events that may cause a change to values held by the object may not cause a change in the object's state, and the diagram may not show them. The events that cause changes to an object can be classified as:

- *Change events*, which occur when a condition becomes true. These events can be described with a 'when' clause. A customer may be entitled to a credit status 'When they have supplied credit references'.

- *Call events* and *signal events*, which occur when the object receives a message that invokes one of its operations.

- *Time events*, which are similar to change events but are denoted by the use of 'after' rather than 'when'. 'After' four weeks from the issue of the invoice could denote a change of state of creditworthiness in a customer.

11.14 Modelling Logic

Systems analysts are often required to understand the logic of a procedure or a set of business rules. When the analyst has to specify a program or define the results that are expected from a set of user acceptance tests this must be done clearly and logically. Dialogues used in call centres can involve the operator in checking a number of conditions to establish the caller's eligibility for a service.

All of these areas need a simple and logically complete method of specifying the conditions and actions that form the rules of the logic, and this can be done using a *decision table*. Decision tables and flowcharts were the original building block of software systems. Although the system behaviour can be modelled at a higher level of abstraction using objects, entities and complete systems, there is still a need to model detailed logic, to test its correctness and to specify the desired outcome of a process before it is created. Decision tables are often used to specify these rules. A decision table is made up of four parts (Figure 11.12):

- the *condition stub*, which lists all the conditions that apply;

- the *condition entry*, which shows the combinations of conditions that must be satisfied, known as *rules*;

- the *action stub*, which lists all actions that can occur;

- the *action entry*, which shows the actions to be taken when particular conditions, or combinations of conditions, are satisfied.

Tables can be completed in one of two ways: *limited entry* and *extended entry*. With a limited entry table, the statement of each condition or action is completely contained in (or limited to) the appropriate stub. The entry portions of this table indicate only whether a particular rule satisfies the condition or requires the action stated. Convention dictates that in the condition entry part of a limited entry table only three symbols are used: Y (for yes) if the condition is satisfied, N (for no) if it is not, and a hyphen if the condition is not pertinent to the rule. Similarly, only two symbols are allowed in the action entry portion. These are X if the action is to be executed, and a blank if it is not.

In an extended entry table, the statements made in the stub portions are incomplete. Both the stub and the entry sections of any particular row in the table must be considered together to decide whether a condition or action is relevant to a given rule. The advantage of the extended entry method is a saving in space,

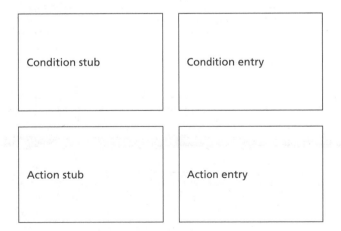

Fig. 11.12 Decision table components

although an extended entry table can always be converted to a limited entry form. Figure 11.13 shows the two methods used to state the same problem.

Limited entry tables may be checked for completeness by a simple mathematical relationship. First count the number of blanks in each condition entry. Call this N, remembering that $N = 0$ when there are no blanks. Then, for each rule in turn, calculate the value of 2 to the power of N. Sum the resulting values. The answer should equal 2 to the power of C, where C is the number of conditions given in the table. If the two answers do not agree, then either some rules are missing or too many rules have been inserted and the table must be re-checked for accuracy. If identical sets of conditions require different actions, then the table is said to be *ambiguous*, and again a check for this must be made. If different sets of conditions lead to the same actions, then the rules may be combined (eliminating redundancies).

There is one additional feature employed in decision tables, which makes the above checking method void. This is known as the *else* rule. It is used when only some of the total number of possible conditions require testing. The required conditions are written as normal rules, and then a final rule having no conditions but entitled 'else' is inserted. The actions for this rule are normally to go to an error routine or to exit from the table. Insertion of this special type of rule is

Limited entry	Rules				
	1	2	3	4	5
Is order valued between £0 and £10?	Y	N	N	N	N
Is order valued between £11 and £100?	–	Y	Y	N	N
Has customer satisfactory credit limit?	–	Y	N	Y	N
Approve order	X	X		X	
Allow discount of 3%		X			
Allow discount of 5%				X	
Refer to supervisor			X		X

Extended entry	Rules				
	1	2	3	4	5
Order value is more than	£100	£100	£10	£10	£0
Credit limit satisfactory	Y	N	Y	N	–
Approve order	X		X		X
Allow discount of	5%		3%		
Refer to supervisor		X		X	

Fig. 11.13 Limited and extended entry methods

an instruction to perform only the tests on stated conditions. If all these are unsatisfied then the 'else' action is taken, without testing every possible rule (i.e. combination of conditions). Although this device can be useful in restricting an otherwise large table, it must be employed with extreme caution to ensure that no conditions that should have been tested have in fact been forgotten.

The problem to which the analyst must specify a solution will normally be written as a narrative description. The wording may be vague, and conditions and actions are likely to be scrambled together. With experience, the analyst will be able to prepare a decision table directly from the narrative without difficulty. For beginners, however, the following method provides a systematic approach to the task:

1 On the narrative, underline all conditions with a solid line and all actions with a dotted line.

2 Enter the first condition on a blank decision table outline immediately above the double line, using extended entries.

3 Enter the first action immediately below the line.

4 Complete the table in extended form. Identify and consolidate similar statements.

5 Check for ambiguity, redundancy and completeness.

6 Insert 'else' rule.

7 See whether the table should be converted to limited entry by checking whether it will still go on to one page, whether any one existing entry will not extend to more than five new lines, and whether there are a reasonable number of entries on at least two lines.

8 Check whether the problem would be better expressed on more than one table.

Figure 11.14 shows an original narrative, its underlined version and the decision table derived from the latter to illustrate the above points.

As a general rule of thumb, it has been suggested that a decision table should be considered when the number of rules multiplied by the number of conditions in the problem gives an answer of six or more. However, the tendency to draw up tables that are too large must be resisted; another general rule is that in a limited entry table of full size, the maximum number of conditions quoted should be four, which will give rise to 16 rules. It is stressed that these are rough guides only, and the analyst must use common sense to detect when a table is too complex and would benefit from being split. Always remember that the aim is to communicate clearly and concisely.

11.15 Size and Frequency Statistics

One final point. It is not sufficient to collect information on what the system must do and then model the processing and data structures and relationships in it. It is

Original narrative

WHEN THE QUANTITY ORDERED FOR A PARTICULAR ITEM DOESN'T EXCEED THE ORDER LIMIT AND THE CREDIT APPROVAL IS 'OK', MOVE THE QUANTITY ORDERED AMOUNT TO THE QUANTITY SHIPPED FIELD THEN GO TO A TABLE TO PREPARE A SHIPMENT RELEASE. OF COURSE, THERE MUST BE A SUFFICIENT QUANTITY ON HAND TO FILL THE ORDER.

WHEN THE QUANTITY ORDERED EXCEEDS THE ORDER LIMIT, GO TO A TABLE NAMED ORDER REJECT. DO THE SAME IF THE CREDIT APPROVAL IS NOT 'OK'.

OCCASIONALLY, THE QUANTITY ORDERED DOESN'T EXCEED THE ORDER LIMIT, CREDIT APPROVAL IS 'OK', BUT THERE IS INSUFFICIENT QUANTITY ON HAND TO FILL THE ORDER, IN THIS CASE, GO TO A TABLE NAMED BACK ORDER.

Underlined version

WHEN THE QUANTITY ORDERED FOR A PARTICULAR ITEM DOESN'T EXCEED THE ORDER LIMIT AND THE CREDIT APPROVAL IS 'OK', MOVE THE QUANTITY ORDERED AMOUNT TO THE QUANTITY SHIPPED FIELD THEN GO TO A TABLE TO PREPARE A SHIPMENT RELEASE. OF COURSE, THERE MUST BE A SUFFICIENT QUANTITY ON HAND TO FILL THE ORDER.

WHEN THE QUANTITY ORDERED EXCEEDS THE ORDER LIMIT, GO TO A TABLE NAMED ORDER REJECT. DO THE SAME IF THE CREDIT APPROVAL IS NOT 'OK'.

OCCASIONALLY, THE QUANTITY ORDERED DOESN'T EXCEED THE ORDER LIMIT, CREDIT APPROVAL IS 'OK', BUT THERE IS INSUFFICIENT QUANTITY ON HAND TO FILL THE ORDER, IN THIS CASE, GO TO A TABLE NAMED BACK ORDER.

Limited entry table		Rules 1	Rules 2	Rules 3	Rules 4
01	Quantity ordered ≤ order limit	Y	N	Y	Y
02	Credit approval = 'OK'	Y		N	Y
03	Quantity on hand ≥ quantity ordered	Y			N
04	Move quantity ordered to quantity shipped	X			
05	Go to release	X			
06	Go to order reject		X	X	
07	Go to back order				X

Fig. 11.14 Preparing a decision table from a narrative

also important to collect business data that may affect *how* it should do things. The basic information required concerns the frequencies of events and the numbers of entities. These, together with an indication of their growth or decline over the life of the system, can be used to provide estimates of performance and capacity demands that are likely to be made on the system. Event frequencies are recorded on function definitions in SSADM and provide the basis for estimates of the frequency with which the functions are likely to be used. Entity volumes are added to the LDM both by recording figures on relationship and entity descriptions and by adding them to the LDS itself. These figures are important in the design phase, where they are used to estimate the amount of disk space required for the system, the traffic on communications lines, and the likely response times and run times of online and offline processes.

11.16 Summary

In this chapter we have described how details of the current system are recorded by producing a current physical data flow model and a current logical data model. We have also described how to record requirements for the new system in a requirements catalogue.

We have explained how this information is interpreted, by creating a logical version of the DFM, and applying the new requirements to it and to the LDM. We then described techniques for entity–event modelling. These are used to analyse and model the internal workings of the new system in more detail by adding a timing, or sequencing, element for update processing.

We have also shown how structured methods can be used to analyse and document the external aspects of the system, the way in which the user wants to access the system. The SSADM function model (Figure 11.10) provides a good summary of the relationship between models of the internal and external aspects of the system. It is at this stage of a software development project that size and frequency statistics must be collected in order to help determine the performance and size criteria that the physical system must meet.

The models described in this chapter help in specifying the detailed requirement for the new system, and are used as the blueprint for its design.

Exercises

11.1 Using the entity description for 'Bill', which is shown below, the case study scenario and the level 1 DFD, identify the events that will affect the 'Bill' entity during the lifetime of an entity occurrence.

Entity description:
Subscriber no
Rental period no
Bill date
Bill amount
Bill type
Payment date
Bill status
Reminder date
Disconnection notice date

Bill type has the values:
Bill due
Request

Bill status has the values:
0 – Bill issued
1 – Payment made following bill
2 – Following reminder
3 – Payment made following disconnection notice.

11.2 Draw a partial entity–event matrix showing the effect of these events on this entity.

11.3 Draw the entity life history (ELH) for 'Bill'.

11.4 Construct a limited entry decision table from the following description of a loan company's activities.

A loan company will offer loans to applicants based upon their age and their employment history. Applicants who are below the age of 25 are required to supply details of a suitable guarantor who can provide security for the loan. An interest rate of 14% per annum is charged, and the loan is offered for a maximum of 5 years. If the applicant is 25 years of age or older then they do not need to provide a guarantor provided they can supply an employer's reference and a reference from their bank. These applicants are charged a rate of 12%, and the loan can be extended to 10 years. If they are unable to supply a bank reference but can provide a guarantor then they will still be allowed to obtain a loan at a 12% interest rate but the loan must be repaid in 5 years. Applicants who are under the age of 25 and who supply a bank reference and employer's reference and a guarantor will be allowed a loan at 12% per annum for up to 10 years. All other applications will be refused.

11.5 Candidates for employment in an engineering company are recruited on the following basis. Construct a limited entry decision table of this process.

Candidates for employment are accepted if they have experience in engineering, provided they manage to pass an interview. Candidates without engineering experience must pass an interview and an aptitude test to be accepted. A satisfactory interview but a failure in the aptitude test will mean rejection except where the candidate has experience of similar work outside engineering, in which case a probationary appointment is made. Candidates who have engineering experience, but have failed to pass an interview, are offered a temporary job only. Candidates who do not meet any of the above criteria are rejected.

11.6 Chapter 1 asked you to construct a physical DFD of the LozCo system. LozCo keep machine maintenance records that they update as shown below. Construct an entity life history (ELH) of the machine maintenance record from the description below.

When a new machine is installed in the machine shop LozCo create a machine maintenance record. This is used to hold a running total of the product produced by the machine. The machine is reserved for the manufacture of a particular group of products, and this is recorded on the maintenance record card.

When the machine is installed, it is passed for service by a quality inspector, who checks that the commissioning and installation have been done correctly. The equipment manufacturers employ these inspectors, and details of inspections are recorded on the maintenance record. If a machine fails this quality check then the check is repeated later until the standard has been reached. The total quantity produced per week is accumulated in the maintenance record, and this figure is incremented each week.

Routine maintenance is conducted twice a year at roughly six-month intervals. The equipment manufacturer's staff undertake the maintenance, and details of the most recent maintenance are held on the record. When a machine is removed from service at the company it is either scrapped or sold second-hand, and its date of removal from service is recorded. The accounts department records any costs or income derived from its disposal at the end of the year.

12 Systems Analysis: Meeting Business Requirements

12.1 Introduction

We have seen that the purpose of systems analysis is to find out what the users of the proposed information system want, prior to beginning its development. However thorough the research is, though, it is necessary to specify the requirements in some form that is:

- accessible and intelligible to the user;
- unambiguous;
- reasonably practical and amenable to execution.

Let's examine these three criteria for a moment, as they are critical to the later success of the system's development.

We have seen in Chapter 2 that one of the major objectives – and the main claimed advantage – of structured methods is that they deliver a specification that the user can understand. It is simply no practical use giving the user a multivolume narrative to read and approve. Even if the user does, apparently, agree to such a specification, there will be endless arguments later over understanding and interpretation. It is, of course, true that it is sometimes difficult – very difficult even – to get users to review and agree specifications. However, securing such agreement is one of the analyst's skills and responsibilities, and without it the development is unlikely to be successful.

First the user has to be persuaded to read the specification. Next, it is important that the user understands it in precisely the same way that the analyst intended. Here again, structured methods offer advantages in that it is less easy to introduce ambiguity into a drawing than into several thousand words of text. Ambiguity can still creep in, however, and every effort must be made by the analyst to ensure that it is eradicated from the final specification. One way of achieving this is to use a formal walkthrough technique, such as a Fagan inspection (see Chapter 4). The users are asked to paraphrase the specification in their own words – and the analyst can see whether the users think what she or he meant them to think.

Finally, the specification has to offer a practical solution. Although, in specifying the requirement, the analyst ought to consider business needs first and technological solutions second, it is not very sensible to specify something that is totally impractical or prohibitively expensive. Here, the analyst has a special responsibility to the user; after all, it is the analyst who should possess the better knowledge of the possibilities of technology, and who must use this knowledge to steer the user in directions where a successful information system can be built.

Having disposed of these general points, let us now consider the specification process itself.

12.2 Agreeing the Options

For any given system requirement, there are always a number of solutions available:

- At the one end will be the very simple solutions, providing a minimum level of functionality but requiring little time and money to develop and implement. Such solutions will be attractive to the users where funds are scarce or where timescales are very tight and it is important to have something, however basic, available as soon as possible.

- At the other extreme are the systems with full wide functionality providing every desired function, complete system help facilities and probably a very attractive user interface. Such a system will cost a lot of money, and take a lot of time to develop. This may well be necessary if the users' business is very complex or an objective is to get others to use the system.

- Between these extremes, there are all sorts of possibilities, including systems that have a limited number of fully developed elements, often referred to as *core functions*, and more rudimentary ways of providing less-used facilities.

The factors that will influence the way the system will be developed include:

- the speed of implementation;

- the funds available;

- the technical environments available, especially where the new systems must operate alongside existing implementations;

- the technical sophistication of the target users. Can they reasonably be expected to grapple with the complexities of a multi-menu system?

A development route that is sometimes followed, especially where funds or timescales are tight, is to identify a *core system* that will be implemented initially, with other functions being added as resources permit. This approach has the obvious advantage of spreading the costs and effort over a longer timescale, but the danger with this is that the business requirements change during the project, so that the features to be developed later do not fit well with the initial facilities. Also, of course, technology moves on, and the users may require more advanced facilities later in the project that cannot easily be reconciled with the more primitive features provided earlier.

12.2.1 Identifying Options

In the initial stages of identifying options, both users and analysts should give themselves complete freedom of thought. In principle, nothing should be ruled out, however 'off the wall' it appears, as the idea is to bring the maximum of creativity to bear at this point.

However, the analyst has an important duty towards the users in this stage. The analyst is the one who should understand the possibilities and limitations of technology, and must make sure that the users:

- do not limit their thinking too much by what they have seen, or had, in previous systems; in particular, the users must be encouraged to think about what they really want their new system to do and not just try to reproduce their old one;

- do not think that just because an idea is suggested in this initial option-identification exercise it can necessarily be implemented; users must realise that cost and time constraints – not to mention the limitations of technology – will constrain the implementation route finally selected.

An excellent way of identifying options is to use the technique of *structured brain-storming*. Get everyone involved together in a room and have them suggest ideas, capturing them on a whiteboard or on Post-it™ notes stuck to the wall; in this initial stage, do not evaluate or judge the ideas, simply note them for later analysis. Then, identify similarities between ideas and rationalise the possibilities, thereby gradually narrowing down the list of possible options. Finally, analyse each option and produce a list of strengths and weaknesses for each. In this way, analysts and users generate an initial 'longlist' of all the possible options.

Before a proper selection exercise can take place, the initial list must be reduced to a shortlist of not more than two or three possibilities, which can be presented to the senior managers who will decide how to proceed. Typically, this shortlist includes one option at each of the extremes already mentioned – high-cost, complex, full-features, and cheap, quick and simple – and a solution that, the users and analysts agree, offers a good balance between cost, complexity and functionality.

There is no magic formula for producing this shortlist – and especially not for identifying the balance or compromise option. Instead, users and analysts must engage in rational discussion and rigorously review the advantages and disadvantages of each possible solution. It is important that the options to be proposed are presented in a way that is:

- clear and concise to those who will make the decisions;
- consistent as between the options offered.

High-level data flow diagrams are useful for illustrating the boundaries and functionality of the proposed systems, and tables present the pros and cons in a comparative way to the decision-makers.

12.2.2 Choosing Between the Options

If the analyst wants a successful outcome to the selection process, it is vitally important to decide who *are* the decision-makers. Quite often we talk about 'the users', but who are they exactly? Are they the people who will sit down at the keyboard and use our new system? Are they these people's managers? Or are they the senior management of the organisation who want a system to support some overall business objective? Very often senior management makes the final decision based on the facts of the case – the evaluated costs and benefits of the proposed solutions – but also advised by those who will use the system directly and who may be influenced by more subjective criteria such as appearance of proposed on-line screens.

Whoever turn out to be the 'users', it is essential that they make the decision on how to proceed, and that this is not left to the analysts. If the analysts feel that the decision is being edged back towards them, they must use their diplomatic skills gently but firmly to push it back where it belongs. Apart from any contractual implications here, it is vital to the success of the development that the users accept ownership of the project and the system, or they will not give their full commitment to its implementation. Without this commitment, the project is almost bound to fail.

The option selected may be one of the two or three proposed, or it will be a composite, embracing some features from each of the options. The selected option must be fully documented, including:

- what decision was reached;
- who made the decision, and when;
- what constraints or limitations were attached to the decision.

This documentation provides the terms of reference for the detailed design work, which can now begin.

12.2.3 The Use of Prototyping

A persistent problem of systems analysis and design is that it is very difficult for the users of the proposed system to envisage, before it is built, what it might look like. Paper-based representations of online screens, for example, do not have the look and feel of the real thing, and it requires a lot of imagination to see how the various menus and screens will work together. In addition, a set of routines that look fine in theory may turn out to be cumbersome to use in practice.

This problem is also recognised in more traditional engineering disciplines, and systems analysis has now adopted one of the techniques of the engineer to overcome it – the building of prototypes to test ideas. In analysis and design there are two distinctly different approaches to prototyping, and it is important that the analysts decide in advance which of these to use:

- *throwaway prototyping*, where a representation of the proposed system, or of parts of it, are created, probably using some screen-painting tool, and used to test out ideas with the users;

- *evolutionary prototyping*, where elements of the system are created in outline in the actual chosen technical environment: these parts are then developed and refined and form part of the finished system.

Whichever approach is adopted, the process needs careful management. With throwaway prototyping, the users must be told, often and loudly, that what they are seeing is a simulation – not the real thing in embryo. They also need to realise that this simulation is not in any way shortening the development process; what it *is* doing is ensuring that the finished system more closely matches their requirements.

With evolutionary prototyping, on the other hand, the users are looking at part of the finished system. However, it is still necessary to manage their expectations, as the part they are seeing – usually the online menus and screens – probably represents the lesser part of the whole system. Still to build, and taking more time, are the complex processing, data manipulation and validation routines that make the system work. In addition, there is the need for unit, system, and volume testing and all the other tasks that make for a soundly built and reliable computer system.

The lessons learned from the prototyping process require documenting, like all other analysis research. In addition, with evolutionary prototyping, the agreed screens must be placed under configuration control as soon as they are agreed so that they can be carried forward properly into the remainder of the development process.

In summary, then, the use of prototyping can prove very valuable in ensuring that the system will be acceptable to its users. But the prototyping process needs careful management to avoid raising over-high expectations either of the product to be delivered or of the delivery timescale.

12.2.4 Quantification of Options

We mentioned before that, when we present our options to the decision-makers, they will want detailed information on which to base their decisions. Providing this information involves the application of some form of cost–benefit analysis to each of our options. Cost–benefit analysis is a very large subject in its own right, certainly beyond the scope of this book. However, if we think first about the costs side of the equation we need to consider the following:

- development costs;
- development timescales;
- hardware costs;
- other costs;
- other impacts;
- lifetime costs.

Development costs

Systems development is a labour-intensive business, so the cost of producing the proposed system will be based largely on the effort involved. The analysts need to produce estimates of the work involved in high-level and detailed design, in program coding and testing, and in system testing, integration testing and implementation.

This is somewhat easier than producing the estimates for analysis, as we now know more about the scope and complexity of the proposed system and we should have some idea of the development environment proposed. In addition, most development organisations have some broad metrics that provide ratios of effort as between analysis and coding and unit testing.

However, the option proposed may involve some new technology or some application of the technology that has not been tried before. This is particularly likely where the system is to achieve some competitive advantage for the organisation. In this case, the developers need to be cautious and careful with estimates and avoid raising the users' expectations unduly or underestimating the difficulties ahead.

Development timescales

These are related both to the effort involved and to the resources that can be made available. Systems development, though, is not like digging a hole in the ground, where the time spent can be reduced just by using more people. There is an optimum size for each development team that enables the task to be accomplished in a reasonable time but which does not incur excessive overheads in co-ordination and control. If very specialist skills are needed for some part of the development – for example to produce an optimal database design – then these will act as a limitation on the possible speed of development. These, and other, constraints should be carefully considered and taken into account before proposing a development timescale for the option.

Hardware costs

Broad-brush hardware costs can usually be arrived at by considering the overall size of the proposed system and what sort of platform is needed to support it. Will it be a mainframe, a minicomputer or a PC? Will it involve a network of some sort? Will the system be proprietary – involving components from one manufacturer – or 'open' – in which case the benefits of competition become available?

At the stage of deciding options, the actual final platform may not be decided, so these approximate figures may be all that can be offered with the options. However, the platform may already have been decided on – perhaps it was a constraint at the project initiation – or the organisation may have a hardware strategy – for example the requirement for open systems – which can be used to narrow down the hardware options. In this case, a more detailed estimate can be provided.

However, one word of warning on estimating for hardware costs. Two common problems seem to beset development estimates here:

- The final system turns out to be more complex and hence to require more computing power than was originally envisaged.

- The hardware itself turns out to have less available power than the sales specifications suggest.

The result is that initial estimates of the size of machine required almost always turn out to be too low. If the machine proposed initially is somewhere low to middling in the range, this is not insurmountable, though it will involve going back to the users for more money. But if the machine proposed is at the top end of the range, the analysts should look at their estimates very hard indeed and consider whether they shouldn't be proposing a more powerful environment in the first place.

Other costs

Development of both software and hardware is not the only area where costs are incurred. Other things the analysts need to consider and include in their options proposals include:

- training of users for the proposed system;

- additional equipment that may be required;

- the need to redesign office layouts;

- the costs of possible parallel running of the old and new systems;

- the need to recruit new staff with special, or additional, skills to operate the new system;

- possible costs of redundancy payments, or retraining costs, for staff displaced by the new system.

Other impacts

Apart from the items that cost money, there are other impacts that the new system might have and which may have to be considered in the decision-making process. We have already suggested that there may well be retraining costs involved because people's jobs will be changed by the new system. The organisation may also have to reconsider the type of people it recruits in future and the training they need. Consider, for example, the situation where an organisation has relied hitherto on receiving orders by post from its customers and entering them – via data entry clerks – into its computer system. If it introduces a system that can handle telephone orders, then its staff will now need to be good on the telephone and able to interact directly with customers.

The management style may also have to change because of the new system. The data entry operation just described requires no more than someone to oversee the process and supervise the clerks. But an operation where people are actively trying to make sales requires management who are sympathetic and encouraging and prepared to train people and develop their skills. Some of these impacts may be intangible; it may not be possible to put a cash figure on them. However, the analyst should bring them to the attention of the user management so that they can make their subjective assessment of them and take them into account when choosing their system option.

Lifetime costs

When presenting the costs of a proposed system, it is important that analysts focus on the lifetime costs of the system, not just on the initial development costs. This is particularly important where a structured development method is being used, as it is acknowledged that such methods do involve more effort, and hence cost, during development. However, the use of structured methods produces systems that are easier and hence cheaper to maintain in the long run.

12.3 Identifying Benefits

When we were discussing the costs of a development, we suggested that there were *hard* (tangible) costs and *soft* (intangible) costs. The same applies to the perceived benefits of a new system, which can be either tangible or intangible depending on whether a monetary value can be placed on them. The analyst needs to remember that, when identifying and presenting benefits, they will appear rather differently according to who is considering them: one person will place more value on a benefit, particularly an intangible one, than another.

Tangible benefits are usually the easiest to identify and quantify, though not always. They could include:

- *increased throughput* – the ability to handle a greater volume of business;

- *greater productivity* – the capacity to handle more work with the same or fewer staff, the reduced salary bill providing the quantifiable benefit;

- *the ability to enter a new market* – the value being the increased turnover or margin that results;

- *reduced running costs* – if the system is replacing one that is very old, operating on unreliable hardware and requiring specialist, and therefore expensive, skills to maintain it.

Getting facts and figures on some of these can be difficult but some things, such as salary costs, should be readily available. You can use salary costs, too, to work out other things, such as the cost of entering a single order in the system. The costs of operating existing systems are sometimes hard to establish. The simplest situation is where the system is run by a bureau, perhaps as part of a facilities management deal, but this is still fairly uncommon. Instead, you will need to get some overall costs for running the computer, including staffing, floorspace, environment, maintenance and so on, and work out what proportion of it is accounted for by the system to be replaced. Computer managers are sometimes reluctant to provide this information, indeed some do not even know themselves, but the analyst's usual persistence should eventually produce some usable figures.

It is very important when assessing benefits not to overstate them. Nothing so undermines the case for a particular course of action than if its proponents are over-optimistic about its benefits. If you are reasonably careful and conservative, and if you document the assumptions on which you have based your calculations, you will be able to present a robust set of costs to support your options. Intangible benefits are much more difficult to deal with. They are rather like an elephant! You have trouble describing it but you'd know one when you saw it. Some intangible benefits that you might want to consider include:

- greater customer satisfaction resulting from the use of the new system;

- lower turnover of staff working with the new technology;

- better company image caused by the use of up-to-date equipment and methods;

- better management decisions based on more up-to-date information;

- the ability to react more quickly to changing circumstances in the marketplace.

Analysts often get themselves into trouble by trying to place a monetary value on these intangible benefits, by asserting for example that greater customer satisfaction will produce so many new orders per year, worth so much money. If the users do not share this assumption, then they will not agree with the analysts' evaluation of them. It is much better for the analyst to identify the *potential* intangible benefits and invite the users to place their own value on it. A managing director currently making many decisions 'in the dark' may rate very highly a proposed system that offers accurate and up-to-date management information. Finally, it is extremely unwise to base the whole case for a particular option on intangible benefits unless the users themselves identified these benefits when initiating the project. It is much better to quantify the tangible benefits and then to list the intangibles as additional potential gains.

12.4 Presenting the Requirement

However good the analyst's ideas, however cogent the arguments for a particular solution, these will not sell themselves. It is very important that the proposed solutions be presented in a way that is:

- clear;
- intelligible;
- pitched at the correct level for the intended audience.

In most cases the selection of options involves some sort of presentation, supported by appropriate written material. Later, the specifications for the proposed system will need to be expressed in paper form. So, the analyst needs to master the skills of expression, both written and oral and, in the latter case, in small groups and to larger gatherings. We have covered these areas in detail in Chapter 3, but we'll consider how they apply to the presentation of system proposals.

The three keys to a good presentation are preparation, preparation and preparation. Successful presentations may look effortless, but that is because they have been planned carefully, and rehearsed thoroughly, in advance. Of course, a presenter needs to be able to 'think on his feet', to field questions from the audience, but the basic structure of the presentation – the order and method in which subjects are introduced – must have been worked out well beforehand.

If, as is usually the case, a team is presenting, then there should be a thorough team briefing, and everyone must be clear about:

- who will say what, in what order;
- who will respond to questions in the various subject areas;
- how questions will be fielded.

Nothing looks worse in a presentation than everyone in the team trying to talk at once or, just as bad, embarrassing silences because no-one had picked up a question.

Visual aids should be considered carefully. Overhead or slide projection can have a major impact but not if they are merely tedious lists of bullet points covering what the speaker is saying. They should illustrate vividly and directly the point the speaker is trying to make – like a pie chart showing the breakdown of costs for a proposed system. You need to practise, too, the use of the visual aids so that they supplement what you are saying, rather than act as a distraction from it.

At the outset of the presentation, it is necessary to establish your credibility. You must understand the level of interest and understanding of your audience and pitch your talk correctly. Computer jargon should be avoided, unless you are addressing a very technical audience. You may reasonably use your audience's own jargon – engineering terms for engineers, for instance – but only if you yourself have sufficient expertise; otherwise, you may well find yourself out of your depth and lose your credibility.

And finally, if you are trying to make a case, do not overemphasise the *features* of your solution; stress the *benefits* of the solution as they would be understood by the audience. So, for example, don't describe the hardware in terms of gigabytes of storage and megahertz of processor power; point out instead that 'the proposed hardware can handle 100 orders an hour more than your current system with no increase in manpower.'

Written reports must also be pitched at the intended audience and use appropriate language. A board-level report, for example, concentrates on high-level issues and overall costs, whereas a program specification contains very detailed and technical implementation information.

If you have some standards for the format and content of a document, use them. You may find the standards a little constraining, but this will be outweighed by the benefits that arise from everyone knowing how and where to find things in the finished document. At all times, you must consider the needs of the reader. The language in a report should be as simple as possible, given the subject matter. Of course, some points are difficult to convey in short, simple sentences, but it can be done and it presents an interesting challenge to the skilled writer. If you are writing a long and detailed report, produce a management summary that distils the major points into a few sentences or paragraphs; it is this summary that arrests the attention, and secures the interest of the senior managers for whom it is intended.

The use of drawings and diagrams can save many hundreds of words and also, of course, helps to break up large areas of text. Use adequate 'white space' as well, to make the document more accessible and so encourage people to read it. If you are preparing a technical specification, then the need to gain the audience's attention is less acute. However, layout and presentation are still important, this time so that important points are not overlooked or buried in acres of text.

Finally, make sure that your document, report, specification or whatever contains adequate cross-references to other relevant documents or publications.

12.5 Writing the Functional Specification

Once the client has selected one of the system proposal options presented by the analyst, the *functional specification* is written. This is a document that specifies in detail the functions to be performed by the new system and describes any constraints that will apply. Box 12.1 represents the suggested contents of this document, with examples of the sort of information contained in each section. This is only a skeleton list, and it is likely that other sections would be added.

In writing this document, the analyst must ensure that it is unambiguous, and that it passes the '5 C's test' by being:

- Clear.
- Complete.
- Consistent.
- Correct.
- Concise.

Box 12.1 The functional specification

- **System Performance**
  Response times, throughput, dealing with hardware & software failures

- **Inputs to the System**
  Sources, types, formats, procedures

- **Outputs from the System**
  Contents, format, layout

- **Constraints**
  Hardware, software, environment and operational

- **Other Aspects**
  System start-up and shut-down, security procedures

The functional specification is passed to the client, who reads it and agrees the content. The client then signs it off as an acceptable deliverable, and work begins on the design phase. Sometimes design may begin before the functional specification has been agreed by the client. In this case, it is unwise to proceed too far with the design in case the functional specification has to be changed in a way that has major implications for the designers.

Before this chapter concludes, we want to introduce some ideas about business analysis, business activity modelling and requirements engineering. Each of these techniques, as well as systems analysis, contributes to meeting and specifying business requirements, which is the main theme of this chapter. Although these techniques provide a broader analysis of an organisation's current business position and its future potential than the systems analyst might expect to create, the strategic importance of information technology has made it imperative that the business analyst is able to view the organisation and its goals in the context of these issues. The techniques are now considered as a significant prerequisite of an IT development project, and we include them in this text for that reason. We'll finish with a further high-level view of the contribution that these techniques can make to strategic information systems development.

12.6 Business Analysis

Business analysis and systems analysis are similar activities, and some organisations use these job titles interchangeably, but systems analysis predates business analysis. When developers recognised the need to view the system as a whole, rather than as a collection of programs, the role of the systems analyst was born. Unfortunately, the system analyst often saw problems in the proposed development, and the role became typified by the sometimes negative attitude of developers wholly preoccupied with the problems of supporting ageing mainframe systems that were unable to take advantage of new technology. In this section we differentiate between the systems analyst and the business analyst by defining the emphasis that each should put on particular stages of the system life cycle. Additionally we contrast the techniques that are fundamental to each role. The systems analyst will be expected to identify requirements in the same way as the business analyst but, having identified requirements, he or she is expected to design the system that will meet them. The systems analyst will be expected to understand the principles and techniques that are used in systems design and be able to use the models we have defined as system behaviour models. Equally, the systems analyst will have a good understanding of the technical systems options that are feasible for the proposed development and be able to use the expertise of technical specialists to select the best of these options for the new system. The systems analyst will construct models of the data structures that the system will require, and will understand the implications of different methods of data access and data storage. The opportunities and the problems associated with the use of telecommunications technology will influence the physical design of the new system, and the specification of the network and the data entry system will be within their view. Screen layouts and output design forms part of systems analysis, as does the design of controls and features that make the system secure and auditable.

The business analyst, however, will concentrate on the business needs of the organisation, and although systems analysis does recognise business needs in the design of a new system, business analysis focuses specifically on this task as a goal in its own right rather than as the first stage in the analysis and design life cycle.

The business analyst will often have a different background from the systems analyst, although both may have similar career aspirations. The business analyst will frequently have been recruited from a business background and perhaps from the user community, often as a result of his or her involvement in a development project as a user representative. Their knowledge of business processes is invaluable when planning change, and their perspective, seeing the system from the user's point of view, is essential to the success of the development. The business analyst's responsibility is the production of clearly stated business requirement definitions, which can be passed to a system designer to be turned into specifications that are the input to the development process.

The skill of business analysis lies in writing business requirement definitions that are understandable to the user and the developer and can be tested to the user's satisfaction when they have been developed. The business analyst will be particularly aware of the system life cycle as a V-shaped process, as illustrated in Figure 12.1.

In this life cycle we look at each stage of the development in terms of the tests that can be applied to confirm the successful completion of the stage. Business analysis defines the tests that will be needed to gain the users' acceptance. The design of the system – the responsibility of the systems analyst or the systems designer – will be tested with integration or suite tests to ensure that modules developed independently will function together. As it is unusual for a system to be created in a 'greenfield' environment, the integration tests are accompanied

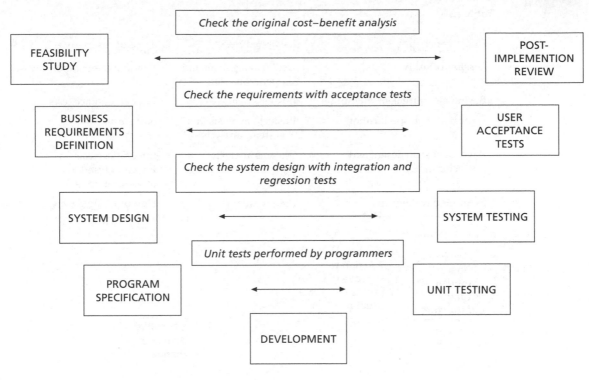

Fig. 12.1 The 'V' model

by regression tests to ensure that any parts of the system that have been modified or incorporated into the new development will still produce the right results when subjected to the tests used when they were first developed. The individual modules or units of development will be tested by the developers themselves using unit or module test data to show that the module will perform to the specification it has been produced from. Organisations that allocate their development tasks in this way will often define the development roles as business analyst – systems designer – programmer. Alternatively, the role of designer is described as an analyst/programmer, recognising that the requirements definition provided by the business analyst will need further development work, which may involve analytical decisions before the technical development can begin. The stages of the V life cycle and the tests and responsibilities are shown in Table 12.1. Although this life cycle is not specifically linked to the role of the business analyst or to business activity modelling, it is described in this context because of the importance of linking a business requirements definition with tests for user acceptance. You will notice that it is not in exactly the same format as the V life cycle model shown in Chapter 6. The model shown in Figure 12.2 is a simplified version to illustrate the place of the business requirements definition, but in other respects it is the same.

The techniques used in business analysis are drawn from several different sources. Perhaps the most influential contributor to the process is Peter Checkland, whose Soft System Methodology underpins much of the thinking

Table 12.1

Life cycle stage	Designed by	Type of test
Feasibility study	User management and operations staff	Post-implementation review
Business requirements definition	Business analysts	User acceptance tests
Logical system specification	Business analysts and systems analysts	Suite tests
Physical system design and specification	Systems analysts	Integration tests Function tests Regression tests
Program development	Programmers	Unit or module tests

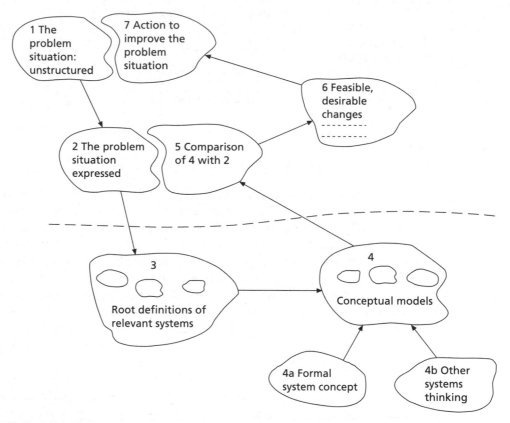

Fig. 12.2 Checkland's model

on business activity modelling and business analysis in the UK. Checkland's methodology formalises an approach to systems analysis that recognises that problem definition and the perspective of the individual creating the definition will have an important impact on the judgements being made. The model of Checkland's view of systems thinking, shown in Figure 12.2, illustrates the link between the ill-defined and unstructured view of the problem in the real world and the formalised and structured view that is created through the application of systems thinking and systems methods. Creating 'Root Definitions' of systems is achieved by analysing a prose description of the system against the acronym CATWOE. There's more about root definitions later, but it is enough at the moment to say that they are a precise statement of the system's reason for existence.

The analyst is seeking to identify the following elements of the system:

- *Clients.* Clients are the beneficiaries of the system. In some cases, a judicial system perhaps, 'beneficiary' might not be the best word to use, but it identifies the individuals who will feel the impact of the system's operation. In the Denton Motor Holdings case study the dealers who receive parts from the company are the obvious clients, but so too are the company's suppliers. The dealer's customers might also be identified as clients as they will benefit from the faster and more reliable supply of spare parts that the system will provide. In each case the client's perspective will vary, one looking for faster service, one for lower prices and one for increased business. Reconciling these requirements will be one of the tasks facing the business analyst.

- *Actors.* The actors are the individuals who are making changes occur through the use of the system. In the case of the warehousing system the clerical staff are actors, but so also are the dealers, as they are using the system to deliver a service to their customers. When identifying actors and clients the business analyst must step back from the problem domain and attempt to view it from as many different perspectives as possible.

- *Transformation.* In simple terms the transformation is what the system does. The transformation will vary according to the system's actors and the clients it is associated with. Clerks will process orders, but dealers will seek to obtain required items, and suppliers will wish to maintain a supply of their parts to the warehouse.

- *Weltanschauung.* The *Weltanschauung* – or world view – is any viewpoint, relevant to the system, that forms part of the accepted culture or attitude of the people involved. These can be difficult to identify because they are often taken for granted. A payroll system deducting national insurance payments assumes a culture of taxation and state pensions, but the same *Weltanschauung* might not apply in a newly formed republic. In the case study the *Weltanschauung* assumes that reducing the stock holding to the minimum required is the most profitable course of action. In an economy experiencing rampant inflation, the opposite might be the case. In university education the expression 'A good staff/student ratio' can be used as an example of the way in which *Weltanschauung* can vary from person to person. The student might view a good ratio as 1 to 1, whereas a government education minister might consider 1 to 20 to be better.

- *Owner.* The owner of the system is sometimes referred to as the *sponsor* of the system. This is the person or even the organisation that is paying for the development. The owner or sponsor has a controlling influence on the development. In the case study, the ownership of the system and its sponsor is the company DMH. A closer examination of the roles of the Chairman and the Managing Director will reveal that one, the Chairman, is focused on expansion with IT as the driving force. The other, the Managing Director, is intent on setting the 'house in order' before engaging in any expansion. These positions could lead to conflict, and the business analyst must identify potential and actual sponsors as early as possible if their requirement's definition is to be accurate.

- *Environment.* The environment is similar to the *Weltanschauung* but is the wider environment in which the system must exist rather than specific cultural norms that the system must accommodate. The environment is similar also to the context defined by a structured systems context diagram, but it's more general and seeks to position the system rather than define its boundaries. The case study environment is one with dealers, customers and suppliers with communications facilities and warehousing capacity available. The view of the environment can vary according to the individuals defining it and, as in the case study, the expansionist views of the Chairman extend the environment to include Internet facilities and an increased number of sales outlets, whereas the narrower views of the Managing Director limit the environment to the operations within DMH. Again the business analyst must reconcile these two positions before making any firm statement about requirements.

The acronym CATWOE, defined above, forms the basis of the system root definition that is written using the elements identified above. The definition seeks to incorporate all of the essential aspects of the perspectives identified using the CATWOE, and this might lead to a definition for our warehousing case study, which suggests that their system is one that:

Enables DMH dealers to obtain the spares they need, ensuring that the company's stock holdings are kept to a minimum, while ensuring that orders are met in full and that order processing staff can process all orders on the day of their receipt.

12.7 Business Activity Modelling

The term *business activity modelling* can be used specifically to refer to one of the particular modelling techniques described below or more generally to refer to a collection of techniques all of which are of importance to the business analyst. We identified earlier a number of business activity modelling techniques that form a part of structured systems analysis and other systems methods. These techniques are all useful and relevant to the work of a business analyst.

Business activity modelling is a more loosely defined modelling technique than the data flow diagram, although there are many similarities. The business activity model identifies major functions and system boundaries and shows associations between different parts of the system without specifically defining

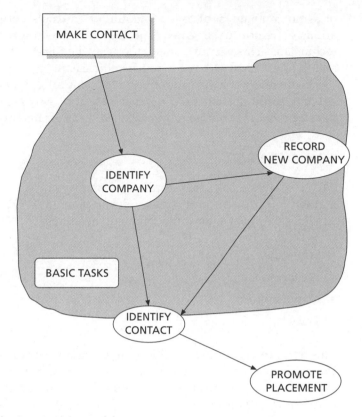

Fig. 12.3 A business activity model

the nature of these associations. Figure 12.3 illustrates the way in which a business activity model using this approach might be drawn for the activities involved in operating an undergraduate placement system for a university sandwich degree. The shaded portion indicates the system boundary; external to this, the rectangle identifies a business event, and within the system boundary the functions or activities that are associated with this event are shown in the form of ovals. Arrows that indicate the order in which the activities occur link these activities. The diagram is not as formal as a data flow diagram but does provide us with an initial system map that will help us to produce more structured diagrams as the investigation proceeds. The business activity model should identify those activities that are data-oriented activities, as these are the ones that the new system will be based on.

12.8 Business Analysis and IT Strategy

The development of an IT strategy is a vital ingredient in the success of any organisation that uses computers. The development of communications and the increased access to computing and digitally stored information and images affects every aspect of the business world. Strategic decision-making is the task of senior management, but a vacuum often exists between the business aspirations of senior management and the enthusiasm for technology felt by the IT technicians. This vacuum can all too easily be filled with unrealistic and unworkable projects spawned by too much enthusiasm.

The business analyst cannot provide technical guidance in the field of IT strategy but, through analysis, can structure and classify aspects of the business or its development to facilitate more reasoned decision-making.

12.8.1 IT SWOT

SWOT analysis has been applied for many years as a structure and tool for marketing proposals and strategy development. SWOT identifies the features of a proposal or idea against the following headings:

- Strengths.
- Weaknesses.
- Opportunities.
- Threats.

This deceptively simple classification technique was developed by Professor Sam Waters into a matrix in which the cells were further subdivided into the critical aspects of the organisation that would affect the proposed developments. The matrix might typically consider strengths, weaknesses, opportunities and threats when applied to the people within the organisation and the customers and suppliers outside it. The money supply, the use of technology and the use and availability of information within the company can all be applied to the matrix. The result can be seen in the example in Figure 12.4.

Waters's approach advises the analyst to see the business domain in four perspectives, which are identified by the shorthand acronyms of:

- W3 – Where we were.
- W2R – Where we are.
- W3 2B – Where we want to be.
- G2GT – Going to get there.

The approach places particular emphasis upon the role of information within the organisation, as this is the focus of any IT development. The information row of the IT SWOT matrix can be analysed by identifying the information flows as shown in Figure 12.5. Some flows pass through the organisation and into the IT system and some flows communicate directly with the IT system. Two further information flows are considered: information flows within the organisation, and information flows within the IT service itself. Viewing each of these flows in terms of its SWOT characteristics helps the business analyst to anticipate difficulties and identify business opportunities, and to enable management to make more informed decisions about the feasibility of the proposed development.

INTERNAL FACTORS			EXTERNAL FACTORS		
Strengths & Weaknesses			**Opportunities & Threats**		
	S	W		O	T
People: Management			**People:** Customers Suppliers		
Money:			**Money:**		
Information:			**Information:**		
Technology:			**Technology:**		

Fig. 12.4 IT SWOT

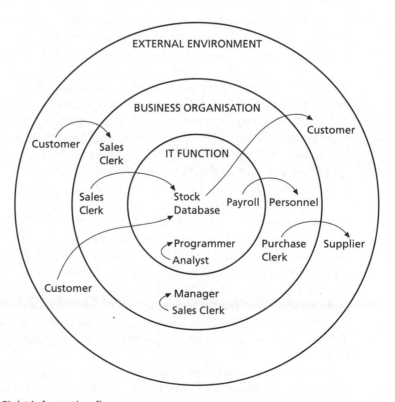

Fig. 12.5 Eight information flows

12.8.2 Requirements Engineering

Requirements engineering is a term used to describe activities that, at first sight, closely resemble systems analysis and design. The techniques used in requirements engineering are the same techniques that we describe as part of systems analysis. Systems models using structured analysis and object-oriented analysis can all be used by the requirements engineer. However, the perspective of the requirements engineer is different from that of the systems analyst. Requirements engineering is a fundamental aspect of business analysis, and it is significant that the ISEB Diploma in Business System Development that specialises in business analysis identifies requirements engineering as one of its core components.

This emphasis on the requirements phase of the life cycle comes from an increasing awareness in organisations involved in the development of computer-based systems that the poor performance, late delivery and high maintenance cost of software systems come from a failure to understand and specify requirements at the outset of the project. The use of the term 'to engineer' adds weight to the view that sees this stage of the life cycle as a formalised and structured activity that underpins the quality of the design.

Requirements engineering is frequently used when the development is of a technical or scientific nature rather than a business-based system. The business-based system often derives its characteristics from the behaviour of the system's users, and the systems analyst is always aware of the importance of the user's acceptance of the way in which the new system will operate. Systems that are developed for technical purposes, such as missile control systems, air traffic control systems or aircraft control systems, must still originate from a set of requirements, but these requirements will be based upon mechanical and physical characteristics rather than human and organisational ones. Recognising the need to apply a structured, documented approach to the identification and definition of these requirements is an important step towards the establishment of professional standards for the software engineer engaged in these developments. The same standards encourage the business analyst to apply an engineering perspective when developing a business system solution that will accommodate the changing patterns of the commercial world.

The life cycle for requirements engineering closely resembles that used by the systems analyst, although the emphasis is on establishing high-level definitions of requirements that provide an overall design, which can then be decomposed into lower-level, more detailed requirements. The system partition is done by requirements, and this can be contrasted with the process partition that is used in structured systems analysis and the object partition that is used in OO analysis and design. The requirements engineer would argue, quite reasonably, that requirements engineering postpones the selection of a development method, and this avoids the creation of a solution that is dictated by the methodology that defines it.

The process of establishing requirements is subdivided into three stages: elicitation, analysis and validation. Requirements *elicitation* is the investigation stage of this process, and the requirements engineer will use the interview, observation and modelling techniques in the same way as the systems analyst. The identification of stakeholders and their classification is an important element in this process. The CATWOE principle described earlier is adapted to allow the engineer to recognise the different perspectives of those who sponsor the system by paying for its development; those who own the system and who will be responsible for its ongoing use and development; those who monitor the quality and the system's conformance to organisational standards; and finally those who have an influence on the system through their position, experience and knowledge of the application area.

The *analysis* of the requirements often concentrates on the resolution of conflicts that can occur naturally amongst these stakeholders. Recognising the need to address and resolve these conflicts is part of the analysis phase of the requirements engineering process. Prioritisation is also considered at this stage. The requirements engineer may apply the acronym MoSCoW to the requirements, judging each one on a scale of:

Must have

Should have

Could have

Won't have

When the analysis of the requirements has been completed and the conflicts have been resolved, *validation* of the requirements specification checks that they have been documented correctly and conform to the organisational standards. The testability of the requirements should be reviewed in conjunction with the system's testers, and the wording is checked for ambiguity. Prototyping, which might have been used earlier in the elicitation phase, can now be repeated to validate the requirements and models; data flow diagrams, entity models and any of the analysis techniques used in the elicitation phase will be checked for consistency.

Although the process of requirements engineering bears a close resemblance to that of systems analysis and design, by emphasising the requirements phase of the life cycle the requirements engineer avoids the pressure to start developing prematurely. The systems analyst, responsible for both the analysis and the design of the system, will frequently be urged by management to make crucial design decisions early in the project life cycle before the implications of the decision have been fully explored. The elicitation, analysis and validation of requirements provide a mechanism for avoiding this.

12.9 Strategic Information Systems

We saw in Chapter 1 the connection between business strategy and information systems, and the way in which strategic information systems can contribute to the competitive advantage that organisations seek to establish. This process can now be taken further by examining the *value chain* – the progressive added value of a product as it moves from one stage in the manufacturing process to another and then on to the customer for installation and maintenance.

Each step in the process adds value to the product, and the IT strategist can make a structured review of the contributions made by different systems to the increase in product value by both the current and proposed systems (Table 12.2). Some business processes are not directly involved with manufacturing although they make a vital contribution to its success. The support processes of human resource management, training and research can also benefit from the use of a strategic information system. The value chain leading to competitive advantage is represented in the form of an arrow as shown in Figure 12.6.

The value chain guides the analyst to each area of the business in turn so that the search for competitive advantage does not overlook any aspect of the manufacturing and support process. The value chain and the competitive forces analysis help us to look for potential business advantages and then relate them to the available hardware and software rather than looking at the technology first and then trying to find an application area that might be able to use it.

The business analyst's role is similar to that of the systems analyst, particularly in the early stages of the life cycle. The business analyst is expected to perform a more rigorous analysis of the business system requirements, to resolve conflicts and prioritise proposals. Business analysis and systems analysis use

Table 12.2 IT applications with their position in the value chain and the benefits they provide

Application	Value chain impact	Improvement or benefit
Stock control	Manufacturing and support	Working capital reduction; better investment; spares availability; faster production
Just in time	Manufacturing	Faster production; less WIP; better plant utilisation; reduced product cost
Supplier contract negotiation	Procurement	Quicker procurement; lower procurement costs; improved supplier product quality
Customer order servicing	Order processing	Better customer response; reduce lost business; customer profiling; monitoring of demand
Breakdown analysis	Maintenance and support	Reduction in faults; improved fault diagnosis; increased product reliability
Computer-aided design	Manufacturing	Reusable designs; quality documentation; subcontract opportunities; improved engineering
Project control	Installation	Quicker completion of installation; better use of staff; greater customer satisfaction

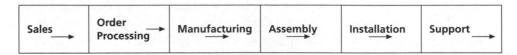

Fig. 12.6 A value chain for a manufacturing organisation

many of the same techniques, and none of the techniques described in this and any other chapter can be viewed as exclusive to one particular job title. The difference between the roles lies in emphasis. IT strategy, although not defined as the remit of either the systems analyst or the business analyst, is supported by techniques that move away from systems analysis techniques towards techniques that are encountered in other functional areas of the organisation. Defining requirements without designing the actual system that will deliver these requirements makes the business analyst responsible for planning and conducting the tests that will lead to the user's acceptance of the system.

The combination of the task of requirements definition with the responsibility for user acceptance testing fits well in organisations that have separate software development centres. The current trend to the 'outsourcing' of development to agencies outside the UK suggests that this role will increase in the future.

12.10 PESTEL Analysis

The business analyst needs to understand the factors that can affect the environment in which the business operates. One framework for doing this is known as a *PESTEL analysis*. PESTEL is an acronym that stands for Political, Economic, Social, Technological, Environmental and Legal. Business analysts wanting to increase their understanding of the organisation they are studying and to identify the factors that will support and impact upon the organisation's strategic planning for the use of information technology can use a PESTEL analysis. Indeed PESTEL analysis can be used in any strategic decision-making.

- *Political*. Political decisions affect all businesses. Government attitudes towards private and state-owned enterprises, international politics, and the impact of conflicts and variations in the price of oil and raw material supplies are among the many factors that can alter the future performance of an organisation.

- *Economic*. Economic factors are closely related to the political influences. Interest rates and currency exchange rates will affect home and international markets. Consumer expenditure is related to inflation and the amount of disposable income present within the different economic groups within a society. This, too, affects long-term planning. The profitability of the organisation, its market share and the predictions about these will also influence the planning process. Decisions taken to enlarge the European Union just before Christmas 2002 will have a profound impact on organisations in the joining countries and on those already inside the EU.

- *Social*. Social aspects may include demographic changes and the changing perceptions of the population, lifestyle changes, and changes in working conditions. Education, transport and family responsibilities are all examples of social issues that can impact on an organisation. An ageing population offers an opportunity to the healthcare sector yet threatens the capability of an economy's welfare structures.

- *Technology*. Technological factors include the availability of new ways of delivering a service through the use of technology, the use of technology to obtain and exploit marketing information, and the ability to extend choice and communicate readily with suppliers, customers and other agencies through the use of internetworking technology.

- *Environmental*. Climate change and the impact of pollution come under the environmental heading. Sustainability of raw material supplies, the use of energy, regional variations of climate, and the impact of the environment on the individual's lifestyle will also affect the way the organisation plans its growth.

- *Legal*. Legal issues link closely with the political, social and environmental aspects of the PESTEL analysis, as the constraints that occur under these headings are enforced through law. Anti-trust and monopoly legislation can be viewed as a political issue or as a legal issue, and similarly laws aimed at the reduction of pollution may be cited as environmental issues or may appear under the legal heading. Specific legislation may impact upon an organisation on account of its location. Planning restrictions may apply to organisations in greenbelt areas, and specific taxation legislation and controls may be applied to financial institutions.

The PESTEL analysis is often combined with a more general statement of an organisations goals and objectives, which is defined using the acronym *MOST*. MOST stands for the Mission, Objectives, Strategy and Tactics. This hierarchical classification of an organisation's goals has appeared in different forms over the years. R.N. Anthony was one of the first authors who identified this as a structure that can be applied to the development of management information systems when he classified planning decisions as strategic, tactical and operational, defining the structure as *Anthony's triangle*, as shown in Figure 12.7.

Although these techniques provide a broader analysis of an organisation's current business position and its future potential than the systems analyst would expect to perform, the strategic importance of information technology has made it imperative that the business analyst is able to view the organisation and its

Fig. 12.7 Anthony's triangle

goals in the context of these issues. The techniques are now considered as a significant pre-requisite of an IT development project and we include them in this text for that reason.

12.11 Summary

It is very important that the users of a proposed system read, understand and agree the specifications and that they are committed to their success. Securing this commitment requires that the specifications be presented clearly and that proper, controlled, methods are used to review them.

There are always options in the way in which a system may be developed, each one offering a different balance of functionality, cost and speed of implementation. Analysts and users must work together to identify options and to present a shortlist of these, together with their perceived costs and benefits to senior management for their decision.

This chapter has attempted to define the way in which the user's business requirements can be identified, specified and evaluated. Specifying a requirement in terms that a user can understand and agree is an essential skill for a systems analyst. As it becomes increasingly common for program development to be done remotely from the business user, so the emphasis on clear and unambiguous specification is increased. We have argued that the difference between the role of the systems analyst and the role of the business analyst is one of emphasis rather than of function, and that successful developments rely on both.

Exercises

12.1 The System Telecom LDS and DFDs that you have seen represent the selected business option: that is, they are for the preferred required system. Consider which areas of processing could have been excluded for reasons of cost. What are the two other options that would consequently be produced?

12.2 Identify the relative benefits and drawbacks of these options.

12.3 Using the Denton Motor Company case study in Appendix 1 perform the following requirements engineering tasks. A specimen answer is shown as an example on the form on p. 268.

  (a)   Identify and briefly name a requirement.
  (b)   Specify the requirement's source.
  (c)   Name the requirement's owner.
  (d)   Define the requirement.
  (e)   List the benefits to be derived from meeting the requirement.
  (f)   Allocate a priority to the requirement (you may use MoSCoW to specify this priority if you wish to).

Requirement Name	Source: Simon Martindate.
	Sales Office Manager
Stock Availability Check	Owner: Sales Department

Requirement Definition
Check each item on an incoming order for availability and allocate stock to the order.

Requirement Benefits
Improve service to the Denton dealers

Priority (MoSCoW)
M

12.4 Using the headings People, Money, Information and Technology complete the SWOT matrix on the Denton Motor Company. The solution has been started below.

SWOT for the Denton Motor Company

INTERNAL FACTORS			EXTERNAL FACTORS		
	Strengths	Weaknesses		Opportunities	Threats
People: Staff and managers	Commited Loyal		**People:** Customers suppliers		Lose customers through poor service
Money: Cash supply in DMH			**Money:** In the marketplace		
Information: Management information			**Information:** External market info	Obtain more customer information through WEB sales	
Technology: As used in DMH			**Technology:** As available outside DMH		

13 From Analysis to Design

13.1 Introduction

Having now used the PARIS model to take us through the five stages of planning the approach, asking questions and collecting data, recording the information, interpreting the information collected, and specifying the requirements, we shall now turn our attention to the process of design, the third stage in the model of systems development introduced earlier and shown here in Figure 13.1.

As we pointed out in Chapter 6, although the model is useful because it indicates the relative position of the stages in the development process, there is frequently an overlap between analysis and design, with high-level design beginning during analysis and analysis continuing as part of design. In the following chapters the design process will be described in detail. This chapter will focus on the transition from analysis to design.

The final deliverable from systems analysis is a document containing an unambiguous statement of the client's requirements for a new system. This document, called the *functional specification*, states what the development project will have to deliver in order to be considered a success. It is written by the analysis team and agreed and signed off by the client. The functional specification is the starting point for the designer, who will rely to a great extent on the accuracy and thoroughness with which the analysts have carried out their task. The analysts' understanding of the business, appreciation of the client's problems and documentation of requirements provide the foundation on which the designer will build a working solution. However, if the design is based on an inadequate understanding of the users' requirements, then the system delivered, however well it works, will not be a quality solution because it will fail to meet

Fig. 13.1 Stages in system development

the real needs of the business. This can lead to a great deal of extra work for the developers, who then have to carry out further analysis, fix the design, and produce and test revised code in order to deliver a system that *does* conform to the client's requirements. This is a costly process, because, as Edward Yourdon once observed, it is easier to make a working system efficient than to make an inefficient system work.

In structured methodologies, a lot of emphasis is placed on the need to spend considerable time and effort ensuring that analysis is rigorous so that the design process, and later the implementation, will be straightforward. A key factor in this approach is the use of structured techniques, and in the next section of this chapter we shall discuss their value in 'bridging the gap' between analysis and design. We shall then consider the objectives of design and the constraints on the process, before concluding the chapter with an overview of the stages in the design of a computer system.

13.2 Bridging the Gap

In traditional approaches to system development there was frequently a gap between the information about the system documented by the analyst and the detailed technical task that lay ahead for the designers. Although the existing physical system was described in detail, usually in the form of a lengthy narrative – sometimes described as a 'Victorian novel' – it still left the designer, who had to produce designs for files or databases, processes, interfaces and controls, with a lot of unanswered questions. Analysis ends with a description of what the new system must do, whereas design must specify how this will be done by selecting one of the many possible ways of doing it. The gap between the end of analysis and the beginning of the design is represented in Figure 13.2.

All structured methodologies share the view that logical models must be integral to the process of systems development in order to ease the transition between analysis and design, and also to enable intermediate views of the system to be discussed with the users. As we described in Chapter 6, a logical model describes exactly what the system does rather than how it is does it, by ignoring the constraints that determine how the current system is physically implemented. A required logical view is created by mapping the customer's requirements for a new information system onto the current logical model. The structured techniques used during analysis that provide this logical view include:

- *data flow diagrams* representing the processes that manipulate the data as it passes through the system;

- an *entity model* showing the relationship between the data items held within the system;

- a *data dictionary* providing an overall consistent definition of the data used by the organisation. This definition can include the content of the data stores, data flows and processes shown on the data flow diagrams, and the entities that make up the entity model.

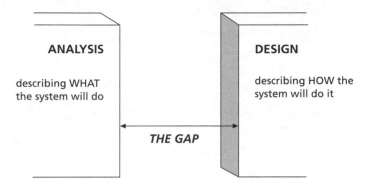

Fig. 13.2 The gap between analysis and design

These logical models provide a sound basis for the process of design, and, as we shall see later, the designer will use, amend and develop these models to create design documentation. For example, the entity model is used in drawing *logical access maps* – also described as data navigation diagrams – which assist in the design of files or databases, whereas the data flow diagram is the starting point for designing inputs to the system such as an order form, outputs from the system such as a sales report, and human–computer interfaces such as an online enquiry screen.

In this way the logical models support both the current system that is in operation and the new system being developed, and can be used to overcome the analysis/design gap by providing a 'bridge' of techniques central to the processes of analysis and design. This is particularly so when using structured systems analysis and design techniques that complement each other and which can be applied to the structured systems life cycle. You can see how this works in Figure 13.3.

The structured systems lifecycle begins with the physical DFD and the initial entity model, which are constructed as a result of the interviews with the users in the investigation phase of the project. The external entities and the datastores identified in the physical DFD indicate the things that the organisation needs to hold data about, and these show us the first of the entities in the entity model. Investigating the current system with the users also provides the input into the business systems requirements. The old physical DFD is converted into an old logical DFD by removing references to physical places, people and documents. Processes are combined where they are joined by data flows, and processes that simply manipulate data – such as photocopying or sorting – are also removed. The datastores on the physical DFD can be rationalised by replacing them with the entity names from the entity model. This removes the duplication of data that might occur in the physical system. The physical DFD might have processes on it that will not form part of the information system when it is automated, and these should be removed and shown as external entities with data flows to them and from them. The data flows can be rationalised to show only the data items that are needed by their destination process. If these flows have too many attributes

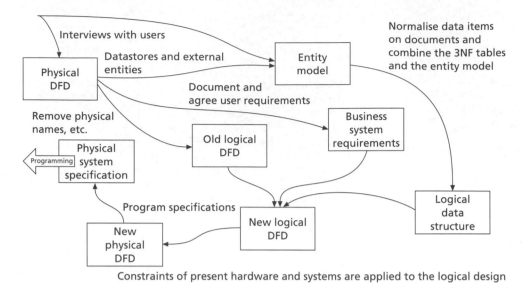

Fig. 13.3 The structured systems life cycle

to be shown on the diagram then it may be necessary to create a data dictionary of them and use a single-word identifier on the DFD. Sometimes processes exist in a system for political or traditional reasons, such as those that involve author-isations of some sort. If these process are no longer essential to the operation of the system then they should be excluded from the logical DFD.

The old logical DFD is combined with the user requirements, and this allows the analysts to produce a new logical DFD to show how the system will work in principle before it is adapted to the hardware, software and physical con-straints of the users business. The input to the new logical DFD is threefold. The old logical DFD, the business systems requirements and the LDS (logical data structure diagram) are the three essential components. Adding and chang-ing the processes creates changes to the data structure as new attributes and new entities are added to the model. The initial entity model will have been extended by the normalisation exercises carried out on documents collected in the investigation stage. The tables that have been developed through this process will be combined with the initial entity model to create a logical data structure diagram capable of supporting the functions described in the new logical DFD.

The logical system must then be adapted to fit the existing hardware and software in use and to meet any overriding business constraints. This produces a new physical DFD. The datastores become tables or files, or are mapped onto existing or modified data structures in the present system. New processes may need to be combined with existing ones as the logical model is incorporated into the present business practices. The final outcome from these structured systems models will be the program specifications that will be used by the developers to produce the new routines.

13.3 Design Objectives and Constraints

13.3.1 Objectives

It is important, right at the start of the design process, for the designer, or design team, to set clear objectives. The primary objective will always be to design a system that delivers the functions required by the client to support the business objectives of their organisation. For example, the system may be required to speed up the production of accurate invoices, so that the company's cash flow can be improved; or to provide up-to-date, detailed management information to improve the managing director's control over the business; or to help senior managers to make strategic decisions. In other words, to be a quality product – as we described in Chapter 4 – the system must conform to the customer's requirements, and be delivered in a way that meets their expectations in terms of service. There are many ways in which these requirements might be met by a physical design solution, but there are a number of other objectives that must be considered if a good design is to be produced:

- *Flexible*. The design should enable future requirements of the business to be incorporated without too much difficulty. Often, during the analysis phase, users may not be clear about the entirety of their needs, but during the evaluation period, after the new system becomes operational, further needs may emerge, and a flexible design will be able to accommodate these new requirements. In addition, businesses change over time, and a good design enables the system to reflect these changes. This is often called 'making the system futureproof'.

- *Maintainable*. This is closely linked to the previous objective because it is about change. A good design is easy to maintain, and this reduces the system's maintenance costs, which usually represent a high proportion of the total lifetime cost of the system.

- *Portable*. Still on the subject of change, a software system may have to run on new hardware. A good design is portable – in other words it is capable of being transferred from one machine environment to another with the minimum amount of effort to convert it.

- *Easy to use*. With the increasing exposure of people to computer applications in the home as well as in the office, expectations of computer systems in terms of their ease of use are also increasing. A good design will result in a system that is 'user friendly' – easy to understand, not difficult to learn how to use, and straightforward to operate. Competing products and services offered through the Internet seek to gain competitive advantage through their site becoming the user's 'site of choice'.

- *Reliable*. This objective is about designing systems that are secure against human error, deliberate misuse or machine failure, and in which data will be stored without corruption. This is desirable in any computer system, but for certain systems in the areas of defence, process control or banking, it will be a key design objective and when balancing time and cost equally during development.

- *Secure*. Security is another objective that must be considered by the designer. In order to protect the confidentiality of the data, particularly if it is commercially sensitive, it may be important to build in methods to restrict access to authorised users only.

- *Cost-effective*. This includes a number of the other objectives, and is about designing a system that delivers the required functionality, ease of use, reliability, security, etc., to the client in the most cost-effective way. This is often more complex than it may appear, as future system costs may be difficult to estimate and benefits difficult to quantify.

13.3.2 Constraints

In addition to thinking about design objectives, the designer must also be aware of the constraints that will have an impact on the design process. The logical models of the system are the starting point for design, but the physical realities of the environment in which the designer is working must be taken into account. In addition to time, which is always limited, and money – the available budget will limit the options available to designers – there are a number of other constraints that need to be taken into consideration. These are listed below:

- *Resources*. An important constraint on any design solution will be the availability of resources to be used in delivering a solution to the client. As hardware costs fall and people costs increase, and as skilled people remain hard to find, the human resource may be the key resource constraint.

- *The client's existing systems*. A major constraint would be the need for a new system to interface with other systems – hardware, software or manual – that already exist and will continue to be used by the client organisation. At the time of writing, the need to link web-enabled front-end systems to old legacy systems and the desire for data warehouse operations emphasise the need for good interoperability between applications.

- *Procedures and methods*. The final design might also be constrained by internal or external procedures, methods or standards. For example it might be a company standard to develop systems in SSADM, or use a specific CASE tool.

- *Knowledge and skills*. This might be an internally or externally imposed constraint. The knowledge and skills of the development team may limit a designer's options, as might the competence or 'computer literacy' of the potential users. Also, financial considerations may be important here – 'how much does it cost to employ two trainees compared with the cost of employing one expert?'

As long as the constraints on the possible design solution are clear to the design team from the beginning of the process, allowances can be made or alternatives considered, in order that the stated objectives of design can be met.

13.4 Summary

In this chapter we have looked at the interface between analysis and design. The value of starting with a set of logical models, produced during analysis, was emphasised, and we described how these models bridge the gap between analysis and design. If analysis has been carried out thoroughly and documented in an unambiguous manner, the designer's chances of delivering a quality system are greatly increased.

It is important that the designer is clear about the objectives of design, and understands the constraints that will affect any proposed design solution. With this in mind, the process of design, which includes the design of:

- controls;
- human–computer interfaces – inputs, outputs and dialogues;
- system interfaces;
- data – logical models, files, databases, and physical storage media;
- processes;

can begin. And of course any design solution must be considered in relation to a number of factors, including the available hardware, software and middleware.

Although analysis and design have been presented as two separate stages in systems development, we have emphasised that there may be considerable overlap between the two, and on large development projects the two processes may be occurring in parallel. The essence of a smooth transition between the analysis and design depends on the quality of the communication that takes place, and structured techniques provide an ideal means of communicating effectively.

14 Systems Design: Information Security

14.1 Introduction

In this chapter we're concerned with two things: protecting the system from external threat, and making sure that the normal day-to-day operation of the system processes data in a controlled way. So, we're trying to ensure secure operation of the information system and safeguard the information and assets stored in this system so that the application systems run properly. We're concerned with information security and application controls.

Typically, information security aims to preserve:

- *Confidentiality*. The only people to see the data are those authorised to see it. Private data is kept private; personal privacy is respected.

- *Integrity*. There are limits on who can change the data.

- *Availability*. Data is available at all times to authorised users.

- *Accountability*. It should be possible to discover after the event who has modified what data.

Information security is of concern to systems analysts but typically not part of their routine. It does, however, have the power to hit the headlines when security breaches are discovered or when viruses are spread over the Internet, and for this reason it is included here. It is the area of application controls that forms the routine part of analysis and design.

Also in this chapter are some aspects of computer fraud and auditing, and disaster recovery – or contingency planning, as it is often called.

There is one final point to be made in this introductory section. For controls to be effective they must operate in a systematic way and be part of an overall control framework. A control policy document should describe this framework and set out general guidelines for:

- *The control context.* A controls policy makes it clear that the control of IS systems is an important business issue, and that disciplinary action will be taken against employees who disregard IS control procedures. It is, for example, now commonplace to find statements in employee conditions of service dealing with the misuse of computers. The downloading of pornography from the Internet now routinely leads to disciplinary action and even dismissal. Within the overall context of information security, good business practices that have been followed since before the introduction of computers still apply. The recruitment process should still deal with assessments of the honesty and integrity of applicants, taking up of references and – in some cases – checking for criminal records and about issues concerning national security. Effective training, supervision and performance management all contribute towards the creation and maintenance of a climate of effective information security. Some organisations now also include statements about the use of laptops and mobile phones in public places.

- *Controls in systems development and maintenance.* These may include a review of the proposed new system design by an audit function, the monitoring and logging of system maintenance and software changes, and audits of the system's documentation.

- There will be similar controls applied to the *operation and maintenance of the system*, and access to the physical storage of data. These will certainly include access controls to data centres and the use of remote terminals, and authentication of registered users.

- *Contingency planning measures* will include firewalls around the systems to prevent deliberate attack, and disaster recovery procedures to deal with maintaining the delivery of information services in the event of a disaster of some kind – fire, flood, explosion, terrorist activity and so on.

All of this costs money, and could be regarded as an overhead cost to the 'normal' running of organisations' information systems. There is therefore a need to balance the investment in information security with the likely risks. The client needs to make this assessment with help from the analyst, risk specialists and information security experts. The parameters of likely risk change all the time as threat profiles change and as requirements change owing to changes in financial regulation, legislation or business need. The effects of the terrorist attacks in New York on September 11, 2001 have still to be realised as far as information security is concerned.

And just in case you're not entirely convinced of the need to treat this subject seriously here are some examples of the kinds of problems being faced.[1]

- At the end of September 2001 the Bush Administration appointed Richard Clarke to head a new office of Cyberspace Security.

1 These examples are drawn from news items in the *Guardian*, *The Nation* (Kenya), *The Times of India*, *The Times*, *Sunday Business*, several Internet sites and surveys including NCC, Ernst & Young, Gartner Group and Peapod.

- In July 2001 the head of the Australian Defence Forces said that more than 30 countries had 'advanced and aggressive programmes for waging war by computer'.

- In the business magazine *Fortune* a risk management firm said that many of the contract staff who fixed Y2K problems in corporate systems were working for overseas intelligence operations.

- The Department of Trade in the UK said that 60% of all UK firms had suffered a security breach in the two years 2000 and 2001, and that many of them did not recognise that their business information was a valuable asset and was sensitive or critical to their business.

- 50% of European employees spend three hours a week on-line on non-work-related websites using their employees' computers and networks.

- Two-thirds of emails going through employers' email systems are not business related.

- There are now six pieces of legislation in the UK detailing an organisation's responsibility for the protection of information from improper use. These are the Data Protection Act, the Human Rights Act, The e-Commerce Directive, The Unfair Contract Terms Act, The Regulation of Regulatory Powers Act, and the Electronic Communications Act.

- The Indian government has introduced new legislation in its Information Technology Act to punish people, who, without authorisation, download data or viruses, tamper with source code, or change computer-held information. Punishments include up to three years in prison.

14.2 Hacking and Viruses

The business and technology pages of the broadsheet papers can usually be relied upon for regular articles about threats to computer security, global cyber attacks and viruses. The simple fact is that every organisation connected to the Internet is vulnerable to hackers and viruses. Hacking and viruses are big business, and illegal – which is why hundreds of Internet sites tell you how to hack or to send out viruses! In the USA there are annual hackers' conferences.

In 2001 ZDNET – an IT Internet news site – reported that Russian and Ukrainian hackers had stolen the details of more than one million credit cards by targeting over 40 e-banking and e-business sites. According to the FBI many of the sites were then blackmailed by the hackers, who threatened to reveal the break-ins and use the credit card details if a ransom wasn't paid. Although the cost of such attacks – whether or not the ransoms were paid – is spread across retailers, credit card companies and consumers, the effect is to create a loss of confidence in e-commerce generally.

A famous case reported in most UK newspapers identified a Welsh teenager who caused a worldwide alert after gaining access to the details of 23 000 credit cards. It was estimated that £2 million of damage was caused to the dot.com companies involved. Eventually it took the British, Canadian and US law enforcement agencies to track him down, leading to his arrest and trial.

Consulting and computing services companies now offer to carry out penetration studies of computer systems and networks. Reported in the *CFO Magazine* in 1998 a senior manager from one large international consulting house described some of the activities in such a study. These included

- attacking the firewall that protects the system from the Internet;

- dialling every extension on the company's network until a computer answers;

- obtaining key information from employees over the phone by posing as an employee.

What advice do the experts give? No business can be entirely secure, but the following things can help:

- Re-examine all policies and procedures about security. Are all employees aware of security policies?

- Carry out audits internally and use occasional penetration surveys.

- Allocate resources to securing systems according to the degree of risk.

- Use the latest versions of anti-virus software and firewall protection.

- Review normal business controls. The two biggest currency trading disasters – one brought down Barings and the other hit AIB for over £500 million – were the result of inadequate internal control mechanisms and supervision.

- Upgrade access controls so that access to systems and data is closely controlled. Unauthorised insider use of systems was reported by 40% of almost 500 users in a Computer Institute Survey in the late 1990s.

14.3 The Purpose of Control

Most modern organisations in the public and private sector depend on their information systems in order to be able to operate reliably. Banks and other financial institutions can't survive a total failure of their IS systems for more than a few days. We are all affected in our daily lives by computer failures in transport systems, utility companies, banks and other financial institutions, hospitals, ambulance dispatching systems, supermarkets and government offices. It's convenient to think that if the hardware and software never malfunctioned then the need for controls in IS systems would be significantly reduced, but problems would still arise owing to unexpected events and the activities of those ever-present humans who use the systems, design, build and modify them. We therefore need to safeguard the systems we design and build.

We can classify the controls needed as follows:

- *Administrative or management controls.* These are concerned with the control of the IS/IT framework. They are not usually developed by systems analysts for specific projects, as they extend across the whole of the IS function and involve other departments as well. There are some essential framework controls that you should expect to see where you work. These include a published controls policy that describes the reasons for controls, responsibility for operating and working within the policy, the penalties of not following the rules – from the organisation's and the individual's standpoint – and advice about what to do should you see breaches of control policies – sometimes called the 'whistleblowers' charter'!

- There should also be *formal procedures, standards manuals and quality procedures* for the systems development and project management processes as well as appropriate manuals and back-up procedures for computer operation.

- Ranging more widely across the organisation there should be policies for the *recruitment and selection of personnel* who pay attention to these issues, and induction training should cover the essentials of IS security and control. These days there are more and more organisations that set policies to establish the organisation's right to monitor and inspect Internet access and email use, and to discipline employees who go beyond what are set down as acceptable limits.

- Finally, these administrative controls should follow the good practices of earlier manual systems and *separate out the different functions* responsible for processing data so that no single individual has complete access to all parts of a process. The process of separating, for example, authorisation of payment, recording the payment and making the payment increases the difficulty with which fraudulent payments can be made.

- *Access and protection controls.* These are usually aimed at preventing unauthorised access to systems and data, and include restricting access to computer rooms and data libraries, and limiting access to networked and Internet systems to those users who have the appropriate access rights. Physical access is usually controlled by swipe cards and passwords and sometimes monitored by a computer system that logs who has had access to specific facilities. Except in areas of particularly high security, physical access controls are generally regarded as not very secure. Employees lend entry passes to visitors and contractors, and passwords are often well known.

- There are often similar problems with *terminal log-on procedures and remote user passwords*, and we saw earlier in this chapter how organised crime and purposeful hacking can make systems vulnerable to unauthorised access.

- *System-specific controls.* These are an analyst/designer's responsibility and are the subject of most of the rest of this chapter. They aim to deal with prevention, detection, minimising loss, recovery from failure and subsequent investigation. Outside the analyst's responsibility lies the audit process. We'll examine controls on input, output, processing and storage.

14.4 Input Controls

In the early years of expansion in IS development there was a popular acronym – GIGO; indeed there was even a film made with GIGO as its title. It stands for *garbage in, garbage out* and was intended to stress the need for controls over input to computer systems. It didn't win an Oscar but was shown to many thousands of users as part of computer appreciation courses and user training programmes. Data input is still the area where most control is applied, as it is here that greatest scope exists for error and fraud. (Input controls aim to ensure the accuracy, completeness and reasonableness of data entering the system.) We can identify the following typical control mechanisms:

* *Format checks.* (These check the structure and format of data items) In the UK, a national insurance number – essentially one's identification number – is made up of two letters, six numbers and one letter. The picture of the data item is therefore AA 999999 A, and an input validation program will expect to see national insurance numbers in this format.

* *Limit checks.* These test that incoming data items fall within expected limits. Typical examples might be that hours worked in a week are less than 100, that the numbers of light bulbs ordered is less than 50, or that the number of gearboxes per order is less than 250.

* *Reasonableness checks.* The data is in the right format and within limits, but does it look reasonable? Salary costs for departments in a bank may range from £10 000 a month for a small department up to £800 000 for a large one. A monthly salary summary input item of £38 000 falls within acceptable limits and is in an acceptable format; however, the average monthly bill is £650 000, so probably the data entered is unreasonable and worth investigating. This is a useful check to employ when data is occasionally supplied from a different source – for example a householder reading the gas meter instead of the regular gas company meter reader.

* *Checking those big numbers!* 14529144009366318 is a long number. It's the account reference code for a householder's electricity supply. There's plenty of scope for entering it wrongly into the system. A good analyst will have split it down into more easily referenced groupings such as 14 529 144 009 366 318, but it's still a big number. Check digits are used to ensure that long account reference codes are checked. Let's choose an easier example. If the code was 6968436, typical entry errors would be 6986436, where two digits are transposed, or perhaps 6968426, where one digit is entered incorrectly. Probably both of these mistakes pass the format and limit checks and, as it is an account code reference number, the reasonableness check is not applicable. Check digit verification detects these errors by adding an extra digit to the code number, derived by a simple calculation. The calculation uses a weight – the multiplier used on each digit in the original code number to arrive at a product – and a modulus – the number that is used to divide the sum of the weighted products to arrive at a remainder. Here's how it works. If the

incoming account reference number is 6968436 and we use weights of 8-7-6-5-4-3-2 and modulus 11 the way of allocating the check digit is as follows:

1 Multiply each digit in turn by its corresponding weight. This gives

$$(6 \times 8)\ (9 \times 7)\ (6 \times 6)\ (8 \times 5)\ (4 \times 4)\ (3 \times 3)\ (6 \times 1)$$
$$48 \quad\ 63 \quad\ 36 \quad\ 40 \quad 16 \quad\ 9 \quad\ 6$$

2 Sum the resultant products: $48 + 63 + 36 + 40 + 16 + 9 + 6 = 218$

3 Divide the sum by the modulus and note the remainder: 210 divided by $11 = 19$ and a remainder of 9.

4 Subtract the remainder from the modulus and the result is the check digit, $11 - 9 = 2$. So the new complete code number becomes 69684362.

Sometimes, the remainder comes out at 10 (for code number 5968436 for example), and in these cases X is used as the check digit.

- *Other checks.* The advent of real-time, online systems has meant that data going into the system can be verified immediately. We all nowadays telephone call centres, give our reference number, membership number or account number and hear the call centre operator confirm back to us our name and address. In other systems, entering data in one field requires data to be entered in another. Typical examples are:

  'If married and female give your maiden name.'
  'If you have moved in the last 12 months give your previous address.'

In batch systems we are also concerned to ensure that all data is processed – that input processing is complete. There are three typical completeness checks:

- *Batch control totals.* Incoming transactions are collected together in batches of transactions. One field is identified as the batch control field – perhaps order amount or invoice amount – and the total order or invoice amounts are calculated manually and compared with the equivalent total generated by the computer for that batch. This isn't a foolproof check, as compensating errors may be made, and manual calculations can also be wrong.

- *Hash totals.* These are similar, but here a meaningless total is calculated manually and by the computer – perhaps all part numbers are summed in a batch of goods received notes.

- Simplest of all is just to *count* the number of items in the batch.

With the growth of real-time systems physical batches no longer exist, and sometimes logical batches are used instead, where the order entry clerk, call centre operator or whoever is the focus, and transactions entered by each one in a day become the 'batch'.

There should also be a record of the transactions entered into the system and of the errors found. It is especially important in batch systems that errors don't bring processing to a halt, so an error log is usually kept. With real-time systems, where input transactions come from many different places a transaction log may well be kept by the system, and in some systems these are used by audit packages to check against fraud.

Finally some comments on form design. All of us I expect are the victims of having to use poorly designed forms, where the spaces for entering the required data are too small – try writing 23 November 2002 in the space available on a UK cheque, where the instructions are confusing, where you have to enter data twice, or where the form asks for what you consider to be unreasonable information. Difficult forms design often reflects the complexities of the system to which the form belongs or, more often, a lack of clarity when specifying the requirements of the system. The following advice, taken from a predecessor book to this one, still holds true.

When designing a form:

- Define the objective.
- Specify the data content.
- Draft a design.
- Try it out.
- Redesign it.
- Try it out in the field.
- Revise it.
- Produce it.

Appearance is important. Forms that look complicated and difficult to complete, or are unattractive to the eye, are not likely to do the job they are intended to do. Be polite. 'Please complete part B . . .' is so much better than 'You must now complete part B . . .' Be prepared to compromise between the needs of a computer system and those of the user. The user's interest should be paramount. It is pointless having efficient processing if every single user finds the input form difficult to use. With the advent of the Internet the ease of data entry by someone at home may easily mean the difference between ordering from Tesco rather than from Sainsbury – or vice versa.

14.5 Output Controls

Output controls aim to ensure that output is complete and accurate and gets to the right people in a timely fashion. Operating procedures will define when output is to be ready and how it is to reach the intended users of it. It would be comforting to think that outputs were only for distribution within the organisation, but with us all now receiving telephone bills, gas, electricity and water bills, bank statements, credit card statements and many other demands as well, and probably every month, computer-produced outputs are now customer service documents or even sales aids. Apart from not having the funds to pay, disputing items on an invoice or protesting that it's not clear or didn't reach me on time are perhaps the commonest reasons for non-payment of bills, and a consequent cash flow issue for the organisation sending them out. Why else would so many organisations insist on payment by variable direct debit?

Typical output controls include:

- *Control totals*. These detect whether or not extra outputs have been produced, or whether some are missing. They assure the user that all of the expected reports and documents have been produced. If the number of input documents triggers the number of output documents to be produced, then an output control should be checkable against the appropriate input control.

- *Spot checks*. All output documents cannot be checked individually, but spot checks on the outputs can detect printing problems or failures in processing that have not been detected by processing controls. Outputs with nil or exceptionally high quantities or values should be checked; they should of course have been reported as exceptions during processing.

- *Pre-numbering*. Some outputs – such as cheques – will be on pre-printed and pre-numbered stationery. All pre-numbered forms need to be accounted for, including any documents spoilt during printer set-up.

14.6 Processing Controls

All controls involve some sort of processing, as their purpose is to control the operation of an information system. There are some controls, however, that focus specifically on protecting data during processing.

There are two main causes of data corruption: the actions of system users and the inadequacy of the original design. Users can be creative in finding ways to make the system do things it was not designed to do, and will make a habit of it if they think the system should be able to do it. Often this is done with the best of intentions, perhaps to save time or recover from a plant failure, and usually without realising that this will cause problems. This can happen only if the system design allows it.

For example, in an automated warehousing system, information about where the pallets were stored chained the records together. The first pallet of product A identified itself as the head of the chain and pointed to the location of the second pallet and so on down the chain to the end. However, the crane mechanisms were notoriously prone to failure. The crane sometimes picked up a pallet to be stored in the warehouse and then stopped in the middle of storing it. The pallet was then manually recovered. Because manual recovery meant switching off the crane, this caused the crane to lose the data about that pallet. This in turn broke the product chain, which made retrieving any following pallets impossible without first fixing the chain. So if there were 50 pallets of product A to be stored and the crane failed on pallet number 32, pallet 31 pointed to a location that was thought to be empty, and pallets 32 to 50 could not be found (Figure 14.1).

Pallet number	Warehouse location	Data stored on the system
1	location full	points to next pallet
2	" "	" " " "
3	" "	" " " "
.	" "	" " " "
.	" "	" " " "
.		
30	location full	points to next pallet
31	location empty	no pointer
32	location full	points to next pallet
33	" "	" " " "
34	" "	" " " "
.	" "	" " " "
.	" "	" " " "
.	" "	" " " "
50	location full	points to next pallet

Fig. 14.1 Data chain broken due to hardware failure

Because the location for the 32nd pallet was empty the pointer to pallet 33's location was blank, and therefore pallets 32 to 50 were not retrievable using the system. These broken chains usually went unnoticed until the warehousemen tried to retrieve pallets of that product to load it onto a delivery lorry. The crane failures were not anticipated, so the software system was not designed to recover from them. The user's method of overcoming the problem then caused data to be inaccessible.

Another typical case can arise where the designed system is badly implemented: for example, where the value reported by the system does not match the value the user expects to see, or a cross-check value held by the system. Let's say that at the end of each monthly billing period a cellular phone system adds up the cost of each call made on that phone for the month. This figure is then checked against a running total that was incremented each time the phone was used. At times, these two figures do not match. Which figure does the client accept as being accurate? This problem arises because, in the design of the system, the part dealing with day-to-day processing of the calls and the part of the system dealing with the monthly billing processing are using the same data in different ways to produce different results.

The effects of a damaged system can be anything from inconvenient to life-critical. Consequences will vary depending on the data problem. If a charity's mailing list has been corrupted and the postcodes are missing, the consequence might be that some mailshots are delivered late or not delivered at all. If a formula for a new type of oil was stored on a system and fell into the hands of competitors, the originators would quickly lose their competitive advantage. If a military aircraft wrongly identified a friendly aircraft as an enemy it could be shot down. This occurred in 1991 when an American warship stationed in the Arabian Gulf identified an Iranian airliner as an Iraqi fighter plane and shot it down.

However, it would be wrong to assume that, simply because an organisation operates in a commercial marketplace, all security problems should be treated as profit-threatening, or that all inconsistencies in a defence establishment threaten lives or political stability. Alongside the technical problems that have to be resolved are the personal issues. If bad design or inadequate advice about the consequences of decisions was the cause, the client may lose confidence in the system and its developers, and this will take months to rebuild. Two issues must be investigated: how is the relationship between the software maintainers, client organisation and system users affected, and how is the relationship between the client organisation and its clients affected?

Consider what happens when an online flight booking system goes down. Prospective travellers might phone back later, but they are as likely to phone another airline. For that airline to decide whether it is cost-effective to prevent this happening, they might use a simple algorithm:

Bookings per hour × hours to recover × probability of risk occurring

However, this takes no account of the subconscious effect on their clients, who might start thinking along the lines of 'If their computer system is unreliable, how reliable are their planes?' or 'If they can't give me instant information, they don't value my custom.' These are less tangible, and the impact lasts much longer than the system downtime.

14.7 Storage Controls

Storage security operates at two levels; physical security to ensure that no damage is done to the files while they are not being used, and file or database processing controls to ensure the integrity of file data.

Physical access controls to file libraries and computer rooms aim to prevent unauthorised access to files. The usual range of access permissions such as swipe cards and keyed entry locks are used, and the roles of the file librarian and the database administrator are critical in setting up and monitoring access to data. Simple things such as physical and software file labels ensure that the correct versions of files are used.

Once the files are available to the system, further protection against loss of data is possible. Magnetic tape files and floppy disks can be set to be read-only files. Machine-readable file labels identify the file at its start point giving at least its name, creation date, last update date and, in the case of disk files, the start and end addresses. Labels at the end of the file – trailer labels – also contain file control totals that can be used to check against control totals produced during processing. There could, for example, be cross-footing totals to show that the file totals for gross pay minus deductions equalled net pay, and that the amounts carried forward by the file balanced against those produced as an output control.

Copies of important files or master files are often held for security purposes. The so-called *grandfather–father–son* method is often used to achieve this. With this method, three versions of a file are available at any one time. File version 3 – the son – is the latest version of the file and was created from file 2 – the father –

which, in turn, was created from file 1 – the grandfather. The advantage of this technique is that recovery is always possible, as the latest run can be repeated as well as the run before that. This recovery system is used mostly with magnetic tape systems, but can also be used with direct access device processing. More usually, however, direct access devices have their files dumped into back-up storage – usually tape based – so that files can be reconstituted in the event of a major file failure. PC-based networks routinely back up files held on servers and rely on users backing up files held on the hard disk.

Remember that the time and effort involved in producing back-ups will only be worthwhile if they are made regularly.

14.8 Audit Controls

There are two types of audit: external audit and internal audit. The *external audit* gives an independent, reliable and expert opinion about financial statements: do the financial statements produced give a true and fair reflection of the state of the business? A typical statement might be as shown in Box 14.1. *Internal audits* aim to prevent fraud by evaluating internal financial control systems, and are a useful resource to help in the development of control procedures for IS systems.

Typically the audit of computer-based systems can be done in two ways. For relatively simple systems the computer processing is regarded as taking place in a 'black box', and auditing concentrates on the inputs and outputs, and checks that the outputs derived from the inputs are correct according to the procedures carried out. With this 'auditing around the computer' there is no attempt made to check on the internal processes of the system. 'Auditing through the computer' checks the external inputs and outputs and the internal processes. Computers' audit software packages are usually used to do this. With the increasing complexity of IS systems and the greater extent to which they used in business, auditing through the computer is now commonplace. This doesn't mean, however, that it is simple to do, and system controls often have to be built into the system to enable reliable auditing to take place. This is another reason for involving the audit function in this aspect of design.

14.9 Contingency Planning

Contingency planning is sometimes described as *information security of the last resort*. It takes care of the unexpected disaster due to breakdown, natural disaster, accident or sabotage. Regrettably, in recent times the threat of sabotage or terrorist action has caused many IS/IT departments in the public and private sectors to pay more attention to contingency planning.

The National Institute of Standards and Technology – a US government agency – describes a seven-step contingency process for organisations to use in the development and maintenance of its contingency plans for its IT systems. It covers seven platform types: desktop and portable systems, websites, servers,

Box 14.1 Typical audit statement

Statement of the independent auditors to the shareholder of XYZ plc
(pursuant to section 251 of the Companies Act 1985).

We have examined the Group Profit and Loss Account and Group Balance Sheet.

Respective responsibilities of directors and auditors

The Directors are responsible for preparing the Annual Review and Summary Financial Statement in accordance with applicable United Kingdom law. Our responsibility is to report to you our opinion on the consistency of the summary financial statement within the Annual Review and Summary Financial Statement with the full annual financial statements and directors' report, and its compliance with the relevant requirements of section 251 of the Companies Act 1985 and the regulations made thereunder. We also read the other information contained in the Annual Review and Financial Statement and consider the implications for our report if we become aware of any apparent misstatements or material inconsistencies with the summary financial statement.

Basis of opinion

We conducted our work in accordance with Bulletin 1999/6 'The auditor's statement on the summary financial statement' issued by the Auditing Practices Board for use in the United Kingdom. Our report on the group's full annual financial statements describes the basis of our audit opinion on those financial statements.

Opinion

In our opinion the summary financial statement is consistent with the full annual financial statements and directors' report of XYZ plc for the year ended 31 December 2002 and complies with the applicable requirements of sections 251 of the Companies Act 1985 and the regulations made thereunder.

Audits InternationalAA

Chartered Accountants
Registered Auditor.

---

local area networks, wide area networks, distributed systems, and mainframe systems.

The first step is to develop a contingency planning policy: this is not likely to be a task for a new systems analyst, but you may be expected to consider how the contingency plans you and your user customers prepare for your application system development fit into the overall policy. Following the establishment of the organisation's contingency plan, the following steps are identified:

1 A business impact analysis identifies and prioritises the critical IT systems and components.

2 Preventive controls can be established to reduce the effects of disruption.

3 Recovery strategies ensure that the system can be recovered quickly and effectively following a disruption.

4 Contingency plans specify how to restore a damaged system.

5 Testing and training plans improve overall effectiveness and ensure that the organisation can respond quickly and thoroughly to an emergency.

6 Regular review and maintenance of the plan keep the plan up to date and enable the organisation to meet changing circumstances.

A sample IT contingency policy statement for a banking and financial service organisation is shown in Box 14.2.

Typical contingency planning strategies include the use of off-site storage for regular back-ups of data, application programs and operating systems together with appropriate operating documentation, procedure manuals, software licences and legal documents. The use of standard hardware and software platforms makes system recovery easier, and for this reason, if for no other, leaving the development of contingency planning measures until the operations phase of the life cycle is too late.

Contingency measures should be identified at all stages of the development life cycle so that design decisions can be taken in the full knowledge of their contingency implications.

Contingency planning almost always includes the use of standby facilities and networks. Moving from the least expensive to the most expensive, these include:

- cold sites, which provide the basic building infrastructure but no IT equipment or software or even office equipment;

- hot sites of office space and facilities, with all the necessary equipment and staff available on a 24 by 7 basis;

- mirrored sites, which give full real-time mirroring of the mission-critical systems for which they are the back-up. A mirrored site is identical to the primary site in every respect, except one: it's in a different place!

Finally, and in keeping with the US flavour of this section, the State of Kansas Department of Information Systems and Communication publishes on the Internet a structure for a typical contingency plan (www.da.state.ks.us). You might care to consider the section on business impact analysis for a service on which you regularly rely at work or at home and think about some of the issues faced by the service you have chosen. You might also care to check out whether

Box 14.2 A sample IT contingency policy statement

The Plouer Banking Corporation (PBC) contingency planning policies are mandatory for all mission-critical systems as set out in Appendix A, and shall meet the needs of these systems in the event of disruptions to service exceeding the threshold times specified in the systems descriptions. The procedures for the execution of the contingency planning capability shall be documented in a formal contingency plan by the IT Contingency Planning Manager, and shall be reviewed and tested according to an annual plan agreed between the IT Contingency Planning Manager and the appropriate business general managers.

Each plan will assign specific responsibilities to designated staff or jobs, and staff responsible for any part of a designated system will receive full and appropriate training.

the service has contingency plans in place that enable you to get the level of service you currently enjoy in the event of an unexpected disaster.

14.10 Summary

In this chapter we have considered various aspects of information security, its purpose, and the increasing need for it as information becomes increasingly recognised as a business resource. The chapter has also identified typical controls for inputs, outputs, files and procedures, and invited you to consider some aspects of contingency planning for a system important to you.

Exercises

14.1 System Telecom relies very much on having its systems up and running when they are needed. How would you formulate a protection policy for the system described in the level 1 DFD? Remember to consider the risks to the system and the risks to the business.

14.2 Field sales representatives in System Telecom all use laptop PCs to send call reports or orders to their local office. They also receive sales information directly from the local office server. What security measures should be taken to protect this activity? Remember that System Telecom's style of operation is 'lean and mean', but equally it regards competitive information as having a high value.

15 Systems Design: Human–Computer Interaction

15.1 Introduction

In this chapter we shall look at the design of the interfaces that make possible the communication between the computer system and the people who use it. Such an interface can be described as the point at which the user and the computer system meet. We shall consider the output the users receive, the input they enter, and the dialogues through which the user and the system talk to each other. The inputs and outputs that are referred to are those which involve people. Inputs to, and outputs from, other systems or other processes in the same system are described in the next chapter.

The specification of outputs, inputs and dialogues forms a key part of the designer's task because of the high visibility of these interfaces to the users of the system. The output produced by the computer is the main reason for developing the new system. If the users are clear what they want from the system, the inputs needed to produce this output can then be identified. Should the output fail to meet the requirements of those who have to use it, the system can be seen as a waste of time by those users, who may have little appreciation of the internal, and therefore invisible, sound design or elegant code. The layout of a screen and the consistency of the dialogue will be important to those users who have to spend a lot of time sitting in front of terminals, and who will base their evaluation of the whole system on these interfaces. If the method of entering data is difficult, because of a poorly designed input form for example, then the chances of inaccurate or incomplete data entering the system will be greatly increased, which in turn will adversely affect the value of the output produced.

Some designers see the design of forms, screens and reports as a less important or less interesting part of their task than grappling with the logical design models. However, the time and effort spent getting the interface design right will enable the designer to meet the design objective, described in Chapter 13, of producing a system that is easy to use. In this chapter we first consider how interfaces are identified as a result of drawing the system boundary, and then go on to discuss the design of outputs, inputs and dialogues. Finally we describe one other area of interface design – the design of the workstation. This is important for the designer because it can significantly affect the performance of the end user, it can be critical in their perception of the system, and it also has health and safety implications.

15.2 Agreeing the System Boundary

In order to identify where in the new system the interfaces will occur, a useful starting point for the analyst or designer is the data flow diagram for the required system. This is a logical view, which was described in detail in Chapter 11. The example shown in Figure 15.1 is a simplified version of a required DFD for an order processing system. The line around the edge represents the system boundary and shows those parts of the system to be automated – inside the line – as well as those parts that will remain outside the new computer system. This boundary must be determined in consultation with the users of the new system, and in the end it is their decision as to which processes are automated, and which require human judgement or intuition and are therefore best done by people. In discussing this with the client, there are three questions to be asked about any process:

- Can it be automated?

- Is it economic to do so? The answer to the first question may be 'yes', but will it be worth the money in terms of the benefit it will bring to the business?

- Is it operationally possible to automate it? In other words will the environment allow it? There may be resistance to the automation, for example from vested interests of some kind.

The designer will present options, but the final decision rests with the client. When the system boundary has been agreed, both the client and the system developer will be able to see clearly what is in and what is out of the new system. In the data flow diagram in Figure 15.1, inputs are represented by data flows entering the system and outputs are those data flows leaving the system. The points at which one of these lines enters or leaves a process box mark the actual interfaces with the system, and procedures have to be designed to handle these. This includes the design of screens and dialogues that allow the users to give instructions or to ask questions about the stored information. The system boundary can also be used to illustrate the phases in the development of a system by extending the original boundary with dotted lines on the DFD to represent the future stages of the project.

15.3 Output Design

Having identified from a logical model of the new system where the outputs will be, by listing those data flows that cross the system boundary as they leave the

An Invoicing and order processing system

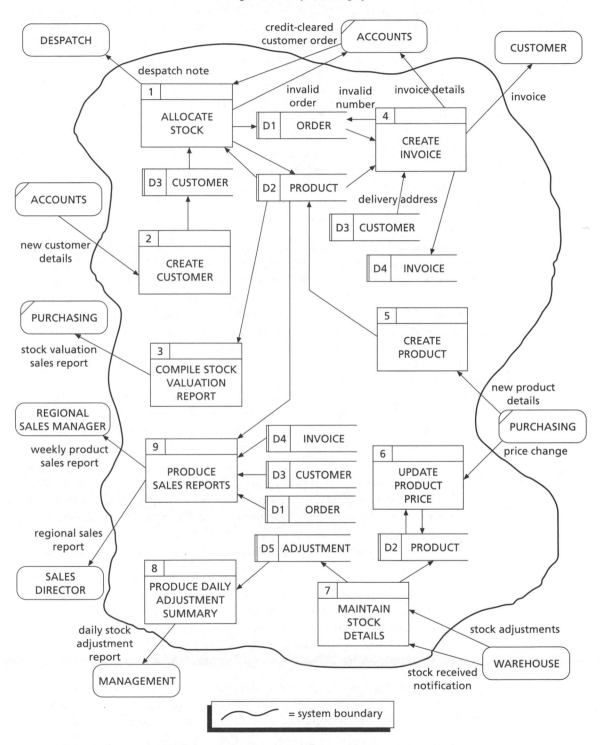

Fig. 15.1 The identification of outputs, inputs and dialogues on a data flow diagram

system, the next stage in the process is to determine their content. Again, structured techniques play a useful role here, because the designer can turn to the data dictionary to find the content of each data flow that represents an output. Let's consider an example from the DFD in Figure 15.1 – the output described as *Stock Valuation Report*. According to the data dictionary, the contents of this data flow are as follows:

Data item	Type	Length
Inventory group	Character	25
Stock code	99999	5
Product description	Character	30
Unit cost	999.99	6
Quantity in stock	99	2
Unit selling price	9999.99	7
Expected sales	999	3

Once the content is known, the designer must select the appropriate method or technology to present the information, and then create the document, report or display that contains the required information. Note that not all of the outputs required by the user may be shown on a data flow diagram. For example, a number of ad-hoc reports may be required on demand from data stored in the system, or exception reports – which show only data items that are unexpected, or above or below a predefined limit – may have been identified as a requirement in the requirements catalogue produced by the systems analyst. These should not be overlooked by the designer.

A quality output is one that meets the requirements of the end user, and which presents the information in a way that is clear, easy to read and visually attractive. In order to decide on an appropriate method of presentation, and a suitable format, a number of questions need to be asked:

- *Who receives the output?* What profile can you create of your target population and their needs? The output may be received, for example, by users within the company, e.g. a listing of accommodation available, or by people outside the organisation, such as customers, e.g. an invoice, or government departments, e.g. Inland Revenue returns, or by management, e.g. a monthly sales report.

- *Under what circumstances will the output be received?* Does the environment place constraints on the technology that can be used? For example, if the output is to be generated on a factory floor, the device used may have to operate effectively in dusty or dirty conditions, or in a noisy environment where an error message 'beep', which would be perfectly audible in an office setting, would be inappropriate.

- *What use will be made by the receivers of the information on the output documents or screens?* If the design of the output is to result in a quality product, then its purpose, from the user's point of view, must be understood by designers.

- *When and how often is the output needed?* What implications will the required frequency of information have for the selection of an output method? For example, a warehouse supervisor may require a daily stock report, whereas senior management may need to receive reports only once a month (although they might also require the facility to make ad-hoc enquiries).

The answers to these questions will help the designer make decisions about whether a display or a printed copy of the output is required, the type of device needed to produce the output required, and the layout of the information that would best meet the needs of the users.

One fundamental rule of human–computer interface design is to base the design on the level of skill and experience of the user. Generally designers will classify users in three broad categories:

- *Dedicated or skilled keyboard users.* These are people whose primary function involves the use of the keyboard or the data entry device. In some cases they may be dedicated solely to data input, and the designer will know that they are capable of achieving input speeds of 8000, 10 000 or even 12 000 key depressions per hour. They will not be involved in decision-making as a result of their keyboard activities, but will be focused on speed and accuracy. The keyboard user will not know the application area that the data is directed towards or comes from, and their only contact with the user might be when errors in keying or transcription of data are corrected

- *Semi-dedicated users.* The semi-dedicated user needs the system to perform their job and will expect to spend more than 50% of their working day using a terminal or input device. They will use the system often as a means of entering and updating data, but they will be involved in decision-making and communication with customers, suppliers or other members of the organisation in their job. The range of applications they will use will be wider than that for the dedicated user, and therefore the functionality they will require will be greater. The design for this category of user will often require a trainee and an experienced user interface, and designers may introduce shortcuts for longer-term users who have become very familiar with the system and wish to maximise the throughput of work they can achieve.

- *Casual or infrequent users.* These users can occur for many different reasons. The user may need to use the system infrequently; a tax assessment system might be used only yearly by members of the public performing their tax returns. Senior managers might wish to access specific pieces of information at infrequent intervals, so the HCI has to be designed in a way that is intuitive to the type of user involved. Help menus and on-screen instruction will be needed to remind the user of the way in which the system works when they return to it after a period of absence.

  In each of these cases the designer must assess the frequency of use, the background and experience of the user, and the nature of the user's expectation. The much-vaunted term 'user friendly' should not be taken as a requirement for endless screen messages and prompts and menus when the user is simply going about a daily, repetitive, well-understood task.

Let's now consider some of the options available to the designer: first a brief review of the technology available, and then an examination of the alternative ways of presenting information.

15.3.1 Output Technology

When considering output devices, there are two main alternatives:

- printing, using any of a variety of different types of printer;
- displaying the information on a screen.

There are two main types of printer: *impact printers*, which work like a typewriter, where a hammer strikes an inked ribbon to produce a character on paper, and *non-impact printers*, which work in a number of different ways to produce a character on paper, without making physical contact with it. Examples of the former are the dot matrix and daisy wheel printers, while examples of the latter include the laser and ink-jet printers. Laser and inkjet printers have become desktop equipment, and the quality of printed output that can be achieved at low cost is impressive. The analyst must be pragmatic in the choice of an output device and recognise that in certain circumstances robust, unattractive devices may provide a better service than some more modern devices. An impact printer attached to a robust if oily purpose-built keyboard in an exhaust-fitting centre acts as a testimony to the correctness of this theory.

A computer screen offers the most common form of output, and standards for screen design are evolving rapidly. The availability of desktop printers supports the facility of displaying on screen first with the option to produce hard copy if required.

In addition to the above two methods, a number of other alternatives are available. Plotters can be used to produce coloured line drawings, such as graphs, diagrams, and maps; output can be transmitted as a facsimile or a digital message; output can be in the form of sounds, such as beeps or clunks for example, music or video images; or if the output is to be stored, rather than being read straight away, it can be recorded onto magnetic media, optical disks or onto microfilm or microfiche. (Microfilm is a strip of film along which individual frames are arranged, and microfiche is a rectangle of film, the size of an index card, containing frames arranged in a grid. In both cases one frame corresponds to a sheet of paper.) Speech output is also possible, either as *concatenation*, by chaining together pre-recorded units of human speech (this is used on telephone services such as the speaking clock), or by a method called *synthesis by rule*, in which artificial speech is produced through the use of rules of pronunciation, intonation and the physical characteristics of human speech. A number of software packages use this method, which although less limited than concatenation can still sound rather artificial. The use of speech output for error messages, instead of the familiar beep, is an attractive idea for designers, because it can not only attract the user's attention to an error, but also state the nature of the error.

15.3.2 Displaying Information on a Screen

Whether the output is printed on paper, or displayed on screen, three important principles apply:

- The first and most important point is about content. The message here is to keep it simple. This is achieved by presenting only that information which is needed by the user. Clearly, if this is to be achieved, it is important to know the answers to the questions suggested earlier, particularly the first three. The designer can be tempted to include on a report all the available information, but this usually proves to be unhelpful to the end users.

- The second principle is to ensure that the page or screen is uncluttered and easy to read. Often reports that are poorly designed have so much crammed onto one page that it is very difficult for the reader to make sense of it. The use of white space on a printed page significantly increases its readability.

- The final point is to arrange the information logically on the page or screen, in such a way that it can be easily and quickly used and understood. Every output screen or report should include a main heading or title that identifies the purpose of the output, and subheadings that identify the various sections within it.

In addition it is helpful to the reader if reports and screens from the same system show consistency in the way that the information is arranged, so that users will know where to look to find the information which is important to them.

Reports can easily be produced with minimum effort using the report writer feature of a 4GL. Report writers are best when used for analysis reports that have subtotals and totals derived from the data sorted by structured key sequences. Totals by sales staff within areas within regions can quickly be generated using these facilities. Users who are familiar with either the report writer or a similar type of software such as a spreadsheet may prefer to create their own reports, or be given the output in a spreadsheet form, which they can then manipulate themselves. Often the end user will be more familiar with the facilities of a spreadsheet package than the analyst or indeed the software developer, and this experience can be a valuable link between the development team and the end user.

15.3.3 The Use of Tables and Graphics

Reports are commonly arranged as tables, especially those containing financial information, and this is appropriate if the detailed information is arranged in discrete, labelled groupings, if totals are included and few explanatory comments are needed. However, the report in Figure 15.2 is an example of poor information design. Although all the data required is present, the layout is cluttered and there is too much redundant information, which reduces the impact of the key data items. All the zeroes, for example, are unhelpful, and the reader needs some way of deciphering the codes on the top line.

Management Reports – VAT Return

Date from : 010180
to : 311299
Page : 1

Code:	T0	T1	T2	T3	T4	T5	T6	T7	T8	T9
Rate:	0.00	15.00	0.00	0.00	0.00	0.00	0.00	0.00	13.04	0.00

Sales Tax Analysis (by Invoice)

	T0	T1	T2	T3	T4	T5	T6	T7	T8	T9
Sales Invoices – Nett	8218.39	38707.02	0.00	0.00	0.00	0.00	0.00	0.00	0.00	603.00
Sales Invoices – Tax	0.00	5806.07	0.00	0.00	0.00	0.00	0.00	0.00	0.00	0.00
Sales Credits – Nett	0.00	0.00	0.00	0.00	0.00	0.00	0.00	0.00	0.00	0.00
Sales Credits – Tax	0.00	0.00	0.00	0.00	0.00	0.00	0.00	0.00	0.00	0.00

Purchase Tax Analysis (by Invoice)

	T0	T1	T2	T3	T4	T5	T6	T7	T8	T9
Purchases Invoices – Nett	2868.60	4933.98	0.00	0.00	0.00	0.00	0.00	0.00	244.41	19882.35
Purchase Invoices – Tax	0.00	740.12	0.00	0.00	0.00	0.00	0.00	0.00	31.88	0.00
Purchase Credits – Nett	0.00	0.00	0.00	0.00	0.00	0.00	0.00	0.00	0.00	0.00
Purchase Credits – Tax	0.00	0.00	0.00	0.00	0.00	0.00	0.00	0.00	0.00	0.00

Nominal Tax Analysis

	T0	T1	T2	T3	T4	T5	T6	T7	T8	T9
Bank Receipts – Nett	0.00	0.00	0.00	0.00	0.00	0.00	0.00	0.00	0.00	0.00
Bank Receipts – Tax	0.00	0.00	0.00	0.00	0.00	0.00	0.00	0.00	0.00	0.00
Bank Payments – Nett	0.00	0.00	0.00	0.00	0.00	0.00	0.00	0.00	0.00	0.00
Bank Payments – Tax	0.00	0.00	0.00	0.00	0.00	0.00	0.00	0.00	0.00	0.00
Cash Receipts – Nett	0.00	0.00	0.00	0.00	0.00	0.00	0.00	0.00	0.00	0.00
Cash Receipts – Tax	0.00	0.00	0.00	0.00	0.00	0.00	0.00	0.00	0.00	0.00
Cash Payments – Nett	0.00	0.00	0.00	0.00	0.00	0.00	0.00	0.00	0.00	0.00
Cash Payments – Tax	0.00	0.00	0.00	0.00	0.00	0.00	0.00	0.00	0.00	0.00
Journal Debits	3260.27	0.00	0.00	0.00	0.00	0.00	0.00	0.00	0.00	0.00
Journal Credits	0.00	0.00	0.00	0.00	0.00	0.00	0.00	0.00	0.00	0.00

Tax Analysis Summary

	T0	T1	T2	T3	T4	T5	T6	T7	T8	T9
Inputs – Nett	2868.60	4933.98	0.00	0.00	0.00	0.00	0.00	0.00	244.41	19882.35
Inputs – Tax	0.00	0.00	0.00	0.00	0.00	0.00	0.00	0.00	0.00	0.00
Outputs – Nett										

Fig. 15.2 A cluttered report

Denton Motor Holdings
Weekly Sales Report

Product Code		1111	Item Description	BOLT	Page 1

Order Number	Date	Customer Number	Customer	Quantity Ordered
4021	13/04/04	2222	SMITHSON	10
4020	12/04/04	1111	WAKEFIELD	12

		Total Number Ordered		22

Date Report Produced   11/09/02

Fig. 15.3 DMH weekly sales report

Figure 15.3, by contrast, shows a report in which the layout is clear and the information unambiguous. This weekly product sales report could be one of the outputs from the order processing system. It is clearly labelled with a title, makes good use of white space, and does not include redundant information.

Graphics can easily be used instead of tables and tabular reports. Here again the use of spreadsheets as the output medium facilitates the creation of graphs, pie charts and bar charts, and Figure 15.4 provides some alternative ways of presenting sales analysis information.

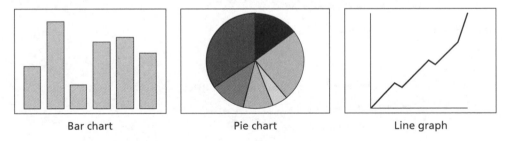

Bar chart	Pie chart	Line graph

Fig. 15.4 Types of business graphics

15.3.4 Specifying Outputs

The use of 4GLs has removed the need for the analyst to create the detailed print layouts that formed part of the specification of a 3GL program. The facilities available with a report generator are illustrated in Figure 15.5. This report is viewed as a number of sections consisting of:

- the report header;
- the page header;
- the detail line(s);

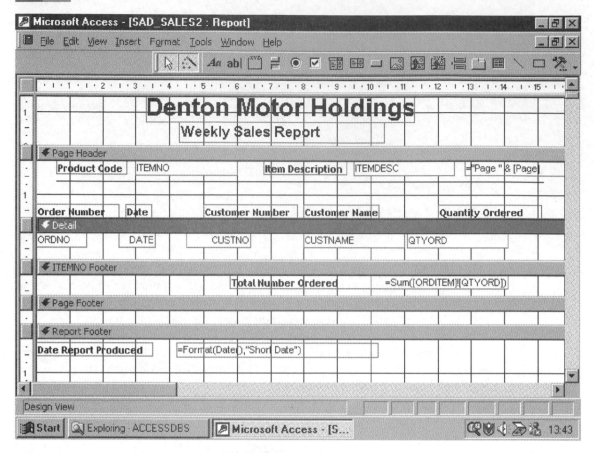

Fig. 15.5 A 4GL output specification

- a total field per group of detail lines (ITEMNO Footer);
- a page footer;
- a report footer.

The 4GL provides a large number of functions that can be incorporated into the report by setting properties for each section and each data item on the report and by specifying formulae that can be used with specified fields.

Here, a report date function [=Format(Date(),"Short Date")] is included in the footer to the report and a page number [="Page" & [Page]] is shown on the header to each page. A total function is used to show the number of items ordered per group [=Sum([ORDITEM]![QTYORD])]. Although the Visual Basic code displayed for these functions can appear intimidating to the non-programmer, the code has in each case been pasted into the appropriate place using a menu and by setting the appropriate properties.

The analyst can produce prototypes of the reports the system will produce and get the user's agreement at a much early stage in the proceedings, and this can act as a vital step in gaining user agreement and identifying business requirements.

15.4 Input Design

When designing input, the objective is to ensure that the data that will be processed by the system is collected and entered into the system efficiently, according to the specified requirements, and with the minimum of errors. In discussion with the client, the designer will choose a method of input that is cost-effective and acceptable to the end users. The process of input design, like output design which was described earlier, consists of four stages:

1 identifying the inputs into the system, by listing the data flows on the required logical data flow diagram that cross the system boundary on their way in;

2 determining the content of these inputs by inspecting the data dictionary;

3 choosing an appropriate input device to change the user's data into a form that can be read and processed by the computer system;

4 completing the detailed design work involved in specifying forms, input screens and any other data collection documents.

We shall examine each of these four stages in turn and look at the design options available and the steps that can be taken to ensure that the objectives of input design are achieved.

The first two steps are linked together, and involve the designer in looking at the data flow diagram for the required logical system, and the data dictionary. If you look back to the DFD in Figure 15.1, a number of inputs for the order processing system can be identified: *new customer details, credit-cleared customer orders, new product details, price changes, stock adjustments* and *stock-received notifications*. If the data dictionary for the system were to be inspected, the contents of the data flows that correspond to these inputs could be determined. For example, the data items that make up the input called *new customer details* are:

> customer number, customer type, sales region, discount code, name, address, and delivery instructions,

whereas *new product details* contains the following data:

> product number, description, manufacturer, origin, inventory group, product class, despatch unit, re-order level, discount prices, VAT code and VAT rate.

In this way the contents of each input can be confirmed, as can information about the source, volume and frequency of the input.

The next stage is to choose the appropriate technology for introducing the data contained in each of these inputs into the system. There are a wide variety of different ways of entering data, and the choice of the appropriate method will depend on a number of factors, the two most important of which can be summarised in the following questions:

• Which method will be most suitable to the needs of the users who have to enter the data? Although a keyboard will be appropriate in many situations, it may not be appropriate for a checkout operator in a supermarket, where speed and accuracy are important.

- Which method will be most suitable for the format and volume of the data to be entered? If an educational institution has a large number of multiple choice answer sheets completed during examinations, and wishes to put these results onto the system, then an optical mark reader – which can read the input directly from the students' answer sheets – would be the most suitable.

Whichever method is chosen, it will include some or all of the following steps:

1 initial recording of significant data by the user;

2 transcription of data onto an input document;

3 conversion of the data from a 'human-readable' into a 'computer-readable' form;

4 verification of this data conversion to pick up any errors;

5 entry of the checked data onto the computer system;

6 validation of the data by the system to ensure it is logically correct;

7 correction of any errors highlighted by the data validation program.

As passing through all these steps makes data entry a costly process, the key guideline for the designer is to make the process as simple as possible. If this can be done in a way that minimises the cost to the user, minimises the chance of data transcription errors occurring, and minimises the delay in entering the data onto the system, then the designer will once again be building quality into the system.

There are a large number of different input devices, but they can be grouped according to the way in which data is entered: by keyboard transcription from clerical documents, by direct input onto the computer system via a peripheral device, by direct entry through intelligent terminals, or by speech or body movement.

15.4.1 Keyboard Transcription from Clerical Documents

This is still the most common way of entering data – from an order form, a time sheet, or an application form for example. The device used is the keyboard or keypad. There are a number of different types, including:

- the *QWERTY keyboard*, which has the keys arranged in a layout invented by Christopher Scholes and used on conventional typewriters;

- the *Dvorak keyboard*, which allows greater speed and lower error rates as a result of frequently used keys being located together;

- the *alphabetic keyboard*, which is very similar in design to the QWERTY keyboard, except that the keys are arranged in alphabetical order;

- the *chord keyboard*, which requires several keys to be pressed simultaneously to form letters or words, and can be extremely fast when used by an experienced operator – an example is the Micro Writer keyboard, which consists of five keys that fit the fingers of the right hand, plus two shift keys, and these seven keys, in various combinations, can produce upper- and lower-case characters, special characters and numbers;

- the *numeric keypad*, which consists only of keys marked with numbers, decimal points, and arithmetic operators, plus an enter key, and is used for the rapid keying of numeric data.

In addition to the keys found on a typewriter, keyboards may also have a number of special-purpose function keys, which are programmed to perform a particular action – such as 'escape' – when pressed, as well as cursor control keys, which are four keys, marked with arrows, used for moving the cursor around the screen. The layout of keys on a typical QWERTY keyboard is shown in Figure 15.6.

If the number of transcription errors are to be minimised when this method of data entry is used, then various steps need to be taken. Some are the responsibility of the user organisation, such as the training of the keyboard operators, whereas others rest with the designer. In the latter category, these steps would include:

- designing an input form that is easy to complete;

- minimising the amount of data that the user needs to record on this form (on a customer order form, for example, the customer's name, address and account number can all be preprinted);

- ensuring that the design of the input screen matches the input form – with the data fields in the same order and the same relative positions.

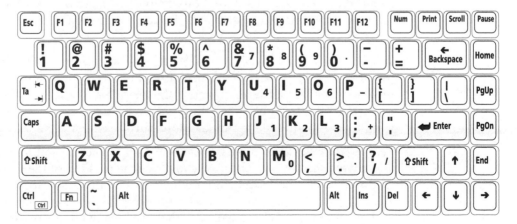

Fig. 15.6 Layout of a keyboard

15.4.2 Direct Input onto the Computer System Via a Peripheral Device

Another approach to minimising the errors introduced into the system is to reduce the possibility for human error by using input devices that require little or no action by the user after the data has been initially recorded. These peripheral devices include:

- *Bar code readers*, which read the input contained in bar codes, and can take the form of pens, as used by librarians when issuing books, or the gun-like versions used in shops. Bar code readers can also be embedded into work surfaces, as is the case at many supermarket checkouts, and read bar codes that are passed over them.

- *Optical character recognition (OCR) devices*, which read printed characters directly from a page, and are widely used to accept input where the volume of data is high, and the input needs to be entered quickly. For example, turnaround documents, such as gas and electricity bills, are produced by a computer system, sent to the customer and then re-accepted as input, when they are read in by OCR devices.

- *Magnetic ink character recognition (MICR) devices* are similar to OCR devices, but are sensitive to the magnetic rather than optical qualities of the characters and are therefore more reliable. This system is used by banks, and characters printed using a special font can be seen at the bottom of every cheque in a cheque book. The ferrite-impregnated ink with which these characters are formed is magnetised by the MICR device, so that the characters can be recognised and accepted by the system.

- *Optical mark recognition (OMR) devices*, which detect the position of hand-drawn or machine-printed marks on documents. These marks are read from specially designed forms so that the marks will be in the correct positions, and these devices are therefore best suited to stable applications where the production of large quantities of these input forms will make the method cost effective.

- *Automatic scanners*, which accept input either as pages of text which can be read into the computer system at high speed, or in the form of pictures or diagrams.

- *Touch-sensitive tablets or screens*, which detect the position of a finger touching them, and interpret this as a particular item of input: for example, in on-screen telephone dialling facilities, touching the telephone number on the screen will cause that number to be automatically dialled. Such devices are very easy for people to use with little training, but the surfaces must be kept clean.

- *Pointing devices*, for example the *mouse*, which can accept continuous input when it is rolled over a flat surface to move the position of the cursor around the input screen, or discrete input when a button on its surface is pressed to select an on-screen object. The *trackerball*, which is a ball embedded in a fixed socket, and the *joystick*, a small stick that can be moved in any direction within a fixed socket, are similar input devices that can be used to move the cursor.

Other direct entry devices include machines that read magnetised plastic badges, or which accept input from the magnetic strips on the back of credit cards.

15.4.3 Direct Entry through Intelligent Terminals

An 'intelligent' terminal is one that has processing power and the ability to store data. There are many examples of this type of input, which eliminates the need for input forms. One example is the point-of-sale (POS) equipment used by many shops. Data is entered directly via a keyboard into an intelligent terminal, often a personal computer of some kind, and validated. It is then either sent directly to the main computer – in an *online* system, such as an airline ticketing operation – or stored on disk, and entered onto the main system at some later stage – a *deferred online system*. This type of direct entry is often a feature of distributed computer systems, where local processing and storage of data are seen as an advantage to the business needs of the organisation. A number of retail outlets carry out stock checking using small, hand-held computers, which can then be connected to the main computer system and the data which is stored in the memory downloaded.

15.4.4 Input by Speech

Input using speech recognition is a desirable method of data entry because it is a natural method of communication, leaving the hands free to carry out other tasks and requiring very little training of data input staff; however, it still has a long way to go in its development. It has been used only in certain specialised applications, and even then is limited to single words or short phrases, and the system has to be 'taught' to recognise the speech patterns of the people whose voices will be used to provide input. This is because speech recognition devices have problems recognising where one word ends and the next one starts, adapting to the voice patterns of different people, and distinguishing between similar-sounding words and expressions (Figure 15.7), and can be confused by background noises. However, some predict that speech input will one day replace the keyboard as the primary method of data input.

Input can also be accepted from devices responsive to head or eye movements of the user, using methods such as the detection of reflected light from the eye, the tracking of head movements, or the recording of muscle contractions through electrodes.

The final stage in input design, having identified the inputs and their content and chosen the appropriate technology, is to do the detailed design work. Many of the principles that were outlined earlier, when discussing output design, are applicable here. The designer should be concerned with keeping the amount of data that has to be input to a minimum by limiting the collection of data to information that is variable, such as the number of items of a particular product ordered, and data that uniquely identifies the item to be processed, for example an indication of whether payment is being made by cash or credit. Data that is constant, or which can be stored or calculated by the system, does not need to be

Fig. 15.7 The problems of speech recognition (from the *Usability Now Guide*, 1990)

entered. To ask the user to do so wastes time, increases the possibility of transcription errors, and makes the job of data input to the system seem like an additional overhead rather than an integral part of an individual's work. When designing input forms and screens the key, as with output design, should be to keep things as simple and uncluttered as possible. A well-designed input form will have a logical sequence to the information requested, will read from left to right and from top to bottom of the page, and will contain sufficient 'white space' to make it easy to read.

15.5 Dialogue Design

For most users of computer systems, the main contact with the system is through an on-screen dialogue, and their perception of how 'friendly' the system is will depend on the characteristics of this dialogue. Ambiguities and difficulties in the dialogue cause problems in training and operation, and lead to systems underperforming. For example, it is important that developers use *style guides* to ensure that screens that are part of the same system, but which are designed or programmed by different individuals, have a consistent layout.

Style guides for *graphical user interface* (GUI) systems are an essential aspect of human–computer interaction (HCI) design. Government, the armed forces and most large commercial organisations have defined style guides to suit their own requirements. These guides, based upon traditional GUI-based systems, focus particularly on information display and the requirements of help, data entry and message boxes. HTML style guides place a greater emphasis on a common look and feel. The web user, moving from site to site, is performing a different task from the user of a business application system. The style guide helps to create consistency in the functions and the appearance of the system, and can be an important part of the creation of an organisation's brand image. The guide should also focus on the usability of the system and should enable development teams to share functions, routines and objects across different applications. The principle of polymorphism – performing the same task on different objects – supports this approach. Typically an HCI style guide will contain guidance on the principles to be adopted in the design of the interface; how to achieve usability; how to provide an appropriate level of functionality; how to use colour; and how to perform standard tasks such as reversing actions and paging between screens and functions. A section of the guide should be devoted to the way in which dialogues are to be constructed; how message boxes should be used; and when to use forms and toolbars. Detailed recommendations on the use of the objects, such as list boxes, option boxes, control buttons, scroll bars and types of caption, will help developers using languages such as Visual Basic to achieve consistency. Multinational companies will require the guide to address issues of international compatibility and the use of terminology and the specification of standards based upon specific proprietary products such as those of Microsoft, Apple or IBM.

15.5.1 Website Design

Website design can be viewed as a specialist area separate from the design of business applications. As the use of intranets for in-house company applications increases, and as the Internet is used for e-commerce applications, the analyst is required to treat a web-based interface in the same way as any other information technology development. The web-based system must take into account the type of user that the site is targeting, and the structure and navigation of the site are essential aspects of the design. The use of topic cards, which the users sort into logical groups to show how they structure the information, can support user interviewing. Site navigation can be documented using hierarchical flow diagrams, which can show the breadth and depth of the site. Some practioners favour broad, flat hierarchies and attempt to avoid going beyond three levels of depth, fearing that users become lost and quit the site if the links are too deep. The presentation of the site, use of scroll bars and other 'on-screen' functions differ little from the presentation of GUI interfaces for general business applications, and the same principles can therefore be applied to both.

The quality of the screen design can have a direct impact on the performance of the users of the system, and the designer needs to consider the format as well as the content of the screens on which the dialogue, or interaction, between the user and the system is based. A number of features of screen design are worth discussing here:

- *Text* – must be easily readable. In addition to choosing an appropriate font and size for the characters, readability can be improved by using lower- and upper-case letters, rather than the approach sometimes adopted in screen design of using all upper case. Evenly spaced text, with an unjustified right margin, is easier to read than right-justified text, which has spaces of varying sizes between the words. The use of concise phrases, familiar vocabulary and appropriate abbreviations makes it easier for the reader to understand the text.

The most visible section of the screen is the upper left-hand corner, and it is a good idea to locate important messages in this area. Again, it is important that the designer understands the characteristics of the end users in order to deliver a quality product. Beginners, who are usually looking at their fingers, will notice error messages that appear on the bottom line of the screen, whereas the top-right corner of the screen is a more appropriate location for experienced keyboard operators.

- *Highlighting* – can be used to make parts of the text stand out from the rest. There are a number of different ways of doing this. The text can be

  in UPPER CASE
  underlined
  in a **bold** typeface
  enclosed in a box
  or in a shadowed box

  or it can be larger than the rest.

  In addition, because the medium is a VDU screen, rather than paper, other techniques can also be used to highlight the important information. It can be made to *flash*, to be *brighter* than the surrounding text, or *reverse video* can be used – creating an effect rather like a photographic negative, with white text on a black background.

- *Colour* – text can be highlighted by being in a different colour from the rest or being enclosed in a coloured box. Background colours can be changed, or a design convention can be used in which different types of information are displayed in different colours. The consistent use of colour on screens within the same system is important, and the designer must be wary of using too many colours or creating lurid combinations, as these will work against the effectiveness of the screen design. In addition, the designer must also be aware of avoiding colour combinations that could cause problems for those users who are colour-blind.

- *Animation* – can be a powerful technique for attracting the attention of the user, because the eye is always drawn to a moving object; to mark the position of an object, for example, a blinking cursor can be used; or to communicate a message, a clock with a moving hand, or an hourglass with moving sand, are simple devices and indicate to the user that they have to wait while some processing is carried out by the machine. Unfortunately, sales promotion web sites have all but destroyed its effectiveness through overuse, and the use of animation in business applications should be approached with care.

15.5.2 Dialogue Types

There are various approaches that can be taken when designing the conversation or dialogue between the user and the computer system. In essence, a dialogue consists of the user responding to a prompt from the computer by providing input. This input is processed by the computer and a response is output to the screen, which in turn may prompt the user for the next input.

The main dialogue types are summarised below. It is up to the designer, having considered the alternatives, to decide which of these is most appropriate, based on the requirements and characteristics of the end users.

Menus

In this approach, the user is presented with a set of alternatives from which one has to be selected. These alternatives can be displayed on screen allowing the user to select the appropriate option with the mouse. An example is shown as Figure 15.8.

Menus are widely used in screen design because they require minimal effort, and skill, on the part of the user. This in turn reduces the training requirement when preparing individuals to use the system. A common approach is to structure the menus hierarchically in a 'nest': selecting an option on the first menu takes the user to a second menu from which another option is chosen, and so

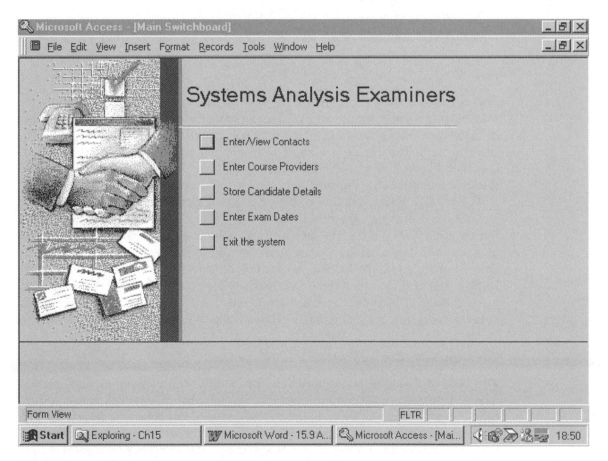

Fig. 15.8 A menu screen

on. This allows the number of alternatives on any one screen to be kept to a minimum. When designing nested menus, it is important to build in short cuts to allow experienced users to move quickly through the system and avoid the frustration of having to go through several menu screens for each transaction, and to allow an exit that doesn't involve travelling back through each of the previous menus. The principles of good design should also be applied by keeping the menus simple, with an upper limit of ten choices per screen; minimising the number of levels of menu through which a user has to navigate; and ensuring consistency in the way options are selected from each of the related menus.

Question and answer

This type of dialogue involves the system prompting the user by asking a question, and then carrying out the processing associated with the user's answer. The questions usually require one of a limited number of answers, e.g. yes or no, which eliminates errors and reduces the amount of validation of answers required. It is another dialogue type that is useful for beginners, but which can be frustrating for experienced users. It is commonly used when checking instructions given to the system. For example:

Do you really want to delete this file?   Type 'Y' or 'N'
(where the default is 'N').

Form-filling

This is particularly appropriate for the user who has to enter information into the system from a paper input form, and a good design will ensure that the layout of the screen resembles the original document as closely as possible to minimise the risk of errors. This type of dialogue is also called a *template*, and an example is shown in Figure 15.9, the screen design for the input *new product details* shown on the DFD in Figure 15.1, the content of which was described earlier.

The areas in which data has to be entered will usually be highlighted in some way to stand out from the background text – using colour shading or graphics for example. When data has been entered, the cursor moves to the next input area. Form-filling is useful when a large amount of similar information has to be entered quickly into the system. A variation of form-filling is panel modification. In this type of dialogue, a screen of data is presented to the user, who can then move around it to amend specific items. This is appropriate if existing records held on the system are being amended by an experienced user.

Command language

This type of dialogue can appear very 'unfriendly' to the inexperienced user as the prompts are usually very limited, and response by the user has to be syntactically correct in order to be accepted by the system. However, it is a very fast and efficient dialogue for the experienced user, and short commands or abbreviated forms of these commands will initiate specific processing. There is a great deal of freedom to move around the application, as the user rather than the system is

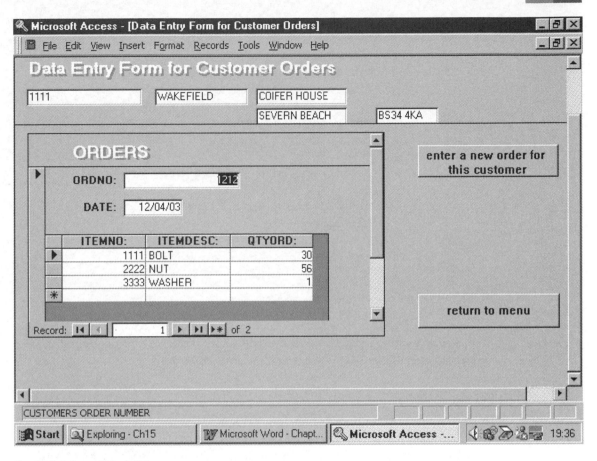

Fig. 15.9 A form-filling dialogue screen

structuring and ordering the conversation. The designer should ensure that there is a visible output on screen to show that the user's input has been accepted by the system, and should endeavour to make error and help messages in such a dialogue as meaningful as possible. An example of a command language dialogue is the MS-DOS window, a sample of which is shown in Figure 15.10.

The earliest and still the cheapest form of screen-based interaction uses a set of menus to implement hierarchical selection, but this technique effectively constrains the operator to making only a limited number of selections. From the operator's viewpoint this can be a slow, cumbersome and tedious way to work, effectively providing a very narrow interface to the system, and menus can be particularly irksome for the experienced operator. A command language, with defaults, is generally preferred by experienced operators. However, there is more to remember and more can go wrong – the operator is not so constrained as by menus and there are opportunities for 'finger trouble'. Hybrid systems use a combination of menu and command techniques for interaction. For example,

```
          Type EXIT to return to Menu
          C:\>A:DIR

          Not ready reading drive A
          Abort, Retry, Fail?R

          Not ready reading drive A
          Abort, Retry, Fail?R

          General failure reading drive A
          Abort, Retry, Fail?F
          Invalid drive specification
          Bad Command or file name

          Type EXIT to return to Menu
          C:\>
```

Fig. 15.10 Example of a command language dialogue

menus may be displayed in 'novice' mode, or by request from the operator, with command specification available as an override or default.

Natural language

In contrast to the command language dialogues, natural language conversations are much closer to the way way people would speak. This type of dialogue relies on artificial intelligence and expert systems that will recognise key words or phrases input by the user and translate them into instructions which can be followed by the computer. The problem with natural language is that most natural languages, like English, are characterised by ambiguity and inconsistency in their syntax. These dialogues therefore require the use of a limited vocabulary and syntax, with which users need to be familiar before they use such a dialogue.

In practice a designer may use a number of these dialogue types in combination when designing the screens for a system, depending on the requirements of the system and the needs and experience of the users.

15.5.3 WIMP Interfaces

The WIMP interface is so called because it incorporates:

WINDOWS, several of which can be opened on screen at the same time,
ICONS, which represent entities such as files and documents,
a MOUSE to select and move icons around the screen and
PULL-DOWN MENUS.

Some years ago Apple Computer Inc published a number of design principles to help designers who are developing products for Macintosh computers. Ten of these principles, from the *Macintosh Human Interface Guidelines* (1992), are summarised below; they are still useful today for any designer creating a WIMP interface for a computer system.

- *Metaphors*. This involves using representations of familiar, concrete ideas from the outside world to help users understand concepts and features that are part of the application: for example, using graphic representations of files and folders to simplify the saving and storing of information.

- *Direct manipulation*. This is one of the key concepts in a WIMP interface. It enables the user to directly control the objects represented on screen. So, for example, a folder can be dragged into a wastebasket in order to delete information held on the system, or a menu can be pulled down from the bar at the top of the screen.

- *See-and-point*. If the user can see what they are doing on screen, and have a pointing device – the mouse – they can select options from a menu, or initiate actions by pointing at objects on screen. In the Macintosh desktop interface the user will point first at an object of interest, called a *noun*, and then at an action from a menu, called the *verb*, in order to initiate a piece of processing. For example, using the mouse, a file can be opened by pointing at the icon for the file (the noun), pulling down the appropriate menu, and then pointing at the 'open' command (the verb).

- *Consistency*. Consistency is just as important when designing WIMP interfaces as it is when designing any other interface – a point that we have emphasised throughout this chapter. It allows users to transfer their skills and knowledge from one application to another, because of the consistency in appearance and behaviour of the interfaces.

- *WYSIWYG*. Another important principle is WYSIWYG, meaning 'what you see is what you get'. This involves, for example, using meaningful names rather than codes or abbreviations on menus, and making sure that there are no major differences between a document as it appears on screen and as it appears when printed on paper.

- *User control*. This means that the designer of an interface ensures that the user, and not the computer, is always in control of the dialogue and is able to initiate chosen actions. This allows the user to be more actively involved in the interaction than if the computer were guiding the user through it.

- *Feedback and dialogue*. It is important to keep users informed about their progress through an application, by providing feedback as soon as they have given a command. This might involve the designer building a visual or aural response into the dialogue, or a message that explains exactly what caused an error. Again this will ensure that the user remains actively engaged throughout the dialogue.

- *Forgiveness*. If actions carried out by the user of a computer system are reversible, the designer has built in 'forgiveness'. This encourages the user to experiment and learn how to get the best out of an application. Messages that notify the user of potentially destructive actions, such as deleting an application or data file, give the user a chance to change course.

- *Perceived stability*. In order to help users to learn to use new applications within a system, familiar, understandable and predictable features of the interface are desirable. The designer should consider the consistency of layout, graphics, colour, etc., which increase the user's perception of stability. For example, when familiar commands on a pull-down menu are unavailable, they can be dimmed rather than deleted from the display.

- *Aesthetic integrity*. This means that information displayed on screen is well organised and visually attractive. As we discussed in the section on screen design, the usability of an interface will be enhanced if layout is simple and clear and the graphics used are appropriate.

15.5.4 User Support

As well as the important principles of simplicity and consistency, which we have stressed throughout this chapter, the designer also needs to consider how to provide help if a user has problems in selecting an option from a menu or in continuing a particular dialogue. Such help may be offline, through the use of documentation or help desks, or online, using screens that explain particular functions to a user.

When designing offline help, which is usually paper-based but which could also be in the form of audio or video tapes, a key principle is to think about the needs of the users who will be referring to them. They will be keen to find a quick solution to their problem and will frequently be anxious and in a hurry. Manuals should therefore be kept simple and not overloaded with information, and should be relevant to the common types of problem encountered by users. The most useful way of developing such material is by working closely with end users and modifying the text in the light of the difficulties they experience when using the system.

Online help can be basic, usually in a concise form with reference to a manual where more detailed information can be obtained; it can be context-sensitive, providing appropriate information about the particular function being used at the time the help is requested; or it can be intelligent, responsive to the route a user has followed while navigating through an application and their needs when the help screen is called.

User support will also take the form of training for those who will be interacting with the computer system. Again, this can be provided offline, in the form of a training event (either a taught course or an open learning programme), or online, as a tutorial that takes the user through the functions of the system and then through a series of structured exercises.

It must not be forgotten, when designing a computer system, that users are part of this system, and can be considered almost as an extension of the computer. Their role must be defined and designed like any other component of the system, and thought must be given early on as to how they can best be supported in carrying out this role.

15.6 Ergonomics and Interface Design

A final area to address in this chapter on interface design is the subject of *ergonomics*. Ergonomics is the study of the physical and mental reactions that people have to their working environment, and computer ergonomics has been the subject of a lot of discussion in recent years. It is an applied science, which draws on the findings of three other areas of study: *anatomy*, which provides information about the dimensions of the body (anthropometry) and the application of forces (biomechanics); *physiology*, which helps explain the expenditure of energy and the effects of the physical environment on the body; and *psychology*, which contributes an understanding of how people process information, make decisions and solve problems (cognitive skills), how they produce and control changes in the environment (perceptual-motor performance), and how they behave and interact with others at work. An ergonomist also needs to understand the computer system and the working environment in which the two will come together.

The findings of ergonomists are useful to system designers, who recognise that computer systems can be effectively implemented only if human factors are taken into account from the beginning of the development process. This is because the reason for developing the system is not just to develop more powerful technology, but to meet a business need by improving communication, providing effective tools and minimising the chance of errors being made.

In addition the design, implementation and use of computer systems is also governed by law, and all video terminals and personal computers must now be designed to good ergonomic standards. With effect from 1 January 1993, a set of regulations has been in force to meet the requirements of EC Directive VDU 90/270. The *Display Screen Equipment Regulations* require employers to perform an analysis of workstations in order to evaluate health and safety conditions to which they give rise for their workers, particularly as regards possible risks to eyesight, physical problems and problems of mental stress, and to take appropriate action to remedy the risks found. There are stiff penalties for non-compliance.

In designing an effective and ergonomically safe workstation, attention must be paid to a number of points, highlighted in the Display Screen Equipment Regulations. The diagram in Figure 15.11, and the accompanying text, summarises these points.

1 The body should be upright and the body weight fully supported on the chair.

2 There should be good lumbar support, and the seat back should be adjustable.

3 The height of the seat should also be adjustable.

4 When the height of the seat is correct, the forearms should be horizontal, the shoulders relaxed and not hunched up, and the angle between forearm and upper arm about 90°. In this position the hands will be in line with the home run (the ASDF row) of the keyboard, and there will be minimum extension, flexion or deviation of the wrists.

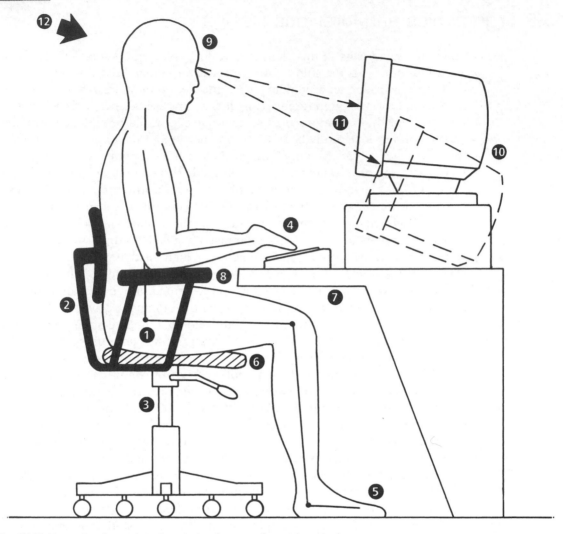

Fig. 15.11 Key points in workstation design (see text for explanation)

5 Feet should be flat on the floor, and a footrest should be provided if required.

6 Thighs should be supported by the front of the chair, but there should be no excess pressure from the chair on the underside of the thighs or the back of the knees.

7 Space should be allowed for changing the position of the legs and obstacles removed from under the desk.

8 Space should be provided in front of the keyboard to support hands and wrists during pauses in keying.

9 The distance between eye and screen should be in the range 350–700 mm, so that data on the screen can be read comfortably without squinting or leaning forward.

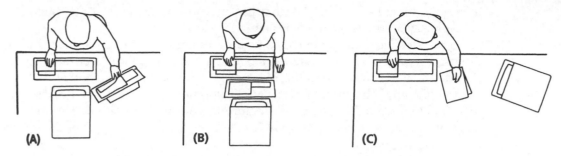

Fig. 15.12 Workstation layout (see text)

10 The height of the VDU screen should be adjusted according to the user's typing proficiency, and the needs of the task.

(a) For those with touch typing skills, or whose work is purely to screen without referencing written material, the top of the screen should be level with the eyes, and should be angled approximately 15–20° to the horizontal.

(b) Users who are not trained touch typists, and switch between screen, keyboard and reference material, should have the screen set in a lower position to avoid eye and neck strain in constantly switching back and forth. The screen plane should be as close as possible to 90° from line of sight.

11 Contrast and brightness controls should be set to produce a display that is comfortable to use, and should be adjusted to take account of varying light conditions during the day.

12 The screen should be positioned to avoid glare from either direct sunlight or artificial light. Where possible, blinds should be used to shield the screen.

The layout of a workstation should be designed to allow the user to maintain an upright body posture without having to repeatedly twist to access supporting material. This involves maintaining a balance between the individual's position, the VDU screen and the keyboard. Figure 15.12 shows two working arrangements that conform to this recommendation (A and B) and another (C) that does not.

15.7 Summary

We have explored a number of different aspects of interface design in this chapter, which is intended to be an introduction to the subject. Much has been written about interface design and human–computer interaction, and particularly about the cognitive approach to HCI, which is outside the scope of this chapter.

The starting point for interface design is the drawing of a system boundary, which allows inputs, outputs and dialogues to be identified. The designer can then determine the content of each input and output, using the data dictionary, and agree appropriate technologies with the user.

To be effective, a dialogue has to be both functional and easy to use, and we discussed issues of screen design, dialogue type and graphical user interface design that would contribute to this objective. It is important to state that dialogue design, like any other part of systems development, is an iterative process, and there may be a number of changes before the design is finalised. The involvement of the user at an early stage is vital to ensure that this aspect of the system meets their requirements.

A key goal of interface design is to maximise the usability of the system by ensuring that users can carry out their tasks effectively, efficiently, safely and enjoyably, and in order to do this a designer has to be aware of the available technology and the needs, tasks and characteristics of the eventual users of the system. Technical developments have enormously widened the range of human–computer interaction possibilities at the hardware level. The major developments include:

- larger, flatter, colour screens;
- new CRT controller chips, which are oriented towards high-speed windowing displays;
- liquid crystal displays;
- coloured LEDs;
- speech synthesis and recognition chips;
- wireless technology for the keyboard and mouse;
- the connection of electronic diaries and organisers directly to the PC;
- remote access by mobile telephone and laptop computer.

The technology now exists to take some account of the psychology of the human being who is operating, and contributing to, the system. Although it can be argued that all this new technology costs money, it must also be remembered that new technologies in the IT industry fall rapidly in price once they have been around and adopted for a year or two, and also that the user interface is the most prominent view of the system the customer has. There are many examples of poor interface design, and it is clear that the time invested in designing interfaces that meet the real needs of the user contributes significantly to the effectiveness of the system delivered to the client.

16 Systems Design: System Interfaces

16.1 Introduction

The design of the user interface is a key element in delivering a system that users like to use, and which enables them to operate efficiently. Behind this interaction are the interfaces between the different parts of the system that make it possible to give the user the kind of interface that works best for them. System, data and application architects all influence the environment within which the analyst/ designer can produce a system that meets user needs. The scope for interface design is limited by the way the system is compartmentalised to enable it to fit into organisation-wide systems planning. In this chapter we look at some of these issues.

16.2 Interfaces Defined

The first step in analysing a complex system is to divide it into a number of smaller, more manageable objects and then analyse each of these smaller objects separately. So, for example, a simple online banking system might be divided into:

- database containing information about the bank's customers and their accounts;
- interaction with a customer.

A set of messages passes between the terminal and the central database. First, a password is sent for validation. Then, after this has been accepted, a balance request is sent and the reply returned – a total of four messages.

This set of messages and the sequences in which they occur, constitute the interface between the terminal and the central database. If the interface is not well understood, then any attempt to analyse the subsystems will be inadequate. For example, suppose in our example that details of the password validation were

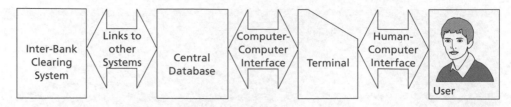

Fig. 16.1 External interfaces

not defined. The designers of the terminal might assume that they had to send the password to the central database for validation. The designers of the central database, on the other hand, might suppose that the validation is performed locally by the terminal. Both designs might work, but they won't work together.

So far, this example has imagined that interfaces are simply ways of dividing a system into manageable parts, but there are other interfaces that are important – interfaces which are concerned with the way the system works. The system must, for example, interact with the outside world. In Figure 16.1 we see that:

- There is an interface between the user and the terminal, called the human–computer interface (HCI).

- There could be another interface that links the central database and the inter-bank clearing system.

As we saw in the previous chapter, the HCI is concerned with the design of screens, the way messages are displayed, the way the user is expected to respond, the use of passwords and cards with a magnetic strip, and so on. The links to other systems are usually thought of under the heading of data communications. Both of these are discussed in more detail in other chapters of this book and are not discussed further here except to emphasise that they are just as much interfaces as a procedure call or shared memory, and can be analysed in just the same way. The complexity of data communications protocols, for example, often leads to the false assumption that there is something qualitatively different about data communications. This is not true.

In this chapter we shall consider the analysis of the boundary that enables the system to be divided into well-defined subsystems, and the mechanisms that might be used to implement an interface. First of all we have to identify the interfaces. There are three ways in which we can do this: partitioning by organisation, partitioning by data flows, and partitioning by data ownership.

Partitioning by organisation

Organisations naturally divide themselves into different parts, either by function or by geography. There may, for example, be a head office, a sales office and some factories, and these may be located in different parts of the country, or simply on different floors of the same building. These functions and locations represent natural divisions within a company. There will be information flows between them. Where the divisions are geographic, the flows of information are normally grouped under the heading *data communications*. Where different functions exist in the same place, there may well be common use of computers. For example, the accounts department and the sales office might have access to the same database.

Where there is a real distinction between uses being made of the computer system, rather than between the departmental function, then there is a natural boundary across which information may flow. This should be reflected in the design of the computer system. If, on the other hand, there is little distinction in the need for computer services, then there is an opportunity for savings by providing a common service. The sales office and the accounts office have very different functions, but if their main use of computers happens to be word processing then there is no distinction in the use and, therefore, no sensible system boundary.

Partitioning by data flows

Partitioning by organisation works well at a high level, but there is also a need to find ways of identifying interfaces between individual computers, between processes within a single computer, and even between the different parts of a single process. The general idea when analysing data flows is to partition the system to localise complex interfaces. Think again of the bank terminal we discussed earlier. Figure 16.2 shows three parts of this system with arrows to indicate the complexity of the interaction between each. The question is: Where should the functions provided by the bank terminal be implemented? Should the terminal hardware provide relatively few functions directly, with most functions being implemented as part of the central banking functions? Alternatively, should the terminal be given more processing power?

Suppose the terminal functions and the central database functions were to be located together, as shown in Figure 16.2. In this case, large numbers of messages pass across the interface, and the closely coupled terminal and database communicate in a much simpler way.

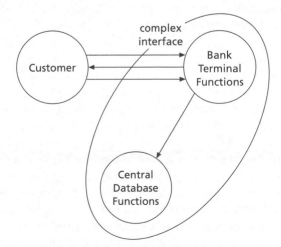

Fig. 16.2 Poor partitioning, which produces a complex interface

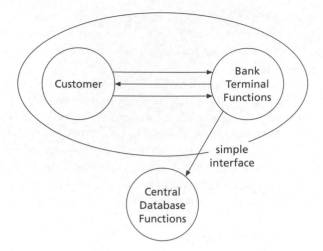

Fig. 16.3 Good partitioning, which produces a simple interface

A better solution, however, would be to place the support of the bank terminal functions with the customer as shown in Figure 16.3. In this case the majority of the communication takes place locally between the customer and the terminal, with relatively little communication over the longer journey to the central services.

Partitioning by data ownership

The partitioning that we have discussed so far is on the basis of the flows of data round a system. Increasingly, the use of object-oriented analysis and design (OOA and OOD) has introduced an alternative view, based on what is known as *data encapsulation*.

Consider an example. Suppose you are a member of your local squash club. You want to arrange a game with another member, Mary, but you don't know her phone number. So you do the obvious thing and ask the club secretary to tell you the number. What you don't do is ask where the secretary stores the members list and in what form – and then go to look for it yourself! This may sound silly, but that is effectively how thousands of computer systems over the years have been designed. Data was considered public. So every part of the system had to understand the structure of the data. If the data structure had to change, to include a new field for example, then every part of the system that accessed the data would have to be rewritten. Back at our squash club, you don't care about how the secretary stores the members list so long as she can answer the question. At some stage she could convert an aged card index system into an online database and you would never know. In programming terms, if the data is 'encapsulated', its structure is known only by the program that owns it. Other programs can only gain access to the data by using access functions provided by the owning program. In a system designed in this way, the key feature is the identification of the data and the partitioning of the system into areas of *data ownership*.

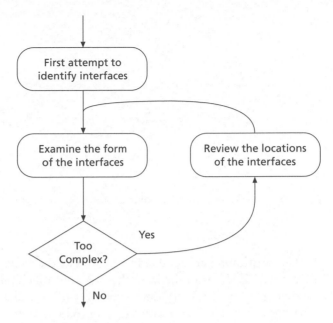

Fig. 16.4 Looking for interfaces

Having identified interfaces, the next step is to understand the different kinds of interface. You should be wary of assuming, however, that this is a simple two-stage procedure involving first identifying the interfaces and then analysing them. As a designer you have some choice over where the interfaces go. If your first attempt to partition the system produces interfaces that turn out to be too complex, you'll need to revisit the partitioning process: move step by step towards partitioning so that interfaces are simple enough to be defined in a clear, unambiguous way. This iterative process is shown in Figure 16.4.

16.3 Analysing Interfaces

The next problem to be tackled, then, is how to analyse an interface.

A point that will be emphasised again later when dealing with data communications is the importance of separating what an interface is used for from the physical form that the interface takes: that is, to separate the reason for having an interface from the choice of mechanism.

The purpose of an interface might be to carry accounts data from the sales office to the accounts office. The forms in which this transfer takes place could vary widely. The two offices could, for example, share access to a computer on which is a database into which the sales office place data and from which the accounts office read it when they want it. Alternatively, there might be a data communications link between separate computers used by the two offices. The same interface could even be implemented by sending a fax from one office to the other. The analysis of the interface will suggest what form the interface should take. So, the decision illustrated in Figure 16.4 can be understood to mean

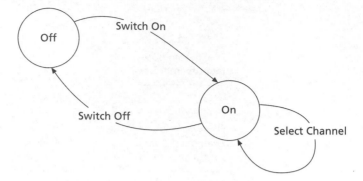

Fig. 16.5 State transition diagram of the control of a television set

'Is the partitioning acceptable in the light of the ways we have to implement the interfaces?' We'll examine later the different mechanisms that are available, but here we'll consider the interface itself in relatively abstract terms.

There are three diagramming methods that are widely used to describe interfaces:

- state transition diagrams;
- time sequence diagrams;
- data flow diagrams.

They are not alternatives, but different tools with different capabilities.

Imagine a system that waits for an event, acts on it, and then waits for another event. Each time it waits there may be a different set of events on which it can act. Interfaces can be described in this way using what is called a *state transition diagram*.

Consider, for example, the interface between you and your television. A possible form of the interface is shown in Figure 16.5. The circles represent the waiting for an event: these are called the *states*. Arrows between them show the *events* that move the interface from one state to another.

The interface starts in a state called Off in which there is only one event that can have any effect: Switch On. Having switched the TV on, the state changes to On. In this new state there are two events to which the interface can respond: Select Channel, which does not cause a change of state, and Switch Off, which causes the state to change back to Off.

A more complex interface might have many more states. An analysis of the interface to a video recorder, with all of its different controls, could have well over 50 states. In such complex circumstances, using a table is often clearer. The events are drawn across the top of the table, and the states down the side. Text in each box in the table then describes the associated processing. In our TV set example this would look something like Figure 16.6. In this example nothing happens in the empty boxes. In a more complex interface they might cause error processing because an event has occurred in the wrong state.

Events States	Switch On	Switch Off	Select Channel
On	• Switch on the power • Change state to 'On'		
Off		• Switch off the power • Change state to 'Off'	• Select another programme

Fig. 16.6 State transition table showing the control of a TV set

State transition diagrams don't tell the whole story, however. They show the events that control the interface, but they don't show any information passing across it. In the case of the TV set, for example, there is no information about a picture being displayed, which, after all, is the whole point. In such cases a time sequence diagram can be useful.

A *time sequence diagram* shows 'things', whether data or control, passing across an interface. Figure 16.7 shows the television set example in this form.

The line down the centre represents the boundary between the user and the TV. The arrows crossing it represent 'things' crossing the interface. An arrow has also been added to the central line to indicate that time is to be thought of as flowing down the page. At the top of the diagram a Switch On signal passes to the TV, which responds by sending a picture back. The user then changes channel, and in response the TV sends a different picture. Finally the user sends a message to Switch Off. This form of diagram captures both the control and data aspects of an interface, but cannot show the more complex sequences. For example, it does not show that having switched off the TV, the user can switch it on again, nor does it show that the user can repeatedly change channels.

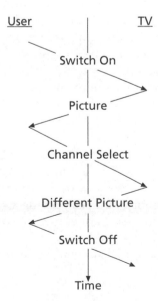

Fig. 16.7 Time sequence diagram of control of a TV set

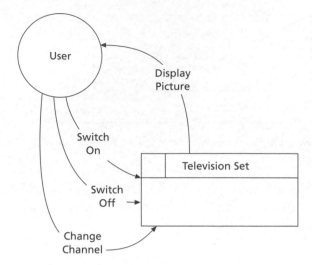

Fig. 16.8 Data flow diagram for the control of a TV set

A *data flow diagram* captures a static view of the communication between parts of the system. It looks superficially similar to a state transition diagram. However, where the state transition diagram shows the control of the system, the data flow diagram, as in Figure 16.8, shows the movement of data. It does not represent state changes or changes in time.

16.4 Physical Forms of Interfaces

This section will examine the mechanisms that are available to implement an interface. It concentrates on communication between processes within a computer. The first mechanism to be discussed, the procedure call, is the simplest in that only one program is running. Later methods such as mailboxes and shared memory assume that more than one program is running at the same time. Finally, to give a taste of the variety of solutions that are available, two special mechanisms are mentioned: the Ada 'Rendezvous' and UNIX 'Standard Input' and 'Standard Output'.

The commonest way to pass information from one part of a program to another is a *procedure call*. In Figure 16.9, the call and return arrows show the flow of control which may or may not be accompanied by data.

The two pieces of communicating code are so closely linked that a subroutine call is almost more a part of the program structure than an interface. However, simple though it is, it does provide a boundary between two processing worlds. In most languages there is careful control over the information that can pass between the two worlds.

There are two ways in which information is passed:

- pass-by-reference;
- pass-by-value.

Calling Routine   **Called Subroutine**

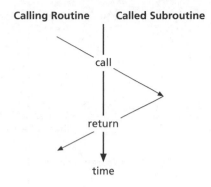

call

return

time

Fig. 16.9 A subroutine call

If a parameter is passed by reference, then the subroutine is given access to the same piece of memory as the calling program. This means that if the subroutine changes the value, then the calling program will see the change. This is the mechanism that was used by default in older languages such as the early versions of FORTRAN. It works perfectly well, but the calling routine has to be able to trust that the subroutine will behave itself and not corrupt things that it should leave unchanged. More recent languages such as C pass parameters by value. That is, a copy of the parameter is made and the subroutine is given access only to the copy. The subroutine can corrupt this as much as it likes because it will be thrown away when control returns to the main program. In C, a programmer wanting to pass a value out of a subroutine must explicitly pass into the subroutine an address in memory. This means that the programmer has to be explicit about what the subroutine is allowed to change. In the Ada language, every parameter must be marked as 'in', 'out' or 'in–out' to identify the direction in which changes to the parameters are allowed to flow.

Older computer systems often ran as what were called *batch systems*, a form of processing that is becoming increasingly rare. Such systems were written as a series of standalone programs. The first would read input, perhaps from punched cards, and write to a file. The next program would take this file as its input and write its output to another file, and so on. The interfaces between the programs were these shared files. There are some disadvantages with this approach, not least of which is the fact that one stage must be completely finished before the next can start.

Instead of sharing a file, two programs running on the same processor can *share a data area within memory*. One program writes to the shared area; the other reads from the same area (see Figure 16.10). This is a particularly useful solution if there is a lot of data passing and processing speed is important, but it is important to prevent clashes between sender and receiver. The reader must be prevented from reading before the writer has completed writing the data, otherwise only part of the data will be read, and the message will be corrupt. This problem did not occur under the older file-based batch systems because the reading program was not run until the writing program had finished writing to the file. The same idea of not allowing access by the reader while the writer is

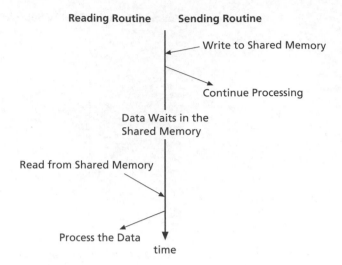

Fig. 16.10 Communication by shared memory

writing still exists. However, the suspension of the reader now takes place for each message, not for the whole file of messages.

Mechanisms are provided by many modern operating systems to pass messages from one program to another through a mailbox. This is rather like one program sending a letter to another program. You can visualise the mailbox as a kind of pigeonhole maintained by the operating system where the message is retained until the recipient reads it.

The kinds of services that could be expected by the user from the operating system are:

- Send a message.
- Read from my mailbox.
- Tell me if there are any messages waiting.
- Advise me immediately when a message arrives.

Messages can be sent synchronously or asynchronously. In synchronous communication the sender cannot proceed until the receiver has received the message, but more often asynchronous communication (Figure 16.11) is used because the programs involved do not keep in step with each other and are usually doing completely different things.

Some modern languages have communications features built in. For example, the Ada language supports its own built-in synchronous communication method called a *Rendezvous* (Figure 16.12). This is rather like accessing a subroutine in one program from a call in another. The functions used are CALL and ACCEPT. The calling program issues a CALL, which must be matched by an ACCEPT in the called program. The programs can issue these calls in any order: the program that issues its call first is suspended until the other catches up and issues its own call. Code specified as part of the ACCEPT is then executed using parameters supplied by the caller. During the Rendezvous, data can pass in both directions.

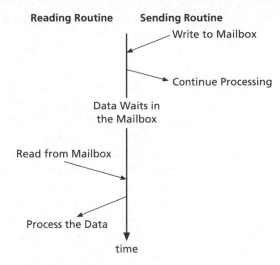

Fig. 16.11 Asynchronous communication by mailbox

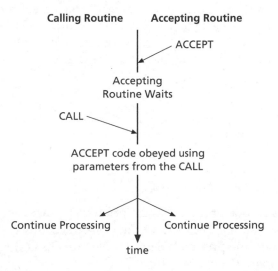

Fig. 16.12 Ada Rendezvous

The UNIX operating system tries to make all interfaces look like files. A program has an input channel called STANDARD INPUT and an output channel called STANDARD OUTPUT. It can read from one and write to the other without knowing whether the messages are coming from a file or from another program. There is, for example, a UNIX command `ls`, which lists the contents of a directory, rather like the `dir` command in MS-DOS that was mentioned earlier. Some of the ways in which it can be used are:

- `ls`   Display the content of the current directory at the terminal.
- `ls > file`   Create a file called `file` and write to it a description of the content of the current directory.

- `ls | more`   Make a description of the content of the directory and pass it to the program `more`, which will display it one screenful at a time.

The point is that in all these cases the `ls` command is identical. In each case the `ls` command thinks it is writing to a file called STANDARD OUTPUT. The last example, `ls | more`, is similar to the MS-DOS `dir | more` command. In the case of UNIX, however, there is no intermediate file created. The data is passed directly from one program to the other: it just looks as if a file is being created.

Most of these forms of interface require *synchronisation* between the reading and writing processes. It would be unwise, for example, for a process to read from shared memory before the message has been completely written. Processes also often need access simultaneously to resources that are by their nature non-shareable. Imagine what would happen if two processes could write to the same printer at the same time! This implies the need for some form of communication between the processes. The communication on this occasion is concerned with the control of those processes, not with passing data between them. Take the example of access to a printer mentioned earlier. If there was a flag that was set to 1 if the printer was available, and to 0 if it was in use, then access could be controlled so long as every process that wanted to access the printer performed its processing along the following lines:

```
IF flag=0
   THEN
      suspend until flag=1
   ENDIF
   set flag to 0
   access the printer
   set flag to 1
```

While one process uses the printer, all other processes are suspended. Then when the flag is reset to 1, all the suspended processes are given the opportunity to access the printer. What actually happens at this point depends on the operating system. Possibilities are:

- The process that has been waiting longest gets the printer.
- The highest-priority process gets the printer.
- Chance! – the first process to run gets the printer.

You should notice, as well, that the problem is not quite as simple as has been implied. Consider what happens if, between testing the flag and finding it set to 1, and trying to reset it to 0, another process runs and sets the flag to 0.

One form of control that can be used to prevent this is often called a *semaphore*. This is a more general version of the idea of a simple flag. Suppose in this case that there are several printers, so that several processes could print at the same time. The flag used in the earlier example could become a count of the number of printers available. The logic then becomes:

```
IF count=0
   THEN
      suspend until flag>0
   ENDIF
   decrement the count
   access a printer
   increment the count
```

Many operating systems provide functions, often called *wait* and *signal*, to support semaphores:

```
wait(s)     IF s = 0
            THEN
               suspend until s>0
            ENDIF
            decrement s
signal(s)   increment s
```

16.5 Interfaces to Peripherals

Historically, computers had relatively few types of peripheral devices attached to them. In the 1960s and 1970s, common computer peripherals consisted of magnetic disk and tape units, printers, terminals, teletypewriters, card readers and not much more. Most of these were relatively slow devices with a simple interface. Today there are many more ways to get data into and out of computers. Mice, tracker-balls, light pens, CD-ROM drives, keyboards, colour VDUs, magnetic disks, scanners, digital cameras, optical fibres, laser printers and LCD projectors spring to mind immediately, and these are just the 'standard' devices. Move into industry and the computer may well be controlling a robot. In your own kitchen there will be some computing in your washing machine, and there is even an Internet fridge advertised! Camera technology has changed, too, with digital cameras allowing the uploading of images for reprocessing before onward transmission or printing.

When discussing interfaces in general, the importance of separating the use of an interface from its implementation has already been noted. Such a distinction is even more important when widely varying peripherals are to be used. It is bad design to have to completely rewrite a piece of software because the user wants a different printer! To achieve this, the operation of the program needs to be separated as far as possible from the real characteristics of the peripherals. It might, for example have available to it a command such as print, which prints a line of text on the printer. However, its knowledge of the behaviour of the particular printer to be used would be limited to such things as the length of the print line. The more it knows about the printer, the more it is likely to be incompatible with some other printers.

At the lowest level, the *device driver* supports the peripheral directly and is aware of the detailed control sequences needed to support it. If you change the printer you will need to change the device driver, but in most cases that is all you would have to change.

The user expects a very high-level interface, but the device driver supplies a very low-level interface. If these are just too incompatible, an intermediate *device handler* could be introduced. This can supply buffering and queueing services as well as providing a more convenient access to the device driver. The device handler exists to bridge the gap between the application and the device driver. It makes the device easier to use.

Although the device handler can hide many of the characteristics of a peripheral, it cannot hide them all. Because peripherals vary so much, it is not possible to give hard and fast rules. The following, therefore, are some issues to be aware of:

- What *speed* does the device operate at? Few peripherals can operate as fast as a computer processor. Some, indeed, are particularly slow. A keyboard, for example, can deliver characters only as fast as someone can type. If the application is doing nothing but processing these characters then it might be acceptable to wait for each character. In general, however, it is better to separate responsibility for the collection of characters into a device handler, which can then either raise an interrupt when a character arrives, or be inspected at regular intervals. Similarly, if characters are to be written to a printer, there is no point in the application waiting for the device after every `print` statement. A device handler that accepts the text and holds it until it can be printed is a better solution. This mechanism by which an intermediate store holds information until a slow device can accept it is called *buffering*. In general, whenever two devices of significantly different speeds are to be linked, there will be a need for buffering.

- What is the *unit of transfer*? That is, what is the form of what is passed into the application program? Some devices communicate in terms of single characters, others in terms of kilobytes of data at a time. Here, the device handler is again important. It would be poor design to allow every application direct access to the structure of the disk: every disk is different. An application is much more likely to want to talk in terms of 'Files' and 'Records within those Files'.

16.6 Summary

A complex system must be partitioned in order to make it easier to understand. In human terms we'd describe this by saying: 'divide and rule'. There are many different kinds of interfaces. Figure 16.13 shows some of them.

When deciding where to make the partitions, care must be taken that:

- Geographically separate processing is not unnecessarily combined.

- It used to be a rule of thumb that the more complex the interface, the more local should be its implementation. This is now less so as better communications enable more complex displays to be transmitted to remote terminal devices.

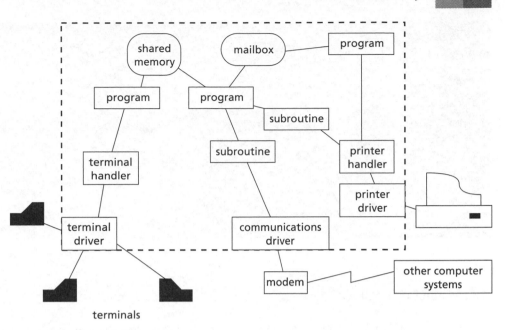

Fig. 16.13 The variety of interfaces

The other key to good interface design is to remember that an interface implies that data is crossing a boundary between two physical entities. Using diagrams to represent the structure of the interfaces graphically helps other software developers and users to picture how it works.

17 Systems Design: Logical Data Design

17.1 Introduction

Data is something that an organisation invests in but which has value to the organisation only when it is accurate and properly controlled. Business processes change frequently, but the underlying data is relatively stable, and unless the core business of an organisation changes, the data it uses will remain unchanged. For example, the processes needed to control a warehouse stock retrieval system may change from being completely manual, where paper records are kept and where stock is stored and retrieved by forklift truck, to being fully automated. In the new system incoming goods are identified to the system by barcodes, the system decides where to store the item, and it controls cranes and automated goods vehicles to transport items to and from locations. The core data, item numbers and locations remain unchanged, even though the processing has changed dramatically.

During the 1960s systems were usually built to follow the current processes, and little attention was paid to data analysis and data design. This approach suited the technical limitations of the times, where many applications used serial magnetic tape files in batch processing systems. Because no thought was given to the fact that data has a right to exist on its own, separately from any processing that used it, it came to be stored in the system only when a process required it. This also resulted in each user holding their own customised version of the data. This meant a proliferation of different names, sizes and formats for the same data item. One piece of data could be held many times in different files in different formats.

With the introduction of structured methods and database techniques, greater attention was paid to data analysis – a method that considers data in its own right, independent of processing limitations or hardware and software constraints. It also ensures that there will be only one version of the data, and that any duplication is explicitly agreed and controlled. The resulting data model provides a complete picture of the data used by the organisation. It consists of:

- data entities;
- key fields for entities;
- a list of attributes for each entity;
- relationships between entities.

17.2 The Top-down View: Entity Modelling

In Chapter 9 we considered entity models in the context of recording information about the existing system. The same principles apply here and are restated with additional examples as part of the overall approach to data design. We begin with some revision about entities, their properties and the relationship between entities. A data entity is something about which an organisation needs to hold data. Data entities are not only tangible and concrete, such as 'person', but may also be active such as 'accident', conceptual such as 'job', permanent such as 'town', and temporary such as 'stock item'. Entities are always labelled in the singular: 'student', never 'students'. Although the system will hold information about more than one student, the analyst is interested in identifying what the system has to know about each occurrence of 'student'. The entity label 'student' is a generic description. An entity must have the following properties:

- It is of interest to the organisation.
- It occurs more than once.
- Each occurrence is uniquely identifiable.
- There is data to be held about the entity.

Entities have attributes. An attribute is a data item that belongs to a data entity. For example, a bank may have a data entity 'customer', which could include the attributes 'account number', 'type', 'name', 'address', 'phone number', 'account balance', 'overdraft limit' and so on. So a data entity is really a group of data items and in concept is closer to a record than to a data field.

An entity must have a key that gives each occurrence of the entity a unique reference. For 'student' we could try to use 'name' as the key, but there could be (for example) more than one John Smith, so 'name' is not unique and therefore can't be used as the key. To find a unique identifier therefore we could make one up and choose the student's admission number because it uniquely identifies each student in the college. This is a *simple key* because it consists of only one data item. If we had not assigned a unique number to each student, we would have to use more than one data item as the key, such as 'name, date of birth, and address'. A key like this, consisting of more than one field, is called a *complex key*. Where possible it is preferable use simple keys.

There are three possible relationships between entities: one-to-one, one-to-many and many-to-many. Only one-to-many relationships are modelled on a data structure. The logical data structure for a college enrolment system is shown in Figure 17.1.

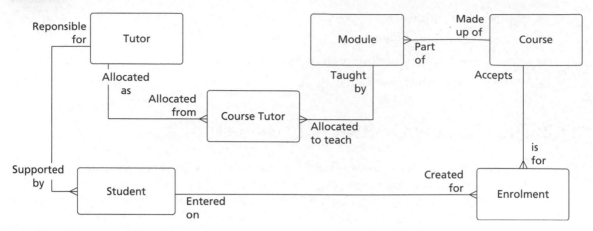

Fig. 17.1 Logical data structure diagram

Student	Tutor	Course
application number	tutor	course code
name	tutor name	course title
address	address	course cost
telephone number	telephone number	
tutor	grade	
year of entry	skills area	
career intention	salary	

Fig. 17.2 Entity descriptions

For each entity shown on the data model the analyst compiles a list of attributes, and checks that the attributes support the relationships defined on the model. Figure 17.2 shows some of the entity descriptions that support the data structure.

Production of the logical data model is an iterative process, which begins with a basic outline model of the current system. This first attempt can be made without having defined the data content of each entity in detail. Gradually, with further fact-finding interviews and cross-checking of the system models, this initial data model will be expanded and refined. The data model(s) that are produced should not be used in isolation. They are just one of the techniques used to understand and define the new system, and should interact with the other models if successful systems development is to take place. The data model is produced in parallel with the process model, and is used to check the data stores accessed by the process model.

17.2.1 The Entity Relationship Matrix

An entity matrix is drawn to establish the 'direct' relationships between entities. It shows that each relationship has been considered and resolved in a way

Entities	tutor	student	enrolment	course	course tutor	module
tutor	x	1:m	-	-	1:m	-
student	m:1	x	1:m	-	-	-
enrolment	-	m:1	x	m:1	-	-
course	-	-	1:m	x	1:m	1:m
course tutor	m:1	-	-	m:1	x	-
module	-	-	-	m:1	-	x

Fig. 17.3 An entity relationship matrix

that satisfies the requirements for the user's new system. To illustrate this, let's take a few candidate entities from the case study system and draw up an entity relationship matrix for them. Normally the matrix is drawn for all entities in the system, but it is possible – and helpful – to show the relationships between entities within one functional area. Optional and exclusive relationships are entered as direct relationships, which means the link must exist on the physical system.

The diagonal axis (Figure 17.3) acts as a mirror, with every relationship on one side of the axis reflected on the other side. That means it is only really necessary to complete one side of the matrix, but it is good practice to complete the whole matrix, and then check it for consistency. An 'x' is placed in the box when the entity has the same name. This is because it is not helpful to say 'student has a 1:1 relationship with student'. Where the relationship is indirect, this is indicated by '-'. For example, each student attends one or more courses, but the relationship is not direct because it is routed through 'enrolment'. If there is a query over whether this is a direct or an indirect relationship, then the customer is consulted to resolve it. It may be necessary to assume it is a direct relationship until data modelling is complete and then question the relationship again. The relationship highlighted reads as 'student has a many-to-one relationship with tutor'. The main benefit of drawing the matrix is to validate the data model.

17.2.2 Summary of Entity Modelling

We can summarise the main points about entity modelling as follows:

- On an entity relationship diagram each entity is represented by a rectangular box.

- A 'direct' relationship between a pair of entities is that which can be described without reference to some other entity on the matrix, and is shown as a line on the diagram.

- The line between two boxes is a relationship, or access path, and corresponds to an entry on the entity relationship matrix.

- A 'crow's foot' at the end of this line denotes the 'many' part of the relationship.

- The 'crow's foot' end of the line denotes a 'member'; the single end denotes an 'owner'.

- An owner may have different types of member.

- A member may have more than one owner.

- A member cannot exist without an owner, unless the relationship is optional.

- A many-to-many relationship is converted to two one-to-many relationships by the addition of junction data.

Logical data modelling provides a solid foundation for any system to be developed, whether file based or using a database. However, the logical data design is an ideal model, so before data is eventually stored in the system the data will be quantified and the model will be flexed to meet the constraints of the physical system.

17.3 The Bottom-up View: Third Normal Form Analysis

Normalisation of data is a process of removing duplication, and grouping related data to minimise interdependence between data groups. The less interdependence that exists between data groups, the less impact a data modification has, such as increasing the size of a data item. This approach to data analysis allows the analyst to build a data model starting with the attributes and subsequently grouping these together to form entities. The analyst then identifies the relationships between those entities. If the proposed system is not replacing an old system, copies of existing input and output will not exist – therefore third normal form analysis cannot be carried out, but there are very few systems in development that do not have predecessor systems.

To take data through third normal form analysis, you first need access to all data the organisation stores in the system. Typically this will be done by collecting one copy of every type of form and report. If there is an existing computer system, screen printouts can also be used. Forms provide the input to the system, reports identify the output, and screens are a combination of the two. From these system inputs and outputs every data item that appears is listed. This gives the complete picture of all of the data that is important. The analyst must then identify how these data items relate to each other. Unlike entity modelling, third normal form analysis is a procedural method of modelling the data. So let's start by listing the steps involved:

1 Identify all system inputs and outputs.
2 For each of these:
   - List all data items and identify a unique key (unnormalised form).
   - Remove repeating groups (first normal form).

- Remove part-key dependences (second normal form).
- Remove inter-data dependences (third normal form).
- Label the relation.

3 Merge entities with the same key.

4 Apply third normal form tests.

5 Draw a logical data model showing the relationships between entities.

Each successive step refines the structure of the data further. To illustrate how this works, we'll normalise the data items found on the student enrolment form.

A university entrance system receives applications for places on the form shown in Figure 17.4. An application may be for more than one course, and each

Student Enrolment Form

Name .... Tutor .... Year of Entry .... Application No. ....

Address: .... Tutor Dept ....

....

....

Telephone ....

GCSE Results	
Subject	Grade
GCSE results validated	
Signed .... Tutor	

Enrolment: Examined Courses				
Course Code	Course Title	Module Code	Module Title	Course Cost
			Total Cost:	

Gareer Intention

Payment Method: V ☐ A ☐ CH ☐ INST ☐

AMOUNT OUTSTANDING: ....

Fig. 17.4 Student enrolment form

application specifies the modules that the applicant wishes to study on each course they are applying for. Their application must also state the GCSE subjects they have been examined for and the grades they achieved. Each course has a cost associated with it, and the total cost of the courses applied for is shown at the bottom of the form. An application is handled by a specific tutor; the applicants are expected to state the method of payment they wish to use, and the form also records the amount of money that remains to be paid for these courses. Applicants are also expected to submit a brief detail of their career intentions.

The next step is to list all the data items and identify the key data items. There are a number of rules to follow when selecting the key. First, it must be unique so that it uniquely identifies all of the remaining data items. It can never be blank, otherwise the remaining data items are not accessible. A short simple numeric key is preferable, as this makes searching and sorting easier. Figure 17.5 shows

UNF Select a key for the document and list all the items	INF Separate the items that repeat into their own tables with compound/composite keys	2NF Create separate tables for items uniquely identified by part of a key only	3NF Create separate tables for items dependent on non-key items
APPLICATION NO NAME ADDRESS TEL NUMBER TUTOR TUTOR DEPT YEAR ENTRY GCSESUBJECT GCSEGRADE RESULTSIGNATURE COURSE CODE COURSE TITLE MODULECODE MODULE TITLE COURSECOST TOTALCOST PAYMENTMETHOD AMTOUTSTANDING CAREER			

Fig. 17.5 Enrolment form data in its unnormalised form

the enrolment form data in its unnormalised form. The key that uniquely identifies this set of data is 'application number' as each student will have a unique admission number.

To move the data into first normal form we remove any repeating groups of data. Looking back to the layout of the enrolment form above, the repeating groups are easy to identify. Subject and grade appear several times, as do module and module code, which themselves are within a repeating group of course code and course title. Having separated out the repeating groups we must identify a key for each group, and this key must maintain the link to the original data set as in Figure 17.6.

We now need to remove part-key dependences, thus structuring the data into second normal form. This means that, if the key to a set of data has two or more

UNF Select a key for the document and list all the items	INF Separate the items that repeat into their own tables with compound/composite keys	2NF Create separate tables for items uniquely identified by part of a key only	3NF Create separate tables for items dependent on non-key items
APPLICATION NO NAME ADDRESS TEL NUMBER TUTOR TUTOR DEPT YEAR ENTRY GCSESUBJECT GCSEGRADE RESULTSIGNATURE COURSE CODE COURSE TITLE MODULECODE MODULE TITLE MODULECOST TOTALCOST PAYMENTMETHOD AMTOUTSTANDING CAREER	APPLICATION NO NAME ADDRESS TEL NUMBER TUTOR TUTOR DEPT YEAR ENTRY GCSESUBJECT GCSEGRADE RESULTSIGNATURE TOTALCOST PAYMENTMETHOD AMTOUTSTANDING CAREER APPLICATION NO GCSESUBJECT GCSEGRADE APPLICATION NO COURSE CODE COURSE TITLE COURSECOST APPLICATION NO COURSECODE MODULECODE MODULE TITLE		

Fig. 17.6 Enrolment form data in first normal form

data items in it, every data item in the set must be tested against the individual parts of the key. For example, we can find the description and cost of a course simply by knowing the course code. We don't need to know the student's application number to find these data items. So we separate it out, as shown in Figure 17.7.

This leaves some relations containing only key data items. These maintain the links between data groups, and will go on to become link entities; also, it is possible that, after normalising other inputs and outputs, we may find attributes for such an entity. We now move the data into third normal form by removing interdata dependences. This is where data items within a set that is already in second normal form are tightly related to each other, but are not directly related to the key. In this case, the tutor's department is dependent on who the tutor is,

UNF *Select a key for the document and list all the items*	INF *Separate the items that repeat into their own tables with compound/composite keys*	2NF *Create separate tables for items uniquely identified by part of a key only*	3NF *Create separate tables for items dependent on non-key items*
APPLICATION NO NAME ADDRESS TEL NUMBER TUTOR TUTOR DEPT YEAR ENTRY GCSESUBJECT GCSEGRADE RESULTSIGNATURE COURSE CODE COURSE TITLE MODULECODE MODULE TITLE COURSECOST TOTALCOST PAYMENTMETHOD AMTOUTSTANDING CAREER	APPLICATION NO NAME ADDRESS TEL NUMBER TUTOR TUTOR DEPT YEAR ENTRY RESULTSIGNATURE TOTALCOST PAYMENTMETHOD AMTOUTSTANDING CAREER APPLICATION NO GCSESUBJECT GCSEGRADE APPLICATION NO COURSE CODE COURSE TITLE COURSECOST APPLICATION NO COURSECODE MODULECODE MODULE TITLE	APPLICATION NO NAME ADDRESS TEL NUMBER TUTOR TUTOR DEPT YEAR ENTRY RESULTSIGNATURE TOTALCOST PAYMENTMETHOD AMTOUTSTANDING CAREER APPLICATION NO GCSESUBJECT GCSEGRADE APPLICATION NO COURSE CODE COURSE CODE COURSE TITLE COURSECOST APPLICATION NO COURSECODE MODULECODE MODULECODE MODULE TITLE	

Fig. 17.7 Enrolment form data in second normal form

not on the student's application number. The data item 'tutor' now appears in one data set where it is the key, and in another data set where it is just an attribute. In the student entity we label tutor as a foreign key to show that it is the key to another data set. Foreign keys are marked with an asterisk (Figure 17.8).

We now label the relations: in this case appropriate entity names are 'student', 'tutor', 'GCSE subject', 'course', 'enrolment', 'course module' and 'module'.

What started out as one long list of interrelated data items has now been structured into a number of discrete entities. This same process is followed for each of the forms, screens and reports in the system. When all system inputs and outputs have been normalised in this way, we combine duplicate entities. Because in our example we've normalised only one form we don't have duplicate

UNF	INF	2NF	3NF
Select a key for the document and list all the items	*Separate the items that repeat into their own tables with compound/composite keys*	*Create separate tables for items uniquely identified by part of a key only*	*Create separate tables for items dependent on non-key items*
APPLICATION NO	APPLICATION NO	APPLICATION NO	APPLICATION NO
NAME	NAME	NAME	NAME
ADDRESS	ADDRESS	ADDRESS	ADDRESS
TEL NUMBER	TEL NUMBER	TEL NUMBER	TEL NUMBER
TUTOR	TUTOR	TUTOR	TUTOR*
TUTOR DEPT	TUTOR DEPT	TUTOR DEPT	YEAR ENTRY
YEAR ENTRY	YEAR ENTRY	YEAR ENTRY	RESULTSIGNATURE
GCSESUBJECT	RESULTSIGNATURE	RESULTSIGNATURE	TOTALCOST
GCSEGRADE	TOTALCOST	TOTALCOST	PAYMENTMETHOD
RESULTSIGNATURE	PAYMENTMETHOD	PAYMENTMETHOD	AMTOUTSTANDING
COURSE CODE	AMTOUTSTANDING	AMTOUTSTANDING	CAREER
COURSE TITLE	CAREER	CAREER	
MODULECODE			TUTOR
MODULE TITLE	APPLICATION NO	APPLICATION NO	TUTOR DEPT
COURSECOST	GCSESUBJECT	GCSESUBJECT	
TOTALCOST	GCSEGRADE	GCSEGRADE	APPLICATION NO*
PAYMENTMETHOD			GCSESUBJECT
AMTOUTSTANDING	APPLICATION NO	APPLICATION NO	GCSEGRADE
CAREER	COURSE CODE	COURSE CODE	
	COURSE TITLE		APPLICATION NO*
	COURSECOST	COURSE CODE	COURSE CODE*
		COURSE TITLE	
	APPLICATION NO	COURSECOST	COURSE CODE
	COURSECODE		COURSE TITLE
	MODULECODE	APPLICATION NO	COURSECOST
	MODULE TITLE	COURSECODE	
		MODULECODE	APPLICATION NO*
			COURSECODE*
			MODULECODE*
		MODULECODE	
		MODULE TITLE	MODULECODE
			MODULE TITLE

Fig. 17.8 Enrolment form data in third normal form

entities. Our next step is to apply the third normal form tests. These tests can be summarised as taking each data item in turn and asking: 'Does finding the value of this item depend on knowing the key, the whole key and nothing but the key?'

The final step is to draw the data model. The 3NF tables can be shown as a data model by making a one-to-many relationship between the primary and foreign keys in the tables. This is a less complex data model because it represents only the direct relationships between entities, and does not explore optional or exclusive relationships. The data model for our example is shown in Figure 17.9.

As this method of data analysis represents a considerable amount of work, it is not recommended as a preferred starting point. Data analysts often start by using the more intuitive entity modelling approach, and then third normal form analysis on those forms or reports that the client identifies as key system inputs or outputs. Third normal form analysis may also be used where information from users is contradictory, so that the data actually used and stored is identified. It models only the current physical system, whereas entity modelling also takes account of what the client wants in the new, required, system. However, for a small system, or to be certain that no data has been missed, data analysts would want to carry out both entity modelling and third normal form analysis. This provides them with two different views of the same data.

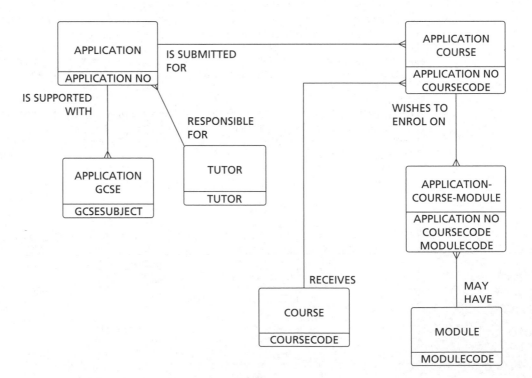

Fig. 17.9 Data model for college enrolment system

17.4 Merging the Data Models

The final stage in logical data design merges the top-down view of the data and the bottom-up view. The aim is to identify any candidate data entities or relationships that need further investigation. We may find that an entity was not identified in the top-down approach but is shown by the results of normalisation to be needed. We may also find that some conceptual entity that was not identified during normalisation is required for the new system. We use this dual approach because if we treat data design as a totally intuitive task we can miss things and, similarly, if we carry out normalisation and don't reflect on the results with a business eye we can also miss things. Again it is the combination of the logical, thorough approach and the business knowledge that produces the most appropriate solution. Figures 17.1 and 17.9 illustrated the two views of the student enrolment system, and as you can see there are significant differences. Merging these two results in the data model shown in Figure 17.10.

In the merged model we have added the entity 'GCSE subject' from the bottom-up data model, and examined the relationships between 'student' and 'GCSE subject' to test for optionality. We did not normalise any documents that gave us information about the 'course tutor' entity so, although it did not exist on the bottom-up data model, it remains as part of the model.

This approach will duplicate effort of course, but double-checking at this stage ensures that the data design is accurate.

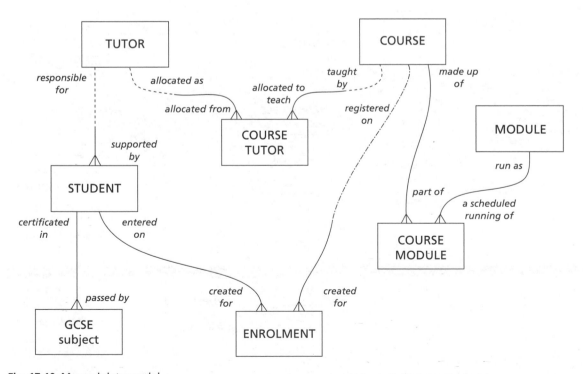

Fig. 17.10 Merged data model

17.5 Testing the Data Model

Having built this idealised form of how the data entities in the system relate to each other, we must now check that this structure will support the business needs of the organisation. To do this we take each input to and output from the system and a copy of the data model, and then draw onto the data model the route through the data structure required to produce each report, and each input. To draw the route for every input and output on the same data model would result in an unreadable diagram. It is therefore simpler to copy the data model several times and draw one access map on one copy of the data model. James Martin's version of this model is called a *data navigation diagram* (DND), whereas the SSADM equivalent is called a *logical access map* (LAM). So to produce a class list for a given course for our example, Figure 17.11 is what the logical access map looks like.

In this example, only three read accesses are needed to produce the class list, which implies that this would be a simple report for the system to produce. Each read access is labelled sequentially, and the initial read data is shown, in this case the course code. It may be that, when drawing an access map, the analyst discovers that a relationship has been missed from the model, or that the route is too circuitous, which would mean reading a lot of data that would not be shown in

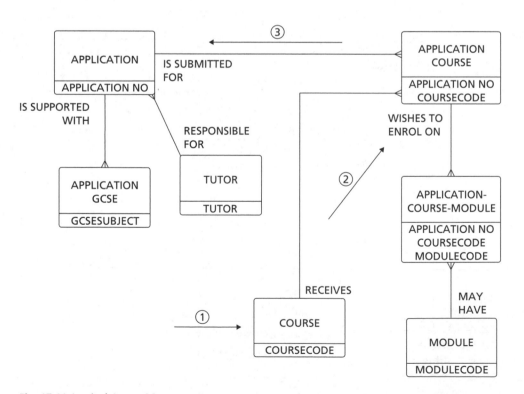

Fig. 17.11 Logical Access Map

the report. This would prompt the designers to reconsider relationships, and possibly add some new ones. This is not a problem; indeed it is the reason for using logical access mapping.

17.6 The Data Dictionary

To be certain that each relationship shown on the data model is accurate, we have to look behind the model at the entity descriptions showing all the attributes. Then we must look more closely at these attributes to ensure that we have not defined the same attribute under two different names. This is where the data dictionary is invaluable. It provides a detailed view of the data, and how that data is used during processing. This gives us, at a very low level, a link between data and processes.

A data dictionary may be used to support a simple file-based system, or a more complex database system. A data dictionary contains metadata: that is, it contains data about data. In its simplest form a data dictionary will hold basic information about each data item, such as: name, size, validation rules. A simple example of this might be student enrolment number. In our example the enrolment number is made up of three data items: the college number, the year of entry, and the admission number. Typical data we might store about this data item is shown in Figure 17.12.

Everything we need to know about each data item is stored in the dictionary because:

- it is easier to trace and maintain data, as each data item is defined once only;

- productivity is increased as a result of the reuse of previously defined data items with consequent avoidance of errors;

- central control allows data to be traced through the system, making maintenance easier.

The dictionary can be a manual one, with one page of data per data item. This means that the data dictionary, even for a small system, can be over a hundred pages. However, there is only one dictionary in the system, regardless of how many databases and/or files there are. The major drawback, however, when using a manual data dictionary is that developers can forget to complete the cross-referencing, or can get it wrong. This causes confusion or errors later. Sometimes developers may use this as an excuse to avoid having a data dictionary at all, especially if the system is small, but the errors and difficulties caused by not having a central data reference usually outweigh those caused by its incorrect use.

The dictionary can of course be automated, and to a large extent this solves the problem of developers forgetting to follow through dictionary updates, because the dictionary automatically updates cross-references and related entries. However, automated dictionaries do have a number of drawbacks. The quantity of data stored and the time taken to check cross-referencing can mean that updating

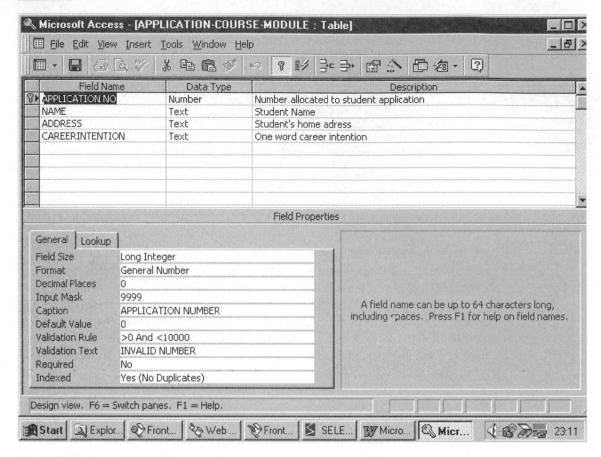

Fig. 17.12 An Access Data Dictionary entry

the dictionary can be a slow process. Where a dictionary is associated with a particular DBMS, such as MS-ACCESS, it is based on the use of that DBMS, so that the database is built from the dictionary. The best automated dictionaries use database management systems for their internal data storage, and thereby support other database facilities, such as full recovery and online multi-user updating. Another benefit of automated dictionaries is that changes made to one screen automatically update any related information, so that if we amend the 'where used' section to add the name of a common routine, the system automatically accesses the data held about that common routine to say that this data item is also used in the routine. This prevents the confusion that might occur if one part of a manual data dictionary is out of step with another.

17.6.1 Advanced Features of a Data Dictionary

As was suggested previously, developers might want a central store holding not just data, but also information about how that data is used. For this reason some data dictionaries allow the user to enter the data definitions, data flows, common processing routines, and layouts for screens, forms and reports.

The information held about a data flow includes:

- names of data items contained;
- the origin and destination of the flow;
- what event triggers the flow.

Data held about common processing is usually

- a description of what it does;
- its inputs and outputs;
- a list of processes it is called by;
- detailed processing such as would be found in a program specification.

If common processes are defined in this way in the data dictionary, there is no need to write program specifications for the routines. Screen layouts, sometimes called *skeletons* or *proformas*, may be defined in the dictionary, but not if they are included in the functional specification. The reason for including them here is because the dictionary is a working document used all the way through development, whereas the functional specification, written in the early stages of design, might become more of a reference document.

17.7 Summary

As data is the key to an organisation, and the techniques for constructing the definitive logical data design are many, it is worth summarising the process step by step.

1. Identify as many candidate entities as possible. During the fact-finding phase of analysis you should document entities in the existing system and add others identified in discussions with the client about their requirements for the new system.

2. Rationalise the entities. Check whether the same entity has been identified twice but under different names. Combine duplicate entities. Check whether an entity exists outside the boundary of the system. Examine the data content of each junction entity to ensure that it is in fact required.

3. Draw an entity relationship matrix as an aid to identifying the direct relationships between the entities.

4. Represent each of the identified entities as rectangles on a sheet of paper.

5. Initially, draw only the definite relationships. Later, having constructed the logical data model, any relationships that were shown on the matrix as being questionable can be reconsidered to decide whether they are in fact required.

6 For each relationship decide which entity is the owner and which is the member. If both appear to be members a many-to-many relationship exists. Identify the junction entity. An entity can be the owner of one relationship and the member of another.

7 We recommend an average of between 8 and 12 entities, and a maximum of 15 on any one model, simply because this makes the model more readable. Large systems will typically have anything between 50 and 200 entities, but to model all of these together would be difficult to do and cumbersome to use.

8 The initial diagram may be untidy, with relationship lines crossing each other. To aid understanding and communication, redraw the diagram to produce a clearer representation. Also, to aid clarity, draw the member entities below the owner entities on the diagram.

9 Test the data structure against the existing system, then against the required system. Check that each form screen and report required can be produced by following a path through the data model.

10 With the client, reconsider any relationships you are not sure should be implemented, and make a final decision. It is important that the true significance of each of the relationships on the model is understood to ensure that the data being retrieved is precisely that which is required. It is important too to exercise care when rationalising the entity model, as it is easy to over-rationalise as a result of having inadequate information about the data content of the entities or the true nature of the relationships between them.

11 Revalidate the rationalised data structure against the user's requirements for the new system. Once the data structure is complete, walk the client through it, and once they have agreed it ask them to sign it off!

Exercises

17.1 Perform third normal form analysis on the following list of unnormalised data.

Subscriber no	Call no
Telephone no	Call date
Rental start date	Number called
Bill start date	Call period
Bill end date	Call charge
Subscriber name	Total amount payable
Service type	

17.2 Name the resultant relations and draw a partial data model.

17.3 Identify the types of key found during this exercise.

17.4 Showtime Cinemas own a number of cinemas that show different films. The data below is a report of the takings from different cinemas. Rearrange this data in 3NF tables.

Film no.	Film name	Cinema ID	Cinema name	Location	Manager no.	Manager name	Takings
23	JAWS IV	AB	PLAZA	NEWCASTLE	01	JONES	£200
		CH	ROXY	NEWTON	01	JONES	£150
		MZ	EMBASSY	CROYDON	03	SMITH	£200
68	BLADE 2	AB	PLAZA	NEWCASTLE	01	JONES	£300
		CH	ROXY	NEWTON	01	JONES	£500
		MZ	EMBASSY	CROYDON	03	SMITH	£600
		BA	PLAZA	EDINBURGH	03	SMITH	£450
31	THE ROCK	AB	PLAZA	NEWCASTLE	01	JONES	£90
		TU	CLASSIC	WOOLWICH	04	ROBSON	£100
76	ROCKY V	CH	ROXY	NEWTON	01	JONES	£150
		MZ	EMBASSY	CROYDON	03	SMITH	£200
		TZ	CLASSIC	PUTNEY	05	WILSON	£250

18 Systems Design: Files

18.1 Introduction

The way in which data is organised and accessed can be crucial to the effectiveness of a computer system. Much of what the computer does is data processing. This involves taking input data, doing some processing on that data, and producing output data. Physically this data consists of alphanumeric characters grouped into data items or fields: for example, a customer name or address. Related fields are grouped into records. A customer record might contain the fields 'customer name', 'address', 'telephone purchase date', 'telephone number' and a 'customer reference number'. A file is an organised collection of related records. System Telecom's customer file would, for example, contain a customer record for every one of System Telecom's customers.

This chapter describes the most common types of data, the ways in which data can be organised, and how records can be accessed. We also look at many of the factors that determine the optimum organisation and access method for a particular application.

18.2 Types of Data

Eight different types of data are described in this section.

Master data is critical to the system and its users. The records contain permanent information of long-term value to an organisation, which is used regularly in the organisation's key systems. System Telecom, for example, might hold data about customers, about the company's own employees, and about call-logging stations. The customer records could contain the following fields:

Customer number	Name	Address	Phone purchase date	Telephone number
0001	M. Jones	9 Uxbridge Road Pinner, Middx HA9 7RD	27.8.03	020 8866 3147

The records in the logging station file might contain these fields:

Log Station reference	Location	Reliability	Last service date	Network service date
LON 0051	Hyde Park Corner Underpass	93%	9.8.02	4.2.03

Transaction data is data relating to business activities, such as telephone calls logged. It is used mainly to update master data. Transaction data usually relates to a particular period of time. For example, a new set of records may be created each day and written to file between system start-up and system shut-down. The next morning, that data will be used to update the master data, and a new transaction file will be created for that day's transactions. Transaction files are sometimes known as *transaction logs*, *log files*, *update files* or *change files*.

Output files contain information for output from the system, such as data for printing as a report. They are usually generated by processing master data and transaction data.

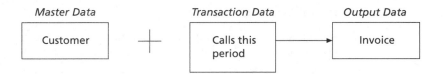

Transfer files carry data from one stage of processing to another. A transaction file, for example, may be the input to a sorting process so that the subsequent sorted data can then be used to create an output file.

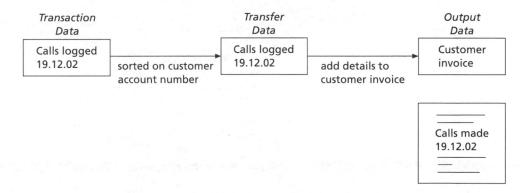

Security or dump files contain copies of data held in the computer at a particular moment. Their purpose is to provide a back-up, to permit recovery in case data is lost or damaged. Therefore security copies are stored offline, on a magnetic tape, disk or other computer.

Archive files contain archive information for long-term storage. System Telecom might want to archive details of payments made by customers over past years. Archiving is often required by law for tax and audit purposes.

Library files contain library routines such as utility programs and system software. The term can encompass any file containing any compiled computer program. For example, our mobile telephone system will need a program that works out which logging station to use. Such a program will be coded and compiled, and may be used by several applications in the system: therefore it could be said to be one of a library of files.

Audit files are used by a computer auditor to check that the programs are functioning correctly, and to trace any change to master files. Such a file contains copies of all transactions that have been applied to the permanent system files.

18.3 Storage Media

Data is stored on backing storage devices. The capacity of these devices increases continually, so data storage capacity is rarely a problem for transaction processing systems.

- The multiple-platter, fixed hard disks illustrated in Figure 18.1 may hold from 10 gigabytes of data to over 200 gigabytes.

- PC systems normally feature a 3.5 inch floppy disk that holds 1.44 megabytes of data, as well as a hard disk.

- Additionally a Zip disk can be used to compress data for storage purposes. Currently a Zip disk can hold up to 750 megabytes of data – the same as 170 floppy disks. A Jaz disk can hold up to 2 gigabytes.

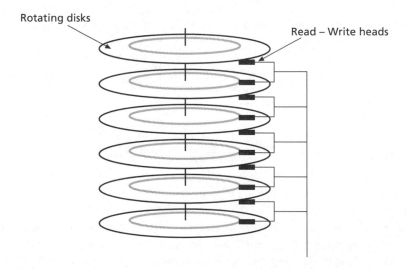

Fig. 18.1 A disk pack

- Zip drives are also a useful addition to laptop and PC systems, and laptop computers are usually equipped with Universal Serial Bus ports, which provide an easy high-speed interface for external devices such as the Zip drive.

- Compact disc read-only memory (CD-ROM) stores data in the form of tiny reflective bumps known as pits and lands, and is read with a laser beam. The CD-ROM holds up to 700 megabytes of data in a single track that spirals from the outside edge to the centre, unlike the concentric tracked storage method used on magnetic disks as described below.

- Digital video disc read-only memory (DVD-ROM) holds the data in a more densely packed format and currently permits the storage of up to 17 gigabytes of data when both sides of the disc are used.

This increase in storage capacity for PC systems is likely to continue as users store video and audio data on their machines.

Conversely, the use of disks for business data processing purposes on larger corporate systems has not changed as dramatically. Capacities and access speeds have improved without major changes occurring in the file-handling techniques used to access and organise the data. In this chapter we look at data storage devices and define the principles used for organising and accessing data on these devices. In Chapter 19 we shall see how the database management software that provides the link between the user's application and its stored data uses these principles.

18.3.1 Magnetic Disk

Hard disks are the main file storage device for most computers. Hard disks are made of metal that is coated with a thin layer of magnetisable oxide. They are often mounted in packs (Figure 18.1).

A typical disk pack contains six disks, which have ten magnetisable surfaces. The outermost two surfaces are not used for recording data. Each of the ten surfaces has its own read–write head. Each surface is divided into tracks (Figure 18.2), and there are typically 200 tracks on each disk.

A track is subdivided into equal-sized blocks, and these blocks are the smallest addressable units of data. This means that, when data passes between the disk and the central processor, a whole block of data is transferred. There are gaps between blocks – inter-block gaps – which contain the block's address. The disk pack revolves continuously while the computer is switched on. To read files from a disk the read–write heads move to the required tracks, and data is sent down a data bus to main storage. The read–write heads all move in unison and are always positioned over equivalent tracks on each disk surface. The tracks that can be accessed for any particular read–write head position form an imaginary cylinder. So we can treat a disk pack as consisting of 200 cylinders, each with 10 recording tracks. Each block contains a number of records. If the block is 256 bytes and the record length is 240 bytes, the block contains one record. Records on disks can be accessed directly using their address, defined in terms of the cylinder, track and block numbers.

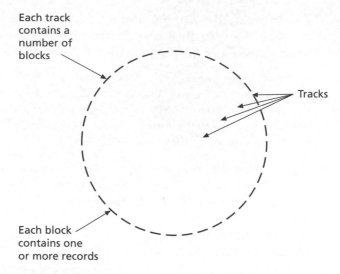

Each track contains a number of blocks

Tracks

Each block contains one or more records

Fig. 18.2 Tracks on a disk surface

To write a record to disk, data passes from main memory through a read–write head, onto a track on the disk surface. Records are stored, one after another, in blocks, on each track.

The time taken to read from or write to disk is made up of the following:

- *Head movement (seek time)*. This is the time to reach the correct track.

- *Rotational delay (latency)*. This is the time taken for the disk to rotate so that the correct record is under the head once the correct track has been found.

- *Head switching*. This is the time taken to activate the head to read or write, and is usually negligible.

- *Channel transfer time*. This is the time taken to transfer information between the processor and the storage device.

With microcomputers, as well as hard disks, floppy disks (diskettes) are also used for storing data, sometimes as backup files for PC systems or for data transfer. They are similar in principle to hard disks but are lighter and non-rigid. Floppy disks are more prone to contamination by dust or heat or magnetic corruption. They have a smaller capacity than hard disks and a slower data transfer rate.

18.4 File Organisation

Discussions about the increase in computer power over the last 30 years resound with stories of the way power has increased and size and cost has diminished. File storage has evolved in a similar way. Disk stores on small mainframes costing £50 000–£100 000 in the 1970s might have held 4 or 8 million bytes. Laptop PCs in the new millennium have capacities measured in gigabytes.

Although storage capacity has increased dramatically, the underlying techniques for storing data on magnetic media have remained consistent. Database management software and file management systems provide a transparent access layer to data stored on discs, and the analyst need not be concerned with the way the software navigates this data. The access mechanisms used by the DBMs remain the same as those used for conventional file processing, and it is therefore appropriate for the developer to recognise the terms used to describe these mechanisims and to be aware of the way the underlying access mechanism will often determine the response time the user sees at the terminal.

18.4.1 Serial Organisation

This is the simplest way in which records can be organised. The records are placed one after another each time a record needs to be stored. No particular sequence is followed – records are not sorted according to the value of a key field, for example. Each record goes into the next available storage space. This method gives maximum utilisation of space, but no room is left for inserting records. It is similar to the way you might record songs on to a tape. You would record song 1, then song 2, then song 3. You would not record songs 1 and 3 and then go back and insert song 2.

Serial organisation can be used for data stored on magnetic tape or magnetic disk. In either case, records are placed on the storage device one after the other, with no regard for sequence. Examples of files that might be organised serially include transaction files, output files, security files and archive files. The main disadvantage of serial organisation is that it does not cater for direct access to records. If the required record is in the fifteenth position in the file, the first 14 must be read prior to accessing record 15. If access is required in any order other than that in which the file was written, the file must be sorted.

18.4.2 Sequential Organisation

Like serial organisation, sequential organisation is also appropriate for data that is to be stored on either tape or disk. In this case, records are sequenced on the value of one or more key fields. For example, customer records might be sequenced in alphabetical order, or in ascending order of some unique customer number (Figure 18.3). Sequential organisation is appropriate for data in a batch processing environment. It is not generally used for online systems demanding fast response, other than for recording data for later analysis 'offline'. This is because it takes too long to find each individual record if the file has to be read from the beginning each time.

The advantages of sequential organisation are:

- It is a simple method of writing data to disk.

- It is the most efficient organisation if the records can be processed in the order in which they are read.

- It can be used for variable-length records as well as fixed-length records.

Customer number	Name	Address	Telephone number	
0001				
0002				
"				
"				
3219				

Fig. 18.3 Records organised sequentially, using customer number as the key field

18.4.3 Indexed Sequential Organisation

Indexed sequential organisation has records stored in sequence like sequential organisation but, in addition, an index is provided to enable individual records to be located directly after reaching the index. Indexed sequential organisation is used with disks but not with magnetic tape. Data held by telephone directory enquiries could be held in indexed sequential format. The index could be used to locate all data for a particular town. The data for that town would be held sequentially, with names sorted into alphabetical order.

When such a file is first created, the records must be sorted so that the value of the key field increases on consecutive records. It is also necessary to think about how much extra space may be needed for record insertions to cater, for example, for new customers being added. Spare space or overflow areas may be needed on each track, and on each cylinder, in case more records need to be inserted. Also, additional cylinders may be required for overflow of the file, to cater for further record insertions. Initially, additional records would be inserted into empty space between existing records on a track in the appropriate position, according to their key fields. When there is no space for a record insertion at the sequentially correct position, the record would be put into track overflow space, and when this is full the record would be put into cylinder overflow.

When the data is stored, indexes are created to enable groups of records to be accessed. The indexes may include, for example, a cylinder index and a track index. The first cylinder on the disk pack typically contains the cylinder index, and the first track on this cylinder contains the track index. These are limit indexes so the highest key value for each track is held in the track index and the highest key for each cylinder is held in the cylinder index. Figure 18.4 illustrates the idea of the track index.

To access a record, the indexes are inspected to determine which track the record is on. This track is then copied into memory where the records are inspected to obtain the one which is required. If the records on the track are in sequence, a binary chop search can be used to reach the desired record. Using this method the designer knows the average and maximum access time for any record. This is described in section 18.5.2. Limit index organisation can also be used when the records on a track are not strictly in sequence (as long as the last record on the track still has the highest key value).

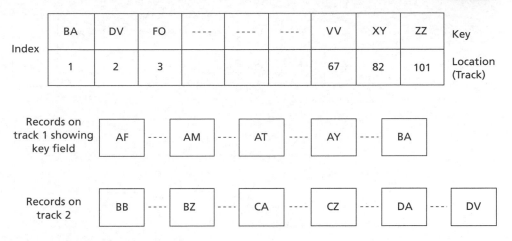

	BA	DV	FO	----	----	----	VV	XY	ZZ	Key
Index	1	2	3				67	82	101	Location (Track)

Records on track 1 showing key field	AF	----	AM	----	AT	----	AY	----	BA

Records on track 2	BB	----	BZ	----	CA	----	CZ	----	DA	----	DV

Fig. 18.4 Limited index organisation

The main advantage of indexed sequential organisation is its versatility. It combines direct access to a group of records with rapid sequential scanning of the group to obtain the record required. The problem with indexed sequential organisation, however, arises when records are inserted into overflow areas. This can slow down access since if a record cannot be found on the track where it would be expected from its key and the limit index, it will be in the overflow areas so these then have to be searched. Depending on the volatility of the data, it may need to be reorganised fairly often, because otherwise too many records will be in the overflow areas and access times will become unacceptably slow.

18.4.4 Random Organisation

Randomly organised data is stored with no regard to the sequence of key fields. Like indexed sequential data, random organisation can only be used with direct access devices and therefore requires direct access media such as magnetic disks, rather than serial media like tape.

A mathematical formula is derived that, when applied to each record key, generates an answer that is used to position the record at a corresponding address. The records are retrieved using the same formula. The main problem is to devise an algorithm that achieves a fairly uniform distribution of records on the disk. Also, variable-length records are difficult to deal with, and 'synonyms' can occur, where several keys result in the same address because the algorithm does not produce a different address for each different key. In these cases, records are put into the next available space.

The main advantages of random organisation are:

- No indexes are required.

- It permits the fastest access times.

- It is suitable for volatile data: records can be inserted or deleted indefinitely without reorganising the dataset.

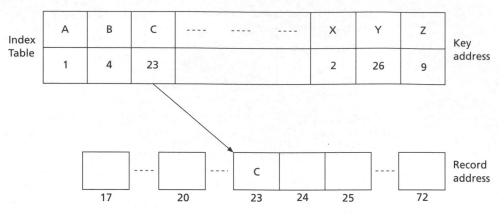

Fig. 18.5 Full index organisation

18.4.5 Full Index Organisation

With a full index (Figure 18.5) there is an entry in the index for every record. This entry gives the address of the record. The index is arranged in ascending order of the keys, although the records themselves can be in any order. There can be an index for each of several key fields, enabling records to be accessed by more than one key. For example, we could access a customer record by customer name or geographical location.

The drawback with full indexing is the size of the index, as it can be large. Space is required to store the index, and it can take a relatively long time to read the index and then access the record from the address.

18.4.6 Chained Data

Data can be stored using pointers to organise the data into chains, like beads on a necklace. This is often done when a combination of direct and sequential access is required. To illustrate the idea, consider a warehouse system used by a food processing company (Figure 18.6). Their warehouse has a number of aisles, each with a number of columns and levels. Each batch of, say, cake mix is coded with a date and pallet number. Samples of the cake mix are tested, which takes up to one day. The batches of cake mix are stored in the most convenient space, not necessarily in physically adjacent locations. If a sample fails the test, the batch must be destroyed, so the locations of each pallet of that particular batch must be known. This can be done with a chain or linked list of addresses.

The system stores a pointer to the start of the chain, in this case 030403 (i.e. aisle 3, row 4, level 3). From the start of the chain it can follow the chain of pointers to the end. The pointer is actually a field within the record containing the address of the next record. In this way the records are organised as a linked list. In this food example the records would be chained as shown in Figure 18.7.

Sometimes, records are chained using forward pointers only, but we have shown a file with forward and backward pointers. The final record in the list is assigned a forward pointer of zero. It is easy to insert or delete records using

LEVELS 4	CHOCCMIX 9302001 0003				CHOCCMIX 9302001 0002
LEVELS 3		CHOCCMIX 9302001 0006		CHOCCMIX 9302001 PALLET NO.1	
LEVELS 2			CHOCCMIX 9302001 0005		
LEVELS 1				CHOCCMIX 9302001 0004	

Fig. 18.6 Warehouse aisle 3

record 1	Ø	CHOCCMIX 93020010001	03 05 04
record 2	03 04 03	CHOCCMIX 93020010002	03 01 04
record 3	03 05 04	CHOCCMIX 93020010003	03 04 01
record 4	03 01 04	CHOCCMIX 93020010004	03 03 02
record 5	03 04 01	CHOCCMIX 93020010005	03 02 03
record 6	03 03 02	CHOCCMIX 93020010006	Ø
	Pointer to previous location	Product details: description, batch number + pallet number	Pointer to next location
		A Ø pointer indicates the head or the tail of the chain.	

Fig. 18.7 A chain file

record 1	Ø	CHOCCMIX 93020010001	03 05 04
record 2	03 04 03	CHOCCMIX 93020010002	**03 04 01**
record 3	**03 05 04**	CHOCCMIX 93020010004	03 03 02
record 4	03 04 01	CHOCCMIX 93020010005	03 02 03
record 5	03 03 02	CHOCCMIX 93020010006	Ø
	Pointer to previous location	Product details: description, batch number + pallet number	Pointer to next location
		A Ø pointer indicates the head or the tail of the chain.	

Fig. 18.8 Amended chain file

chaining, simply by modifying the pointer in the preceding and following records: if we removed record 3, we would amend the forward pointer in record 2 to point to pallet number 4, and the backward pointer in record 4 to point to pallet number 2.

Figure 18.8 shows the chained records showing where the chocolate cake mix is stored after pallet 3 is removed. So the chained data maintains a link from one pallet to the next. The two data items that had to change are highlighted in bold.

Using chains in this way allows for flexible use of the storage area. If there was no chocolate cake mix in the warehouse, no storage space is reserved for it. If there are 600 pallets of cake mix the system handles it in exactly the same way as it handles 6 pallets. Data designers have to make a decision about whether deletions can be made only at the head or tail of the chain or whether mid-chain data can be deleted. For example, if a pallet of cake mix was badly damaged owing to a crane breakdown you would want to remove the pallet and delete any reference to it in the data files.

18.5 Access Methods

Organising data and accessing it are two different aspects of data management: the method used to organise the data may not always be the best method to access the data. This is because the order in which data is processed and the amount of a dataset that is accessed in one processing operation can vary according to the processing task.

For example, a dataset will need to be processed in a key sequence when it is being used to produce reports, or when an update operation is being performed on every record. However, the same dataset might be required for ad hoc enquiries, and in these circumstances the application will require direct access to a single specific record. Holding the data sequentially with an index such as a limit index for direct access will allow these two requirements to be met. Also, when backups are being made a dataset will be accessed in a serial mode as it is only being copied in its entirety to a new file space.

The fastest access method to locate an individual method is through the use of a key transformation algorithm, as a single calculation will provide the address of the required record, which can then be retrieved with a single access. This method is appropriate for applications that involve the use of large datasets with continual online enquiry processing. Airline booking and social security systems are often quoted in this respect. The difficulty arises only when the data requires processing in a key sequence. Two options are available. The entire dataset can be copied and sorted, to allow the process to be performed, or the designer must specify a secondary index for the dataset that stores the key values in sequence with a pointer to each record. Both alternatives carry processing penalties, and the database administrator must balance these penalties against the importance and frequency of the application.

The systems analyst may not choose the method of data access and data organisation for a particular dataset. Designing systems using database management software inevitably leads to the use of shared data, and the organisation method for the data will be based upon the requirements of all the applications that will process it. Database management software is usually the responsibility of a database administrator, and the analyst can become distanced from decisions about the organisation and access method to be used.

We have included this description of these methods because they are the underlying mechanisms of all data management software. Database tuning involves the exploitation of these methods of access and organisation, and the logical data structure of an application is only one input into this process. Data access maps provide the database administrator with the processing paths and details of the frequency of access that the application will require. Understanding the mechanisms derived from these maps underpins the analyst's approach to their development.

18.6 Factors Influencing File Design

There are many factors that determine the best organisation and access method for a particular application. The most important of these are discussed in this section.

The *purpose* of the file is likely to be the major factor in determining the most appropriate organisation and the best method of accessing records. If it is to be used for online enquiry, for example, direct access is needed, and the data must be organised for this, perhaps using indexed organisation or random organisation with key transformation techniques. It may be that the data has to be processed in a variety of ways. For example, data may be accessed online during normal day-time running, but used to produce reports overnight as a batch process. An organisation must be chosen for both methods if it is decided not to have two or more differently organised versions. Data that is to be used for batch processing only, and where many of the records need to be processed, should be organised serially or sequentially as this is most efficient in these circumstances.

It is important to identify any constraints imposed by the existing system. Does the legacy system support a particular method of organisation and access? What data storage media are available? Remember that serial devices support only serial and sequential file organisation and serial access.

Updating of data is usually either 'in-situ' or using the 'grandfather–father–son' method. In-situ updating involves updating, inserting or deleting records online, without retaining the old version. There should, of course, be back-up copies of the old version, in case something goes wrong, or as archive files. In-situ updating of records in a random order requires direct access to the data. However, an organisation that allows in-situ updating may make record accesses inefficient after several record insertions or deletions.

The father–son method involves a new version of the data, thus resulting in having two generations of it, the father and son generations. Father–son updating is more secure than in-situ updating, because if the system fails the old version of the data should be unharmed. The updating can then be repeated when the system has been restarted. Three generations of the data, 'grandfather, father and son', are often created, before the oldest version is destroyed and the storage space re-used.

A file designer needs to consider the *frequency of access* for enquiry or for updating. How many records will have to be accessed in one process? This is termed the *hit rate*. For example, if 100 records are processed each day out of 1000 records, the hit rate is 10%. If the hit rate is high, batch updating of a sequential file may be the most efficient design. To decide whether the hit rate is 'high', the designer must calculate the 'average' time to access 100 records, and then calculate the time to read through all 1000 records. If it takes less time to process all the data sequentially, that would be the more efficient choice. It is not as simple as saying that a 45% hit rate is 'low' and a 55% hit rate is 'high'.

Sometimes the data changes infrequently, and sometimes it changes minute by minute. Therefore, in design it is important to consider how often records will need to be inserted, amended or deleted. This is termed *volatility*.

In systems that have online or real-time aspects, the *response time* to an external event may be critical to the performance of the overall system. Such systems include military or other safety-critical systems, and process control systems supervising machinery. Fast processing of records can also be important in large batch systems because of the sheer number of records involved. Where fast response or fast processing times are required, the speed of access to records can be the dominant factor for the design, and this usually means using direct access methods with key transformation. If an indexed file is required then the system might be tailored so that the file index is stored in main memory, thus reducing access time to the index.

The *volume of records* and predicted growth pattern can have a significant effect on the design of the system. A file that extends over more than one disk can cause operational problems, particularly during system recovery, when it may be time-consuming and difficult to copy the file. It is also slower to access a large file. In general, if a file has to be large it is better to use an organisation that does not use an index, because of the time taken to search the index. Random organisation using key transformation is likely to give quicker access to large files than, say, indexed sequential, which would require several levels of index and would be time-consuming to search. It may be better to restructure a large file to split it into several smaller files.

File records may be of either fixed or variable length. Variable-length records can be dealt with straightforwardly in sequential file organisation but can present problems for direct access files because they might be too big for the space available. In general it is quicker to access records that are of fixed length. The system application will dictate the requirement for fixed- or variable-length records and for the record size. The choice of record size can also affect the speed of access and the efficiency of storage. A fixed-length record format must be large enough to accommodate the largest record to be stored. This may result in much wasted space in the other records that are smaller. These concepts are illustrated in Figure 18.9, which shows fixed-length blocks containing variable-length records, and the wasted space at the end of each block.

Systems may need to be *restarted* following failure caused by hardware, software or power problems. The most efficient restart begins exactly from the point of previous failure, as this means that no processing has to be redone. To achieve this situation would require a constant capture of the state of the system at every moment. This is clearly not possible. However, we do need a *base point* – or *checkpoint* as it is sometimes called – from which the system can be restarted. In a batch processing system we can begin the run again using the same transaction file and a back-up copy of the master file. For systems with very long runs this could be wasteful, and we may therefore choose to set up checkpoints at stages through the processing. These effectively break down a long batch-processing

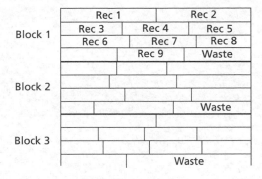

Fig. 18.9 A file comprising blocks of variable-length records

run into several short runs. For transaction processing systems with multiple terminals online to a system restart requirements are more complex, but at least logs of the transactions can be made and snapshots made of master file records before updating, so that the system can be restarted after failure.

18.7 Summary

Although databases are becoming increasingly popular, there will always be a place for conventional files in computer systems. They are needed for real-time applications, where searching a database would take too long. They are also needed for many batch processing systems and for security, archive, library and audit files. In this chapter we have looked at ways of organising files and of accessing records on the files. We considered factors that help us to choose the best organisation and access method for a particular application. We have also proposed a way of specifying file design. This involves a translation from the way humans see and understand data to the way it is seen and understood by a computer system. The main things to consider when specifying data sets are the application, the system environment, the file size, its volatility and what time is acceptable for accessing data from the file.

Exercises

18.1 What are the main issues to be considered when choosing a file organisation? What circumstances would make an indexed sequential organisation appropriate for a master file? Is there such a file in the System Telecom applications described in the case study?

19 Systems Design: Databases

19.1 Introduction

The purpose of this chapter is to introduce the concept of databases and the various types of database currently in use, and then to describe the approach taken to designing database systems. The concept of physical data modelling is continued, and is intended to pave the way for an understanding of physical data design in the following chapter.

The concept of files has already been introduced as a way of storing data. Groups of files – containing data related to each other from the business viewpoint – are often described as a database. The purists would argue that these are not true databases, however, as databases have a number of characteristics that are not shared by such groups of files. It is these characteristics that will be illustrated in this chapter.

By definition, a database is a single collection of structured data stored with the minimum of duplication of data items, to provide a consistent and controlled pool of data. The data contained in the database is sharable by all users having the authority to access it, and is independent of the programs that process the data. The main benefits of a database are that programs do not necessarily need to be changed when the data structure changes, and that data structures do not need to change when programs are changed.

The facilities provided by a database management system (DBMS) can be seen as the three 'I's. These are:

- integration;
- integrity;
- independence.

Data integration allows applications to share data and avoids the need for data duplication and the inconstancies this can cause. The DBMS provides ways of specifying the links between data items so that each application can access the appropriate subset of the database. As different applications and different users are accessing the database concurrently the DBMS must also resolve concurrent access conflicts – two users trying to update the same data simultaneously. *Data integrity* is also derived from the removal of duplication, as the inconsistencies that can arise when duplicated data is updated at different times are removed. Data integrity is also provided by the security systems and password protection offered by the DBMS, and the data validation rules that are specified in the DBMS's data dictionary help to ensure that the data in the database is correct and complete. *Data independence*, as mentioned above, allows the developer to modify the structure of the database without changing all the application programs that use it. Additional columns may be added to a table in an RDBMS and this will not affect the operation of any existing functions that do not need to use them. In the legacy DBMSs described in the next section this feature is an essential aspect of the development process when a 3GL language such as COBOL is being used.

As we have seen elsewhere in this book, organisations have often developed systems in a relatively piecemeal fashion, typically designing systems in isolation and then transferring them to the computer: each system with its suite of programs, files, input and outputs. One disadvantage of this approach is that the systems do not truly represent the way in which organisations operate, as most organisations have business functions that are interdependent, where the exchange of information is crucial to their operation. For example, in System Telecom, customer invoicing is related to the customer details, to the charge rate details, and to the number of call units used. If this information was in separate systems, then the manual effort required to collate the information for customer invoicing would be incredibly tedious.

Information obtained from a series of isolated files does not provide a complete picture of the state of the business at a point in time, as the data cannot easily be gathered or joined in an effective manner. Programs in these systems typically have to define the structure of the data in the files in order for processing to take place, which in turn creates a maintenance burden for the organisation whenever changes to the functionality or the data occur.

19.2 Database Concepts

A database system consists of two main components. First, the physical and logical organisation of a database is controlled by a *database management system* – DBMS – as shown in Figure 19.1. The DBMS constructs, maintains and controls access to the database. It is not normally possible to access the data except via the DBMS. Second, the database application code enables the data in the database to be retrieved, modified and updated. This code 'executes' a particular process or function, as also shown in the diagram.

The data in a database is available for use by several users or application programs simultaneously. Each user may have a different view or picture of the data, depending on the requirements of the application. In general, an item of data is stored only once. Logically the data is a single, integrated structure, which is how it is normally envisaged by the users, as shown in Figure 19.2. Physically, however, a database may be organised into discrete units, containing data pertinent to

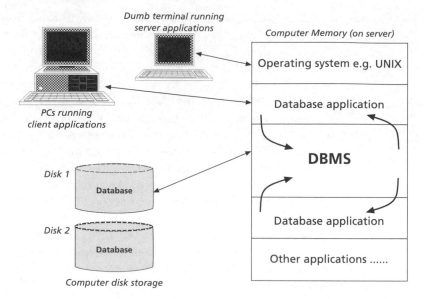

Fig. 19.1 Schematic view of a database

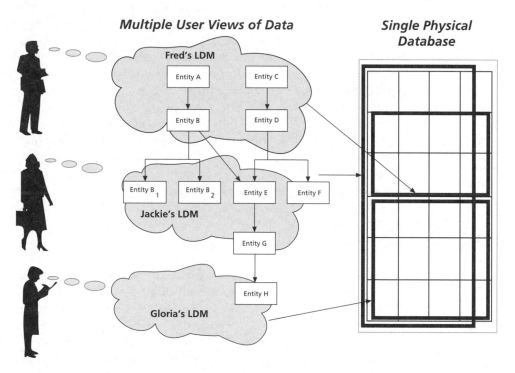

Fig. 19.2 User perspective of a database

a local group of users. This is known as a *distributed database*, which may span several machines or 'nodes', linked together using a computer network. Nevertheless, it can still be regarded as a single database. The objective is to locate the data closest to its point of use, to reduce response times and communication costs, without sacrificing the ability to process data as a single, logical database.

19.3 Database Models

The data in a database is organised according to the data structure 'imposed' upon it by the physical data model. This physical data model is normally produced during the physical data design stage in the development life cycle and tailored specifically to the selected, or imposed, database type.

Before producing a physical database design, the designer must have a detailed knowledge of the database to be used for the implementation of the physical data model. The rules regarding this implementation and its subsequent optimisation will vary widely according to the type of DBMS. Rules are described in this chapter for a relational database.

Data independence is achieved by separating the logical structure of the data from its physical implementation. Data models are not affected by any changes in the way that data is physically stored, which gives the data model a certain degree of flexibility. The DBMS software is the vehicle that enables the data model to be mapped onto the physical storage of the data. If the storage medium or data location is changed, only the associated storage mapping needs to be modified, via the appropriate DBMS utilities.

The database management systems available today can be grouped into four types:

- file management systems (FMS);

- hierarchical databases (HDS);

- network databases (NDS);

- relational databases (RDBMS).

The most common databases found today are relational databases. RDBMS implementations are rapidly outnumbering both HDS and NDS as organisations strive to produce more flexible systems with less coding and maintenance effort. Many organisations are moving away from their large-scale database systems for their business requirements, by 'downsizing' their systems to a number of smaller RDBMSs. The main enabling force behind this drive to downsize is the emergence of Open Systems standards and technology, which allow many different types of system to intercommunicate via computer networks.

Each database model is a conceptual description – the architecture – of how the database is constructed and operates. Specifically the model describes how the data may be accessed and presented to both end-user and programmer. A database model also describes the relationships between the data items: for example, in a System Telecom database each item of information such as customer account number is related to the particular customer that the whole record describes. That particular customer record may also be related to other items in the database such as sales area and invoice details.

With the exception of file management systems, the database models do not describe how the data is stored on disk. This is handled by the DBMS. However, in some circumstances, a model may indirectly place constraints on how the data is stored if the DBMS is to meet all the requirements that comprise that particular model.

In *non-relational databases*, the complete definition of a database is sometimes known as its *schema*. The schema relates or 'maps' the logical data structure to the actual physical organisation of the data. All data items are defined to the DBMS in the schema, which is held in a data dictionary. When a user or program needs data, the DBMS will look in the schema to discover where to find the data and how to retrieve it. A subschema is a logical subset of the schema, comprising selected groups of records, record types and fields. Any number of subschemas can be defined and are coded into the program modules as data access routines. Users and programmers are usually constrained to access the database through a particular subschema. A subschema defines the particular view of the data structure that a program may access, and may differ between applications that require different access views of the data. A subschema can have security controls associated with it, such as read-only to ensure, for example, that programmers cannot inadvertently allow certain fields in the subschema to be updated. Access to the database is provided via operators such as READ, FETCH, FIND and WRITE, which operate on both RECORDs and SETs. These terms will be described in more detail in the network database section later.

In *relational databases* the table and column definitions are effectively the same as the schema described above, except that they are tabular in nature and are normally defined in the DBMS's internal data dictionary (see Figure 19.3).

The RDBMS's internal data dictionary typically contains information relating to the location of the database components, users, access requirements, individual file or table structures and application definitions. Additionally, this dictionary often holds statistics regarding data value distribution, in the form of a histogram. Statistics are collected for use by the database.

Note that the DBMS's internal data dictionary should not be confused with external data dictionaries, which are typically central repositories of information for systems within which the logical and physical data models may be defined and maintained in addition to descriptions of processing elements in the system. Subschemas are not defined in relational programming languages, known as 4GLs – fourth generation languages, as the organisation of data and access to the data are controlled by the database, and hence the application does not need to know about the physical structure, which results in less program coding for most relational systems. Relational databases are accessed using *SQL* (Structured Query Language), and SQL has become the database access language used by most RDBMSs.

19.4 File Management Systems

File management systems (FMS) are the easiest database model to understand, and the only one to describe how data is physically stored. In the FMS model each field or data item is stored sequentially on disk in one large file. In order to find a particular record the application must start reading from the beginning of the file until a match is found. FMS was the first method used to store data in a

Customer Table

CUSTNO	CUSTNAME	CUSTADD1	CUSTADD2	POSTCODE
1111	WAKEFIELD	CONIFER HOUSE	PILIKIN STREET	BS12 3JJ
1212	WITHERS	ESSEX MANSIONS	STONE GRAY	WR1 1CW
2222	TURPIN	DENNIS ISLAND	THE BEACH	SB2 5PL
3333	DOYLE	MORE GAGE LANE	KEHTAL HOUSE	TN1 9BK
4444	TRIMSTUCK	CORNER SHOP	PARTON	PB5 6YY
5555	CRYSTAL	BLOCK ROAD	MANDO	LN1 3XA

Item Table

ITEMNO	ITEMDESC	ITEMPRICE	QTYINSTK
1	BOLT	12	10
2	NUT	10	10
3	WASHER	20	12
4	VALVE	23	4

Order Table

ORDNO	DATE	CUSTNO
4020	12/04/95	1111
4021	13/04/95	2222
4022	06/04/96	1111
4023	12/05/95	2222
4024	03/03/95	4444

Orditem Table

ITEMNO	ORDNO	QTYORD
1	4020	12
1	4021	10
2	4020	4
2	4021	4
2	4022	4
4	4023	4

Fig. 19.3 A set of relational tables in an RDBMS

database, and simplicity is its only advantage over the other types. Figure 19.4 illustrates how the customer file might look in an FMS database.

The disadvantages of this model become immediately apparent. First, there is no indication of the relationships between the data items, so the user and the programmer have to know exactly how the data is stored in order to manipulate it.

Fig. 19.4 File management system model

Second, data integrity is not enforced, requiring the programmer to build this into each module of code in a consistent manner. Third, there is no way of locating a particular record quickly, as every record must be examined to find a match. It may be possible to store pointers against the file to avoid having to search from the beginning each time, but as the file is not 'organised' this may not be practical. The data could be sorted, for example, on customer surname, but this would have to be done after every new record insertion. A more efficient method for locating the data is to generate an index file that contains one or more of the fields from each record and a pointer to the physical record in the customer file. Another major disadvantage of this model is that the file and associated index(es) must be completely recreated if the data structure changes, such as when a new field is added.

19.5 Hierarchical Database Systems

The hierarchical database system (HDS) is organised as a tree structure that originates from a root. Each level or class of data is located at different levels below that root. The data structure at each class level is known as a *node*, and the last node in the series is known as a *leaf*. The tree structure of the HDS defines the parent–child (master–detail) relationships between the various data items in the database. Figure 19.5 demonstrates this structure.

The HDS model demonstrates the advantages over the FMS model in terms of a clearly defined parent–child or master–detail relationship. It also demonstrates that searching for specific data items is a more efficient and faster process: for example, if the user wants to find out all of the items on a particular customer's order then this can be done by locating the customer record, which is the root segment of this hierarchy, locating the orders attached to this, and then finding all the items attached to each order.

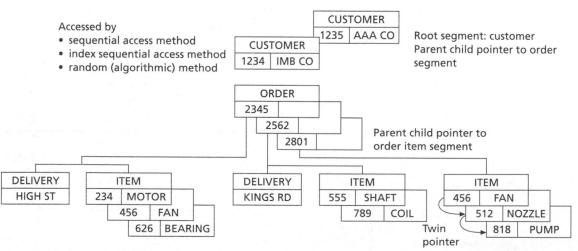

Fig. 19.5 Hierarchical Database tree structure

The physical structure of the data on disk is not important in the HDS model, as the DBMS normally stores the data as linked lists of fields with pointers from parent to child and between children, ending in a null or terminal pointer to signify the last leaf. The HDS structure enables new fields to be added at any level, as the method for achieving this consists of changing pointers to point to the new field.

One disadvantage of this model is the internal structure of the database, which is defined by the designer/programmer when the database is created. If the nature of parent–child relationships is subsequently changed, then the entire structure must be rebuilt. An example of this would be where the customers are to be subdivided by sales area. As a result of this overhead, programmers often add additional fields to a particular level in order to satisfy the new requirement by adding sales area to the customer record, and in doing so the data is often duplicated, thus leading to a maintenance overhead.

Perhaps the most significant disadvantage of the HDS model is its lack of ability to support many-to-many relationships, which makes it the most complicated to convert from logical to physical design. An example might be where, in a company, employees may also be managers or supervisors, in which case a slightly illogical parent–child relationship might exist between a manager and themselves. This was described in detail in Chapter 9. The usual solution to this would be to create a new field in the employee file identifying the manager for each employee, but this adds to the data duplication problem and slows down searches.

Another approach to this parent–child problem might be to add second parent–child and child–child pointers to the structure, creating circular relationships. As these relationships become more complex, the architecture gradually evolves into the network model, where each child can have more than one parent.

19.6 Network Database Systems

Network database systems (NDS) are often referred to as CODASYL database systems. This is an acronym for Conference on Data System Languages. This was convened in 1959 to define and recommend standards for computing languages. Its initial task was to define a Common and Business Oriented Language, resulting in COBOL, a procedural programming language. The Database Task Group of CODASYL published its first paper in October 1969, and a revised paper in April 1971. This has formed the basis of the design and development of many subsequent CODASYL databases. The name 'Network' bears no relation to the type of architecture where the system is implemented – a computer communications network (see Chapter 21). The network model conceptually describes databases in which many-to-many relationships exist.

Logical data is described in terms of data items, data aggregates, records and sets. A *data item* or *field* is the lowest addressable unit of data. It usually corresponds to a real-world attribute such as customer account number. Data is stored in an NDS as occurrences within a record type. The relationships between the

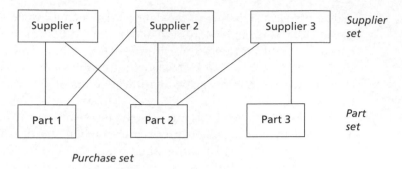

Fig. 19.6 Network database model

different data items are known as *sets*. A set defines a logical relationship between two or more record types, and represents a real-world relationship between two or more entities such as that between customer and account. One record type in a set is the owner, the others are set members. There are zero or more member records for each owner record. A set occurrence comprises one occurrence of the owner record and all its related members. Sets are implemented by means of *pointer chaining*, whereby each owner record is connected to its related members by pointers from one record to the next.

An NDS relies on either straight-line or cyclical pointers to map the relationships between the different data items. Figure 19.6 demonstrates a simple straight-line relationship between suppliers and parts. A company manager can find out who sells a particular product by searching the Parts set and then following the pointers to the Suppliers. This approach is very flexible as the NDS can also consider the combination of Suppliers and Parts as a Purchase set thereby providing two views of the same data.

There are no restrictions governing the way sets can be defined to link record types. This means that the relationships that can be supported by a CODASYL DBMS enable a full network structure to be defined and accessed. The logical data model can, if required, be mapped directly onto the physical database design without change.

The rules for converting the logical design into a CODASYL design are very simple, although there are a number of rules concerning placement of RECORDs. Initially, all data groups and operational masters become RECORDs. RECORDs may be placed in one of two ways:

- CALC places the RECORD on the disk by applying a hashing algorithm – providing rapid full-key access – to the key of the RECORD to give a physical disk address at which the RECORD is stored.

- VIA places the RECORD as near as possible to its master in the specified SET.

All RECORDs at the top of the data structure, which have no masters, and RECORDs on which direct access/entry points are required, are placed by CALC. All other RECORDs must be placed by SET.

Physical data is described in terms of AREAs and PAGEs. An area is a physical subset of the database. It is usually a constraint of the DBMS that all records of a particular record type must reside in the same area. An area is divided into pages, which is the CODASYL term for a physical block, which means the unit of retrieval from disk. With most CODASYL DBMSs, any given page may contain records of different record types. The division of the database enables areas to be taken offline when not in use, enabling only affected areas to be recovered after a crash and enabling the designer to control placement of the data. Each area usually resides on a separate physical file.

The flexibility of the NDS model in showing many-to-many relationships is its greatest strength, although that flexibility can be difficult to code. The interrelationships between the various sets can become very complex and difficult to map out, requiring the programmer to write the application code – usually in COBOL – to navigate the different data chains and pointers. Like HDSs, network databases can be very fast, especially if secondary indexes are available to be used to point directly to the physical records. Unlike HDSs, network databases go further in reducing the need to hold duplicated data by allowing many-to-many relationships. The network model also shares the main disadvantage of the HDS model when structural changes are required. Once the initial structure is created, any changes to the sets require the programmer to create an entirely new structure. Adding new data items is not such a chore as with an HDS, however, as a new set can be created and the various pointers established to generate the required relationships. The 'true' relationship model has, to date, only appeared in the relational database, which will be described in the next section.

19.7 Relational Database Systems

In 1968, Dr Ted Codd of IBM produced a paper on the mathematical concept of relational SETs, laying down 12 basic rules that he believed should be applied to such a model. A database system called *System R* was subsequently released, and resulted in an emergence of various relational databases, mainly from American universities. The relational database model (RDM) has been continually refined since these early products were introduced, to such an extent that in 1990 Ted Codd produced a new paper outlining 333 rules for relational databases!

19.7.1 Data Structure

The RDM abandons the concept of parent–child relationships between different data items, organising the data instead into tabular structures, where each field becomes a column in a table and each record becomes a row, as in Figure 19.3.

Figure 19.3 illustrates the relational tables that could be used to store data in an order processing application. The relationship between the tables is defined by the use of foreign keys, and it is important that the tables are stored in third normal form as defined in Chapter 17. The primary key of the customer table is used as a foreign key in the order table. In this way the full details of the customer are not entered into the system and stored with every order that customer places. The primary key of the order table is the column called ORDNO, and this appears as part of the key used for the ORDITEM table. This table is more difficult to understand. The primary key for it is constructed from two columns: ORDNO and ITEMNO. These two fields are in fact primary keys in their own right. They have been used together as the key to ORDITEM so that we can store the quantities ordered without repeating the description of the items or the details of the order for each item on a particular order.

Tables often contain columns that exist in other tables. The actual naming of these columns is not critical in the relational model, although it is considered good practice to keep the names consistent with the design entity and attribute names, provided the data in these common columns is of the same domain. Domains are essentially a method for specifying the permissible range of values for a particular column type. The datatype 'Date' could be described as one such domain, provided that all occurrences are of the same format.

There are six special properties of relational tables:

- *Entries in columns are single-valued*. This property implies that columns contain no repeating groups: in other words they have been normalised.

- *Entries in columns are of the same kind*. In relational terms, this means that all values in a column are drawn from the same domain.

- *Each row is unique*. This ensures that no two rows are identical and that there is at least one column – usually the storage or prime key – that uniquely identifies that row.

- *The sequence of columns is insignificant*. There is no hidden meaning implied by the order in which columns are stored. Each user can retrieve the columns in any order, even if this means sorting the entire table first.

- *The sequence of rows is insignificant*. This property is analogous to property the previous property, where rows can be retrieved in any order.

- *Each column has a unique name*. Columns are referenced by name and not position. As the data model attributes are mapped to the columns, it also follows that columns should have unique names across the whole database and not just within each table, so if a customer has a Mailing Address and a Delivery Address, both columns should not be called Address.

These properties are important, as they make the structure more intuitive for users, easier to validate, and flexible with respect to access requirements.

19.7.2 Data Manipulation

All of the operations needed to manipulate data in a relational database can be performed by SQL, and these operations are performed at a table level rather than a record-by-record level. This can cause complications when an application's procedure is conditionally based upon results produced by an earlier SQL query. Also, processing data in batches can involve the creation and deletion of temporary tables, which can make the logic of the application appear to be complicated. Although SQL is defined as being a 'non-procedural' language and is known as a relational calculus, some of these problems are overcome by using a procedural version of the language known as PL/SQL. This language has been developed by the Oracle corporation and provides procedural commands such as `IF, BEGIN, END, LOOP` and `RETURN` to allow the programmer control over the flow of the program. Alternatively the developer can embed SQL commands into a 3GL such as C or COBOL, although this often involves the use of a *cursor* that acts as a database pointer to store the position that an application has reached when processing a particular table or view.

The syntax of basic SQL commands can be illustrated with the `SELECT` command. This is used to specify data that is to be retrieved from the database. The syntax for the command is

```
SELECT fields required
FROM the tables they are in
WHERE the conditions that the selection is to be based
upon
```

A query using SQL in MS-Access to retrieve a specific customer record from the customer table shown in Figure 19.3 would be written as:

```
SELECT CUSTOMERS.CUSTNO, CUSTOMERS.CUSTNAME,
   CUSTOMERS.CUSTADD1,
CUSTOMERS.CUSTADD2, CUSTOMERS.POSTCODE
FROM CUSTOMERS
WHERE (((CUSTOMERS.CUSTNAME)= [ENTER NAME]));
```

The final part of the query `[ENTER NAME]));` is specific to the MS-Access 4GL and is a query object that will appear on screen when the SQL is executed, prompting the user to enter the name of the customer whose record is required. Figure 19.7 illustrates this.

The `SELECT` command can be executed with certain aggregate functions that can provide a valuable data interrogation facility. The aggregation commands include: `MIN`, which returns the smallest value in a given column; `MAX`, which returns the largest value in a given column; `SUM`, which returns the sum of the numeric values in a given column; `AVG`, which returns the average value of a given column; `COUNT`, which returns the total number of values in a given column; and `COUNT(*)`, which returns the number of rows in a table:

```
SELECT COUNT(*)
FROM ITEMS;
```

will return the value 4 from the tables shown in Figure 19.3.

SQL queries provide a means of *joining* tables to create views of data drawn from different tables. Joins are described as either *inner* or *outer joins*. If we want to see the customer name, the order number and the date of all orders that have been placed by each customer in our database in Figure 19.3 then the inner `JOIN` query would be written as shown below:

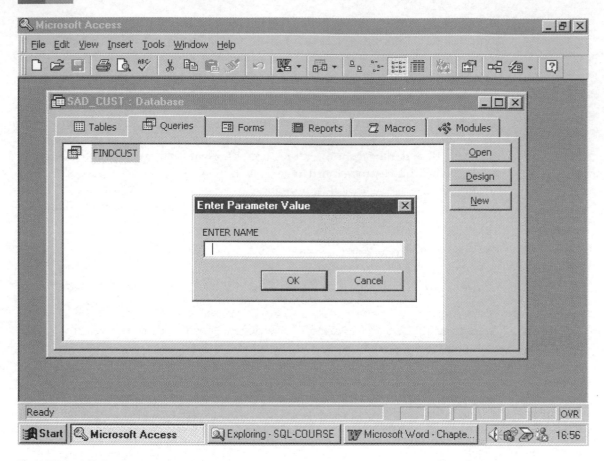

Fig. 19.7 An MS-Access SELECT query

```
SELECT CUSTOMERS.CUSTNAME, ORDERS.ORDNO, ORDERS.DATE
FROM CUSTOMERS INNER JOIN ORDERS ON CUSTOMERS.CUSTNO
= ORDERS.CUSTNO;
```

An alternative to this is to specify the tables in the FROM clause and the joins in the WHERE clause. The syntax for this would be:

```
SELECT CUSTOMERS.CUSTNAME, ORDERS.ORDNO, ORDERS.DATE
FROM CUSTOMERS, ORDERS
WHERE CUSTOMERS.CUSTNO = ORDERS.CUSTNO;
```

In either case the resulting view would be as shown in Figure 19.8. This join, defined as an *inner join* or an *equijoin*, selects only the rows that have equal values in the CUSTNO field in both tables. By specifying an outer join the unmatched rows from one or other of the tables can be included. The syntax used by MS-Access for this allows a left or a right outer join to be requested. The example below shows the left outer join, which displays all the customers in the database, not just those who have placed orders:

CUSTNAME	ORDNO	DATE
WAKEFIELD	4020	12/04/95
WAKEFIELD	4022	06/04/96
SMITHSON	4021	13/04/95
SMITHSON	4023	12/05/95
TRIMSTUCK	4024	03/03/95

Fig. 19.8 The result from the SELECT query with an inner join

CUSTNAME	ORDNO	DATE
WAKEFIELD	4020	12/04/95
WAKEFIELD	4022	06/04/96
BASKERVILLE		
SMITHSON	4021	13/04/95
SMITHSON	4023	12/05/95
BLACKWARD		
TRIMSTUCK	4024	03/03/95
CRYSTAL		

Fig. 19.9 The result of a left outer join on the order processing tables

```
SELECT CUSTOMERS.CUSTNAME, ORDERS.ORDNO, ORDERS.DATE
FROM CUSTOMERS LEFT JOIN ORDERS ON CUSTOMERS.CUSTNO
= ORDERS.CUSTNO;
```

The result is shown in Figure 19.9.

Calculations can be performed on values stored in the database by the inclusion of arithmetic expressions in an SQL command. The operators are + (add), − (subtract), * (multiply) and / (divide). Care must be taken to recognise the higher precedence of the multiplication and division operators when writing these queries. In the example below the quantity ordered is multiplied by the item price to give the amount for the order. Bracketing the words QTY * PRICE directs the interpreter to recognise this as a string and to use it as the column heading for the calculation.

```
SELECT ORDITEM.ORDNO, ITEMS.ITEMDESC, ITEMS.ITEMPRICE,
ORDITEM.QTYORD,
(ITEMS.ITEMPRICE * ORDITEM.QTYORD ) AS [QTY * PRICE]
FROM ITEMS INNER JOIN ORDITEM ON ITEMS.ITEMNO =
ORDITEM.ITEMNO;
```

The result of this query is shown in Figure 19.10.

A group function can be combined with an arithmetic operator to produce a summarised output. Here is the SQL summarising the value of each order by calculating the price times the quantity and summing these results by the ORDNO field:

ORDNO	ITEMDESC	ITEMPRICE	QTYORD	QTY*PRICE
4020	BOLT	12	12	144
4021	BOLT	12	10	120
4020	NUT	10	4	40
4021	NUT	10	4	40
4022	NUT	10	4	40
4023	VALVE	23	4	92

Fig. 19.10 A SELECT SQL command using arithmetic parameters

```
SELECT ORDITEM.ORDNO, SUM(ORDITEM.QTYORD *
ITEMS.ITEMPRICE) AS TOTAL
FROM ITEMS INNER JOIN ORDITEM ON ITEMS.ITEMNO =
ORDITEM.ITEMNO
GROUP BY ORDITEM.ORDNO;
```

The result of this query is shown in Figure 19.11.

ORDNO	TOTAL
4020	184
4021	160
4022	40
4023	92

Fig. 19.11 SQL using a group function

19.8 RDBMS Design

Today's relational databases adhere to the RDM and SQL standards in varying degrees. Although there is an ANSI (American National Standards Institute) standard SQL, most product vendors supply their own SQL extensions to make their product appear more attractive. An example of this is the provision of a single SQL statement that encompasses several standard SQL and 4GL statements to increase efficiency both in terms of coding and execution. Oracle's DECODE function is one such example, which would take many lines of 4GL to accomplish the same result. In practice, however, these extensions can compromise the openness of a product, which may make it less attractive in open systems environments, where portability of both hardware and software is crucial.

The primary goal of the RDM is to preserve data integrity. To be considered truly relational, a DBMS must completely prevent access to the data by any means other than by the DBMS itself. The main advantages of the RDM are:

* ease of database design from the logical design;

* developer and database administrator productivity;

* flexibility – particularly for changing data structures and code as the business changes.

RDMs enhance developer and end-user productivity in providing set-oriented access to data, independent of the underlying storage structures. The SQL language enables some consistency across products, enabling applications and designs to be ported – with some customisation – between different products. This ability is known as *database vendor independence*.

Relational products show greatest variation in the underlying mechanism used for data storage and retrieval. Although these are largely hidden from the SQL programmer and end-user, they have a great impact on the performance of the system. Some RDBMS products fail to adhere to all properties of the RDM and are often less effective in meeting the business requirements of an organisation. Designers and developers must therefore make up for product short-comings by building customised support into the database and/or the application, which adds to development time, increases the maintenance overhead, and may adversely affect performance.

It is essential to follow a design methodology in building any database system, to ensure that the design is carried out using the prescribed rules and steps for the specific database being used so that the designer constructs a robust but flexible solution. If a design methodology is not followed, then the consequences are usually that the design does not satisfy the functional and performance requirements and that the best use of the specific database is not being realised. In practice, database design is an iterative process, which begins with an initial mapping of entities to tables, attributes to columns and identification of keys. This is called the *first-cut* design. The design is then refined to ensure that all functional and performance requirements can be met. Design methodologies specify a number of design *rules* that describe how the data-driven approach to relational design is achieved.

Although design methodologies often specify more than a dozen rules, there are seven basic rules for achieving a relational database design, some of which constitute denormalising the database design to optimise performance. These basic rules are described briefly below.

1. *Translate the logical data structure.* Initially the process of converting logical to physical occurs independently from any access path requirements, transaction volumes or security requirements. This means that no attempt is made to optimise performance for the first-cut design. The steps entail identification of tables, columns, primary keys and secondary indexes, followed by the choice of appropriate storage structures.

2. *Translate the logical data integrity.* This process entails the enforcement of business rules and integrity constraints. The steps entail designing for business rules about entities and relationships, and for additional business rules about attributes. This may entail designing special segments of 4GL and SQL or 'database procedures' into the database itself to enforce the business rules and integrity requirements if the particular RDBMS supports these procedures.

3. *Tune for access requirements.* Tuning is crucial to any database design, and can make the difference between a successful and an unsuccessful database

implementation. Tuning techniques vary according to the facilities provided by the RDBMS and include the enabling of table *scans* for querying, data *clustering* techniques for efficient access, key *hashing* for optimising record access, and adding *indexes* to tables to optimise retrievals. In particular, a novice to relational design should place emphasis upon prototyping different access techniques using a particular RDBMS to gain knowledge of the product's strengths and weaknesses.

4. *Tune by adding secondary indexes.* Secondary indexes are optional access structures that can complement scanning, clustering and hashing to significantly increase the ratio of rows returned by a query to the number of rows searched. They achieve this by enabling direct access to individual rows, by reducing the number of rows searched, by avoiding sorts on the rows searched, and by eliminating table scans altogether.

5. *Tune by introducing controlled redundancy.* This entails altering the database structure to accommodate functional and performance requirements. The caveats of such changes are that they deviate from the logical design and often add complexity or detract from flexibility. Controlled redundancy is often implemented by adding columns from other tables to facilitate data retrieval by avoiding table joins. Adding duplicate data does offer distinct advantages to the business, however, especially where response time requirements are short and where the speed of retrieving all the relevant data items may be critical to the success of the business.

6. *Tune by redefining the database structure.* This process involves redefining columns and tables to optimise the performance for queries and updates. For example, long text columns that are seldom referenced may be split off from the main table into a lookup table. This has the effect of reducing the size of the main table, enabling many more rows to be retrieved in a physical I/O operation. In some cases tables may be split horizontally, such as by date, or vertically, such as by all regularly-used columns and all seldom-used columns, or they may be combined with other tables such as Customer and Account to become Customer Account.

7. *Tune for special circumstances.* This last stage deals with special features rather than design steps, but is considered equally important in database design. This stage includes the provision for end-user ad-hoc requirements, implementation of security features, and tuning for very large databases.

19.9 Futures

Although there has been considerable interest in new types of DBMS, the relational model still accounts for most business and administrative computing. Databases capable of storing objects (OODBMS) rather than formatted records have an impact on the storage and retrieval of graphical images and digitised sound, but this still constitutes a very small part of the information systems business. The introduction of a standard known as *Open Database Connectivity*

(ODBC) has made it commonplace for an MS-Access application to manipulate an Oracle or DB2 database and for other 4GLs to process databases that conform to this standard. Temporal databases recognised that databases represented snapshots of reality within specific timeframes, and they sought to embed time stamping into the changes that occurred to the data and also to the metadata that defined the database structure and its rules of behaviour.

19.10 Summary

In this chapter you have learned what databases are, and how they are managed by database management systems (DBMSs). Database management systems construct, maintain and control access to the data, and different users of the data have different views of it depending on the application that uses it. DBMSs allow applications to share data and provide links between items so that each application accesses the appropriate subset of the database. Data integrity is preserved through security systems, and the structure of the database can be modified without the need to modify the application programs that use it.

There are different types of database management system: file management systems, hierarchical database management systems, networked database management systems, and relational database management systems. The most widespread for business and administrative applications are relational database management systems, and SQL (Structured Query Language) is a popular tool for manipulating data in a relational database.

Some basic rules for the design of databases have been described, and the chapter concluded with a look forward at possible future alternatives to relational databases and the possibility of storing objects, images and sound.

20 Systems Design: Physical Data Design

20.1 Introduction

There can be a big difference between a logical data design and the data model that is eventually implemented in the physical system. This is because the logical data model is constructed with no reference to physical constraints. It might therefore seem that the time and effort spent in logical modelling is largely wasted, but this is not so. Logical data modelling provides the analysts and designers with a clear understanding of which data is important to an organisation and how that data is used to support the business needs. It does this by working through the first three steps in the model in Figure 20.1.

The longer the analysts can keep physical constraints out of their analysis, the freer the client is to make an informed choice when the time comes, and if the system has to be ported to a different hardware or software platform the

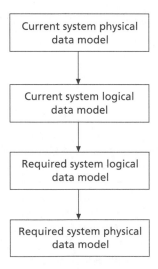

Fig. 20.1 Steps in data modelling

designers don't need to rework the logical design. In this chapter we focus on the last step of Figure 20.1, modelling the data for the required physical system.

Structured methods produce a high-level view of the data, in the shape of the physical data model, and show clearly how this differs from the logical data model. Throughout the chapter we assume that the physical implementation will be either a database or a number of files, and only where there are different implications will we specify one or the other.

The first step is to explain how the initial physical data model is built; we then explore the factors that help designers to tune the model to the best fit for the given hardware and the client's needs.

Before physical data modelling can begin, there are three main issues to be investigated and resolved:

- quantifying the data in order to assess storage requirements;
- resolving any difficulties regarding response time or performance;
- collecting information on the hardware and software platforms to be used.

We shall begin by looking at each of these in turn, before going through the process of transforming the logical data model to its physical representation.

20.2 Quantifying the Data Storage Requirements

Typically, an assessment of the volume of data to be stored and transferred will have been made before the hardware was chosen. The required system logical data model has given us a picture of how the data should be structured to serve the organisation best, but even the best data structure does not help the designer know how much storage space the data will require. Discovering the volume of data demands a different approach.

The current system is the best place to start. For example, the organisation may currently hold details of 50,000 customers. In the past 3 years the customer base has grown by around 6% each year, but the organisation is now planning some major investment and expects its customer base to grow by up to 10% each year for the next 10 years. So using hard facts about past growth and the present, coupled with strategic forecasts, allows the analyst to produce initial storage volume estimates. If no such figures are available, an alternative source of data from within the current system is the existing data files and archives. They provide the same type of information, but without a forecast of future growth. It is important not to rely solely on the user's estimates without validating them in some way. This is because each user asked may volunteer a different estimate. The best way to check user information is to carry out a limited manual file check. This means duplicating effort, but the consequences of not doing so could be that memory space required by the new system is seriously underestimated.

These initial data volume estimates are at a high level because the type of question we are asking the users is 'How many customers do you have?' To decide on how much storage space is actually required we have to ask an additional question: 'How many bytes of data are held about each customer?' It would be inappropriate to ask users to answer that question, partly because it's not their job to know about bytes, and partly because they can only answer based on the current system. We are interested in the required system, which will be different either because new data will be stored or because duplicated data will no longer be included, and so we'll need to refer to the data dictionary.

Performance-monitoring tools can assist the database administrator to maintain the level of service specified in the service-level agreement that has been reached with the user. This may specify the overall availability in hours per week with target availability in percentage terms during this period. Response times, currency of data, disaster recovery and batch job completion times may all form part of the agreement.

The performance-monitoring tool may need to record performance in a distributed environment with different servers running different DBMS systems. Such tools may be supplied by the DBMS vendor, as is the case with the Oracle tools, or may be provided by third-party vendors. The *database administrator* (DBA) needs to be able to identify where the performance problem is and to differentiate between a system-wide problem and a single user or single application problem. The cause of the problem could be network traffic, disk fragmentation, indexing, operating system performance or even changes occurring in the user community – all need to be investigated. It is important that the analyst has performed the basic tasks of estimating data storage requirements correctly in the physical data design stage of the life cycle.

Let's take 'customer' as an example. We know what data items are associated with the 'customer' entity, so we can add these together and multiply this total by the number of times the entity occurs, thus giving us a total for 'customer'. This is shown in Figure 20.2.

The total in Figure 20.2 is of course only for the current number of customers, so an allowance must be made for expected growth. If this is a file system the designer will then calculate how many blocks are required to store the customer data. The designer carries out this exercise for each entity in turn to build an estimate of how many bytes are required to store all the required data.

For designers using relational database systems, the system may do some of this work for you. For example, Oracle provides a tool that, when supplied with the raw data, calculates the size of the database automatically.

20.3 Assessing the Required System Performance

Having established the size of the system, the designers must now work with the users to define performance obectives, especially for critical functions. In the past, systems were developed and installed and only during commissioning were performance problems discovered: users had to wait too long for a system response, or the system crashed because it was unable to handle the number of users it was designed for. The London Stock Exchange in 1987 crashed within minutes of starting up because the system could not handle the number of users

Data item name	Number of bytes
Customer name	30
Customer type	1
Customer billing address	100
Customer mailing address	100
Customer phone number	4
Contact name	30
Sales area	1
Account balance	4
	——
Total bytes per customer	270
Add to this the data management overheads of 50%	130
	——
	400

Therefore:
Quantity of customer data = no. of customers × bytes/customer
= 50,000 × 400
= 20,000,000 bytes

Fig. 20.2 How data is quantified

who logged on. A London Ambulance Service system installed in 1993 also failed because it could not handle the number of requests for ambulances. Such mistakes are costly and, to avoid replicating these errors, analysts and designers not only have to define target system performance, but must ensure that there are few if any performance issues left unresolved when program and data specification begins. During the analysis phase, each process in the required system will have been discussed with the users, and target performance figures will have been agreed for the critical processes. Performance will be defined in terms of transaction processing time, or throughput for a volume of data, such as 100 customer orders per hour. Some of these targets will be non-negotiable requirements, but others will have a defined range within which performance is acceptable. You can reduce processing time by making the code faster using lines of assembler code embedded in a 3GL or 4GL program; the only way to make significant improvements is to make the data handling more efficient. To do this you must first investigate the likely demands on the new system.

When defining performance targets developers must always ask 'What is the consequence of not meeting this target?' If the consequence of not processing data from a sensor in a chemical plant within 0.02 seconds is that we risk a dangerous chemical reaction, this performance target is non-negotiable and indeed we would aim to err on the safe side. If a user waits 6 seconds instead of 5 for a system response the user may not notice. It is often because designers are unsure of acceptable system performance, or because unrealistic targets are set, that over-engineering occurs. So make sure that the targets are realistic and clearly understood.

20.3.1 Factors Affecting System Performance

There are a number of factors that will have an effect on the system's performance. A system will perform differently under different conditions or loads. System loading is influenced by:

- the quantity of data stored;
- the number of users logged on;
- the number of peripheral devices active;
- the speed of the network;
- the volume of traffic.

Analysing their combined effect is probably not possible. What we are aiming for here is to ensure that we have quantified the effect of each, identified any target performance figures which risk not being met, and taken action to overcome the potential problem.

Asking the users for initial estimates of data volumes is the best place to start discussing system performance because it involves the users in the process and encourages them to think more about the functionality they want. Let's assume the user says all data is to stay on the system and not be archived. The analyst can then illustrate the impact this decision will have on performance say after six months, after 2 years and after 5 years. Once the implications are understood, the client is able to make an informed decision. One issue that can affect performance in terms of system loading is a disparity in estimates. Let's say we ask 'How many orders are processed per day?' The manager may give one figure, which is the average number of confirmed orders per day. The sales team may give a higher figure, which is the average plus the number of incomplete orders – orders started, but not confirmed. Although we don't have to be concerned about allocating storage space for these non-confirmed orders, we may need to know this information to fully assess system loading.

Another view that might be of interest is cyclic behaviour. By investigating management reports and files, the analyst might discover that the average daily number of orders triples in early December. This again has no impact on the quantity of data stored, but will have a significant impact on system performance at peak periods. Therefore, while looking for a definitive estimate for data quantity, the analyst must always record these other issues that might be mentioned in passing by users because, if they are overlooked, they will cause problems later, and because they each have consequences for the final system.

Response times can be influenced by many different factors. The number of users, the network speed and topology and the types of applications can all affect performance. There has been considerable debate about the advantages/disadvantages of the two main network standards – *token ring networks* and the collision detection networking standard known as *Ethernet*. Generally the token ring networking systems are more expensive than Ethernet networks, and this perhaps accounts for the fact that there are three times as many Ethernet systems in existence as there are token ring ones. The token ring network, specified in IEE 802.5, does not have a speed standard although it is most commonly installed as a 16 Mbps on IBM hardware. To transmit on this network the PC must await the arrival of the 24-bit token and then attach its data to this with the appropriate destination address. Speed of the network is constant, irrespective of the volume of traffic; only the size of the network determines the response time for the user.

The Ethernet access methodology, known as a CSMA//CD approach, can lead to great variations in response time as this method is a *collision detect* one. Any PC can test the network to see whether it can transmit (carrier sensing, CS), and if the network is free it has access to it (multiple access, MA). If, when it transmits, a collision occurs with a message from a different PC that has also tested the network at the same time, then both are backed off and can retransmit after a randomly calculated waiting period. The result of this approach is to provide extremely fast access when the network is lightly loaded. Users can, however, experience long delays when they attempt to access the network simultaneously.

20.3.2 Overheads that Adversely Affect System Performance

The data-handling mechanisms will affect the speed at which data is transferred.

Factors that are exclusive to database systems are those that depend on how the DBMS handles:

- overheads for page management;
- overheads for pointers, indices and hashing;
- data type handling;
- data compaction.

    For file systems the factors are similar:

- the time taken to locate the required block of data;
- the read time, which will be longer if the required block is stored in an overflow area;
- write time;
- page sizes and buffer sizes;
- the time taken to swap tasks in and out of the CPU;
- how much context data will be saved.

The context data of a task might simply be the values held in registers, the program counter, the program status word and the stack pointer, which amounts to only a few words of data, but if the system has to carry out space management, such as swapping tasks out and locating free space to assign to the incoming task, the overhead will be significant. Badly designed systems can spend more time swapping tasks in and out than actually processing the application programs.

Other overheads result from the need to satisfy the requirements for restart and recovery of the system, for data integrity and for maintaining audit trails. For restart and recovery the system may write all, or part of, the database to another device at given time intervals, or may record significant events. Data integrity may require that the system buffers a number of related data entries until the transaction is complete before committing the whole transaction to the database. This is known as *commit/backout buffering* because if at any time the user exits the transaction leaving it incomplete, the database remains unchanged. The half-complete transaction is discarded. Legal or quality registration audit trails may impose the need for transaction logging where every action carried out by a user is logged to a file that auditors can search through to check that procedures are followed correctly.

20.4 Investigating the Chosen Hardware/Software Platform

Once the required system performance is understood, the designer will need to investigate the chosen hardware and software platform on which the new system will run. Software, in this instance, refers to the DBMS or manufacturer-supplied data-handling mechanisms. Designers must accept the limitations, and exploit some of the opportunities of the chosen platform, all the time remembering that a design that is too intricate or harware-dependent may quickly become unmaintainable. The objectives of physical data design are to minimise:

- storage space;
- runtime processor usage;
- sccess times;
- development effort;
- the need to reorganise data when modifying it;

whilst at the same time achieving a simple user interface! Some of these objectives may appear contradictory: for example, the designer might pack data to minimise storage space but this adds to runtime processor usage because the data has to be unpacked on retrieval, and packed again before restoring.

In investigating the physical environment, the designer must ask three questions:

- How much data can the system store, and in what way?
- How fast does the system transfer data?
- How is data handling affected by the programming language used?

We shall consider each of these three areas.

20.4.1 Data Storage

Installing a completely new network with workstations, servers and perhaps even a mainframe acting as a data repository is unusual unless the application area is one that is totally new, or the organisation – a state pension department in a former Soviet country, for example – is one that has been forced into existence by political change. Frequently the new development will involve a combination of new client–server hardware dedicated specifically to the new application area, links to other server-based networks performing related tasks, and a link to a legacy mainframe system that acts as a repository for 'mission-critical' data. The systems analyst will not have the skills and technical knowledge to calculate performance and response times in these circumstances but will be able to provide the figures that will be used by the DBA and the network administrator to make their calculations. For this reason the analyst is expected to have some knowledge of the principles behind performance estimating.

Data storage is influenced by the block or page size used by the operating system. The block or page size implemented in the final system depends on the operating system or DBMS used, the size of the most commonly used groups, and the CPU space the blocks or pages take up. The designer must identify which block sizes the operating system naturally handles, or which page sizes the DBMS naturally handles. Some systems are designed to handle only one size, whereas others will allow a number of possible sizes, but will read or write their natural size significantly faster than any other. Often in relational database systems the DBMS defines the page size, and the database administrator has to work with that as a constraint. Even if a system can be configured to use a different block or page size, this will have a cost in terms of disk management and read/ write overheads. So while it may be possible to select a different block or page size, this will require more processing effort to transfer data, which will slow the system down. The designer must therefore decide whether the convenience of using a different size justifies the impact on system performance.

One way of improving performance is to group related data entities, and to store them physically close to each other. Related data could be a collection of table items or data records, and storing these close to each other maintains the relationships between them. Both DBMSs and file handlers allow related items to be grouped in the same page or block but may be restrictive, and may not allow you to store different record types together. The designer has to decide which of the available mechanisms to use. The most convenient block or page size for a developer is one that is large enough to store the largest group. If the system's natural size is smaller than this, the group must be split into two or more groups. However if two data entities have a high interdependence, such as 'customer order' and 'order line detail', we would try to keep these together. This is because separating these would result in two accesses each time we processed a customer order, which would increase the processing time.

Another reason for storing related entities together as a physical group is to improve performance by maintaining the access paths. For example if you store master and detail entities together such as 'customer order' and 'order line detail' you access the root entity directly by its key. This also supports the primary relationship between master and detail entities. All systems represent relationships using logical or physical keys. A physical key points to the physical memory area where the related data is stored. A logical key is known as a *symbolic pointer*; it doesn't give a memory address, and it is interpreted in a predefined way. It will be handled sequentially, using binary search, hashing, indexing or any other indexed sequential access method. Wherever possible we would implement logical pointers rather than physical ones because although the use of physical pointers is faster, it removes data independence. A system with data independence can change hardware, data handling software or applications code without affecting the data design. For this reason data independence is fundamental to system design; it allows us to isolate data from changes to the physical environment.

20.4.2 Data Transfer

During each read or write, the operating system's data-handling mechanisms perform a physical data access. The unit of physical access is a block, and this is what the hardware transfers. The unit of logical access is a record, and this is the quantity of data transferred by each software access. There will usually be one or more records per block. For DBMS systems the unit of physical access is a page, and the unit of logical access is a table. Figure 20.3 shows the difference between a physical read and a logical read for file systems.

The operating system buffers any records that are resident in the block but are not yet required by the program. So if we want to change the credit limit for customer number 93-00023, we first need to read the customer's details into a space in memory where we can access it. The program is unaware that a number of

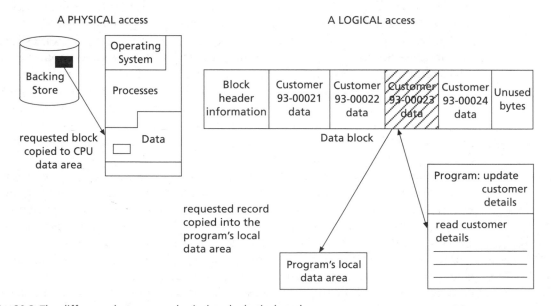

Fig. 20.3 The difference between a physical and a logical read

other customers' details have been retrieved. Customer 93-00023's details are stored locally by the program while it updates the credit limit field.

The difficulty in estimating how quickly the chosen system will perform a specified task is that different manufacturers measure performance differently. They may base their timing estimates on the assumption that you are using their standard defined block or page size, or their brand of peripheral devices, or a prescribed database, or a stated communications standard. Their estimates cannot take account of the impact of any third party hardware or software or of data transfer between devices. All of this makes the task of estimating harder, and of course the reason why manufacturers don't use the same benchmark is that they can then present their products in the best possible light.

20.4.3 The Programming Language Used

The programming language has an impact on performance because different languages will take different lengths of time to perform the same instruction. It may be that one 3GL handles multiplication quickly but swaps between tasks too slowly, and a different 3GL is better at both but is not acceptable to the organisation. Let's illustrate the difference a language can make. If we want to add two numbers together and we are using a 4GL, it will access a code template. The code template may use floating-point arithmetic, which is more complex than fixed-point arithmetic. This involves carrying out more instructions and more complex instructions than fixed-point arithmetic. If we wrote the code in assembler we could speed this up. This addition is a very simple operation, and probably not one that we would need to improve. However, by identifying the operations that are inefficiently handled by the chosen programming language, we can select operations where an embedded 3GL or 2GL could be used. Although assembler languages are increasingly rarely used in commercial systems, they are still appropriate for system communications or real-time systems.

In conclusion, then, designers try to keep the physical data design as close to the original logical model as possible, because in this form the data is easy to understand, to access and to maintain. But the model does have to change to take account of the hardware platform and the capabilities of the operating system, database and programming language used, working within and around the constraints and exploiting opportunities.

20.5 Moving from Logical to Physical Data Design

Having resolved the hardware and software issues we can now consider creating the physical design. The inputs to the process of creating a physical data design are relevant information about the required system, and about the target hardware/software platform. Earlier we looked at quantifying the volume of data to be stored and the importance of setting performance targets, and we discussed the memory capacity and performance details of the hardware. The output from this process is an optimised data design, so now let's look at what the process involves.

20.5.1 Creating a Physical Data Design

The transformation from the required logical data design to the required physical data design begins with some simple steps. For file systems each entity on the logical model becomes a record type. Each attribute of the entity becomes a data field, and the relationships between entities are maintained by identifying keys that are handled by the applications programs. For databases each entity becomes a table, and each attribute becomes a column. The relationships between entities are maintained by using database pointers, which are always logical pointers. The DBMS itself decides on how these logical pointers will be physically implemented.

At this point the designer decides whether more than one entity – more than one record type or table – is to be stored together in the same block or page. Any entities that have a master–detail or one-to-many relationship are candidates for being stored together. Figure 20.4 shows a possible entity group for the student enrolment example used in Chapter 17.

This grouping uses the fact that 'course code' appears in the key of each of these entities. The entity 'course tutor' could alternatively be grouped together with 'tutor' because 'tutor' appears in both keys. Similarly 'enrolment' could be grouped with 'course' because 'course code' is part of the key to the 'enrolment' entity.

In Figure 20.4 optional relationships have been changed to become mandatory ones. Initially all optional relationships are implemented, despite storage overheads. In this way the physical data model still supports the user's logical view of the data, which makes maintenance simpler. Later, after any difficulties

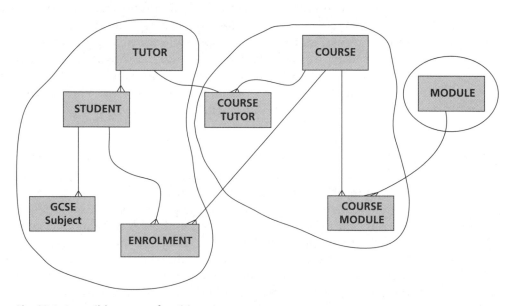

Fig. 20.4 A possible group of entities

in meeting storage or performance requirements have been identified, optional relationships may be reviewed. If the relationship is rarely used, the overhead in maintaining the logical pointer may not be acceptable, so the link may be removed. Users must be involved in such a decision because it will change their view of the data.

20.5.2 Data Access Diagrams

A data access diagram is a useful model to produce when the analyst is assessing the way in which each transaction will access the database. The starting point for the diagram is to create a logical access map that shows the path each transaction will take to obtain the data it requires. In the case of the student–tutor data model used in Chapter 17, if we wish to identify the tutor who enrolled all the students on a particular course then we follow the arrows in Figure 20.5. First we locate the course. This leads us to the applications for that course and thence to the student. Each student application is linked to the tutor who enrolled them, and this then gives us the information we want. This type of record-to-record navigation is common in hierarchical and network databases and in file systems that use multiple indexes. The database administrator will be required to make decisions on the physical storage of record types to minimise data access times. Although the access methods in an RDBMS are based upon the use of SQL commands that define the set of data required rather than the access path to that

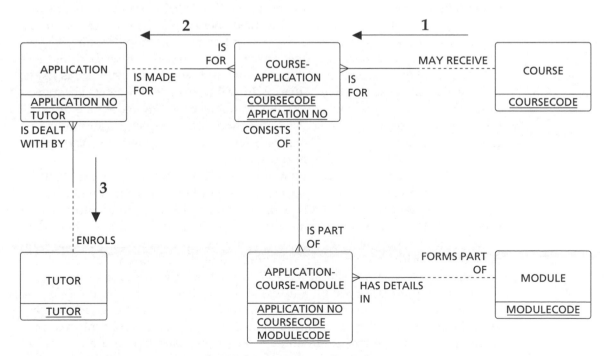

Fig. 20.5 Finding the tutor who enrolled all the students on a particular course

data, the same constraints apply. Tables are clustered in an RDBMS to minimise the time required when they are joined over common columns to produce the required dataset. The arrows on the data access diagram show the table joins that would be required by the transaction. The clustering of the tables will depend on factors such as the frequency of the transaction, the service levels promised to the user, the business reasons for achieving fast access, and the priority afforded to the transaction. The data access diagram will also indicate to the database administrator the extent to which the tables need to be 'denormalised' to improve the performance.

20.5.3 Refining the Physical Data Design

Although optimising one function might reduce processing time for related functions, the main problem in developing a physical data design is that optimising one area can negatively affect another. If the frequently used critical processes are speeded up, and routine batch processes are slowed down, this might not adversely affect the users. However, it would not be acceptable to halve the speed of an overnight batch program, causing a significant increase in online response times.

If merging entities still doesn't allow the data to meet its requirements, there are three other possibilities. The first is packing the data, although this may not be possible on DBMS systems. This means storing character strings, which would usually be held one character per byte, as numerics. This means that each program that accesses the character string has to decode the data to read it, and pack it again before restoring it. The second possibility is to create two versions of a file. If an organisation's staff file held 50 fields per employee, yet most programs accessing that file only wanted to read or update four fields, by creating a short version and a full version we reduce space usage and access time. Both of these entail risk. What the designer and users must do is consider whether this risk is manageable and cost-effective. After all, in real terms hardware gets cheaper as time goes on, so a better and safer solution might be to buy more memory. The third option is to change the accessing method: for example, if using indices is too slow, try using hashing. Using a different accessing method may reduce transfer times, but this is hardware and software dependent.

Prototyping may be a useful technique in checking that the estimates that designers are coming up with on paper are close to how the system will actually perform. The best way to do this is to work with the users to identify critical processing. This might be processes that have to handle large quantities of data within tight performance targets, or it could be processes that access several data areas. Performance tests are designed using the maximum volume of live data that these functions should be able to process. It would also be helpful to run such a performance test on a fully loaded system, so that you not only test this function to its limit, but do so when the system is simultaneously coping with the maximum number of users logged on, the maximum number of processes active, and the maximum number of peripherals active. If the targets can be met under these conditions, there won't be any performance problems when the system goes live. However, it takes a lot of time and effort to design, code and test the prototypes and simulator programs required by such thorough tests, so prototyping to this degree is still the exception. 4GL environments do allow prototyping of single functions relatively easily, and although this isn't testing the function to its limits, it will help to identify whether the function *definitely cannot* meet its performance targets.

Whatever the decisions made, the designers must remember to update relevant documentation, such as the system requirement specification or program specifications, to show what decision has been made and why. This is especially true if the designers had to find processing ways around the problem or if performance targets have been reduced.

20.6 Summary

The physical data model is a progression from the logical data model, but it does not replace it. Developers must maintain a logical view of relationships between data, because the logical model still explains the client's business functions. If they lose this, they risk building back into the system the uncontrolled redundancy and duplication that they spent so much effort stripping out.

The further the physical model is from the logical model at development time, and the more modifications that occur thereafter, the greater the likelihood of reduced or unpredictable system performance. To ensure that the system meets the objectives of physical data design, the designer must focus on:

- identifying the mandatory and high-priority performance requirements;
- resolving performance problems rather than storage space, if both cannot be met, because hardware gets cheaper;
- meeting each program's target run times;
- meeting the system's specified response times;
- maintaining the user's view of data.

As one of the purposes of DBMSs is to simplify the task of data design, it removes a lot of the control, and therefore much of the risk of error, from the data designer. Designers of file systems may not take full advantage of the operating system's data-handling mechanisms because to do so might not allow this design to be portable to another system. This must be an explicit decision, not left to chance.

Exercises

20.1 Convert the System Telecom LDS shown on p. 398 into an initial physical data design. Consider which primary and secondary key accesses may be required.

20.2 Consider which secondary key accesses may be required in this system.

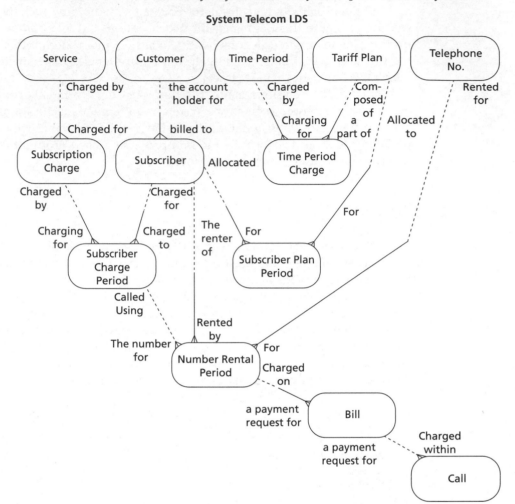

System Telecom LDS

21 Systems Design: Data Communications

21.1 Introduction

Two hundred years ago long-distance communication could take days or even weeks. Armies might have used semaphores and signal fires but, for most people, instantaneous communication could only take place over the distance that someone could shout. Then, in 1844, the first commercial telegraph service was set up, and in 1876 Alexander Graham Bell invented the telephone.

Networking has become the accepted means of communication between businesses and their customers (B2C), and between businesses and their suppliers (B2B). The seamless nature of communication links has produced specialist service providers who will facilitate these links and provide electronic marketplaces that no business can afford to ignore. The analyst must be able to exploit this technology, identifying the business benefits that can accrue from it without opting for technology for its own sake. This chapter looks at the techniques and the technology of data communications and how to use it. Whole books have been written about the theory and practice of this subject. This chapter cannot attempt to cover the whole of that ground. Rather, it will introduce the concepts and the jargon without going into too much detail.

21.2 Basic Concepts

This section introduces some of the terms used in the communications business. It's not intended to be exhaustive, but it's all you'll need at this stage.

Serial and parallel links

A simple piece of wire can carry only one bit at a time. To send characters down the line it is necessary to carry several bits. There are two ways to achieve this. A serial link carries the bits one at a time, perhaps on a single piece of wire. On a parallel link the bits making up a character are transmitted at the same time, each on a different piece of wire. Parallel links are widely used to connect desktop computers to printers. For longer connections the cost of providing a separate conductor for each bit is too great, so serial links are used.

Multiplexing

This is a way of allowing several independent users to make connections over the same link. Computers tend to send data in bursts with large gaps in between. This means that for much of the time the connection is not used. Sharing the connection between several users can therefore make more efficient use of the connection. There are two ways of sharing the link: time division multiplexing and frequency division multiplexing.

- *Time division multiplexing (TDM)* allows each user in turn access to the full capacity of the link for a short period of time. If there were ten users sharing the link, each might be allowed to transmit for one tenth of a second in each second. If the link could carry data at 1200 bits per second (bps), each user would be able to transmit at 1200 bps during this tenth of a second. In practice, from the user's point of view, a speed of 120 bps would appear to be available all the time.

- *Frequency division multiplexing (FDM)*, unlike TDM, allows users to transmit at any time but at fewer bits per second than the full link is capable of. It can be compared to the use of the radio spectrum by radio stations. They all transmit at the same time, but in different frequency bands. A filter circuit enables any particular station to be selected from out of the babble of simultaneous transmissions. Cable TV transmissions use FDM in the same way to carry many TV signals over one wire.

Data rates

The rate at which data can be transmitted is measured in *bits per second* (bps). The term *bandwidth* is sometimes used, but this is a loose use of an engineering term. A high-bandwidth link can carry more bits per second than a low-bandwidth link. The distinction between bits per second and baud is a source of perennial confusion. Bauds are concerned with the rate at which a connection changes from one physical state to another (from one voltage to another, for example). It is quite possible for the rate at which the line changes its physical state to differ from the rate at which bits can be carried.

Reliability

It is important to be able to guarantee the reliability of data transmitted across a link. This is achieved by adding to the data a code derived from the data. This is then transmitted and, on receipt, checked. If the check is passed, then the data is accepted. If the check fails then some remedial action is taken. The particular kind of remedial action will depend on the particular link protocol being used. The data may simply be discarded, or a retransmission of the data may be requested.

Checksum

The idea of a checksum is to treat a message as a sequence of numbers. These numbers are added together and the sum is transmitted along with the message as a check. There is no single way to calculate a checksum, and the particular method chosen may well be based on the type of data being carried.

Parity

This is the commonest form of check. It is easy to implement and in widespread use. It consists of a single 'bit' usually added to a character. The setting of the check bit is designed to make the number of 'ones' in the character either odd or even. Either can be used, so long as both ends of the communications link agree.

Cyclic redundancy codes

CRCs are a form of check applied to a block rather than to individual characters. The method of calculating and checking the codes is complex in software but easy in hardware. CRCs are more reliable than parity checks.

Network topology

A computer network is a set of computers connected to each other. It is not necessary for every computer to be connected to every other. Two computers may still be able to communicate, even if not directly connected, if there are intervening computers that can act as relays. There are many different ways of connecting computers together. The commonest are (see Figure 21.1):

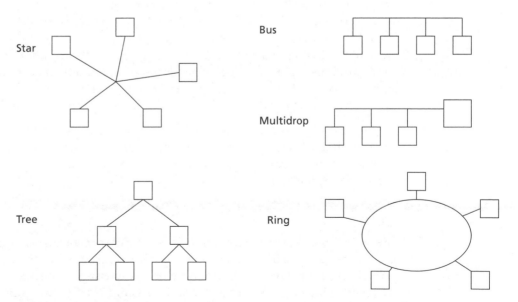

Fig. 21.1 Network topology

- *Star*. In a star, one machine forms a *hub* to which all other machines are connected. The machines on the *periphery* are connected only to the hub, not to each other. This has the advantage that the central machine can easily control and monitor the use and performance of the network. Its weakness is that, if the hub machine fails, the whole network fails. A typical example of a star network is a PC server with many remote terminals connected directly to it.

- *Tree*. This is related to the star. A hub machine has a number of periphery machines connected to it. Each periphery machine may then form the hub of a further star. This may continue for several layers as the network expands.

- *Bus*. This is widely used with Ethernet local area networks (LANs). All computers are connected to a single transmission medium, and all could transmit at the same time. One of the functions of a protocol in such a network is to prevent confusion arising from simultaneous transmissions.

- *Multidrop*. This approach is related to a bus. A central computer may be connected to many smaller machines or terminals, several of which share a single connection to the main computer.

- *Ring*. In a ring, each computer is connected to two others to form a circle. Rings are often used for token passing LANs.

Switching

In a complex network, messages may have to pass over many different links. Switching is the process by which physical links are chosen.

- *Circuit switching* is used on the telephone network. While communication is in progress, there is a physical connection between the two ends of the link. The connection is totally dedicated to that connection and cannot be used for any other purpose until the call is over. A network that uses circuit switching is ideal for carrying voice. Voice traffic is fairly continuous so it makes sense to dedicate a circuit to its use. However, computer communications tend not to be continuous. Data might be carried for a second and then nothing for the next 10 seconds. For computers, circuit switching is not ideal. What is required is a way of switching the use of a circuit rather than the circuit itself.

- *Packet switching* requires data to be divided into packets of a few hundred bytes each. Packets from several different users can then be sent one after another down the same connection. In this way, several users can use the same connection at the same time.

Layering

Communications systems are often thought of as layers of software, the software in each layer being distributed across the different machines. Each layer communicates only with the layers above and below. A message is passed to the uppermost layer, which passes it on, and so on. Eventually the lowest layer controls the physical link itself. The message then passes across the link and up through the corresponding layers on the receiver until it can be delivered. The parts of each layer on different machines will, in most cases, need to communicate with each other. This conversation is called a *protocol*. Although the protocol seems to be carried within a layer, the only 'real' connection is at the bottom of the stack. So the protocol in one layer is carried as messages by the next layer down. The effect is to produce a set of nested protocols, each concerned with a particular aspect of the link. Layering is often used to build communications software. It enables well-established 'communications' practice to be implemented in a clearly defined way. The different protocols can be separated from each other, and from processing-orientated functions. On the other hand, size and perform-ance can suffer.

21.3 The Use and Provision of Networks

From the analyst's point of view, layering can help to separate different aspects of the problem. In particular, it can be used to separate the use being made of a network from the problems of providing the network. Imagine you are making a phone call. You care about what you want to say. You don't care about whether your voice is carried by microwave or copper wire, or the number of telephone exchanges that the connection must pass through. The telephone company, on the other hand, does care about how the connection is made, but does not care about your conversation (Figure 21.2).

The same distinction, between use and provision, can be made between pro-grams that use network connections and programs that provide them. In this case, however, the two programs could well be running alongside each other in the same computer. The programs that use the connection will be aware only of the end-to-end connection. Intermediate points where, perhaps, the packets are switched would be invisible.

In Figure 21.3, the arrows represent protocols. The lower-layer protocols are concerned with the provision of the network and with the distance over which information has to be carried, something considered in more detail in sections 21.4 and 21.5. The upper-layer protocols are directly concerned with the needs of the application. If, for example, the application concerned banking, this protocol might be concerned with checking that credit cards are valid, or that a withdrawal will not exceed the overdraft limit.

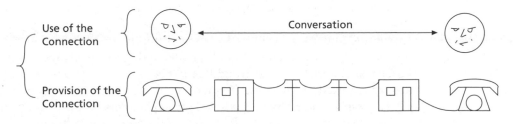

Fig. 21.2 The use and provision of a connection

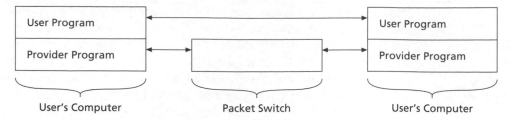

Fig. 21.3 User and provider keys

If these 'user' and 'provider' layers are not separated, then a change to the way the information is carried could require a change to the application itself. It is as if, in a telephone network, a change to the local telephone exchange required you to speak in a different language!

Both the upper and lower layers can be complex and are often divided into several smaller layers. As we shall see in section 21.5, the OSI Reference Model uses seven layers in addition to the application itself.

21.4 Carrying Information Across Networks

Networks can be categorised, according to their size, into *wide area networks* (WANs) and *local area networks* (LANs). The differences lie not only in the physical distances involved, but in the speed and number of the channels provided. A typical Ethernet LAN would provide a speed of up to 100 megabits per second for a maximum distance of about 2.5 km. While there are, in practice, ways of linking Ethernets over much longer distances, there are still limits. WANs are big. The size of a WAN is limited only by the ability to provide a physical medium on which to transmit. A WAN might provide only a few kilobits per second but could provide it from one side of the Earth to the other. Unlike a LAN, the rules for using a WAN do not set a limit on the overall size of the network. So, you might use a LAN within an office, and a WAN to link offices together.

21.4.1 Local Area Networks

You can think of local area networks (LANs) in terms of the protocols used or in terms of the way in which the physical link is used. There are two ways in which the physical link can be used, known as broadband and baseband. A *broadband network* has a very great capacity and uses frequency division multiplexing to provide a number of separate logical channels. The channels may be of different capacities and may be used for very different purposes. You might use one for carrying a video signal, another for analogue voice, and treat a third as a baseband channel in its own right. A *baseband network* is one in which all signals are transmitted at their *base* frequency: that is, they are not combined with any *carrier frequency* to provide separate logical channels on the physical link.

The simplest way to coordinate a small network is polling. One computer is designated the *master* and the others the *slaves*. No slave may transmit until given permission to do so by the master. The master will ask each slave in turn whether it has anything to transmit. The slave may then transmit, or relinquish the right until polled again. This simple procedure prevents contention, but may lead to a backlog of messages if the master fails to poll for some time. For more complex LANs, token passing and Ethernet are the available options.

In a *token passing network* the connections to the network have a predefined sequence. The ends of this sequence are joined to form a logical circle round which the information flows. In the case of a *Token Ring* the physical sequence of connections to the ring is used. There are several different protocols used for token passing, but the principle is that a bit pattern called a *token* is passed like a relay baton round the circle. Only the user who has the token can transmit, and rules of the protocol guarantee that the token reaches each user in turn. *Ethernet* is the popular name for a protocol more correctly known as CSMA/CD. The acronym CSMA/CD stands for Carrier Sense Multiple Access with Collision Detect. The general idea is that anyone wishing to transmit must first listen and wait for a gap in the conversation. When a gap in the conversation is found, the user can start transmitting. The message might be transmitted successfully. Alternatively, another user will also have listened to the line, heard the gap in the conversation, and started to transmit. In this case, the two messages will collide. Both messages will be garbled and will be unrecognisable. If messages collide, the two would-be-users of the line each wait for a random length of time and try again. If the times are selected well, the chance of them colliding again is very small.

21.4.2 Wide Area Networks

For good historical reasons most communications links in place in the world are designed for voice traffic. This is unfortunate for the transmission of data because the requirements for data and voice are very different.

Let's consider a few of the differences. In the first place, telephone conversations are always two-way but data transmissions may be two-way or one-way. When data traffic is two-way it is often 'both ways at the same time'. Two-way voice traffic tends to alternate in direction: at any given time only one person is speaking. Second, data must be transmitted without noise. Voice traffic, however, as we know to our cost, is assumed to be able to cope with all the crackles and pops that the circuit can deliver. We can usually make sense from a noisy message, but a computer usually can't. Also computer data tends to be transmitted in bursts. Telephone traffic is fairly continuous; gaps where neither person is speaking are rare. We also prefer voice traffic to be delivered immediately. A gap of only a few seconds when no one is speaking seems like a lifetime and is often intolerable. Some data has this characteristic too, but most can be delivered later – like a letter sent by post. Finally, the way in which bits are represented on an electrical connection differs greatly from the way in which voice is represented. The effect is that a telephone line, which is designed to carry voice, distorts data to the point where, after only a short distance, it is unrecognisable.

You can, however, use voice lines to carry data. The process of making data suitable for transmission over telephone lines is called *modulation*. Interpreting the tones at the receiving end is called *demodulation*. Hence the acronym MODEM used to refer to the boxes that perform the MOdulation-DEModulation. Modems vary very much in complexity: the longer the distance over which data is to be sent, and the faster the data has to be sent, the more complex the modem. For low-distance and low-speed transmissions a simple device called a *line driver* may be adequate. This consists of little more than an amplifier. For longer distances and higher speeds the way the digital signal is modulated is more complex. The form of this modulation is specified in a number of internationally recognised recommendations. Effectively, the job of a modem is to 'disguise' the data as a signal that 'sounds like' voice and, thereby, to reduce the distortion.

21.5 Standards and Standards-making Bodies

An *open system* is a system that is available to everyone: that is, it is not closed to people who don't, for example, buy from one particular hardware manufacturer. The idea of Open Systems Interconnection (OSI) is that any two open systems should be able to exchange data with the minimum of difficulty. This requires standards. Some standards exist because everyone decided to copy a particular approach. So, for example, the widespread use of the IBM-compatible personal computer is a consequence of other manufacturers choosing to standardise on this design, not because some international standards organisation told them to conform. In data communications, however, it is the standards organisations that reign supreme. Whenever someone uses jargon such as X.25, IEEE 802.3 or RS-232 they are using the reference numbers of particular standards documents.

There are two organisations that are particularly important in data communications. They are the International Standards Organisation (ISO) and the Comité Consultatif International Téléphonique et Télégraphique (CCITT). The members of CCITT are telecommunications providers and are concerned mainly with how connections should be made to and between networks, rather than how networks should actually work. For our immediate concern, ISO is the important body.

21.5.1 The OSI Reference Model

When the ISO decided to produce standards for Open Systems Interconnection (OSI), it very soon found that the problem was too complex for a single standard. The problem had to be broken down into a number of smaller problems. The Reference Model was the result. Each of the seven layers of the Reference Model has a particular function to perform. It will usually be the case that the communications network, whether OSI or not, will be supplied. Even so, the seven layers provide a useful checklist of the concerns which a network designer must address.

The upper three layers are concerned with the needs of the application; the lower three with making the connection. In the middle, the transport layer exists to overcome possible mismatch between the service requested by the upper layers and the service provided by the lower layers.

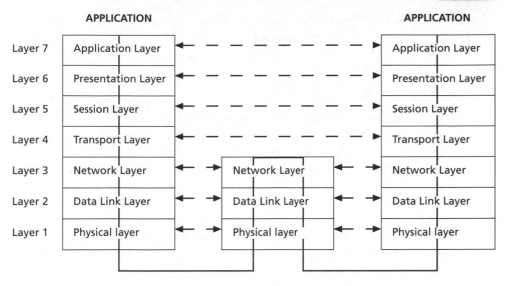

Fig. 21.4 The seven-layer model

Figure 21.4 illustrates these seven layers of software. This form of diagram, with the layers of software shown piled on top of each other, has led to the use of the term *protocol stack*. The dotted lines show where the protocols in each layer seem to be exchanging information directly. So, for example, the application on one machine seems to be exchanging information directly with the application on the other machine. In practice, however, the path along which the real data passes is shown by the heavy line.

The three-layer stack in the middle is a *switch*. The lower layers are aware of and talk to the switch; the upper layers are not aware of it, and talk directly from one end to the other.

21.5.2 The Upper Layers

Layer 7: Application Layer

The Application Layer is the interface between the communications system and the application processes. The main services of the Application Layer are:

- *File transfer, access and management*, which describes how to send files from one place to another.

- *Virtual terminal*, which involves message exchanges in which small amounts of data are transported in both directions. Virtual terminal concerns itself with the characteristics of different types of display. There is no point, for example, in sending colour graphics information to a monochrome VDU.

- *Electronic mail*. The CCITT X.400 Message Handling System (MHS) recommendations describe what in popular parlance is known as electronic mail.

- *Directory services.* To complement the X.400 recommendation on electronic mail, there is a series of recommendations called X.500, which describe how to maintain and distribute directories of users of electronic mail.

Layer 6: Presentation Layer

An open network might contain many different types of computer using different, and conflicting, ways to represent data. Some computers, for example, might represent letters of the Roman alphabet with an ASCII representation, others might use EBCDIC. The purpose of the Presentation Layer is to resolve these conflicts. It is concerned with data representation during transmission between open systems.

A connection between two similar machines may not need a Presentation Layer. If the machines differ greatly it may be necessary for the designer to simplify the data formats in order to make the Presentation Layer manageable.

Layer 5: Session Layer

The Session Layer controls how connections are made. Connections can be duplex or half duplex. A *duplex* connection is one in which both parties can transmit at the same time. A *half duplex* connection still allows communication in both directions, but not at the same time like a telephone conversation. The term *simplex* is also used. This refers to a link on which communication may take place in only one direction, as in radio and television.

The structure of a conversation over a duplex connection is usually left to the application program. A half duplex connection, on the other hand, may well be coordinated by the Session Layer. It is necessary for the two ends of a half duplex conversation to know at all times who is transmitting, and who is receiving. One way of arranging this is to use a token such as those used to coordinate token-passing networks. The token represents 'permission to transmit' and is passed between the parts of the session layer at each end of the link.

Since the computers at two ends of a link run independently, neither can predict the stage that processing has reached on the other machine. If synchronisation is required it could be provided by the Session Layer. The machines on the two ends of the link agree to a number of synchronisation points in the processing, which they should reach at the same time. If one machine is ahead, it might wait for the other to catch up, or in some cases might 'backspace' back to the other machine.

21.5.3 The Lower Layers

These layers provide the connection. If the network is a LAN, then these layers implement the Ethernet or token-passing protocols. If the network is a WAN, then these layers would be concerned with the connection to the network. In this later case, a standard known as *X.25* is widely used. It describes the protocols used by these three lower layers when a user's computer is to be connected to a packet switched network.

Layer 1: Physical Layer

The Physical Layer is concerned with the physical form of the transmission medium: the wire, optical fibre, microwave link or smoke signal. It is concerned with the way in which bits are represented on the physical link. We touched on this earlier when discussing modems. A modem is used to convert the signal into a form that can be carried by a telephone line.

Layer 2: Data Link Layer

The Physical Layer transmits data but makes no guarantees about the accuracy of the transmitted data. The Data Link Layer provides that guarantee. The Data Link Layer is not concerned with the content of the data being transmitted or received; its only concern is that the data is delivered with no errors.

Layer 3: Network Layer

It is the responsibility of the Network Layer to ensure that the correct point-to-point links are chosen. Route selection can be based on many different criteria. The ultimate destination is obviously important, but so is the current network loading. If a particular link is overloaded it may be best to send data to its destination indirectly. Not all communication links, however, conform to the definitions of the Physical and Data Link Layers. There are many communication systems such as the conventional telephone system that were created before the ISO–OSI Reference Model was devised, and a communications strategy that refused to use these systems for data communication would be severely limiting. One function of the Network Layer is to bridge these differences – to bring them all up to a common network service. This can involve joining together a number of different subnetworks to provide a single end-to-end network. In theory the Transport Layer need not know what actual communications service is being used. In practice different transport protocols (called *classes*) are used to bridge networks of different reliability.

The extent to which the actual communications services must be enhanced to produce the required network service varies. The telephone system, for example, provides little more than a physical link, whereas the X.25 protocol for connecting computers to public packet-switched networks comes very close to providing the required service. Very little additional enhancement is needed in this case.

21.5.4 The Transport Layer

The job of the Transport Layer is to bridge the gap between the services provided by the Network (that is, the service provided across the interface between the Network and Transport Layers), and the services required by the Application (that is, the service required across the interface between the Session and Transport Layers).

Depending on how big the gap is between the requirements of the Session Layer and the service provided by the Network Layer, several different transport protocols, called classes, can be used. The commonest are Class 2, which assumes a reliable network, and Class 4, which allows multiplexing over an unreliable network.

21.5.5 The X and V Series Recommendations

The X series recommendations are produced by the CCITT to describe the use of digital networks. The V series are concerned with analogue communication including modems. X.25 is a protocol for connecting computers to public packet-switched networks. It corresponds to the lower three layers of the OSI model. Its importance lies in the fact that, if you want to use a public packet-switched network such as PSS from British Telecom, you will have to use this protocol. The X.25 recommendation assumes that a user's computer is capable of supporting the protocol. Not all computers are this powerful. In these cases some kind of interface device is required. Such a device is called a *PAD* (packet assembler/disassembler). A PAD can receive data over an asynchronous connection, convert the data into packets, and transmit them over the network. Similarly it can receive packets, strip off the protocol, and transmit the data to the user on an asynchronous connection. RS-232 and V.24 are, respectively, the IEEE and CCITT definitions of how to connect devices together using D connectors. RS-232, the American terminology, tends to dominate over V.24, which is often seen as a more European approach. Each D connector has many different circuits. Some of these are used to carry data, whereas others carry control and timing information. Both standards envisage a situation in which devices such as a computers, terminals or printers are connected via modems, as in Figure 21.5 for example.

Fig. 21.5 Computers connected by modems

In this case the modems are given the name *DCE* (Data Circuit-terminating Equipment) and the computer and printer the name *DTE* (Data Terminating Equipment). RS-232 and V.24, therefore, describe how to connect a DTE to a DCE. Unfortunately, the most common use of RS-232 and V.24 is to connect a DTE (such as a computer) directly to another DTE (such as a printer). The process of re-interpreting the standards in order to achieve a DTE to DTE link is seen by many as a 'magic art'.

21.5.6 TCP/IP

TCP/IP (Transmission Control Protocol/Internet Protocol) is a standard that was developed in the USA before the OSI standards became available. It corresponds roughly to the OSI Network and Transport Layers. It is important because it is both widely used and widely supported, particularly in the USA. TCP/IP was originally devised by the US Department of Defense to be used over a WAN linking many sites across the United States. The network still exists, now known as ARPANET, linking universities. Today, with transatlantic links, many European universities are also connected. As indicated earlier, the upper layers of a communications stack are not concerned with distance, but with the needs of the application. It is not surprising, therefore, to find TCP/IP also used over LANs.

21.6 LANs, WANs and the Internet

It is unlikely that you'll be called upon to design a network unless you become a network specialist. Technically, and from a systems design viewpoint, it is a very specialised work area. Mostly you're likely to be working on systems that are, or presuppose, a network. Nonetheless there are some important networking concepts that are worth understanding. These are:

- the business reasons for using networks;
- client/server architecture;
- local area networks (LANs) and wide area networks (WANs);
- intranets and extranets;
- ISDN and broadband;
- the Internet and the World Wide Web;
- Wireless Application Protocol (WAP);
- value added networks and virtual private networks.

First, then, what are the business reasons for using networks? At the simplest level, an office network with PCs, printers, fax machines and scanners connected together means that PCs and their owners can share the printers, fax machine and scanners. A project team of five or six can share a printer and, with more powerful printers and more users, connection to the printer can be through a server, which can also back up users' files at the end of the day. So networks reduce hardware costs by enabling hardware to be shared. Making communication easier and more reliable can also reduce costs. Networks that support videoconferencing reduce the costs of travel and make possible communication that would otherwise not take place. A tutor at Henley Management College can run a tutorial with participants on a corporate MBA who are scattered across the world. It's also a network that enables an oilrig worker on a rig at sea to share an expensive drilling problem with a technical expert back at base and get a solution. It is also networks that enable organisational teams in Asia, Europe and the USA to share work between them and to hand it on from one time zone to the next. Dealing with a global client anywhere in the world, our commercial people can access information about what we do for that client across the world, and about the terms of business for all products and services. Managing corporate clients is a practical proposition these days only with the use of computer and networks.

21.6.1 Client/Server Architecture

The client is a computer connected to a network that can get some resource or service from a server located elsewhere on the network. A home PC connected to an Internet service provider (ISP) is a *client* to the ISP's host computer. Processing is shared between the client and the server. Most networked applications operate on a client/server basis. The analyst's/designer's job is to decide how to divide the data and the processing between the servers and the clients on the network.

Client/server systems use *local area networks* (LANs). Typically a LAN is a small network or a segment of a larger network connected to the same server. LANs can be slow or fast according to the bandwidth – or capacity – of the network and the traffic on it. By contrast to the 'local' nature of a LAN, a *wide area network* (WAN) typically connects LANs together across sites, countries and organisations, and is an internetwork. The biggest and most well known internetwork is the *Internet*. It is a huge client/server network originally conceived in the late 1960s in the USA to link together defence agencies, suppliers and researchers. It expanded during the Reagan administration, was progressively opened up to more and more organisations, and eventually became as it is now. This is the Internet – with a capital I – which is run and maintained by a collection of non-governmental organisations. An internet – small I – is a network of networks that connects users of these networks together so that they can share data and work together. Where this connection and sharing is confined to the employees of one organisation this brand of internet is called an *intranet*. Where it extends beyond the organisation to suppliers, customers and others it is called an *extranet*. The *World Wide Web* shouldn't be confused with the Internet. The WWW is a set of standards that enable material to be published and read by anyone with access to the Internet. The Internet is the carrier but the WWW is the content.

Organisations not wanting to build their own networks can use *value added networks* (VANs) or *virtual private networks* (VPNs). Network service providers who rent out capacity to network customers build VANs and offer the customer the added value of not having to build and maintain their own network. A VPN is similar in concept except that it uses the existing public telecommunications infrastructure and the Internet. Wireless Application Protocol (WAP) enables mobile phone users to access web pages and email.

How does the Internet reach us at home? It comes via a dial-up line, ISDN or broadband. *ISDN* (Integrated Services Digital Network) is a public digital data network intended to replace existing analogue telephone systems and give faster and more reliable connections. It is in widespread use in Japan, continental Europe, Singapore and Australia. In the UK it is in danger of being overtaken by *broadband* technologies using cable lines that carry TV, voice and data, and – according to the latest mailshot from NTL – offers downloading speeds from the Internet up to ten times faster than dial-up.

21.7 Markup Languages

Networks and data communications offer the system developer the goal of instantaneous, paperless transactions for the purchase and sale of goods, for the exchange of money, and for the provision of services. Before the advent of the Internet the use of *electronic data interchange* (EDI) with a *value added network* (VAN) was the prerogative of large businesses with substantial investment in IT systems. Exchanging purchase orders and payments with some of their suppliers became possible only where the suppliers were sufficiently well established to be able to develop compatible systems with agreed standards for the interchange of data. However, these developments were impeded by the lack of universal standards for data interchange and by the need for proprietary software for data communication purposes. The Internet provided an opportunity for even the smallest supplier to communicate directly with other businesses (B2B) or with their own customers (B2C). This brought about the development and spread of markup languages, which are the tools that allow the system developer to define the content of a document or a message so that it can be processed automatically on its receipt following transmission.

Markup languages make it feasible to develop systems that exploit the power of the Internet by specifying standard formats for data being transmitted so that any recipient of that data can identify exactly the content of the message. Markup languages have been used in printing for many years and the codes used to indicate the formatting of text are a familiar feature in printing and publishing. In 1969 Charles Goldfarb, Ed Mosher and Ray Lorie, working at IBM Labs in Cambridge, MA, developed *Text Description Language*. This was renamed to *Generalised Markup Language* (GML) and enhanced further to become *Standard GML* (SGML). SGML is a meta-language, not a language. This means that SGML is used to create languages and is not itself used as a means of marking up documents. It's a mechanism for constructing particular items – markup languages – rather than a mechanism for doing things to documents. Each distinct markup language developed using SGML conforms to a formal description of its construction and rules – its *document type definition* (DTD). Markup languages typically use 'tags', words defined with particular meanings and presented between angle brackets. *HyperText Markup Language* (HTML) is probably the most widely used markup language developed using SGML. It was developed and published in 1989 by Tim Berners-Lee, then working at CERN, in Geneva, and made the World Wide Web possible.

HTML is an actual language. It specifies the tags that can be embedded in a document so that it can be formatted and displayed on the screen of a computer. As such, HTML is a presentation markup language rather than a content language. It has become the standard for documents available through the Internet. HTML does not easily extend into other application areas and in particular into the definition of the content of a document so that it can be processed automatically. Although the facilities provided by HTML enable the display of transmitted documents, the exchange of data needs standards defining the contents of the document, and the standard that has become accepted for this purpose is known as *XML*.

XML or eXtensible Markup Language is a subset of SGML and is therefore a meta-language itself. It provides a simpler means of defining languages that can be used to describe the content of different types of document that may be tranmitted over the Internet. As XML is a meta-language there is no limit to the number of document types that can be described by an XML-derived language. An XML language can have a document type definition that specifies the structure of the document and the tags that are used within that structure. Any document that conforms to this structure is known as a *valid document*. It is also possible to define a document simply by using a set of tags consistently, and this is described as a *'well-formed'* document.

21.8 Summary

There are a few key points that you need to remember. First, in most cases, a potential user of a communications network will already be solving the networking problems in some way. There can be many different ways in which this can happen:

- uncoordinated leased lines;
- dial-up connection;
- the postal service;
- motor cycle courier;
- fax.

These existing information flows indicate places where the user has found a need to provide ad hoc solutions to parts of the networking problem. They are places where the analyst must pay particular attention and get answers to the following questions:

- How much data has to be carried?
- How often?
- How far?

Second, having decided where the information must flow, start the network design by separating the layers of the network. The lower layers will normally be provided by the computer manufacturer. The upper layers, however, will be concerned with what the user wants to do. The upper layers are where you will spend most effort. This is where the application problems must be solved. The first stage in solving these problems is to recognise that the analysis of a communications problem is no different from the analysis of any other problem. The user has a problem. You have to understand it. Having understood the problem as a whole, you will be able to see where there are requirements to carry data from one place to another. At this point you need to start to consider the technology to be employed to carry the data. That is, you need to start to consider the lower layers:

- Does the volume of data merit a dedicated line?
- Do the distances involved suggest a LAN, a WAN, or both?
- What communications products are offered by the user's existing suppliers?

The answers to these questions will give some idea of the structure of the network and the products that might be used to build it.

Having obtained some idea of the requirement and of the structure of a network which could satisfy it, return to the design of the upper layers. Use the OSI Reference Model as a checklist:

- Application Layer:
  Is the problem one involving simply file transfer, or is a more complex interaction required?
  Is there a need to provide an electronic mail service that may need to store messages within the network?

- Presentation Layer:
  Are there several different types of computer involved?
  If so, are their data formats compatible?

- Session Layer:
  How will the connection be managed?
  Who will make the connections, and who will break them?
  What needs to be done if a connection fails?

Finally, don't forget the costs. It is difficult to give any guidance in this area, as prices are continually changing. However, if you are building a complex WAN it is usually cheaper to buy your own switches, and to rent the links between them. Also, office workers tend to move desks often, so, ideally, a LAN should be easily reconfigured. The trade-off is between the initial high cost of structured wiring and the higher continuing cost of reconfiguring an inflexible installation.

This last point leads to one final consideration, which must always be borne in mind. The objective is not to install a communications system, but to use a communications system to solve a problem. The cost of the communications system must always be seen in the light of the benefits to the user in terms of solving the problem. A sophisticated network is no use if it doesn't solve the original problem, or if the user can't afford it.

Exercises

21.1 Describe three different local area network protocols and identify the circumstances for their likely use.

21.2 LANS and WANS are used in different circumstances. What are the different circumstances for using them? When is one more appropriate than another?

21.3 One of the regional offices of System Telecom operates in South Western France as an 'Agence'. It sells System Telecom products and services as well as other telecommunication products such as pagers, answerphones and mobile phones. It now wishes to install a computer system for office administration. It could have a centralised machine or a LAN-connected PC network. What are some of the factors to be considered in deciding which to install?

22   Systems Implementation

22.1 Introduction

The implementation phase of the development life cycle is described as those activities that begin when the system design has been completed and end when the development team have withdrawn from the project and the user acceptance has been 'signed off'. Some practitioners prefer to split this stage of the life cycle into two stages: *development*, which they define as coding, unit testing and system testing; and *implementation*, which they define as the cutover from the current to the new system. We have adopted the broader definition of the term to cover coding, testing and cutover.

This stage of the project is costly in terms of labour, and projects often overrun their budgets and timescales at this stage. The practitioner using the structured approach that we have focused on in this book can take advantage of the associated technique of MKII function point analysis to help in the difficult task of estimating the time and effort needed to bring the project to a successful conclusion.

22.2 Coding and Unit Test

This is the first step in the implementation stage after low-level design. There are two ways of producing the software code. There is, and probably always will be, the traditional method of employing a programmer to code, test and debug each software module. The greatest cost to most projects is during this activity because there are more people to pay, and with that comes a higher probability of confusion, inconsistency and slippage and the need for more management. The alternative to using programmers is to use a code generator. A *code generator* is a suite of programs that matches the input to an appropriate code template and from these produces modules of code. To prevent errors, the input is necessarily tightly defined. Some code generators can take diagrams such as structure charts as their input, whereas others require a formal structured English. Of course both methods – programmers or code generators – have advantages and disadvantages, so it is essential to return to the system requirements before making the choice.

22.2.1 Employing Programmers to Write Code

First-generation programming languages are the languages the processors understand: predefined binary patterns. We still refer to *machine code* when talking about the collection of 0s and 1s that are indecipherable to us, but essential to the processor. No-one programs in machine code today because of the high probability of error (it's easy to inadvertently swap a 0 for a 1), and the low probability of tracing such an error (there are no machine language level debugging aids).

Second-generation programming languages are usually called *assemblers* or *macro code*. A second-generation language is specific to a particular hardware and may not even be portable across different hardware from the same manufacturer.

Third-generation programming languages came into existence in the late 1950s and 1960s when the need for software portability and transferable skills grew. In the 1960s it was estimated that around 70% of systems development projects were never completed, and of the 30% that were delivered few, if any, were error free. Nowadays the customer takes it for granted not only that the system will be delivered, but that it will work.

Fourth-generation programming languages came into being in the late 1970s and began to be widely used in the 1980s. There are two main reasons for their success. Businesses were experiencing rapid growth, and needed systems delivered and updated quickly to support that growth. Advances in technology led users to expect user-friendly systems that they could develop or modify themselves. Anyone with experience of using a computer can learn enough about a 4GL in one day to write some basic report and screen input programs. 4GLs take, as their input, one line of near-English and pick up the appropriate code templates to produce the required results (Figure 22.1). Because each template may contain redundant code, a program developed in a 4GL is not as tuned to the user's problem as a 2GL or 3GL program. The final system will therefore have a percentage of unused code, which takes up memory space and slows down the system performance.

One line of a 4GL is equivalent to about 10 lines of a 3GL; each line of a 3GL in its turn is equivalent to about 10 lines of a 2GL, each of which is equivalent to about 10 lines of machine code. So each generation gets closer to English, and is exponentially more powerful than the preceding generation.

Taking account of the non-coding activities of program design, test and documentation, it is estimated that the average programmer produces ten lines of working code per day. The more powerful the language, therefore, the more productive the programmer. The short learning curve and high output associated with 4GLs should mean that there is less need for specialist programmers, and that users can write their own systems. The reality, however, is that instead of 4GLs making programmers redundant, programmers with 4GL experience are in more demand than 3GL programmers.

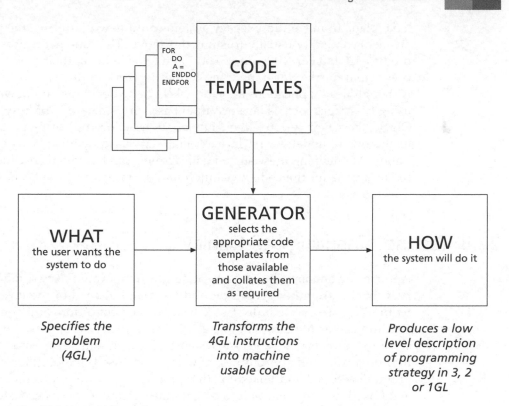

Fig. 22.1 How a 4GL works

The main benefits of employing programmers are:

- The programmer is a trained expert in the programming language, and perhaps in the hardware and operating system, to be used.

- Programmers think, and they make connections. They might see how something in one program conflicts with something in another program, and by raising the issue they can save time, trouble and money.

Obviously there are problems with employing programmers – they are human! They may not have the skills to do the job, which could mean training them; they may not want to do it, which could mean supporting and motivating them; they may leave, which could generate recruitment and familiarisation costs. The biggest problem in employing programmers is that, just like everyone else, their human behaviour is unpredictable!

22.2.2 Using Code Generators

Code generators were used extensively to develop mainframe systems in the 1980s and 1990s. Although organisations owning mainframe computers usually have plans to move these legacy systems onto new platforms, the problems of business continuity usually frustrate this move. The code generators are used to produce COBOL or RPG source code, and knowledge of their mode of operation is essential for the developer who wishes to work in this type of environment. Although new applications are more likely to be developed on powerful servers using languages such as Java or Visual Basic, or using an RDBMS system such as Oracle, these new systems frequently use transaction-processing programs on the mainframe to update or retrieve essential data used by other parts of the organisation. Maintaining these shared data systems can become increasingly costly as the user base for the code generation tool decreases and the licence fees for its use increase.

22.3 Testing: Ensuring the Quality

An error or anomaly in program code can remain undetected indefinitely. To prevent this from happening the code is tested at each of the levels shown in Figure 22.2. To successfully test a system, each condition, and combination of conditions, has to be tested. Just as the system was decomposed by the analysts into more manageable subsystems or functional areas and then further into programs and subroutines, now these are used like building blocks. Each program is tested and linked to other programs. This unit of programs is tested, and linked to other units and so on until the full system has been tested.

The first level of test is *unit testing*. The purpose of unit testing is to ensure that each program is fully tested. To do this the programmer writes a test plan. The plan consists of a number of test runs, such as the valid paths through the code, and the exception and error-handling paths. For each test run there is a list of conditions tested, the test data used, and results expected. A designer or team

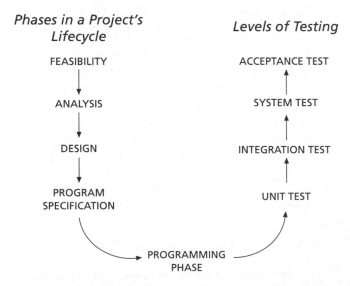

Fig. 22.2 Levels of decomposition and testing

Video Cassette Recorder Conditions list	
CONDITION	COMMENT
1 key pressed 1a record 1b play 1c rewind 1d fast forward 1e eject 1f stop 1g pause	The sequence and timing of key presses cannot be predicted
2 current state of VCR 2a recording 2b playing 2c rewinding 2d fast forwarding 2e stopped 2f paused	The system may be left in this 'current state' by a previous test run or the tester may have to set the VCR into this state before running their test
3 VCR tape status 3a non-write-protected tape inserted in VCR 3b write-protected tape inserted in VCR 3c no tape in VCR	Check whether tape is write-protected before insertion
4	
5	

	Condition tested	Expected response	Actual response
1	2e, 1f	VCR remains stopped	✓ worked as expected 25.7.03
2	2e, 3a, 1b	tape plays, picture appears on TV screen	✓ worked 26.7.03
3	2e, 3c, 1b	VCR remains 'stopped', indicates 'tape not inserted'	✓ worked 26.7.03
4	2e, 3b, 1a	VCR remains 'stopped', indicates 'write protected'	X VCR started recording

Fig. 22.3 A sample test plan

leader then reviews the plan to check that each path through the code will be tested correctly. The programmer is responsible for creating, or selecting from a ready prepared pool, test data that will produce the required test conditions. An example from a test plan is shown in Figure 22.3.

Following testing, all errors are investigated by the programmer with the support of a reviewer. The errors may be in the program code, the test data used, or even in the expected results if these were incorrectly specified. The deliverable from this phase is a working program, its design documentation and the related test plan including expected and actual results proving that the program works as specified.

The next step is *integration testing*. Sometimes this is called link, subsystem or level 1 testing, and it is an intermediate step between testing each program in isolation and testing the whole system. The purpose of integration testing is to test the interfaces between programs in the same functional area. The output from unit testing becomes the input to integration testing. The tests are defined by designers and are carried out under their supervision. Each program is linked to all the other programs with which it interacts. What is being tested is not only that the data is correct and in the correct format, but that it happens in the specified sequence and within the specified response time. The deliverable from this phase is a number of integrated subsystems, again accompanied by test plans, expected and actual results.

All of the applications programs are now linked together for *system testing*. The purpose of system testing is to test the whole system exhaustively, including any additional housekeeping functions such as file archiving. This is the developers' last opportunity to check that the system works before asking the client to accept it. For large systems, system test is run by teams of programmers supervised by analysts or designers, who may have to resolve, with client representatives, any issues that arise. Because the test plan must be followed without any deviation, non-technical staff such as data entry clerks are sometimes used as system test runners. They run the tests, collate the results, and identify mismatches between actual and expected results. In reality no system is ever completely tested, usually because of time constraints but also because it is impossible to predict and accurately simulate every combination and every sequence of events that may happen in the live environment.

As system testing is more complex than unit or integration testing, it is often split between test running and bug fixing. This helps to ensure adequate control over the way corrections are applied to the system, and system test version control documents are kept as in Figure 22.4. The system testers document the errors, each bug is assigned a priority, the bug fixers amend the code, and a new version of the system is released. This doesn't mean that all top-priority bugs will be fixed before the next system release. Some may not be completed in

	Error number & description	Test document reference	Priority	To be released in system version	
1	VCR records onto write-protected tape	REC/04	1	3	Oct 04
52	'write-protected' indicator does not flash	INS/17	3	2	Aug 04

Fig. 22.4 System test control

time. Also, some lower-priority bugs may be included in the next release because they can be fixed quickly and easily, or as a by-product of fixing a high-priority bug.

System testing incorporates a number of other classes of testing: performance testing, volume/soak testing, and regression testing. Each of these three requires that the whole system has been tested before they can begin. The purpose of *performance testing* is to validate that all response times or transaction periods specified in the functional specification can be met by the system, especially when it is fully loaded. This will include timing how long the system takes to respond to a user request, timing normal case paths through processing, and exception cases. *Volume* or *soak testing* ensures that the system can handle the expected number of users or transactions. Let's say a system is to have 10 keyboard operators logged on, processing up to 5000 transactions per day, with a growth factor of 20%. Then a volume test of this system would be 12 users logged on, processing 6000 transactions. As this would be labour intensive, it helps to write a program that simulates system use by the required number of people over a specified number of hours. The final stages of system test usually involve a *regression test*. This may comprise a selection of system test runs, or may be specifically written to test only key functions. The purpose of regression testing is to ensure that corrections during system test have not introduced other bugs. This test may be kept for later use by the maintenance team to check that any enhancements they carry out do not introduce any errors into the system. The deliverable from the system test phase is a fully operational system, accompanied by the system test planning documents, test scripts, and expected and actual results.

The user formally accepts the system when it has sucessfully passed the *acceptance test*. The purpose of an acceptance test is to prove to the client that the system meets the business requirements agreed in the functional specification. Simulator programs may still be used in place of third party systems, but where possible these are replaced by the real systems. Any remaining test data is replaced with live data provided by the client. The acceptance tests are run by client staff or under client supervision to ensure that the developers are using the system as the eventual users will use it.

During the course of acceptance testing the client records all errors, discrepancies and aspects of the system with which they are unhappy. These are then discussed with the project manager to identify why they happened and who bears the cost of correction – the client or the developer. Errors are usually corrected at the expense of the software developers, whereas changes are incorporated at the expense of the client, and the tests are rerun. When all problems have been resolved, the client signs for acceptance of the system. The deliverable from this phase is a system that works to the satisfaction of the client as defined in the requirements specification document and any related change request documents.

22.4 Data Take-on and Conversion

In the transition from the old system to the new it is essential that the data the organisation already has is safely transferred to the new system. It is unlikely that the format of the data on the two systems will be the same, as the organisation may, for example, be moving from file-based data to a database system.

One of the number of ways of getting the data onto the new system in its new format is to employ data entry clerks who can quickly enter quantities of data. This was the traditional method when moving from a manual system to an automated one, and it is still used in some cases. However, because of the repetitive nature of the task, errors do occur and can be difficult to trace. Data can also be entered onto the system by the users. This is a useful way of building users' skills with the new system, and is often done as part of their familiarisation and training. If it is done early enough in the project life cycle it can save programmers, designers and analysts time defining test data, and can provide them with a plentiful supply of normal-case data. Error and exception case data would still have to be defined. Helpful as it is, there are two major drawbacks with this method. First, it is the most error-prone method because it is being carried out by user staff whose priority is to learn how to use the system. They may not be checking the accuracy of their input, as they are just getting used to and appraising the user interface. Second, if live data is taken on early in the project development to be used as test data, and the system goes live months or years later, some of that data may be out of date.

An approach to data take-on that is less prone to error is *data conversion*. Data in the old format is run through a program, or series of programs, to convert it into the new format. The conversion program is not part of the application code and has nothing to do with the application under development. It is written to enable the transition from one system to another, and once that transition is successful it will never be needed again. The conversion programs have to be analysed, designed, specified, coded, tested and reviewed like any other small system, and may therefore be costed separately from the cost of developing the application system.

Conversion can also be from one hardware medium to another. An independent bureau is usually employed to do this. These bureaux are companies whose business is to take input data in one form and return it to their customer stored on another medium in the appropriate format. To illustrate this, imagine someone buys a new hi-fi comprising a CD player, cassette player and radio. What do they do with their old records? A hardware conversion solution would be to hook up their existing record player to the cassette player and record the LPs onto cassette tapes. Some organisations use bureau services regularly, for example to archive data from magnetic tape onto microfiche. Other organisations will require these services only at times of changing from one hardware platform to another.

At the same time it is also important to consider whether archived data should be converted to the new format, or whether it is better to maintain a method of accessing archived data in the old format. In our example that would mean keeping the record player and using it whenever the owner wanted to listen to that music. If the client decides that some or all of their archived data should be accessible to the new system, it is not necessary to wait until after the system is installed. Conversion can be done beforehand, but not if it diverts essential manpower at a critical time, for example if it would postpone the 'going live' date.

Each situation is different. The key is to make sure that nothing is overlooked. If data on the old system is changing right up to the time when the old system is switched off and the new one is switched on, it's important to know how those changes will be recognised and added to the new system in the correct format. The logistics of this would be difficult if data conversion relied solely on bureau services.

These are the main points to consider for a sucessful data take-on:

- How much memory storage area will the data require, including any archived data that may be required on backing store?

- Will the client require archived data on 'going live'?

- Is it cheaper to provide a system prototype and ask users to enter a quantity of live data, or allow time for designers to create test data?

- Which approach to data conversion suits the client's and the developers' needs best? Using bureau services? Using specifically written software?

Errors made during conversion are serious. The new system cannot go live with corrupt or partially complete data areas, and if system changeover fails owing to incorrect data there must be a contingency plan. This might involve running a minimum service on the new system, or reverting to the old system.

22.5 User Training

To be successful, user training requires a learning environment that includes competent trainers, and enough time to train properly, based on well-defined training objectives.

The training should include training not only in the day-to-day functions but in all the functions the system offers. Training takes place over a long enough period of time to allow users to feel competent with each skill area before developing the next. Where possible, users should be trained in the live environment or at least in a simulated one. This is especially helpful when learning how to use fallback procedures because if the users ever have to do this in practice they will be under pressure and not feel confident in their skills.

When deciding who trains the users there are three possibilities: the system developers, more experienced client staff, or a professional training company. Systems developers are sometimes employed to train the users because they understand how the system works, but they often have a technical bias and train the users by constantly focusing on the technical operations of the system, rather than on how to use the system to serve their business needs. It is tempting to think that experienced staff, perhaps supervisors or managers, make the best trainers, but this is often not true either. Although experienced client staff will have a greater knowledge of the business they may be so far removed from the user's abilities and difficulties that they don't see them, and if the user doesn't feel free to admit to difficulties because the boss is the trainer the training will fail. Often professional training companies sell the fact that they don't know the system as their major strength. Because they have no pre-knowledge, they make no assumptions and they can see things from the users' point of view. They don't use the technical jargon of systems developers, and once they have learnt about the system they can communicate that knowledge to the users in a way that is helpful to them.

This last option is usually the most expensive, but to ensure that a system is fully used and is well received by the users it could prove to be money well spent. A painful introduction to a new system will prejudice users against it for a long time afterwards.

There remains the question of whether to train all system users, or to train a few key users, who will then train staff in their area. The first option allows for all users to make mistakes in a safe environment, but if there are a lot of users to be trained it can take a long time. The second option is cheaper but makes it critical that those who are trained develop a sound knowledge of all the functions of the system.

Training should be scheduled to take place during the transition from the current system to the new one. Learning from a training programme that takes place weeks or months before work with the live system will fade. If the training takes place after the user has already worked with the system they may be able to iron out some difficulties they have experienced. Conversely the users may have already acquired some bad habits.

Improving the system's user interface will also ease the transition from the old system to the new. The aim is to allow the user to sit at a terminal and within a short time be able to use the system. Any difficulties the user encounters are dealt with by the system's context-sensitive help functions. These identify the problem and suggest steps to resolve it. In this way the user learns about the system as and when they need it. A good user interface means that less formal training is required. However, providing a user-friendly interface but no training, or a poor interface and thorough training, is not helpful. Both areas need to be user-centred to provide the best results. These issues are explored further in the next chapter.

22.6 Going Live

Thorough preparation for going live is essential to ensure the success of the system. The steps in this process are:

- installation on site;
- site commissioning;
- system changeover.

The task of installing a new system has degrees of difficulty depending on whether the hardware is already in place and installation is simply a matter of loading new software, or the hardware and software both have to be installed.

If the hardware is already running then only the new software system has to be installed. This type of installation might occur where the hardware was previously installed for earlier applications, or if maintenance programmers are releasing a new version of the system to implement a change. If hardware has to be installed then there are issues of site preparation to be considered. The main ones are:

- Is the area big enough?
- Is the layout appropriate?
- Is the environment appropriate? air conditioned? dust free?
- What communications lines need to be installed?
- What other hardware has to be linked to the new system?
- Does it require a separate, or backup, electricity supply?
- Is the site secure? from people? from natural disasters?
- How will the hardware be transported?
- When will it be delivered to site?

Installation must be planned like a project to ensure that all tasks are carried out in the appropriate sequence and within the timescale, and may well be managed by an estates department or by a clerk of works. The risk is that the site may not be ready on time.

Site commissioning occurs after the system has been accepted as complete by the client and has been installed on site and connected up to any third party components. For example, a railway station control system could consist of plant management software that can be connected to other subsystems as in Figure 22.5.

The system may have been accepted by the client when the control system ran using simulator programs that behaved in the way the signal, train location and points control subsystems were expected to behave. However, the way the subsystems are expected to behave, and how they actually behave, may be quite different. This is why site commissioning tests are run, to identify all discrepancies in the interfaces between systems and to correct them.

The first activity involved in commissioning a system is monitoring the interfaces. In this example this entails connecting the station control system to the signal subsystem, attaching a data line monitor to the communications link between the two systems. Having set the hardware up in this way, the installers then check that for each message sent the specified reply is recieved within the defined time period. The interfaces between all subsystems are checked in the same way. All errors are corrected before the acceptance tests are run again. This time the real subsystems take the place of simulators. Commissioning can also be done by running the systems live, but it must be remembered that work produced in this way may be wrong, or will at least take longer to complete than true live running. This is because the main reason for this live running is to test the interfaces, not to run the organisation's day-to-day business. Until the system is proved to work, that is a secondary consideration.

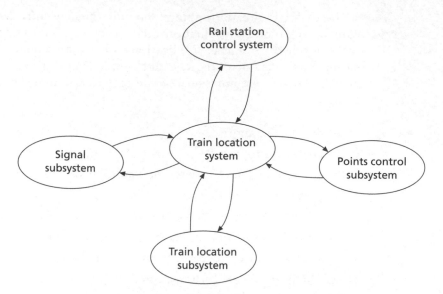

- Are 'hand shakes' between the subsystems and the control system the same as between the simulator and the control system?

- Are message formats the same?

- Is the sequence of messages received by the control system as tested using simulators in place of the subsystems?

- Do the subsystems handle error/exception conditions as expected?

Fig. 22.5 Commissioning a system

System changeover

Some decisions about development, user training and data takeon will be affected by the method of system changeover the user has selected. The choices are phased installation, direct changeover or parallel running, and this will need to have been agreed before the analysis phase is complete because it will affect the system design and will impact on project planning.

Let's assume the latest possible date for a system to go live is 1 December 2005. Figure 22.6 shows what the three possible types of changeover might look like.

In *phased installation*, one part of a system is installed and run live for a period of time. Then a second part of the system is added, and both are run live for a period. Any remaining parts of the system are dealt with in the same way. Systems can be phased by functionality and by geographical location.

If changeover is phased by functionality, the core functions of the system are developed and installed, and as phase 1 development nears completion, phase 2 development begins. As phase 2 nears completion, phase 3 development begins. This allows the user to become familiar with the basic system, then resolve the integration problems between the part of the system already installed and the newly installed phase. The user might have a number of reasons for choosing this type of changeover:

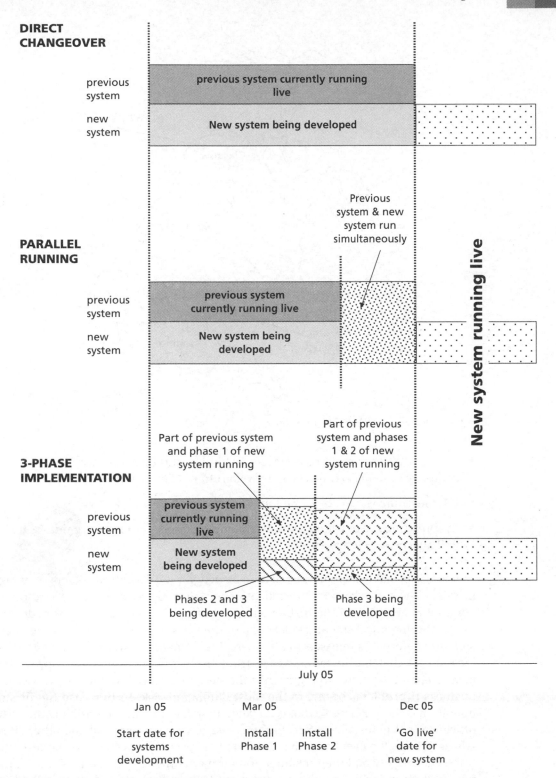

Fig. 22.6 The three types of system changeover

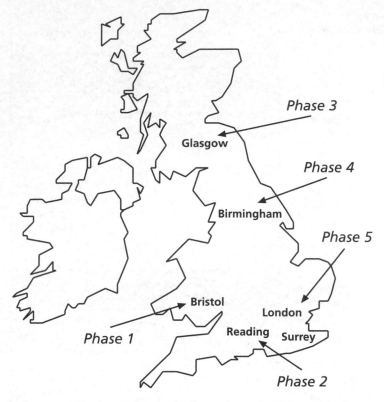

Fig. 22.7 Installation phased by location

- They get the core part of the system faster than if they had to wait for the complete system, so the system may start to pay for itself earlier.

- User learning is spread over a longer period of time, so it is less stressful.

- In spreading the development over a longer period, the client organisation will also be able to spread the cost.

It is also possible to phase installation by geographical location, as shown in Figure 22.7. The software is first installed on one site and any problems are resolved before it is installed on the further sites, one after the other. Some clients do this by identifying a test site and select one of their branches to receive and test new software before it is released to all other sites. Sometimes systems are phased by location so that the installers learn from the first experience and apply that at subsequent locations. In Figure 22.7 the sites are ranked from lowest risk to the business if problems occur, to the most damaging risk. In this case the Bristol operation is the smallest, so that is installed first; the London operation is the head office, so that is installed after all the errors have been found at the other sites. Alternatively, the client may have decided to install the system on the test site, test it thoroughly and then install it at their main office to get the most out of the new system quickly. The client must identify the objectives when installing by location to ensure that the sequence and timing of installations is the best possible.

Direct changeover occurs when, at a given time on a given date, one system must end and its replacement must start. This type of changeover often results from changes in legislation. Most new financial legislation comes into effect at the beginning of a new financial year; changes that may require significant alterations to computer systems to support the new policy must be ready on time.

There are advantages to this type of changeover. It is the cheapest option, and it provides a clean break between the old and the new. But when it goes wrong it can leave the client unable to carry out normal business. This was what happened on the day of the 'Big Bang' when the London stock market was deregulated. Trading started, the systems could not cope with the number of people logged on, and the systems crashed. Because this kind of failure during a direct changeover is so widely publicised, the system and its developers get a bad reputation, and the users are instantly wary about using it. Developers need to have a contingency plan in place so that they know what to do if the system fails irretrievably on changeover.

Parallel running is the most expensive changeover option, and as such may be beyond the financial resources of the client. It requires that both the old system and the new run side by side over a period of time. This time period should be chosen to ensure that cyclic variations such as end-of-month processing are covered.

The aim of parallel running is to validate the new system by checking the results it produces against the results produced by the old system. Obviously, if the results are not directly comparable this option isn't appropriate. To validate the new system in this way it is not necessary to run all the daily transactions through the new system. It is possible to replicate a percentage, say every tenth or every hundredth transaction, and check the results of these. Alternatively a number of each type of transaction could be selected and followed through the system. Of course, to be totally certain every transaction would have to be carried out twice: first on the existing system and then on the new system.

Parallel running means that both systems must be staffed, and this issue alone may well influence the decision about whether every transaction or only a selection of them are run twice. The client will have to employ temporary staff and decide where to use them. Is it best to run the old system using temporary staff, which could be less efficient than using the permanent staff and may introduce errors, or to use them to run the new system, and deprive the permanent staff of a valuable learning opportunity? Whichever option is chosen, the challenge is to manage the staffing to best effect.

22.7 The Maintenance Cycle

However long the development period, the maintenance cycle will be several times longer. This is because the system must first of all pay for itself, and then it must provide a return on the investment. Development is complete and the system is now in daily use, serving the business needs of the client organisation. Initially the client and developers may negotiate a warranty contract. This is similar to guarantees that accompany hardware, with the important difference

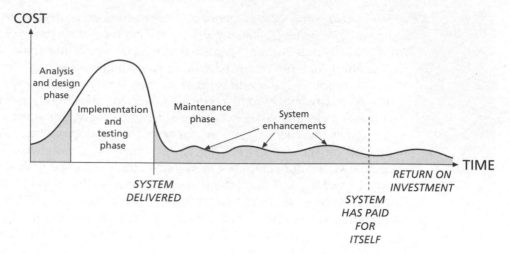

Fig. 22.8 Lifetime system costs and return

that no warranty work is done free of charge. The client estimates how much support they are likely to need, and a monthly or quarterly schedule of payment is agreed. If the client uses less than they contracted for, they are still liable to pay for the full contract, although this is often negotiable. If the system is relatively stable the contract is reduced, and if the client wants some major enhancements the contract is increased. So, even after the system has been delivered it still costs the client money.

Operation is the normal everyday use of the system by the users. As they operate the system under business conditions, they recognise what they like and don't like about it. They evaluate it. This is especially true if they encounter errors or difficulties. Occasionally they will suggest improvements, additions or amendments that would make their job easier. This evaluation phase often provides more work for the software developers, and so the maintenance cycle continues into a new inception phase, and so on round the loop once again, as shown in the b-model in Chapter 6.

22.8 Summary

Implementation is the longest phase on the project and the most labour intensive. The deliverables of this may seem less significant to the developers, and the tasks more repetitive. Each developer may have a limited view of the system, understanding only the area they are working on. For all of these reasons the major difficulty during system implementation is managing the software developers. Analysts and designers have already defined the system, the working methods, procedures, and standards to be followed. Implementation can succeed only if these are followed. This means that much of the implementation effort is spent in reviewing and testing.

23 Change Management

23.1 Introduction

Up to now the focus of this book has been on the technical issues surrounding software development projects. The preceding chapters have attempted to provide a thorough grounding in the concepts underlying systems analysis and design, as well as plenty of practice in using structured methods. However, there are a number of non-technical issues that organisations must address in order to make the transition from old system to new as smooth as possible. Indeed, there is mounting evidence that, unless these non-technical issues are handled carefully, the system will not deliver the benefits it was designed to achieve.

In the 1960s and 1970s, when the automation of back-office tasks was the primary objective of many IT systems, IT delivered tangible gains in productivity. Today, the picture is less bright. Many organisations are reporting disappointment in the payoffs from their IT investment. In 1988, the Organisation for Economic Co-operation and Development (OECD) stated: 'IT is not linked to overall productivity increases.' This conclusion was echoed in the same year by the Kobler Unit, whose researchers found no correlation between the overall IT spend and business efficiency. A major survey in 1990 of senior IT executives from businesses across Europe found that only 27% felt that their organisations were very successful at exploiting IT. And in 1991 the *Financial Times* ran a story about the failure of banks to get the desired benefit out of their new systems. This situation continues up to the present day.

All this is in stark contrast to the optimistic claims made for IT by theorists and practitioners. According to some, IT should not just be helping an organisation reduce headcounts, it should be supporting improvements in service, linking customers and suppliers, providing high-quality information to managers, and so on. But apparently very few organisations even get close to realising these wider benefits of IT. What is happening here? Why are so many IT systems seemingly unable to deliver the goods? Is there any way of reversing this trend? And what is the role of the systems analyst or designer in all this? In this chapter we discuss some of these non-technical reasons, and suggest that for every technical project there needs to be a parallel people project. This people project will be concerned with the management of change, and so this chapter introduces the theory of change management and describes some of the activities that must be carried out and the role that analysts and designers can play in the management of change.

23.2 Information Technology and People

The crisis outlined above has arisen largely because IT professionals and managers in organisations seeking to benefit from investments in technology have overlooked a critical success factor: the people who actually use IT systems. Without adequate consideration of their needs the system being introduced is likely to fail no matter how well-designed it is. For example, we need to be very clear about:

- who they are;
- how they are motivated;
- what they know about the system they're getting;
- the aspects of the change to a new system they are likely to resist, or embrace;
- the skills and guidance they will need so as to get maximum benefit out of the new system.

The best way to make sure that these issues are addressed is to develop a people project in parallel with the technical IT project. This people project would use the theory of change management as its framework. It would aim to make the impact of new IT systems on an organisation as positive as possible, by ensuring that users and managers:

- understand the objectives of the change to a new system, and are committed to achieving them;
- have realistic expectations of what life with the new system will be like;
- know exactly what will be required of them before, during and after implementation;
- get the right level of support throughout the change.

To highlight the importance of the people project, let's look at a typical organisation that's just implemented a new computer system. Two weeks after implementation the office is in disarray. Clerical staff are floundering in a sea of paper because an enormous backlog of work has built up, and whenever a customer rings in with a query, they're told: 'Sorry, we've got a new computer, I'll have to call you back.' Disagreements about who is responsible for updating a key piece of data have led to disagreements between the customer service and marketing departments. One group is actually staging an informal strike. The system doesn't work the way it was supposed to; their representative says 'We were promised things 18 months ago but now they won't be delivered till Phase 2. When is Phase 2?' Meanwhile, the supervisors have disappeared into their offices, dazed and confused. All the tasks they used to do – checking their subordinates' work, giving expert advice, authorising payments – are now done automatically by the computer. As far as they can tell, supervisors no longer have any role to play. Upstairs in the conference room, senior managers are demanding an explanation from the IT director. Why doesn't the computer system work? It works perfectly, replies the IT director, and it does work perfectly but the people who need to use it are not ready, willing or able to use it.

Now let's imagine the alternative. Two weeks after implementation, the office is running smoothly, though it's a very different place from what it was before the new system was installed. Clerical staff have organised a telephone section to deal with enquiries from the public, leaving the computer users to work without interruption, at their own pace. Issues of data ownership have all been resolved by a task force of users drawn from the different departments affected by computerisation. Key users are on call to help with any difficulties that staff experience; as the first line of support, they're able to filter out 90% of the minor problems that would otherwise be flooding into the computer department help desk. Staff who won't be affected by the changeover until Phase 2 have had a few months to get used to the idea and understand why things are being done in this order, and are taking the opportunity to learn from their colleagues' experience. Meanwhile the supervisors are monitoring workflows and making a note of best practices for a seminar with their colleagues from another site. Upstairs, the IT director is receiving the congratulations of senior managers. The system works well, the IT director agrees. But it's the people that are really making the difference. These scenarios are not exaggerations or caricatures; they are drawn from life. A people project really can make the difference between a successful IT system implementation and a disastrous one.

The foundation for a sound people project is effective communication. A good communication plan is therefore an important part of any change management programme. In Chapter 3 we discussed some of the skills that people need in order to communicate effectively with one another, but in the people project effective communication has the specific goals of:

- raising awareness of the objectives and potential benefits of a change;

- giving users information about what to expect from a new system, and what their role will be;

- ensuring that people know what support is available, and how to access it.

Remember too that communicating means influencing people as much as informing them, helping to shape their attitudes, building their commitment and gaining their cooperation.

23.2.1 The Role of Analysts and Designers

The primary role of systems analysts and designers is, of course, to produce a computer system solution to a problem that meets the customer's requirements. This task can easily be so absorbing in itself that there is seemingly no time left over for thinking about the non-technical issues surrounding the introduction of a new IT system, much less for setting up a people project to address them.

So even if the people project is not driven by analysts, designers, or even IT managers, it needs their active support. Many of the tasks carried out by analysts in the early stages of an IT development project have outputs that the people project will need to draw on. For example, the process of creating data models and data flow diagrams may raise questions of data ownership, which need to be fed to the people project to resolve, perhaps through a redefinition of roles and responsibilities or the introduction of a new procedure. Likewise, if systems analysts have done a detailed assessment of costs and benefits, this will give the people project some idea of the messages they can use to sell the new IT system to users and managers.

Analysts can also draw on the people project for valuable help in areas such as human–computer interface design, discussed in Chapter 15. The look and feel of the HCI can be one of the most significant factors in determining a user's response to a system. The people project can help create the conditions in which HCI design can be done collaboratively, thus ensuring that both sides get what they need from this all-important aspect of the system.

Very often, analysts and designers do more communicating about an IT project than any other group. Analysts have extensive contact with the people who will ultimately use the system, as well as with the budget-holders who are actually paying for and steering the development project. They probably know more about the user community's expectations and desires than line managers. They are often more up to date on decisions about the final size and shape of the system, when it will be implemented, even what it will be called, than anyone else outside the project steering group. In short, by virtue of their position and responsibilities on the project, they hold a great deal of information, and can play a major role in influencing the user community. For this reason analysts must consider carefully their own communications to users, helping to manage user expectations of the system throughout its development. In practice this means being aware of key messages about the project that its sponsors hope to deliver, and reinforcing these messages whenever possible, by word as well as deed, and in any case never contradicting them.

In some organisations the distinction between IT and the business has blurred sufficiently for a new breed of change agents or internal consultants to emerge. These people have backgrounds in either IT or the business, or both, and can therefore provide a range of services, such as advising the board of directors on issues and opportunities in IT, writing specifications, designing new business procedures, and organising training. Clearly, where such people exist, they have a large part to play in managing the change driven by a new IT system.

23.3 Change Management

The theory of change management draws on a body of research from areas such as group dynamics and organisational development, as well as a vast pool of ideas based on the practical experience of managers. It is not concerned with the rights and wrongs of any particular change. It looks at the process of change itself. We need to begin with two ideas that are particularly useful in understanding the process of change, and defining change management. These are the S-curve and the concept of unfreezing.

For many years the consultants Nolan, Norton have been using a very simple model of what happens in a change process. In this model, which is called the *S-curve*, the *x* axis is time and the *y* axis is performance, profit and happiness (Figure 23.1).

After the implementation of a new system, performance dips at first because the change has disrupted things. Gradually, the organisation begins to get benefits from the change, but after a while there tends to be a levelling-off, as people get used to things. There might even be a slight decline in performance. At this point the organisation tends to start its next change. Change management is about optimising the curve. It's not concerned with whether the change is the right one; it aims to:

- minimise the depth of the dip, A, on the diagram;
- optimise the angle of ascent, B on the diagram, so as to
- prevent or minimise the second dip, C, on the diagram.

This S-curve is a rather mathematical view of change. The psychologist Kurt Lewin, who worked in the 1930s and 1940s on the behaviour of groups of people at work, developed a different approach.

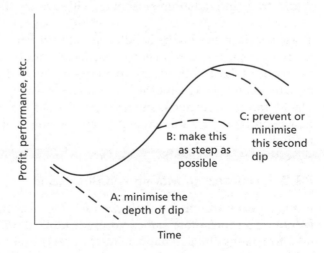

Fig. 23.1 The S-curve

Lewin's theory says that there are three stages to helping people change. First, you need to *unfreeze* them, make them feel restless and dissatisfied with the present situation. Next, you *move* them and show them the way forward. Finally, you need to *refreeze* them into the new circumstances. Usually, organisations concentrate on the middle step and put lots of time and money into trying to move people to accept new ideas or behaviours. They often fail to convince people of the need to change, and also do not stabilise them once the change has been accomplished. Consequently, the change does not work and people revert to their old ways of working because they feel no motivation to change. To some extent this model maps onto the Nolan, Norton S-curve. The initial dip may be the inevitable cost of unfreezing, the climb is where the real moving happens, and if refreezing does not take place the climb is held back.

Both models have one assumption in common: it is that people resist change. In common with other observations that are so true as to hardly deserve mentioning, this one is typically overlooked. The sponsors of a change often assume that everyone will share their enthusiasm for it, or at the very least accept that it is needed. This is rarely the case. Among the reasons that people give for resisting a change to a new computer system are:

- scepticism about the ability of any computer system to understand their job;

- reluctance to trust the machine with information that might get lost;

- anxiety about making a mistake that will break the system;

- anxiety about making too many mistakes, and being exposed as ignorant or inefficient;

- anger at becoming deskilled and a slave to the machine;

- fear that the new system will cost them a job;

- fear that the new system, or rather the host of computer-related disorders it may bring, such as headaches, repetitive strain injury, lower back pain, eyestrain and radiation poisoning, will severely damage their quality of life.

These concerns need to be handled sensitively, but in many cases what underlies them all is simply fear of change itself. Organisational change, whether or not it is driven by IT, can threaten a person's status and job security. It brings about new roles and responsibilities, and forces new modes of behaviour on people. The literature of change management furnishes many examples of the old saying that people prefer a known evil to an unknown one; in fact, they will fight to retain it.

23.3.1 Unfreezing, Moving and Refreezing

But is it really true that people are really so resistant to change? If it were, life would be a much more static and predictable affair than it is. People do undertake to change things about themselves and their world all the time. The key difference is that people don't mind change, so long as it's not imposed on them.

If it is, they will resist. If, on the other hand, they feel as though they own the change, they will be more comfortable with it, and be less likely to offer resistance. That's why the first step in Kurt Lewin's model, *unfreezing*, is about giving people a reason to change and enabling them to see the necessity for it themselves. The reasons that organisations have for changing – world recession, demographic trends, the growing power of consumers, a new-found interest in the environment – by no means dictate the action that organisations should take. That would be too easy. In fact, once a business, a corporation or a government department has accepted the need to change, there are any number of paths it could follow, each one hedged with uncertainties. Some of the questions asked are:

- Why have we chosen to build a new computer system, rather than buy one?
- Why now?
- How will it help us achieve our business objectives?
- Why are we computerising some functions and not others?
- What will my job be like?

These questions aren't new or surprising, but what is often surprising is the urgency and passion behind them. It is the job of senior managers to deal with these questions and to communicate the way forward as clearly as possible. Without this communication, staff will very quickly become bewildered and anxious, and won't be able to contribute as much as they should to bringing the new world into existence. The dip in the S-curve will be steep and, indeed, there may be no climbing out of it.

The second step in Lewin's model, *moving*, is about telling people why one particular route has been chosen over all others, and preparing them to go down it. People don't change overnight. However much we consciously applaud and embrace the new world, deep down we may still be clinging to the old one. Psychologists talk about the tendency of people under pressure to revert to forms of behaviour that they believe themselves to have outgrown. Observers of the change process make the same point: it's human nature to drop back into familiar patterns of living and working, no matter how obvious the need to change. It is this tendency to revert to old ways after a change has supposedly been accomplished that causes the S-curve to level out early, before any real benefits have been achieved. Users of a new computer system may revert to old ways for any number of reasons. Problems with using the system may give them an excuse to mistrust it. Difficulties getting through to the help desk may leave them feeling stranded or out on a limb. Lack of recognition or positive feedback about the benefits achieved so far may cause them to wonder if this change is worth the trouble. And so on, until one day someone discovers that staff throughout the organisation are running their old, paper-based system in parallel with, or instead of, the computer-based system.

The final stage of the change process is *refreezing* people, stabilising them in relation to the change. This can be done by catching and solving problems fast, giving people information that reinforces their training, measuring success and sharing information about best practices. In short, by offering plenty of support. This is not to say that refreezing should prevent further change. If it did, the new regime would become as repressive as the old.

Although we said earlier that the first step in helping people change, unfreezing, was about overcoming resistance, in truth all the steps are about overcoming resistance. Resistance to change can come from any quarter, at any time. People who once embraced the change become willing to say anything for the sake of appearances but fundamentally remain uncommitted. Perhaps they back out at the last minute, or their commitment dwindles owing to lack of positive reinforcement, and they gradually slip back into the old ways. On a computer project, resistance may take various forms. Sometimes, users and managers may:

- spread negative rumours about the new system;
- stay away from the walkthroughs and project reviews;
- leave data conversion until it's almost too late;
- even go on strike.

But careful change management in the form of an effective people project can minimise the risk of these things occurring.

23.4 The People Project

The people project has four stages:

1 creating involvement;
2 building commitment;
3 providing skills;
4 managing the benefits.

Let's look in turn at each of these stages.

23.4.1 Creating Involvement

The main activities during this first stage of the people project include:

- appointing a sponsor;
- setting up steering groups, focus groups, and so on;
- selecting change agents;
- examining the implications of the change to a new computer system for customers both internal and external;
- interpreting user requirements;

- setting high-level business objectives for the project;

- designing new procedures.

A *sponsor* is a senior manager from the business side who acts as change manager and leader of the entire project. Sponsors are a powerful influence on the project, and often become identified with its success or failure. They must be willing to work closely with their IT colleagues, sell the system to other senior managers, and generate enthusiasm among users and managers. It is an extremely challenging job, but an essential one. A survey by the Amdahl Institute found that all the stories of outstanding achievement with IT always had a specific individual associated with them who had the vision and drive that made it happen.

Focus groups are small groups of consumers whose role is to give feedback to the suppliers of a service or product. The term originated in market research, but is now applied to groups within organisations that have some or all of these characteristics:

- a medium to long-term lifespan (six months or more);

- an advisory rather than a decision-making role;

- a membership drawn from the ranks of middle management, to give managers some influence over a change that they might otherwise feel victimised by;

- the potential for commissioning work to tackle problems.

A focus group on a computer project might give feedback on priorities for development, evaluate proposals for training users, or help plan the timing of the roll-out to district offices.

No matter how inspiring the sponsor, no matter how helpful the focus group, large-scale change cannot simply be created from above and cascaded through an organisation. The process works best when there are supporters at every level and every site. Ideally, they should be people who are proven influencers, known and respected by their colleagues. In addition, organisations are increasingly recognising that change works best when those most affected participate in its design. *Change agents* may be champions whose role is to influence their peers, or they may be full-time members of the project team whose role is to create the change. On an IT project, for example, they may define new business processes, specify requirements, or design an awareness programme for staff.

The other activities typically carried out during this first stage – examining the impact on customers, interpreting user requirements, setting objectives, and establishing new business procedures – may all draw on work done by systems analysts in the early days of the project. It is important for analysts to bear in mind the aims of the people project to win commitment from everyone affected by the system, to make sure people are adequately prepared for the change, and to follow through on the change with the right level of support while carrying out their own research into customer and user requirements, or preparing a cost–benefit case, or identifying data flows. The following checklist of questions may be useful:

- Who are the customers for the system, both internal and external? How will they be affected by the introduction of the system? Will they need to provide new or different data? Will the format of reports change?

- Is the user's understanding of the statement of requirements/functional specification the same as yours? Are the users really prepared to put time into this project, or are they showing signs of resisting?

- Are the objectives for this project clear, measurable, and specific? Do they mean anything to users? Is there more than one objective? If so, are some objectives likely to be more important to one group than another? How do the objectives translate into benefits that can be used to sell the system?

- Are there any questions of data ownership? Is there a process in place to resolve them? Is the resolution likely to entail procedural changes, or just a clarification of roles and responsibilities?

23.4.2 Building Commitment

The main activities during this stage of the people project include:

- drawing up a communication plan;
- educating branch/unit managers on the implications of the change;
- marketing the change to everyone affected;
- collaboratively designing the user interface and office layouts.

A *communication plan* sets out the project's approach to communicating the introduction of the system to everyone involved. Earlier we said that effective communication is a key element of any change management programme, and this simple truth cannot be overemphasised. A communication plan specifies the key messages to be delivered to each group of people affected by the change, and the methods to be used for delivering them. It is informed by a detailed analysis of the audiences for communication about the project, the actions required of them, the barriers that may have to be overcome to persuade them to carry out these actions, and the benefits that will result if they do. Clearly, the preparation of a communication plan is another area to which analysts and designers, with their detailed knowledge of who will be affected by the system, can contribute.

A good communication plan will specify who is responsible for communicating to whom. Analysts are often in a position to communicate project news to users about changes in the scope of a system, or revisions to the development timetable, but it's important that users hear this type of news from the right source. This is best done by their own manager, or by someone identified with the business rather than with IT. Unless this happens, users may feel that IT is imposing decisions on them, and when the news is bad – perhaps about the scope of the project being reduced or about it falling behind – it can damage the IT department's image and relationship with users. Analysts and designers should therefore be wary of falling into the trap of delivering bad news to users. Good news and bad should be delivered by user management.

Educating branch or unit managers about the implications of the new system is particularly important, as it is often this group that offers most resistance to change. It is not difficult to see why. IT has often had the effect of empowering frontline staff, of breaking down departmental barriers, or of reorganising a business away from the old functional departments. All these impacts may threaten middle managers, and, if they are not fully involved, the project may fail.

Marketing the change can involve face-to-face selling by the sponsor to individuals affected. This might include a corporate video that paints a picture of the brave new world that the change will create, or the design of a unique identity – a logo or an image – that helps give the project a special profile, and so on. Very often it will involve all these things and many more in a coordinated programme of carefully designed and targeted communication. Marketing a new computer-based system may be different from marketing a car, but the objective is the same: to persuade people to buy. They show that they have bought by investing time and effort in learning what the system can do and how to use it.

The design of the *user interface* is typically the responsibility of system designers, but a moment's thought will make it clear that human–computer interaction has an extremely important non-technical dimension. Involving users in HCI design can help ensure that the system looks inviting and works in a way that makes sense. Even if the design cannot be truly collaborative, users will welcome the chance to be involved, and this will increase their commitment and satisfaction with the system once it's delivered. And the same lessons apply to the planning of *office layouts*: if these can be designed collaboratively, user commitment and satisfaction will rise.

23.4.3 Providing Skills

The third stage of the people project includes such activities as:

- carrying out a task analysis;
- writing learning objectives;
- designing training materials, including tutorial guides;
- designing user guidance materials;
- training those affected, and planning continuing education.

Task analysis is an essential step in producing practical user guides and training material. The aim is to understand exactly who uses the system, and how they use it. It is then possible to tailor the user guidance and training to suit the needs of different groups of users. For the purposes of designing effective user guidance and training, task analysis should have the following outputs:

- list of user groups;
- brief description of each job;
- list of all tasks carried out on the system;
- details of what triggers each task and how regularly this task happens;

- flowchart that shows where the computer tasks fit into clerical procedures;
- list of everything that will change or be difficult for each user group once the new system is introduced;
- matrix showing which user groups perform which tasks;
- matrix showing which system modules or menu options they use to perform each task.

Systems analysts may have already carried out some task analysis before the people project is under way. Usually it falls to the people project to examine the impact of the system, but it may be that lists of user groups and tasks can be made available by systems analysts.

Learning objectives define what a person will know or be able to do at the end of a training session. For systems training, learning objectives usually have a practical value for students in their work context. For example, the learning objectives of an introductory session in using a new office computer might be:

- to be able to log on or off the system;
- to know which application to use and under what circumstances;
- to be able to move through menus to get to the screen needed.

Once defined, learning objectives feed into the design of *training materials* such as tutorial guides and workbooks. These should relate very closely to *user guidance material* such as reference guides, problem-solving guides, keyboard templates, and other desktop reminders. In general, users work better if the documentation they receive is task-based rather than system-based, as this reflects the users' reality. Moreover, they need guidance only on the tasks they themselves will carry out, which cuts down the size of the manuals they need, and makes them more friendly.

Training of users has been discussed already in Chapter 22, but it is worth considering how different approaches to training may map onto the model of change management that we have been using. Training people away from their workplace, for example in learning centres, can help the process of unfreezing. Workshops and walkthroughs can help move people in a common direction. Finally, workplace training is good for meshing learning into day-to-day work, in other words for bringing about refreezing. Effective refreezing is also the goal of continuing education, which may take the form of refresher training, best-practice seminars, or advanced courses that encourage and enable people to extend their knowledge of the system and get more benefit from it.

23.4.4 Managing the Benefits

The final stage in the people project life cycle involves:

- running a help desk;
- post-implementation reviews;

- education or consultancy to help branch/unit managers to manage the benefits;

- collecting learning points from this project for the next one.

By this stage, the system has been running for some time, and the objective is to ensure that any problems are caught quickly so that people don't become demotivated and that knowledge about benefits and best practices is spread as widely as possible. The *help desk* clearly has a major role to play in both these areas. As the focus for feedback about the system, the help desk can identify bugs in the system as well as remedial training needs. It can also capture ideas for using the system effectively, and share these throughout the organisation.

Education of managers is essential to ensuring that the benefits achieved are actual, rather than notional. Finally, reviews and the collection of *learning points* at specially designed seminars or workshops can help ensure that future changes, whether they involve the implementation of the next system, a move to a new building, or the reorganisation of departments, are handled as smoothly as this one was.

23.5 The Change Management Pay-off

The four stages in the people project life cycle may, of course, overlap, and the list of activities just given for each stage is by no means exhaustive. However, the scope of these activities, and their significance to the success of a new system, will now we hope be evident. Two things in particular should be clear: that the people project is of equal importance to the ultimate success of the system as the development project, and that the two projects complement each other. The people project, and the numerous strands of activity associated with it, imply that a great deal of time and effort must be focused outside software development in order for a new IT system to succeed. The cost of all this influencing, communicating, and support is by no means negligible, although compared with the cost of developing the system itself it will probably seem very small indeed. Nevertheless, it must be justified in some way. There are two difficulties. First, in most cases, you have only one chance to implement a system. It's difficult to compare how things went with how things would have gone if a people project had been set up. Second, there are very few objective ways of measuring success. To some extent, you have to rely on subjective evaluations of success.

To overcome the first difficulty, some organisations have taken to using standard questionnaires on IT implementations, which enable one implementation to be judged against another. The questionnaires attempt to track progress against the original business objectives, as well as gathering perceptions from users and customers about the quality of the system, the fit between expectations and reality, the smoothness of the implementation, the level of training and communication, and the responsiveness and efficiency of post-implementation support functions. Over time, it becomes possible to state critical success factors for any IT investment. Many of these, as we have already stated, are non-technical. The best system ever designed may fail to make any difference to an organisation's bottom line if users are not committed, organised, trained or supported.

Overcoming the second difficulty requires us to acknowledge that hard measures that can be translated more or less directly into money are simply not appropriate here. IT systems are successful because the people who use them are motivated and confident. It would be meaningless to try and put a value in pounds on motivation and confidence. In some cases a few minutes at the start of every team meeting spent discussing the imminent arrival of a new computer system may be enough to keep users feeling enthusiastic and involved. In others, outside professionals may be required to coordinate and help deliver a marketing campaign complete with videos, newsletters, training packs, and management seminars.

The key is to focus on the areas that will make the most difference. You will never be able to eliminate resistance to change altogether. Try to identify the main sources of resistance – middle managers anxious about their new role, or users disillusioned by past experience, or anyone else – and concentrate on winning them over. The Pareto principle states that if there are 100 levers you could pull, there are almost certainly 20 or so that will achieve 80% of what you want.

The truth is, organisations that do not attempt to manage change when developing a new IT system are not avoiding the non-technical issues; they are simply addressing them in a bad way, and that is where the real money goes. Unhappy users make mistakes, boycott the system, spread negative rumours, go on strike, hold the entire organisation back. The incremental cost of addressing their issues in a sensitive and thorough-going way is trivial. A good change management programme will help ensure that the system is implemented smoothly, and yields the benefits for which it was designed.

23.6 Summary

To sum up this chapter on the role of change management in an IT project, we've seen that there is a crisis in IT. Computer systems are not delivering the benefits for which they were designed. One important reason for this is that *people* have been overlooked. All technical projects should therefore be accompanied by a people project, designed to help users and managers make the most of new computer systems. Change management theory gives us insights into how such a people project should be set up and run. Effective communication is a key part of any change management programme. Systems analysts and designers can feed into the people project in a number of areas, and need to support the all-important communication effort, helping to ensure a smooth transition to the new system.

The discipline of change management studies the process of change to see whether there are ways of helping it succeed. Two models – the S-curve, and the concept of change as a three-stage process of unfreezing, moving, and refreezing – are particularly helpful. On an IT project, success may be partially equated with overcoming resistance among users and managers to the changes wrought by a new computer system. Resistance can be overcome by giving people ownership of the change, providing them with a vision of the new world and the knowledge and skills to master it, and supporting them to ensure they do not revert to old ways.

The people project can be divided into four main stages. Creating involvement requires appointing a sponsor, setting up focus groups, and selecting change agents, as well as checking the user requirements and setting business object-ives that everyone can understand. Building commitment can be done through coordinated communication and marketing efforts and collaborative work on interface design and office layouts; the focus of much activity in this stage is on middle management. Providing skills includes training people and produc-ing effective user guidance materials. Finally, managing the benefits involves catching and solving problems fast through an adequately resourced and well-briefed help desk, and spreading good practices throughout the organisation.

The benefits of all this change management activity are hard to quantify. How-ever, unless the people issues are addressed in a sensitive and thorough way, those IT projects that ignore them will continue to fail to meet their objectives.

24 What Next?

24.1 Introduction

So far in this book we've addressed three aspects of the time dimension of analysis and design. First, we've looked at the unchanging aspects of analysis and design and, for example, considered fact-finding interviews and communication. Second, we've examined some of the aspects of the analyst's job that have changed as a greater understanding has been gained about methods and techniques. The chapters dealing with structured methods and the management of change are examples of this aspect. Finally there are chapters where the content is driven by technological change and the opportunities it offers to improve the solutions we offer to system problems. This final chapter deals with a different time dimension. It deals with the future – not the immediate technological future but with the broad sweeps of change that will affect business and information systems over the next 10 or 20 years. It's important to recognise that all of the ideas, forecasts, suggestions and predictions do not fit neatly together. It is a turbulent world that lies ahead. You need to decide for yourself, in your situation, the parts of this chapter that offer you an opportunity to improve what you do. Judgement is required; there are different views of the future. Although you should expect this chapter to offer a sound view of likely trends, it won't all be right.

In this edition, in addition to our own views, this chapter includes the views of senior industry practitioners who have generously agreed to contribute their ideas about the future. Scattered through the chapter are some 'panel profiles' of our panellists, and their ideas about the future appear towards the end of the chapter.

24.2 How Did We Get Here?

Information processing is concerned with processing data to generate information. Information systems receive input, store it, process it and output information; nowadays they also transmit or communicate locally or remotely. These functions have existed for a long time and have been in business use for at least a hundred years since the US Census in 1890. Developments in the 1960s and 1970s concentrated on making these functions go faster and cost less. Many people suggest that this 'more speed, less cost' phenomenon began with the 1939–45 World War. A key difference, however, between IT and other office technologies – the typewriter or the adding machine for example – is that whereas other office technologies generated cost savings when introduced, only IT has consistently generated year-on-year cost savings through technological developments and progressively increased functionality. As we so often use Japanese industry as a model for the effective implementation of new technologies let's take two Japanese examples – one of reduced cost and one of increased functionality – and see how information technology has dramatically affected two older technologies that, like the typewriter and the adding machine, would not have been changed otherwise.

The first example concerns the watch industry, effectively controlled by the Swiss with their intricate and beautifully crafted clockwork mechanisms until the late 1970s/early 1980s when Japanese digital watches using chip technology flooded the market and, costing less than 10% of Swiss products, decimated the Swiss watch market. The other example is the fax, the facsimile transmitter, which was revolutionised by the Japanese for whom, with their image-based language, the older telegraph technology with its use of Morse code was unsuited. Nowadays, of course, with the ever-falling cost of hardware it is possible to plug a portable computer into a hotel telephone socket and transmit text and drawings to a hard copy printer in another continent.

Over time, information technology has been a driver for change in isolation and when linked with other technologies. The development and use of IT has been revolutionary. We can see this most clearly by looking at the business impact of Internet technologies and the use of the World Wide Web.

The *Internet* is a global network of networks with member networks all connecting to the global Internet through a defined protocol. Its origins lie in the Cold War of the 1960s, when the USA determined to set up a data network, with high reliability, to connect together military and academic collaborators. It was driven in the 1990s by the development of effective web browsers that enabled documents to be accessed and read even though they were stored in different places. By the end of 2001 it was estimated that there were 445 million Internet users.

The Internet and the World Wide Web are enabling organisations in the public and private sector to make revolutionary changes in the way they do business. These new ways are not without problems, however, as the dot.com boom of the late 1990s showed when it was followed by the subsequent dot.com crash. Nonetheless, there are sound business propositions that are made possible only by Internet technologies. Amazon.com is perhaps the most famous e-retailer selling books, CDs, DVDs, etc., directly to the public at reduced prices with delivery to your door, and is the best known B2C (business to consumer) business.

We can also examine the business value chain to identify how Internet technologies bring business benefit. We need to draw a distinction here between the Internet as we've already described it and the intranet. *Intranets* are private networks, usually organisation specific, that use the protocols and standards of the Internet. In between the private intranet and the public Internet lies something not so private as the first but not so public as the second, as the company intranet is extended outwards to customers, suppliers and business partners. This *extranet*, as it is sometimes called, still has password protection and other security measures but allows bona fide customers to make their purchases on line, access their bank accounts, and deal with their utility bills.

So, in the value chain, procurement and inbound logistics activities use the extranet to link to suppliers; operations use the intranet to share production and assembly information; outward logistics reaches out to customers. All of these use intranets. It's really only in sales and marketing that the public websites reach out to potential customers.

The extension of the use of Internet technologies will be an important topic for our expert panel.

24.3 What's Happening to Work?

IT is also revolutionising the nature of work. Until the 1960s and 1970s the organisation of work was all about planning and control, and Adam Smith and Frederick Winslow Taylor relived their lives in factories and offices throughout the world. Taylor's view was that there was a best way of accomplishing every task. This best way was worked out by managers and technical experts, who then instructed the workforce to 'do it this way'. Managers knew best, the workers knew nothing, the system ruled operations, and supervision and personnel systems focused on enforcing this way of life through the use of the carrot and the stick: beat the donkey most of the time, and occasionally let it reach the carrot and take a bite of it.

The key assumption of the Taylorist model is that the workforce has nothing to contribute to the production process, to the system. This view is advocated by some people on the grounds of technical efficiency, but others say that it found favour – and still does – because it enables management to control the workforce by removing knowledge, and hence power, from the shop or office floor.

There are of course alternative perspectives based on quite different views about people, jobs and the role of management. Many of these views are grouped into what is often called *sociotechnical systems design*. Their general thrust is that productivity rises if job design, social needs and technology are considered in an holistic way. More recently, as we shall see later, people have talked about *empowerment* and *inverting the triangle*. Although we can see a general evolution away from Taylorist principles towards more higher-skill work, we shouldn't suppose that all implementation of new IT systems is designed on this basis. Just as there are implementations that give greater freedom and more opportunity for initiative to system users, so there are those that still deskill the users' jobs.

IT systems have some importantly different characteristics from other technologies, and these characteristics have significant implications for the way work is organised. IT systems break down organisational barriers and enable organisations to be restructured in quite different ways.

To take advantage of the potential of this technology, smarter employees need to be able to work with data and with systems, and there is a greater need for employers to train and for managers to coach employees so that their full potential is realised.

24.4 How Shall We Survive?

So if IT systems will impel so many changes, how shall we survive? All organisations are interested in their future. Survival is the first rule of business; it comes even before profit. There is a lot of evidence about how technology is changing the way organisations operate. The great improvements in productivity in the 1980s came from the application of technology, and this has continued up to the present. But where is technology taking us, and in particular where is information technology taking us? To answer this question, the *Management in the 1990s* Research Programme (MIT90s) was set up to

> develop a better understanding of the managerial issues of the 1990s and how to deal most effectively with them, particularly as these issues revolve around anticipated advances in information technology.

It therefore addresses the future shape of business and the development of computer-based systems, and is therefore central to the organisation and management climate that analysts could expect to find in the future. To help in this research, the team at the Sloan School of Management at MIT (Massachusetts Institute of Technology) created a model which they called the *MIT90s Paradigm* – the MIT90s example or pattern. This is shown in Figure 24.1.

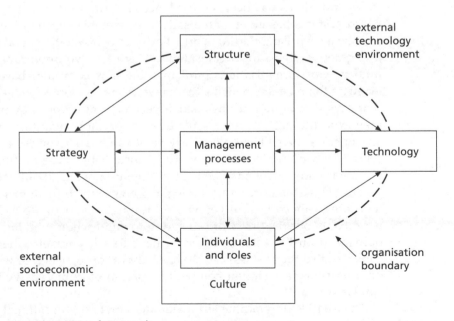

Fig. 24.1 The MIT90s framework

The limit of the organisation is shown by the dotted line. Outside it is the technical environment and the socio-economic environment, both of which cause change inside the organisation. Changes in information technology have, for example, shifted the balance of power in organisations away from technology-led central computer departments to user departments with microcomputers and local area networks. In Europe at the time of writing there is a recession and the economic climate is one of retrenchment, of downsizing in organisations and reductions in investment in new computer-based systems. Central to the MIT90s paradigm are the management processes that link together corporate strategy and information technology. The paradigm therefore emphasises the need for IT to be viewed as a strategic resource. Note the importance of management – or business – processes and how they are separated from the structure of the organisation. As we shall see later in section 24.5, this separation has important implications.

One of the UK sponsors of this research programme was ICL (International Computers Ltd) – now part of Fujitsu – and this company identified nine important top-level issues from the research output. All of these findings are interesting, but two are particularly relevant to this book.

First, there is unlikely to be any reduction in the rate of development of technology in electronics or computing. This will lead to ever-increasing computer power becoming available in smaller and smaller boxes at reducing cost. Applications that were previously uneconomic will become possible, and computer technology will be incorporated more and more into manufacturing processes and products. The main difficulties will be in developing software quickly and cheaply to enable this capability to be used. As consumers increasingly expect products to be 'smart' we shall see increasing demand for software developments using fuzzy logic and expert systems.

Second, there has been no evidence that the implementation of computer-based systems has given organisations sustainable competitive advantage. This may be a surprising finding, particularly for people who spend their lives developing new systems for organisations. There are two important facts that lie behind it. Most organisations implementing new computer-based systems don't evaluate the business benefits that new systems generate. Indeed there is a view that says that organisations make a very poor attempt to quantify the benefits they expect to get. Whether that's true or not, more quantification of the results and business benefits would clearly be of value. There is also a significant qualifying word in the finding: the word is 'sustainable'. The finding says that some temporary advantage may be gained, but sustainable advantage is not achieved because IT systems are easily copied. It seems to us difficult to accept that 'IT systems are easily copied'. If you've read through this book up to here then 'easily' is probably not the first word to spring to mind when thinking about the development of an IT system. Also, you have to ask yourself whether systems are copied so that the business can be changed as a consequence, or whether competing organisations face similar competitive pressures, which drive them to develop similar systems.

The MIT90s programme also paid attention to organisational change issues as well as issues of technological change, and the implementation of change was seen as the key challenge. We've already looked at this in the previous chapter, where we emphasised the need for a people project to run alongside the system development project. The MIT90s project offers a wider, more management-oriented view in the context of the whole organisation, and suggests that unless the technology and the organisation are aligned together then there cannot be an effective implementation of IT. This concept of *alignment* comes from the evidence that the requirements of the IT system must be matched by the capabilities of the organisation. So systems that need highly committed users who can engage in complex diagnostic tasks will call for highly motivated, well-educated and trained staff. Similarly, *alignment* means that the requirements of the organisation are supported by the design of the IT systems. Decentralised organisational structures with local decision-making means that systems need to deliver to the managers' desks the information they need to take their local decisions. This issue of alignment is examined from a project manager's viewpoint in *Project Management for Information Systems* (3rd edn, 2001).

Four groups of people play an important role in aligning the technology and the organisation. Top management has to provide a clear vision of the kind of organisation it wants and the steps needed to get to it. Middle management – the group that is most at risk in today's organisations – has a crucial role. Typically they are instrumental in guiding IT projects from feasibility to implementation, yet the impact of organisational change is often to eliminate management at this level. Throughout this book we've referred to the importance of user involvement in the development of new systems. The ideas – in the previous chapter – of a people project further emphasise its importance. This group – the users, or customers, or clients – of the new system are the third key group. Finally, new technology cannot be introduced successfully where unions represent users unless the unions are involved.

These four groups will operate in the future in completely different environments from those that have previously been familiar. There are several pieces of research or sources of new ideas that you could consider as likely to influence the way business life will be in the next 3–5 years, and we ask you to consider:

- the impact of globalisation and the part that the Internet plays;
- the work–life balance and the increasing importance of home and family and a decline in the importance of 'going to work'! What will this mean for businesses, systems and systems analysts?
- the connection between work–life balance issues and the continued drive towards self-managed work;
- the impact of new technology on the way organisations are organised. Does this mark the final death throes of the hierarchical organisation and the command and control manager?

24.4.1 Globalisation

From the beginning of the 1980s commercial life has become increasingly global. Increased political and economic freedom, particularly the ending of the Cold

War and the increasing integration of the countries of Europe, have made much easier the flow of goods, services and knowledge. Capital is now raised on a global basis, companies organise themselves globally, and managers and technologists move freely across the world. All this is made possible by worldwide travel and logistics, and supported by worldwide computer-based communication. All of this is to meet worldwide markets and to generate competitive advantage in them. Global manufacturing businesses operate where it is most cost-effective for them to do so. Usually this means where labour is cheap, where government grants are high, and where an absence of planning constraints means that manufacturing plants can be built quickly. The technology and the management know-how are imported from headquarters functions located elsewhere. Business systems and processes respond to the different shapes of these global enterprises, but with a global network and Internet technologies all parts of the organisation can speak to one another. Without global information systems, the modern global organisation couldn't exist. However, designing and implementing – via a global roll-out programme no doubt – the latest system for Megacorp is not without its challenges. There will be issues of:

- *national culture*, where the different local countries have different cultural norms about attitudes to uncertainty, hierarchy and power, family and work and the ways in which decisions are taken;

- *political risk*, with uncertainly about the stability of local governments, likely adverse legislation and the political climate in general. In August 2002 *The Times* reported on a survey that ranked 102 countries according to the degree to which corruption is perceived to exist among public officials and politicians; business is clearly thought to be done differently across the world!

- *economic development* and the stability of the banking system, the availability of a skilled workforce and technological differences.

Writing this chapter in the Spring of 2003, with the circumstances surrounding financial collapse in Argentina, the Enron accounting scandal and banking fraud in the USA, political pressures and violence in the agricultural sector in Zimbabwe, and a stagnant economy in Japan, it is only too clear that globalisation of business means that businesses face threats wherever they operate, and will expect their information systems to be sufficiently flexible to cope with the changes necessary to counter these threats.

Work–life balance issues are widely different across the world, and result partly from the stage of economic development that's been reached and from national cultures. In some cultures people are defined by their work or by their employer, and in these cases work and life are closely overlapping. In Western Europe, however, blue- and white-collar employees seek more harmony in the balance between work and life. This is marked in France by labour demands for earlier retirement and the introduction of the 35-hour basic working week, and in the UK by greater attention to holidays, pensions and retirement as negotiating issues. So strongly is this felt in the community that has to deal with it that a collection of employers in the UK has founded the *Employers for Work–Life Balance*.

This alliance of companies – for they are all in the private sector – believes that the introduction of work–life policies has benefited their organisations.

A survey carried out for the Alliance by one of its members and reported in case studies from the Industrial Society showed that work–life balance schemes:

- improve motivation;
- encourage graduates to stay longer;
- help in the recruitment of managers;
- improve productivity;
- improve the quality of work performed;
- reduce absence.

There are implications here for systems analysts – apart from the fact that they might be benefiting from work–life balance policies themselves! How would a highly motivated set of users, working part time, job sharing and working from home at hours of their choosing impact on the information systems you design? And – if this is the way that employment patterns are moving – what kind of systems need to be built to support them?

24.4.2 Technology and Organisation Design

The nature of work is changing partly to meet the aspirations of employees and partly so that new designs of organisation can be constructed to meet rapidly changing global markets.

The Royal Society for the encouragement of Arts, Manufactures and Commerce (RSA) was founded in 1754 to stimulate discussion, develop ideas and encourage action. In the late 1990s it initiated a debate about the future of work. In a published summary there were recommendations for government, education services and employers. Among the conclusions was the following:

> If there is a consensus, in Britain at least, it is that in the twenty years or so (by 2018 or so) that we are considering; there are unlikely to be enough jobs to go round, if that means sufficient jobs in the mainstream economy for all who want them, where and when they want them.

> The new world of work will be a spectrum. There will still be conventional jobs but these will include employment carried out in almost infinitely varied forms, for flexible working patterns will be general.

The report also asked whether 'individuals recognise their responsibility to develop their own employability, and is the right support available to keep them to do so.'

It seems to us that the notion of employability is central to the future of systems analysts. Often recruited as graduates, trained at an employer's expense and then seeking the benefits of work–life balance employment policies, the need to maintain their own employability by continuous professional development is essential. In the buoyant economies there is always work for the analysts and designers of information systems but, as we have seen, buoyant economies are no longer the norm and only those analysts most skilled – in technical and in human relations terms – can expect continually rewarding careers.

If the nature of work is changing, then so is the shape of the organisations. A recently published book by Frances Cairncross has looked at the effect of information systems on the structure of organisations. She sees several changes taking place:

- The cost of handling information will continue to fall.

- Companies will be less hierarchical and will make more use of outsourcing.

- Communications within organisations will need to increase, with much more feedback into the organisation from customer contact and product support people.

In parallel with these conclusions Michael Moynagh and Richard Worsley report on a survey of over 100 opinion-formers about the future of our working lives in the decades up to 2020. They identify in their book *Tomorrows Workplace* four changes to the ways in which work is organised:

- There will be a phase of radical outsourcing, where organisations in the public and private sectors will concentrate on their core activities and progressively outsource their support activities. Will BMW concentrate on its brand and outsource manufacturing? Will the NHS become a brand, commissioning services from a variety of hospitals, consultants and clinics?

- Technology will make jobs more skilled, and the close supervision of jobs will become more difficult. Each of us will know more about our jobs, our customers, than our managers will know.

- There will be new methods of management: rules and controls will be replaced by targets, individual performance measures and financial incentives.

- A growing number of people will expect to be allowed to manage their own work.

What might all of this mean to the ways in which organisations are designed? Recent research by the Wharton Business School in the USA and in particular by their *Emerging Technologies Management Research Program 2000* identifies that future organisations may take many different forms. They may be

- *virtual organisations* where employees, suppliers and customers are geographically dispersed but united by technology. In this context, a vertical organisation gives way to lateral relationships where everyone works towards a common goal;

- *networked organisations* with a small headquarters and a flat structure, a global strategy and culture and common values;

- *spin-out organisations* where parent organisations launch new enterprises that are then 'spun off' and set up as new businesses. The parent acts as a protective incubator and manages a portfolio of businesses;

- *ambidextrous organisations* where old and new businesses flourish side by side and where new technologies are fostered and grow to support the organisation as old technologies decline;

- the *front/back organisation*. This is familiar to those of us who use call centres. Customer-facing staff are at the front and the organisation's manufacturing and supply functions are hidden behind them. In management schools they talk of the *inverted triangle* where the broad base is the most important part and where the previously thought of higher functions of management and control support these customer-facing activities;

- the *sense and respond organisation* where change is rapid and unpredictable and the organisation focuses on meeting this ever-changing demand.

All of this research demonstrates the importance of the organisational form as an important competitive advantage. The future for organisations of all kinds may lie in their ability to change their shape to meet changing customer demands and employee pressures.

So, how shall we survive? Let's recognise that:

- The future will not be an extrapolation of the past, except in hardware. The future software requirements of excellent organisations will not be for centralised, deterministic systems. Decentralised, heuristic, personal, flexible and responsive will be the key characteristics.

- Empowerment of individuals will be the key; control will be the death knell. This chapter has already said something about the nature of work. Modern views about the nature of organisation suggest that the old triangular structures of a senior manager sitting on top of junior managers who in turn sit on top of workers will be replaced by flatter inverted triangles where empowered workers exercise greater responsibility and are supported by their manager.

- Finally there will be greater partnership between the suppliers of IT solutions and their customers. This will be true whether the supplier is the in-house department or an external organisation.

Survival then depends, even more in the future than in the past, on taking a proactive rather than a reactive view about change.

24.5 Business Process Reengineering

One important proactive approach to business and systems development aims to completely break apart the way organisations are structured and to reorganise them in a completely new way. This approach is called *business process reengineering* (BPR). Information technology is the key enabler in this new approach.

We need to begin by looking back over 200 years to Adam Smith's *Wealth of Nations*, which was published in 1776. This book described how the then industrial revolution could be used to increase productivity by orders of magnitude. The single principle that underpinned the new approach was the division or specialisation of labour and the consequent fragmentation of work into small tasks. Smith described each as coming from an increase in the dexterity of individuals who worked more efficiently because the scope of their job was limited, from the saving in time that resulted when people didn't have to change from one task to another, and finally from the invention of machinery to automate the now simple and relatively deskilled tasks. Mass production became possible. The same principle was used by Henry Ford to establish his automobile empire, and Alfred Sloan developed new management principles that applied the division of labour in the management of the huge individual enterprises. Still later, in the 1950s and 1960s, organisations grew by continually expanding operations at the base of the organisational pyramid and filling the missing management layers.

The thrust of BPR is that these old ways of organising business simply don't work any more. Business process reengineering, say Hammer and Champy (*Reengineering the Corporation*, 1999), is 'the fundamental rethinking and radical design of business processes to achieve dramatic improvements in critical, contemporary measures of performance such as cost, quality, service and speed'. It is about:

- *Fundamental change*. It doesn't ask the question about how to do some things better, but about why do we do it at all.

- *Radical change*. When we know what we have to do, what is the best way of doing it, irrespective of how it might be done now or how we are organised now?

- *Dramatic improvement*. BPR is for organisations that are in deep trouble, or which see trouble coming, or which are in good shape and well managed and want to put their competitors in deep trouble.

One of the big UK accounting and consulting practices in the UK has a 'top ten checklist' to help identify whether or not an organisation is ripe for BPR. 'If you recognise four or more of the following signs then you should be looking at BPR' they say:

- You don't know how your competitors do what they do.

- Customer complaints are rising.

- There's no common understanding of your organisation's key performance measures.

- You still do things the old way, and haven't introduced significant new technology in the last three years.

- Similarly, you've not been first in the market with a new product or service in the last three years.

- No one would recognise senior managers if they walked round the sites or offices.

- Individual managers have their own agendas and empires.

- Individuals from different departments rarely work together.

- You haven't reorganised in the last three years.

- Staff development is based on improving technical skills rather than on developing a broad range of experience.

Finally, BPR is about *processes*. This is the most difficult part of BPR to understand because most managements are focused on tasks. A process is a collection of activities that takes various inputs and then creates an output that's valuable to a customer. In a training centre for example, 'course scheduling' can be a task or a process:

- If it's a task it's a list of courses, with dates and venues that don't clash.

- If it's a process it's a list of courses, with dates and venues, and assigned trainers, with joining instructions for the student, course materials for trainers and students, a class list for the receptionist, and a billing list for the accounts department so that the customer gets invoiced. In other words it is complete, it's done because it has to be done, and it has value to the customer.

BPR stands the Adam Smith and FW Taylor models on their heads. Instead of having hundreds of simple tasks linked together by complex processes, what we need are simple processes that enable the organisation to do what it needs to do. In reengineered organisations:

- *Jobs are combined*. The person who sells you the idea and then designs and estimates your new kitchen using Kitchenco Ltd products also schedules the installer, checks that the work has been done, and sends you the bill. This change from job specialisation to job integration is called moving to a *case worker process*.

- *Workers make decisions*. The man who calls to install your new gas meter doesn't say 'I'll have to ask the supervisor, I'll be back in the morning', but makes his own decision about the installation as he is empowered to do through a less complex process.

- *Work is done where it makes most sense to do it*. This may well mean relocating work across organisational boundaries to improve the overall performance of the process.

- *Checks and controls are reduced*. Reengineered processes use controls only to the extent that they make economic sense. Expense claims in a company have to be signed by a division's financial controller if they are for more than £100. He's based at a different site so the claim is copied in case the original goes astray. When the financial controller gets the claim – assuming he's not away – he authorises it and sends it to the central DP site for processing. This happens at the end of the week, and a few days later the individual is paid. The process takes up to three weeks, by which time the individual is on the road again. He gets fed up with funding the company's cash balance so uses the 'advance on expenses' procedure as well in order to get a cash advance. This also involves forms, and signatures and controls. It's a clear case for reengineering the way employees' travel costs are covered.

Modern information technology is part of the reengineering effort, but only if it is part of the revolution. Using IT to do faster what we already do now is not using IT to help reengineer the organisation. The key question is 'How can we use IT to do things that we're not doing now?'

24.6 Conversations and Conclusions

As well as giving their personal views about issues that they think are important, panel members were asked to comment on some of the topics in this chapter and in particular on how they saw the nature of work changing, on how IS/IT might influence organisation structures, on new application areas for IS development, and on the Internet.

There were no surprises when it came to discussing the changing nature of work. Organisations will seek to eliminate 'non-productive' jobs, there will be a greater emphasis on having the best people close to the customer and in product development, and opportunities to work at home will increase. There will be a greater requirement for team working and managing the business through projects.

The move towards matrix organisation structures will continue in large organisations, and technology will continue to support downsizing, globalisation and customer focus. Not everyone saw the extreme customer-centric organisation postulated by Ezingeard as a practical proposition, but organisation structures will change. In spite of some dinosaur command and control structures continuing to exist, future structures will be increasingly networked, with the use of virtual teams becoming commonplace. The panel thought that the limits of the organisation would become blurred where it overlapped with its IT provider or supply chain partners, and although the virtual organisation as set out in Figure 24.2 may be a little way off, there are clear moves towards it.

There were different views about new application areas and the Internet. One view was that there was no new 'killer application' that would fuel IT investment, and another was that greater and greater customer focus would lead to significant change. The development of knowledge management systems was seen as essential in order to compete globally. Early implications had failed to materialise because of lack of fit with corporate cultures, and because of entrenched attitudes about power, but effective applications in the future will be essential for

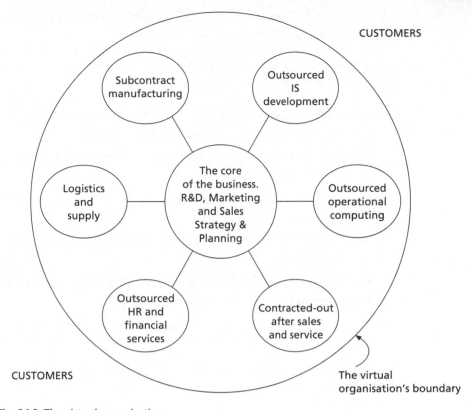

Fig. 24.2 The virtual organisation

global players. There was also an expectation that mobile applications would increase as workforces themselves become more scattered and increasingly mobile.

What of the Internet? There was a universal agreement that the Internet will change the way business is done. It is already changing the way we shop, and book holidays, plane travel and car hire. 'Reaction against the Internet is just an over-reaction, as was the dot.com boom for it,' said one of our panel. There were differences of opinion about where it's going and how fast it's moving. Will we use it for product research and then buy our new car from a showroom, or will we do the opposite and view the models in the showroom and buy online from the lowest-cost provider? Will the most profitable and dramatic applications be business to business (B2B) or business to consumer (B2C)? Certainly B2B applications have had a dramatic impact, with huge volumes of business being transacted, where the cost of the sale is low and the value is high.

Nigel Underwood

Nigel is the Chief Information Officer and a member of the Executive Board of Exel plc, the worldwide logistics company. He has about 1000 IT professionals working for him across the globe. IT is central to Exel's business and an increasingly important component in the solutions they offer to customers. Before joining Exel, Nigel worked for Boots and Mars, Coca Cola Schweppes and the

Hilton Group. Outside work he's passionate about soccer, and he's a qualified Football Association referee and coach.

Based on his experiences with the blue chip employers where he's worked, Nigel was asked whether he has some 'golden rules for analysts in the 21st century'. He suggests the following:

- Work in an organisation where the work is interesting and exciting. You'll have to work hard, so you might as well enjoy it.

- Think about your customer's customer and the business benefit of the systems you're developing.

- In your approach, deliver benefits early. Show the answer, don't just describe the needs.

- Benchmark what you do against the best, not just against similar organisations.

- Develop your skills all the time – soft skills as well as technical ones, and broad-based business skills and knowledge.

- Be a team player. Develop team skills and learn how to manage teams. Build a strong network of contacts in your organisation and in the IT industry.

- As well as doing all of this, aim to get the balance right between work and family or leisure time.

Nigel also highlighted a couple of the technological challenges facing systems analysts. 'First, there's the issue of bespoke development versus the use of packages. The use of packages will increase. These may be enterprise-wide integrated solutions, but for companies like Exel, where IS is part of the solution we offer, there will be an increasing use of company-developed solutions that can be customised. Traditionally I think that analysts have regarded the implementation of packages and products as less demanding than bespoke solution development. But, with the increased emphasis on low-risk quick implementations and the impact that this has for organisational change, I believe that analysts' skills will be fully taxed!'

The second issue he raised was the increasing use of browser-based applications that give universal access to corporate data and systems. Applications now reach out to suppliers, business partners, customers and the general public, and there are huge security implications.

Finally he wanted to emphasise a point about the way analysts and designers do their work. It's not the same everywhere. Different organisations demand the analysts work differently. The organisation's size, the industry it's in, its spread nationally or internationally, the whole organisational culture mean that analysts have to be skilled enough to understand the context within which they'll be applying their skills. In particular, 'for Exel and other global IT-intensive organisations more and more work is done directly for customers. This has implications for the skills analysts need. In this kind of world, IS is not an overhead, it's a revenue-enhancing activity.'

Debra Paul

Debbie has worked in the IT business for 20 years, in the public sector, in computing services and as a self-employer trainer and consultant. She is now a partner in Assist Knowledge Development in the UK. She is particularly involved in business analysis consultancy and training, and contributes to UK national training initiatives in this area through her work with the Information Systems Examination Board's work in setting syllabuses and organising examination for systems analysts. Together with her husband Alan, she contributed to *Project Management for Information Systems*, also published by Pearson.

Her immediate concerns for systems analysts are that, although research consistently shows that projects fail to deliver because of poor requirements analysis, the trend seems to be to reduce analysis effort still further, and that newer approaches are aimed at speeding up analysis rather than improving quality. To her clients she emphasises the need for analysts to understand the business and to develop their interpersonal skills, and to analysts everywhere she emphasises the need to take charge of and be responsible for their own development. This last point connects strongly to the notion of employability mentioned elsewhere in this chapter.

She believes that the big issues for the future are around the integration of systems and the way systems talk to each other, and the flexibility with which systems are designed. Increased globalisation, mergers and acquisitions bring a need for fast integration of systems. The need to rebalance the organisation and to change the ways it works mean that systems need to be flexible enough to meet ever-changing organisation structures.

Frank Jones

Frank is Chairman of Schlumberger plc, a worldwide oilfield and computing services organisation. As a new graduate in the early 1970s he joined a computer manufacturer, working first as a programmer on customer sites, and then worked for computer users as a systems analyst and manager of system development teams ranging in size from 10 to 250. A move into computing services brought him into the Sema Group – an Anglo-French organisation – where he was responsible for global outsourcing, and all local business in Asia and Northern Europe. He took on his Schlumberger appointment following their acquisition of Sema Group.

Looking back over 30 years in IT, Frank's view is that, in spite of the huge changes in technology, the fundamentals of systems analysis haven't changed all that much. The essence of it he says is that 'you're going to analyse and change the way business processes are carried out. The new processes may be faster, more productive or more cost-effective, and new technologies offer many more possibilities for solutions, but above everything you have to meet the user's requirements.' He sees that there is a greater pressure now to get systems developed and implemented quickly, and that although collaborative development processes with users or application packages contribute to this, there is a danger that this results in fragmented systems development.

'This in turn has led to new developments aimed at solving the "fragmentation issue". The first is the development of the systems architecture function in an attempt to ensure that all new systems will be able to communicate with each other. The buzz word here is "interoperability". Second, a range of middleware products have come into being designed to link together independently developed systems. The third approach is that organisations sign up to enterprise-wide integrated software solutions where the integration problems have already been solved'.

Frank also makes the same point as Debbie Paul and Richard Bevan about the overriding need for analysts to 'have very good interpersonal skills' to ensure that the intended users 'buy in' to the development process and to the resultant new system.

Jean-Noel Ezingeard

Dr Jean-Noel Ezingeard is a tutor and researcher in information management and performance management at Henley Management College in the UK – one of Europe's premier business schools. He teaches on the worldwide MBA programme and on corporate programmes for clients in Europe. He is currently researching into the business objectives of customer relationship management systems, and on IT security and the board of directors. His personal statement about customer-centric organisations, IS strategy and requirements is shown as Box 24.1.

Box 24.1 Towards the customer-centric information system

Many organisations have implemented CRM (customer relationship management) software to support their operations and marketing activities, but some have gone further and have reinvented themselves as *customer-centric*. In the late 1990s, for instance, industrial giant ABB found that its customers across the world no longer wanted to see a different salesperson for each group of products they bought from the company. ABB reacted quickly and reinvented itself as a customer-centric organisation serving its markets through key account managers, and forced its decentralised operations to cooperate. It also meant that the company had to reinvent the way it managed information, previously spread around over 500 ERP systems.

Similar stories take place every day in public institutions. Many public services across the world are also being reorganised to offer 'one-stop shops' for citizens. It does not make sense from either a customer service point of view or a resource utilisation point of view to expect people to register separately at their local sports centre, local library and local swimming pool when the same local authority manages all three services. Having a one-stop registration process, however, means that information systems have to be reinvented to support more than just 'products'.

The drive towards customer-centric information systems is not only a result of customers no longer tolerating clumsy customer service processes.

More and more companies realise that being customer-centric can be a powerful source of competitive advantage by enhancing the value of relationships between an organisation and its customers. This is at three levels: first by making the acquisition of new customers cheaper, second by increasing the retention rate of existing customers, and third by increasing the value of this relationship, through reduced costs of servicing or enhanced revenue. This drive towards more customer-centricity in IS is having a profound impact about how organisations think about IS. It means thinking about customer needs throughout the development of the system, and is therefore having an impact at four key stages of systems life cycles: IS strategy development, requirements analysis, implementation, and evaluation.

At the level of the *IS strategy*, the well-rehearsed issue of alignment between business strategy and IS strategy remains critical, but how does a focus on the customer influence IS strategy? At a fundamental level, understanding customers means having enough information about them. This information needs to be collected over time. Such a customer-centric IS strategy will therefore also acknowledge that any outsourcing decision will need to cover information collection and ownership principles. In August 2001 Centrica announced that it had paid £85 million (€133 m) for a database of 1.1 million files of its Goldfish credit card customers. Goldfish was already a Centrica brand, but it had outsourced the operations of the credit card to HFC bank, which also owned the database of customer information. When the relationship between HFC bank and Centrica soured, finding a new partner to run the operations was easy for Centrica, but the company found it also needed information that it didn't own. Replacing the technology partner was easy, but a hefty price had to be paid for the customer information. A customer-oriented IS strategy will therefore be one that acknowledges that *customer information is a valuable asset*.

When looking at *requirements analysis*, customer orientation is having an important impact at two levels

- *The need to manage requirements uncertainty*. If the system is going to be opened to customers, what will the requirements of these customers be? In some cases some are fairly clear. For example, online shoppers expect easy user interfaces, fast download times, and secure transactions. But in other areas of web-enabled IS much uncertainty has to be managed at the system development level about how users are actually going to use the site. Let's think for instance of a patient information website run by a local hospital, allowing patients to access test results or book appointments online. Will patients expect the web site to remember them when they come back for their next visit, or will they be more concerned about protecting their privacy?

- *The need to build for an unclear future*. Will the system developed still meet the needs of the organisation's customers? When UK bank First Direct introduced PC banking in the late 1990s, it did so using a client–server model that required customers to dial a dedicated phone number to establish a dedicated conneition between the bank's servers and the customers' PC. It became clear 2 years later, with the widespread availability of Internet banking, that customers expected to be able to access the bank without a dedicated connection, over the Internet. Fortunately, the systems used by the bank used browser/web-server technology to support PC banking, and the bank was able to offer Internet access almost at the flick of a switch.

At the *implementation* level, being customer-centric often means the need to ensure *seamless integration of information* from and to all customer 'touch points'. Few companies have the luxury of a greenfield start-up operation, and need to work with legacy systems and legacy information. When UK bank the Woolwich launched its Openplan product, it had to think about how it could integrate all customer information into a top-level view of the customer's financial affairs that could be accessed from any touch point (digital TV, Internet, branches, mobile phones). Most of the bank's existing products (current accounts, mortgages, loans, credit cards) were supported by separate IT systems. It also meant that the bank had to think about how to support a wide array of interfaces, ranging from small WAP-phone screens to call centre PCs.

Evaluating customer-centric IS also requires a new mindset. By definition such systems are designed to influence interactions with customers and enhance the relationship between the organisation and buyers. The impact of the system must therefore be sought and evaluated beyond the boundaries of the organisation. Traditional systems evaluation techniques based on user satisfaction, productivity enhancements or return on investment may not be sufficient. How can we capture, for instance, the impact of an information system on trust and commitment of customers towards the organisation?

Being more radical, it is also interesting to speculate about what taking customer-centricity to the extreme could mean in IS terms. Ultimately, it is possible to imagine organisations wanting to tailor their business processes for each of their customers. This would mean (a) an intimate knowledge of what the customer's requirements are, and (b) an extremely flexible IS capable of supporting an infinite variety (or at least a very large number) of business processes. Even if we're being more conservative, bringing customer-centricity to IS development is increasingly likely to become a competitive necessity for many organisations. This is as much about changing mind sets as it is about changing development tools and techniques. Customer-centricity means thinking about how the system will look in the eyes of the customer, whether this customer is in contact with the system directly or not. It means thinking about how the business process supported (or created) by the system will look to customers, from the customers' point of view. It means thinking about how the relationship with the customer could develop in the long term and what resulting information requirements emerge.

Richard Bevan

Richard is the Director of IT for Pearson Education in the UK – the publisher of this book. He is also the Customer Management Director responsible for a call centre and order processing: in his words it 'brings him closer to the heart of the business'. It is often said that the IT function should be represented at board level, so that it can be fully integrated in top-level business decision-making processes, so it is interesting to see an IT director also operating as a line director responsible for part of Pearson Education's value chain.

Beginning his IT life in the late 1980s, Richard has been a computer operator, a programmer and a project manager, and developed his career 'up the management ladder' in the publishing sector. As you might expect from someone who has developed his career in this way, he's a great believer in self-development, having read for an MBA from the Open University and qualified as a Master Practitioner in Neuro Linguistic Programming. 'NLP informs your whole approach to dealing with people,' he says, 'and this will become increasingly important in the future.'

Richard believes that fewer people in organisations will become busier and busier. The spread of their responsibilities will increase, and inevitably they will not have the time to know the detail of their business. Also they will have less and less time to become involved in systems development. Analysts therefore will need to become very effective in managing their interactions with the user community. This illustrates his view that the 'more people-orientated analysts are, the greater the value they bring.'

He also has some ideas about new areas of application development, and believes that there will be two key areas of change in application development. He says:

> Following the huge investments in applications that were made leading up to the Year 2000, a lull in systems investment has quite naturally occurred. It is my view that this lull will draw to a close in early 2003 and, although there are no new killer applications out there for organisations to be drawn to, it is my belief that investment will instead be driven to towards truly integrating the applications they are already using.
>
> The second key area of change will be around the way in which new applications are generated. As organisations become truly more virtual, with an increase in multi-located teams with home working and hot desking, the current model of face-to-face contact between systems analysts and their business users will have to adapt and change. In addition, in most businesses, the continued drive to become leaner will mean that staff identified to represent the business on developments of new applications will have to spend more of their time on their 'day jobs'.
>
> A consequence of this change will be a fundamental shift in the emphasis of skills required of a system analyst. Limited time and restrictions on the amount of face-to-face meetings with business users will necessitate increased emphasis on softer people skills. It will be critical to build rapport and confidence with business users quickly and effectively – earning credibility with the business community will have to be a more dynamic process. The

cultivation of a good network of key business resources, which can be drawn on, and more importantly trusted to deliver what is required, will be a primary concern. All of this can be achieved only with the right people skills and by achieving the balance between soft and technical abilities.

In my opinion, there are five points for the next generation of systems analyst to focus on:

- Think people and not just systems – close, effective relationships with the business will help to build new systems that the business community feel they own and are committed to implement and use.

- Become skilled at gathering the information you need from phone and email communication – face-to-face meetings will become an expensive luxury.

- Take personal responsibility for effective communication – the message is only as effective as the response you get. Don't assume that because you have asked someone to do something they will; always check for understanding, making sure the users really understand what is required from them.

- Don't be afraid to 'spoon feed' information to your business users – they have a limited amount of time to work on your projects and will be glad to have well-prepared information delivered to them.

- Check for your own understanding on information delivered back to you – where necessary you may have to interpret the answer given. Look for the hidden messages that are not necessarily held with the words spoken or written – only 7% of communication is verbal; listen to voice tonality, and if you are in face-to-face meetings watch physiology to discover what people are really thinking.

Essentially, the message I am delivering here is to concentrate on developing in the softer skills areas, as well as being the best systems analyst you can be. Never underestimate your ability to influence your career, critically don't wait for others to come along and offer you opportunities to develop, seek them out for yourself. The better your communication, influencing and rapport-building skills and the more flexible you can be around people, the more likely you are to be able to get people to see your point of view. Never forget that all of your success will be driven by other people's opinions of you and your ability to effect and shape those opinions.

Consistent with his views on self-development, since we had our conversation Richard has set up his own business called Transcend Excellence and now spends all of his time putting his ideas into practice working on organisational development, team dynamics and executive coaching.

This chapter has tried to encourage you to question why things are the way they are, and to suggest that the life of a systems analyst will be different in the future. The future will not be like the past.

Firstly, the business reasons for investing in IT were:

- from the 1960s onwards they were to improve productivity;

- from the 1970s onwards – to improve managerial effectiveness;

- from the 1980s onwards – to create competitive advantage;

- from the 1990s onwards – to do business differently by reducing costs and improving; quality, by improving customer service and by increasing flexibility to improve responsiveness to change;

- in the 21st century the Internet and the Intranet will change the way business is done and the way organisations are organised.

These reasons for investing in IT will operate within a framework of organisational transformation that will see:

- the orientation of business move from product to customer;

- mass production be replaced by flexible, on-demand production;

- increasing value come from intangibles like customer satisfaction and quality;

- an organisation's intellectual assets being with knowledge workers and not with management;

- rewards given for performance and not for loyalty and seniority;

- competition that is global and not national;

- organisation structures that move from functional or hierarchical structures to networked and matrix structures;

- economic relationships that move from take-overs and vertical integration to alliances.

It is within these new and radically different circumstances that new analysts will work.

Bibliography and Web References

We have not attempted to provide an exhaustive list of web references or of suggested reading. The web changes frequently, and the danger is that sites that we might recommend today may not be useful when you come to look at them. Also we don't think that a long bibliography is helpful. Listing dozens of articles and books isn't necessarily helpful either in what we hope is a practical book like this one.

So, we've suggested a few websites that we find helpful and useful that might appeal to you, plus a few books that will give you the opportunity to take your interests in systems analysis and design further after you've gained some practical experience to add to your reading of the book.

Websites

www.dilbert.com

We all need to lighten up sometimes, and joining in the surreal world of Dilbert, who loves technology for the sake of it, Dogbert, The Boss with the spiky hair and the passion for the bottom line, Wally and Alice will help us to do that. More worryingly, however, the cartoon strip has useful messages for everyone in business.

www.bcs.org.uk

This is the home page of the British Computer Society – the only chartered engineering institution for IS professionals. It has over 38 000 members and is the leading professional and learned society in computing and IS. You should at least view the site regularly, and if you're not yet a member you might also consider joining by taking advantage of the new and more inclusive grades of membership.

www.iseb.org.uk

This is the home page for the Information Systems Examinations Board. It is part of the BCS and provides industry-recognised qualifications that measure competence, ability and performance in many areas of IS with the aim of promoting career development. Subject areas include business and management skills, systems development, data protection, DSDM, information and computer technology, information security management, IS consultancy practice, and project management.

www.brook/its/cei

For more about ethical issues try the Computer Ethics Institute at the Brookings Institution in Washington DC. Also, the University of British Colombia in Canada has things to say at www.ethics.ubc.ca

www.acm.org

The Association of Computing Machinery was founded in 1947 in the USA. It has 75 000 members. The site is well worth a visit. As a student member you get free access to online courses.

www.whatis.techtarget.com

To find out 'what is spam?' – unsolicited email on the Internet – and how to deal with it use this site. It is a good starting point for definitions, explanations and links to other sites.

www.zdnet.co.uk

This is a technology news site. As well as hard news it has career planning information that looked interesting when we reviewed it.

www.google.co.uk

Finally of course there's www.google.co.uk. Google is more useful in many ways than 'whatis', but you need to use it carefully. It came up with 24 000 matches from the UK alone for 'entity life history' including an ELH for a bank account together with a 20 PowerPoint slide presentation describing how the ELH worked.

www.computer.org

This is the American Institute of Electrical and Electronic Engineers Computer Society. It is a good source of technical information, news and comment. It has a free distance learning campus and many non-US members, so it is worth a look.

www.smartdraw.com

Smartdraw is a software-drawing package, but the site also has information and tutorials. Look under 'cool examples' on the Home page for links to entity relationship diagrams, SSADM, DFSs, etc.

www.cio.com

This is a website for chief information officers and has been in operation since 1995. It has good news, comment and feature content, and an 'analyst corner'.

There is a research centre that, when we looked at it, had information on data mining and e-business.

www.computing.co.uk

News, comment and features from *Computing* newspaper.

Remember that, with all of these sites, you need to log on regularly if you are to get the best use out of them.

Further reading

Philip L. Weaver, Nick Lambrou and Matthew Walkley, *Practical SSADM Version 4+: A Complete Tutorial Guide*, 2nd edn, London: Financial Times Pitman, 1998
Gives a more detailed treatment of the SSADM approach.

Simon Bennett, Steve McRobb and Ray Farmer, *Object Oriented Systems Analysis and Design using UML*, London: McGraw-Hill, 1999
For a more detailed treatment of the OO approach.

Kenneth C. Laudon and Jane P. Laudon, *Management Information Systems: Organization and Technology in the Networked Enterprise*, 6th edn, Upper Saddle River, NJ: Prentice Hall, 1999
Gives a more general background on the information and communications technology aspects of the ISEB syllabus.

Wendy Robson, *Strategic Management and Information Systems: An Integrated Approach*, 2nd edn, London: Pitman, 1997
Deals with a strategic approach to the development of information systems, seen from the management point of view.

Timothy Cleary, *Business Information Technology*, London: Pitman, 1998
Quite a useful text on hardware and software aspects of the ISEB syllabus.

Paul Bocij *et al.*, *Business Information Systems: Technology, Development and Management for the e-Business*, 2nd edn (ed. Dave Chaffey), Harlow: Financial Times/Prentice Hall, 2003
Covers hardware, IS development and management issues.

James Cadle and Donald Yeates, *Project Management for Information Systems*, 3rd edn, Harlow: Financial Times/Prentice Hall, 2001
A practical book that gives a more detailed coverage of the project management issues that arise in the development life cycle.

David Avison and Guy Fitzgerald, *Information Systems Development: Methodologies, Techniques and Tools*, 3rd edn, London: McGraw-Hill, 2002
For a good general overview of the different approaches to systems analysis.

Efraim Turban and David R. King, *Introduction to e-Commerce*, Upper Saddle River, NJ: Prentice Hall, 2003
Gives more detailed knowledge about the features of the Internet and the way in which e-commerce operates. This text is aimed at the business analyst level rather than the technologist.

Peter Coad. and Edward Yourdon *Object-Oriented Analysis* (2nd Ed.), Englewood Cliffs, NJ: Yourdon Press; Prentice-Hall, 1990
A well-known text on OO analysis.

Apple Computers Inc. *Macintosh Human Interface Guidelines* Addison-Wesley, 1993

Appendix 1
An Analysis and Design
Case Study Using
Structured Methods

Using the Denton Motor Holdings Case Study

The job of the systems analyst involves dealing with people as much as, perhaps more than, dealing with computers, databases and software. Interviewing users, understanding the concerns and requirements of managers, and communicating these requirements to programmers and developers are tasks that rely on the communication skills rather than the technical knowledge of the analyst. This case study is used to illustrate some of the themes pursued in this book. It opens with a description of the Denton Motor Company, a business that supplies spare parts to motorcyclists. The description focuses on the company's managers, identifying their roles and responsibilities and briefly describing their personalities.

The case study has been written to be used on an individual or class basis. An individual reader might adopt the position of a consultant systems analyst who has been asked to investigate the requirements of the Denton Motor Company, and a class could use the material as the basis for role plays, presentations and the development of a structured picture of the way the company works followed by recommendations for new systems. Figure A1.1 shows some of the things you could do.

In both cases there is a list of deliverables that you could prepare about Denton Motor Holdings.

An Introduction to Denton Motor Holdings plc

Denton Motor Holdings plc (DMH) is a holding company for a group of companies supplying services to motorcyclists. The holding company has been in existence for six months following a restructuring exercise that has been carried out on a small independent motorcycle manufacturing concern known as Denton Motors Ltd. Denton Motors originally consisted of two divisions – a manufacturing division and a spares division. The company originally started by manufacturing motorcycles and scooters from components, most of which were bought in

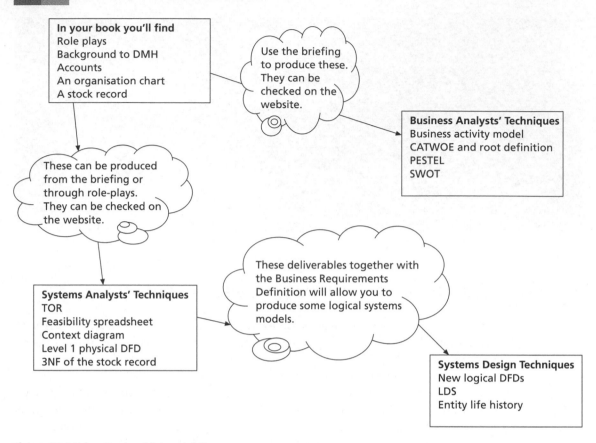

In your book you'll find
Role plays
Background to DMH
Accounts
An organisation chart
A stock record

Use the briefing to produce these. They can be checked on the website.

Business Analysts' Techniques
Business activity model
CATWOE and root definition
PESTEL
SWOT

These can be produced from the briefing or through role-plays. They can be checked on the website.

Systems Analysts' Techniques
TOR
Feasibility spreadsheet
Context diagram
Level 1 physical DFD
3NF of the stock record

These deliverables together with the Business Requirements Definition will allow you to produce some logical systems models.

Systems Design Techniques
New logical DFDs
LDS
Entity life history

Figure A1.1 Using Denton Motor Holdings

from other manufacturers. They provided a spares service from the stock they bought in or manufactured for production purposes. As demand increased they extended their range to include a high-performance super-bike aimed at the higher end of the market. Although this was well received by motorcycling enthusiasts it was not a profitable line and, after losing money on the super-bike for eight years, the company reluctantly decided to concentrate on their 'bread and butter' models that were still selling well. As sales increased they encountered problems, with demands from dealers for spares being in conflict with their requirements for production.

Around this time the company embarked on a number of exercises aimed at improving their overall efficiency, and following the advice of consultants KDW it was decided that they should split into two divisions, one division being responsible for manufacturing, and a new division being created to capitalise on the increasingly profitable sale of spares.

This spares division was established as a separate company – known as Denton Spares – with its own site and staff. Although a senior management committee drawn from the manufacturing company staff was set up, the spares division continued to experience problems, many of which stemmed from the large stockholding they inherited at the outset and from the antiquated methods used for processing orders and controlling stocks. A consultants' report from that period illustrated the volumes and problems the company experienced.

Several different approaches were attempted by Denton Spares to solve these problems. Initially they introduced a manual card-based forecasting system; this needless to say rapidly failed owing to the volume of calculation required. Subsequently they introduced a stock-recording system on the mainframe used by the Denton manufacturing division. This latter system is still in operation, although it is still not solving their problems.

The DMH Chairman is John Milton, whose background is in corporate finance rather than the motor trade. It is generally understood that the need to change has stemmed from him, and that he favours a rapid rate of change that will show immediate benefits. There is plenty of evidence to suggest that he is not afraid of spending money, but any investments must quickly show a return. Other senior posts include: the Managing Director Denton Spares, Richard Chievley; the Sales Manager Denton Spares, John Mattison; the Order Office Manager, Simon Martindale; the Stock Control Manager, Tom Taylor; the Purchasing Manager, Robert Somers; and the Warehouse Manager, Henry Johnson.

DMH Roles and Responsibilities

John Milton, Chairman

John Milton is 44 years old and was appointed chairman of the DMH board when the holding company was formed six months ago. The merchant bank Stein McGregor brought DMH to the market, and the group's share price rose in the first six months of trading. John Milton started his career as a Courtaulds management trainee, having obtained a first-class honours degree in economics at Nottingham University. At the age of 29 he became the youngest Managing Director of any Courtaulds subsidiary, and following a four-year period in

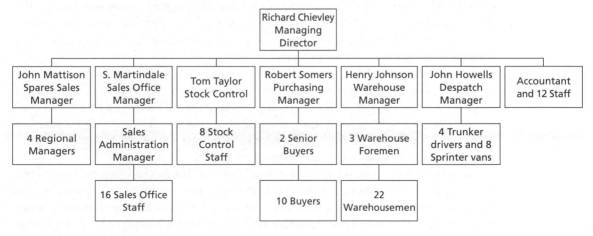

Figure A1.2 Company Organisation

America with General Electric he returned to the UK and joined Stein UK, a medium-sized merchant bank. Specialising in the financing of medium-scale engineering companies, he was appointed a director of Stein after five years, with special responsibility for finance in the manufacturing sector. In this capacity he has been seconded to government working parties on industrial development on several occasions. Following a serious car accident two years ago he became disenchanted with his position in the bank, and when Stein's merged with the Scottish bank McGregor's he resigned. In his position as Chairman he is inclined to attempt to take an executive role by influencing other board members.

John Milton is on trial. He has a good record in finance and as a consultant, but he has not been in the role of a plc Chairman before. He has, however, hounded a few chairmen in his time with Stein's. Although DMH is valued well on account of its assets, the spares company is not performing well, and he feels that he has to turn it round quickly. An opportunity exists to buy a chain of retail outlets, which would greatly increase the turnover of the company without a large increase in costs, provided the administration can be brought under control.

His vision is to expand into retail spares and introduce a streamlined order-processing system that will also provide more realistic control of stock levels. He envisages direct ordering from the retail outlets, and would include a direct ordering system for the existing dealers. He believes it is essential for the manufacturing company and the spares company to function as two entirely independent units.

Richard Chievley, Managing Director

Richard Chievley is an accountant by training, and was promoted to the position of Managing Director of Denton Spares when DMH was formed. He had previously been Chief Accountant for DMC with responsibility for both the spares division and the manufacturing division. For some years he had been advocating change within the spares division but the changes had always been thwarted by internal disagreements. The legacy stock recording system, which is run on the manufacturing company's mainframe, was introduced through his efforts some years ago, but planned enhancements to the system have never taken place and this has consequently reduced its effectiveness.

Currently he is solely concerned with the control of the stockholding within Denton Spares. Although the stock-recording system was set up to reduce the stock levels, the reorder levels – which were taken from the original stock cards – were hopelessly out of date, and reordering is still largely under the control of Henry Johnson, the Warehouse Manager. Richard Chievley is attempting to restructure the company to gain more control of this.

He is fairly conservative by nature, and looks at the bottom line when making his judgements on a business proposition. He is not a natural enthusiast, and is rather a quiet person. He is aware that Denton Spares needs to be turned around, and that he will need to work on this with the group Chairman. He is in favour of correcting the present system before becoming involved in any expansion.

John Mattison, Sales Manager

John Mattison is Denton Spares Sales Manager. He has experience of the spares-ordering system, having previously spent many years in charge of the sales order office in the spares division. He has a good knowledge of the dealers, and is used to dealing with their problems. He has absolutely no knowledge of the spares business outside this, and is having difficulty coming to terms with the idea that Denton Spares will deal with a wider range of customers.

He is responsible for generating sales for spares from the dealers. He spent 10 years managing the Sales Order Office, and has good relationships with the dealers, although he has very little experience in sales. He has four Regional Managers who visit dealers to discuss with them their requirements from Denton Spares and to encourage them to maintain satisfactory stock levels of accessory items to avoid too many small orders. He has not established any set routines, and is at times 'at a loss' to know exactly what he should be doing in his new role. Although the Regional Managers visit the dealers, the dealers all deal directly with the Sales Order Office when they are placing orders.

Simon Martindale, Sales Order Office Manager

Simon Martindale was appointed Sales Order Office Manager when John Mattison became Sales Manager. He is 28 and has had experience outside Denton, having worked for a DMH dealer for eight years. He completed a motor trade apprenticeship during this time, and has also obtained a Diploma in Business Studies through evening classes. Simon Martindale is a PC enthusiast. He is fairly knowledgeable about PC software and is keen to expand his empire in this direction.

He is responsible for the running of the Sales Order Office. The office has installed a networked PC system that was intended to act as an order entry system for all orders. The system uses MS-Access and was written by Simon Martindale with the help of an industrial placement student and a contract programmer over the past two years. The system was intended to take orders and to allow the order office to respond to dealers' queries on stock availability by using a link to the mainframe. The orders entered locally on the PCs were then going to be transmitted to the mainframe to update the stock file and to produce dealer invoices.

Several problems have been encountered in introducing this system. The access to the mainframe has been problematical. The DM manufacturing division personnel have not taken a lot of interest in the development of the spares division stock-recording system, and have regarded the requests of the order-processing section as a nuisance. They have offered some half-hearted advice to Simon Martindale on the use of a 4GL to interrogate the stock file, but they have not been very helpful on the downloading of the stock file. On the one occasion they managed to do this the DM manufacturing systems programmer took a whole day on site at the spares division and, making numerous phone calls to the computer room, managed to download the file onto a PC that was intended to act as a file server. Simon and the placement student tried several times to repeat this transfer but they were unable to make it work.

Currently the order office works in two ways. Some of the clerks found it difficult to adapt to the new PC system, and it was eventually decided to retain a group of them to write picking notes by hand using a top copy and a separate sheet for each item. The clerks working in this way arrange the item sheets in bin number sequence to allow the storemen to pick items from the shelf in the order that they are stored. Some orders are, however, keyed into the PCs and they are then sorted into the DM bin number sequence, this being the part number used by the company. Picking notes and dispatch notes are then printed. These picking/dispatch notes are then sent to the warehouse as they are created, and the sales order office clerk retains the order in a temporary file on their own PC. The clerks have recently set up a system whereby they pass some of their larger orders on floppy disks to the stock control department so that the data does not have to be re-entered to update the stock file. This has helped to keep up with the considerable increase in workload that this department has had to absorb following the introduction of the stock records on the mainframe. The handwritten orders need a dispatch note before they can be sent; they are returned to the Sales Order Office after they have been picked, and they are then entered as PC orders to obtain a dispatch note. The dispatch note has then to be taken to the stores and attached to the goods before the goods can be delivered to the dealer.

The split of orders between the manual system and the PC system varies according to the number of large orders received. The orders are received in two batches through the post, with a few orders being brought in manually by the Regional Managers. This is a hangover from the days when spares and manufacturing were one company and the salesforce covered both car sales and spares sales. In general the split is about 50/50 between manual and PC based.

Unfulfilled manual orders are refiled under the dealer name as they were before the PC system was introduced. The PC system orders are handled in the same way except for the fact that the PC order has the quantity to follow marked alongside each item on the order form. The staff in the order office generally agree that reducing the amount of paper they handle has made their job considerably easier.

Tom Taylor, Stock Control Manager

Tom Taylor has worked for Denton for eight years. He was originally brought into the company to run a manual forecasting system that was aimed at reducing the company's stockholding by manually forecasting demand. This system rapidly failed, and he was reduced to maintaining a system based on manual stock cards that seemed to be perpetually wrong. When it was decided three years ago that the number of clerical staff would have to be reduced dramatically, Tom Taylor was given the task of transferring the company's manual records onto the mainframe system. This was achieved successfully, and the present recording system can give an accurate stock valuation on a regular basis. The sales analysis system produces monthly turnover figures showing the volume of sales per stock item per period.

Part No: A106					Delivery Period: *2 Weeks*	Re-order level: *28*
					Av. daily use:	Danger level:
Date	Goods in serial No	Dispatch note serial No	Quantity IN	Quantity OUT	Actual stock check	Balance

Figure A1.3 Stock record card

The Spares Stock Control Department is really a data entry section rather than a stock control department. Tom Taylor's main task is to ensure that the details of the day's orders are correctly entered into the system to update the stock records on the mainframe. Currently the data is taken on a daily basis to DMH Manufacturing on floppy disks. The department has eight keyboard operators, who enter the dispatch details either from the handwritten picking notes or from the PC produced picking notes.

Tom Taylor is a little cynical about Denton Motor Holdings, but would respond to the provision of a system that would genuinely allow him to control the stockholding. The dispatch notes he receives from the warehouse have invariably been altered because of the items that are out of stock, and so he always re-enters all of the order data, and has now ceased to use the floppy disks that are sent to him from the Sales Order Office. Sometimes, when an order has been changed a lot, he will produce a new copy of the dispatch note to go with the goods.

All the goods inwards documentation comes through Tom Taylor's office. These details are also keyed onto the floppy disks. When the Stock Control Office have finished with the order document they return them to the Sales Order Office. The goods inwards notes are sent to the Purchasing Department.

Robert Somers, Purchasing Manager

Robert Somers, the Purchasing Manager, has never been in a position to exercise very much control over the stock replenishment policy. Replenishment orders are raised from a tabulation that is produced on a weekly basis by the mainframe system, although it is common practice for the Warehouse Manager to contact him during the week and advise him of urgent requirements. Currently there is some confusion and duplication over the reordering process, and Somers is aware of this.

The weekly reorder tabulation is received from the mainframe system on Friday. Clerical staff prepare purchase orders and mark each order number on the tabulation, which is returned to the mainframe data input section, where the purchase order data is entered and the stock record is updated.

Goods inwards notes are reconciled with purchase orders when time permits. They are received from the Stock Control Department after the data has been captured and sent to the mainframe for stock recording.

Henry Johnson, Warehouse Manager

Henry Johnson is the Warehouse Manager, and still retains a considerable measure of control over the way the company operates although, officially, the reordering process has been taken out of his hands. For a number of years he has operated a three-bin system, and although the mainframe stock-recording system has replaced it, the three-bin operation still survives in a limited way.

Picking documents are received from the Sales Order Office, and these may be printed or handwritten on the dispatch instruction cover sheet and dispatch instruction detail sheet sets. These manual orders are sent back to Simon Martindale after they have been picked so that a dispatch note can be produced. The picking notes/dispatch notes are printed as two copies, one for picking in the warehouse and one to go with the goods.

Henry Johnson is responsible for picking the orders and moving them through to the dispatch foreman, who arranges the deliveries. He is also responsible for moving the new stock from the goods inwards bay to the warehouse and for putting it into the correct warehouse location.

He favours the removal of the present computer system and a return to the three-bin system.

Denton Spares' Present Systems

The systems that Denton Spares use are ones that have evolved over the years rather than ones that have been developed for a specific purpose. They have an enormous warehouse that contains over 50 000 different line items. They have always retained parts for their older machines because there is a market for spares for older bikes in the UK, and because the older designs of their bikes have been manufactured under licence in other countries and Denton Spares supplies them with spares. The warehouse is laid out in bin number sequence, and they have numbered their parts to match the bin numbers. They have four different categories of parts. Engine components are category A; fuel systems, braking systems, suspension units and other major assemblies are category B; electrical components, alternators and security systems are category C; and accessories are category D. In each category the bins are numbered sequentially, and the part number is therefore made up of the category code and the numerical bin number. This enables the warehouse staff to pick items from the store in sequence by sorting the picking lists into bin number order before they start to pick the items.

There have always been problems with the level of stockholding. In the past, manual records were kept, although Denton Spares' present arrangement uses the mainframe computer at the DM manufacturing plant, which is situated 3 miles from the warehouse. The data items on the stock record were all transferred to the mainframe system at DM manufacturing when they automated the system some years ago. This system provides the purchasing department with a weekly printout of the items below reorder level, and this is used in the production of supplier purchase orders. The Purchasing Office record the date these orders are raised on the printout and send it back to the mainframe installation so that the part record can be kept up to date with details of the latest orders that have been placed.

All the other data sent to the mainframe system is sent via the stock control office. A PC is used to capture dispatch data and stock receipt data, which is transferred off-line to the mainframe using floppy disks containing the day's receipts and issues.

The Sales Order Office also has some PC systems. Traditionally, DMH used a paper-based system copied from another spares warehousing company in their area. The details of each item ordered were written on a single dispatch instruction document, and these were sorted into bin number order and sent to the warehouse in a special cover often referred to as a *dispatch instruction cover*. The new Sales Order Office Manager, Simon Martindale, transferred this to a PC system, and now about half of the orders are done on two-part order sets, one part of which is used as the dispatch note. The PCs are used only to sort the items into bin number sequence so that the warehouse staff can pick the items in the order in which they are stored. Simon Martindale always intended to network the PCs and hold stock records on a server on a network. Although he still talks about this, there has been little evidence of any real progress recently. A link between a PC and the mainframe was tested on one occasion by the IT Services at DMH Manufacturing, but generally they have too many other commitments to allow them to progress this system, and the Denton Spares staff lack the technical expertise. Unfortunately, some of Simon Martindale's staff are a little reluctant to use the PCs and still prefer to write out the orders by hand. This doesn't really help very much, as it leaves the orders without a dispatch note when the stores have picked them, and the Stock Control Department is always being called on to produce these so that the goods can be dispatched. Attempts have been made to pass the order data from the Sales Order Office to stock control using floppy disks. However, so many items are found to be out of stock when the orders are picked that these disks are really more trouble than they are worth. Although DMH handles on average only between 100 and 150 orders a day, each of these can be quite large: typically an average order will have 150 items on it, and some can be as large as 750 items.

Any items that are not currently in stock are treated as back orders, and when the order documentation has been processed by the Stock Control Department it is returned to the Sales Order Office so that it can be included in the next order received from that customer. The stock receipts, known as GINs (*goods inwards notes*), also come to the Stock Control Department after the goods have been checked into the stores. When the Stock Control Department has processed them they are sent on to the Purchasing Department to be reconciled with the purchase order and the supplier's invoice when it arrives. The Stock Control Department is little more than a data entry facility, as they do not hold any stock records themselves since these are all held remotely on the mainframe and they have no direct access to them. They collect the orders, goods inwards and goods returned data on a daily basis, key it to disk using PCs, and send the disks by hand to the central mainframe computer department. Again, the possibility of a data communication link has been discussed, but as the mainframe system is batch based and is run nightly there is little benefit to be derived from a link.

Although the stock-recording system on the mainframe computer issues the instructions to purchase to the Purchasing Department, the warehouse has always kept its own system of monitoring stock levels by using a three-bin system. When the reorder point is reached in a particular bin the Warehouse Manager will tell the Purchasing Manager, who often authorises a purchase order immediately. This is because the delay in the turnaround of the purchasing tabulation causes stock-outs.

Denton Motor Holdings
Profit and Loss Account for the Year Ended This Year

	This year £000	Last year £000
Sales	38,200	38,616
Trading profit for the year	2,380	2,960
Income from investments	12	12
Miscellaneous income	8	–
Profit before taxation	2,400	2,972
Taxation (based on profit for the year)	690	892
Profit for the year after taxation – for Appropriation	1,710	2,080
Dividends		
Preference	168	160
Ordinary	552	460
Profit retained in the business	990	1,460

Denton Motor Holdings
Balance Sheet

	This year (£000)	Last year (£000)
Fixed assets		
Land and buildings	2,500	2,500
Fixtures and vehicles	832	780
	--------	--------
	3,332	3,280
Current assets		
Stock (at valuation)	15,000	13,852
Debtors	5,800	5,900
	--------	--------
	20,800	19,752
Current liabilities		
Creditors	3,110	2,400
Bank overdraft	20	518
Dividends	720	620
Taxation	690	892
	--------	--------
	4,540	4,430
Net current assets	16,260	15,322
Net assets employed	19,592	18,602
Financed by:		
Ordinary share capital	13,000	13,000
Preference share capital	4,600	4,600
Profit and loss account	1,992	1,002
	--------	--------
	19,592	18,602

Denton Motor Holdings

The Investigation Stage

The first deliverable that you should produce from the case study is a set of Terms of Reference. Chapter 7 provides guidelines for this. There could be some difference of opinion between senior members of the company about the goals and objectives of your study, and the scope of your study must be agreed. Identify the headings you should use, and prepare a set of terms of reference to be approved by the Board of DMH.

Data Flow Diagrams

Chapter 8 describes how an analyst asks questions and collects data. If you have an opportunity to interview role players then this will give you a more complete picture of the way Denton Motor Spares operates and will give you some useful experience in interviewing users. Alternatively the briefing provides enough information for you to produce DFDs and an entity model depicting the present system.

Current physical data flow diagram

The briefing for the case study provides sufficient information for you to create a current physical data flow diagram of the system showing all the problems and duplications that exist in the present system. Chapter 9 discusses how the information about a current system using data flow diagrams and entity models can be recorded.

Current logical data flow diagram

The second step in the analysis is the conversion of the old physical DFD into an old logical DFD. This will allow you to compare the way DMH actually run their business with the way they intended to run it.

Data Modelling

Entity model

Entity models are initially created from the information acquired during the investigation phase, and there is sufficient detail in the briefing for you to produce an initial entity model.

Normalisation

The stock record card is an ideal document to normalise so as to understand the underlying data structures at DMH. Chapter 17 on logical data design provides the background for this.

Feasibility

A balance sheet and a profit and loss account give you some idea of the financial performance at DMH. From these figures it is possible to consider a financial case for the new system. At this stage you haven't got any realistic estimates of the cost of the development. If you use an assumed figure for the 'once-off' set-up costs and for the ongoing operational costs then you can develop some estimates of the feasibility of the system. Take the initial costs as £250 000 for the hardware and the software and the operational costs as £150 000 a year. Do the figures in the balance sheet indicate that this would be a feasible project and, if so, how soon would it show a return on the investment?

Business Analysis Exercises

CATWOE and root definitions

Chapter 12 describes some of the techniques used by the business analyst. The root definition for the DMH operation can be produced from the perspective of the dealers who use the service, the end customers who run the motorcycles, or the DMH staff. Each definition will be based on a different CATWOE. Create a CATWOE for one of these perspectives and turn it into a root definition.

Business activity modelling

Business activity modelling is described in Chapter 12 along with the strategic analysis frameworks that the business analyst can use.

1 Using the headings People, Money, Information, Technology, analyse the strengths, weaknesses, opportunities and threats (SWOT) that DMH face with this new project.

2 Identify the political, economic, social, technical, environmental and legislative issues (PESTEL) that may impact upon the DMH project.

3 Identify the main areas of business activity in DMH and show diagrammatically (BAM) the associations between them.

Logical Systems Modelling

The transition from analysis to design is achieved by combining the business requirements with the old logical data flow diagram so that the new functions can be added to a logical model of the system. These exercises start by providing the business requirements definition created by the business analyst who investigated the DMH system. These requirements should be combined with your old logical DFD to create a new logical system that will meet DMH's needs. The deliverables from this part of the case study exercise are:

1 New logical DFDs for the DMH system.

2 An entity model with the necessary attributes that the new system requires.

3 An entity life history diagram for the entity 'Stock Item'.

Chapter 13 describes the transition from analysis to design; logical data design is in Chapter 17 and Chapter 11 covers the behaviour modelling for the ELH diagram.

DMH Business Requirements Definition

If you have carried out role-play interviews, then you should have gathered some or all of the following information. If you have it all, and if you've organised it in the following way, well done! An alternative approach could be to use this information as the basis for confirming the findings in a series of interviews where you concentrate on understanding the reasons for these requirements. If you are not able to carry out role-pay interviews, then use these statements as the basis for subsequent exercises.

Order processing requirements

1 Accept and store dealer orders, checking the current state of dealer credit.

2 Identify orders that take dealers beyond their credit limit; store such orders until the Sales Manager has supplied authorisation for their progress.

3 Produce picking lists in bin number sequence for all items on a dealer order currently in stock.

4 Issue picking lists, twice per day, of items that could not be supplied when the dealer orders were first received.

Warehousing system requirements

1 Confirm the availability of items on the dealer picking lists after items have been picked in the stores.

2 Accept amendments to the picking lists when items are unexpectedly found to be out of stock.

3 Amend back order data when items are unexpectedly found to be out of stock.

4 Allow goods inwards storekeepers to enter details of items received from suppliers and to reconcile these details with the appropriate purchase order issued to the supplier.

5 Allow Goods inwards storekeepers to enter details of any differences found between:

(a) the quantity of an item supplied and the quantity stated as being supplied on the supplier dispatch documentation;

(b) the quantity of an item supplied and the quantity ordered on the original purchase order;

(c) the quantity of an item stated as supplied on the supplier documentation and the number of items received in good condition.

Purchasing system requirements

1 Automatically vary the reorder level of all items in response to variations in demand and supply.

2 Identify items that have fallen below their reorder level and issue the appropriate purchase order documentation.

3 Check supplier prices on purchase invoices against quoted prices on purchase orders.

4 Hold the current purchase price of all items held in stock.

5 Identify the value of purchases made from each supplier on a monthly and a yearly basis.

6 Identify purchase orders that have not been met inside their expected lead-time.

Accounting system requirements

1 Issue priced invoices on the same day that goods are dispatched.

2 Accept payments from dealers and maintain details of their outstanding debt and their credit limit.

3 Issue monthly statements of account to dealers within two days of the end of each accounting period.

4 Issue payments to suppliers when all items on a particular purchase order have been supplied satisfactorily.

5 Issue credit notes to dealers for items returned to the warehouse in good condition.

6 Monitor the sales prices of items supplied to maintain a minimum of 30% margin of profit between purchase and sales price.

Dispatch requirements

1 Produce dispatch notes with the correct dealer name and address and correct quantities picked and dealer order data immediately goods have been picked in the warehouse.

2 Record the confirmation of the receipt of goods by the dealer, and record any differences between the goods accepted by the dealer and the goods dispatched from the warehouse.

General requirements

1 Include any additional management information and or control procedures that may be deemed necessary to ensure the successful operation of these systems.

Appendix 2
ISEB Qualifications

The Information Systems Examinations Board (ISEB) offers examinations for a range of certificates and diplomas that are recognised qualifications for professionals in the IT and IS business. There are five different Diplomas in Business Systems Development. To obtain a diploma, candidates are required to pass five one-hour, open book examinations in relevant topics. A certificate is awarded for each examination passed, and when candidates have obtained five certificates they may present themselves for an oral examination for the award of the diploma. This book is focused on the Diploma in Business Systems Development specialising in Systems Analysis and Design. To obtain this diploma the student must sit one-hour open book examinations in:

- Analysis and Design Techniques.
- Business Systems Investigation.
- Business Organisation.
- Systems Design and Implementation.

The examination in Information and Communication Technology is the only closed book examination in this set of certificates, and it completes the certificate examinations. Successful candidates can then apply to ISEB for the opportunity to be examined for the Diploma. Sample papers can be found on the ISEB website.

Certificate in analysis and design techniques

This certificate requires the candidate to be able to demonstrate an ability to draw a business process model (typically a DFD) and a static structure model (typically an entity model). Candidates are allowed to take their textbooks into the examination. The Analysis and Design Techniques examination is based on a scenario similar to the LozCo case study. The Analysis and Design examination candidate is expected to have an understanding of the project life cycle, and this is covered in detail in Chapter 6 and referred to throughout the text.

Certificate in business systems investigation

This certificate examines the analyst's ability to investigate and analyse a business system and establish the feasibility of a systems proposal. The syllabus for the certificate includes fact-finding and investigation, which we discuss in Chapter 3, when we consider the analyst's needs for communication skills, and in Chapter 8. Although Chapter 9 underpins the previous certificate there is a close association between the techniques used for analysis and design and the way in which the analyst investigates and documents an existing system, and the examination candidate for this certificate should at very least be familiar with the techniques covered by Chapter 9. Business requirements definition is found in Chapter 12, where we look at the role of the business analyst. The extended case study on the Denton Motor Company provides a further insight into investigation and requirements engineering. Finally for this certificate feasibility and cost justification is addressed in the case study and in Chapter 12.

The examination for the Certificate in Business Systems Investigation is again based on a scenario and is also in an open book format. Typical exam questions will ask a candidate to define the terms of reference for a particular investigation or to identify the stakeholders and participants in an organisation under investigation. Creating a business requirement definition, identifying the critical factors in a particular application area under study and/or proposing the benefits that might be expected to accrue from a development based on the scenario are also typical of the questions found in this examination. Candidates who have completed the Denton Motor Company case study, or a similar one, with role-play interviews and a presentation of their proposals, will probably have experienced the type of training programme this certificate requires.

Certificate in business organisation

Throughout this book we have attempted to emphasise the need for the analyst to view system development from a business perspective. Chapter 1 addresses the topics found in this certificate. The candidate for this examination must understand the purpose and nature of management information in the planning and control of an organisation, and be able to demonstrate an understanding of common business functions. The strategic role played by information systems in a business organisation are addressed in this chapter, and are found also in Chapter 12 when we look at the techniques that can be used for strategic analysis of IT developments.

Certificate in system design and implementation

The syllabus for this certificate is the largest in the set of certificates leading to the Systems Analysis and Design Diploma. The candidate should understand the things that need to be specified for a system to enter the software development phase of the life cycle. We look at the transition from analysis to design in Chapter 13, and we consider the security aspects of system design in Chapter 14. Candidates being examined for this certificate might be presented with a logical data flow diagram of a proposed new system. They might be asked to discuss the file access mechanisms suitable for a particular process or the types of screen designs or dialogue designs that would be suited to a particular data entry aspect of the system. These topics are in Chapters 15 and 18. The method of change over from the old system to the new system and the reasons for the choice of method are found in Chapter 22, and applying these to the proposed new development described in the data flow diagram referred to above enables the analyst to demonstrate an understanding of the factors that affect decisions at this stage of the life cycle.

Certificate in information and communications technology

We have made the point in this book that the analyst must have an understanding of technology and sufficient knowledge to interact with technical specialists to be able to obtain and understand the impact that technology will have on the proposed development. This is the level of knowledge that this certificate seeks to identify. The principles of programming languages are found in Chapter 24, which discusses 3GLs and 4GLs, and the types of database management software are found in Chapter 19. Chapter 21 provides the basic principles of data communications and some of the principles behind web development. This certificate is the only one in this set that is examined under closed book conditions. This textbook provides the theory behind the important basic topics of hardware, software, database management systems and data communications, which the examination is based upon. In our further reading list we have identified additional sources of material for this certificate.

Conclusion

One objective of this book is to provide, as far as possible, a single text that addresses the requirements for these certificates. Each certificate forms part of the complete diploma, and for this reason certain topics are encountered in more than one examination. We hope that the reader will recognise the need to view the techniques and approaches as part of a complete development life cycle even though it is examined and presented in stages. In our further reading list we have suggested some texts that may help examination candidates who wish to study particular aspects of the life cycle in more depth.

Index

business (*continued*)
  requirements specification
      242–68
    benefits identification 249–50
    business activity modelling
        258–9
    business analysis 253–8
    business analysis and IT
        strategy 259–63
    functional specification
        252–3
    options agreement 243–9
    PESTEL analyis 265–7
    requirement presentation
        251–2
    strategic information systems
        263–5
  systems model 35, 48
  to business (B2B) 399, 413, 461
  to customer (B2C) 399, 413, 449,
      461

C language 377
Cairncross, F. 456
call events 234
Cameron, J. 53
Canada 279
carrier frequency 404
CATWOE acronym 257–8, 263
CD-ROM 355
Central Computing and
    Telecommunications
    Authority 48, 49
Centrica 465
CFO Magazine 279
chained data 360–2
chairperson 100, 101
Champy 458
change:
  agents 441
  control 127–8
  events 234
  files *see* transaction data
  management 433–47
    information technology and
        people 434–6
    pay-off 445–6
    people project 440–5
    unfreezing, moving and
        refreezing 438–40
  marketing 443
channel transfer time 356
check point 364–5
Checkland, P. 255–6
checksum 401
clarification 82
Clarke, P. 159
Clarke, R. 277

class:
  diagram 39–40
  inheritance diagrams 206–10
classification section 173
Clerical Document Specification
    177
clients 23, 257, 412
closed questions 166
Coad 201
COBOL 121, 367, 373, 375, 377, 420
Cocomo 122, 124
CODASYL 55, 374–5
Codd, T. 375
coding 417–20
collaboration 57
  diagrams 210, 214–15
collision detect method 389
colour 308
Comite Consultatif International
    Telephonique et
    Telegraphique 406, 410
command language 310
commercial off the shelf 111
commit/backout buffering 390
commitment building 442–3
Common and Business Oriented
    Language 373
communication 63–83
  barriers 67–70
  plan 442
  procedures 151
  skills improvement 70–82
  types 64–7
Companies Act (1985) 288
competitive advantage 4, 8–14
Computer Institute Survey 279
Computer Misuse Act 22
computer run chart 37–8
Computer Services Association
    84
computer-aided software
    engineering 48, 50, 51, 149,
    181, 274
  approaches to analysis and
      design 58
  information recording 194
  modelling systems behaviour
      228
  object-oriented design (OO) 204,
      205, 207, 214
concatenation 295
concepts of systems analysis
    131–43
  definition of systems analysis
      131–3
  development life cycles 134–40
  PARIS model 142–3
  structured approach 140–2

conceptual data/process model
    55
concrete classes 208–10
condition entry/stub 235
confidentiality 276
configuration management 57, 128
confirming 168
consistency 313
constraints 5–8, 148–51
context:
  for analysis and design 1–33
    business analysis 2–4
    competitive advantage 8–14
    constraints 5–8
    ethical considerations 21–4
    role of analyst and designer
        19–21
    successful systems 15–19
  diagram 186–7
  questions 160–1
contingency planning 277, 287–90
control:
  context 277
  purpose 279–80
  totals 284
controlled redundancy 382
conversion 423–5
cooperation 57
core system 243–4
cost 13, 248
  appraisal 89–90
  -benefits analysis 155
  external failure 91–2
  hard (tangible) 249
  hardware 247–8
  internal failure 90–1
  lifetime 249
  soft (intangible) 249
critical success factors 4
Crosby, P. 87–8
CSMA/CD 389, 405
culture 454
current logical system 45, 140
current physical system 45, 140
customer 85
  -centricity 464, 466
  contacts 150
  relationship management 464
  service 4
cyclic redundancy codes 401
Cyperspace Security 277

data:
  access diagrams 395–6
  catalogue 195
  circuit-terminating equipment
      410
  clustering 382